and

Black Letter Series

of

WEST PUBLISHING

P.O. Box 64526

St. Paul, Minnesota 55164–0526

Accounting

FARIS' ACCOUNTING AND LAW IN A NUTSHELL, 377 pages, 1984. Softcover. (Text)

Administrative Law

AMAN AND MAYTON'S HORNBOOK ON ADMINISTRATIVE LAW, 917 pages, 1993. (Text)

GELLHORN AND LEVIN'S ADMINISTRATIVE LAW AND PROCESS IN A NUTSHELL, Third Edition, 479 pages, 1990. Softcover. (Text)

Admiralty

MARAIST'S ADMIRALTY IN A NUTSHELL, Second Edition, 379 pages, 1988. Softcover. (Text)

SCHOENBAUM'S HORNBOOK ON ADMIRALTY AND MARITIME LAW, Student Edition, 692 pages, 1987 with 1992 pocket part. (Text)

Agency—Partnership

REUSCHLEIN AND GREGORY'S HORNBOOK ON THE LAW OF AGENCY AND PARTNERSHIP, Second Edition, 683 pages, 1990. (Text)

STEFFEN'S AGENCY–PARTNERSHIP IN A NUTSHELL, 364 pages, 1977. Softcover. (Text)

Alternative Dispute Resolution

NOLAN–HALEY'S ALTERNATIVE DISPUTE RESOLUTION IN A NUTSHELL, 298 pages, 1992. Softcover. (Text)

RISKIN'S DISPUTE RESOLUTION FOR LAWYERS VIDEO TAPES, 1992. (Available for purchase by schools and libraries.)

American Indian Law

CANBY'S AMERICAN INDIAN LAW IN A NUTSHELL, Second Edition,

American Indian Law—Continued

336 pages, 1988. Softcover. (Text)

Antitrust—see also Regulated Industries, Trade Regulation

GELLHORN AND KOVACIC'S ANTITRUST LAW AND ECONOMICS IN A NUTSHELL, Fourth Edition, approximately 475 pages, 1993. Softcover. (Text)

HOVENKAMP'S BLACK LETTER ON ANTITRUST, Second Edition, 347 pages, 1993. Softcover. (Review)

HOVENKAMP'S HORNBOOK ON ECONOMICS AND FEDERAL ANTITRUST LAW, Student Edition, 414 pages, 1985. (Text)

SULLIVAN'S HORNBOOK OF THE LAW OF ANTITRUST, 886 pages, 1977. (Text)

Appellate Advocacy—see Trial and Appellate Advocacy

Art Law

DUBOFF'S ART LAW IN A NUTSHELL, Second Edition, 350 pages, 1993. Softcover. (Text)

Banking Law

LOVETT'S BANKING AND FINANCIAL INSTITUTIONS LAW IN A NUTSHELL, Third Edition, 470 pages, 1992. Softcover. (Text)

Civil Procedure—see also Federal Jurisdiction and Procedure

CLERMONT'S BLACK LETTER ON CIVIL PROCEDURE, Third Edition, 318 pages, 1993. Softcover. (Review)

FRIEDENTHAL, KANE AND MILLER'S HORNBOOK ON CIVIL PROCEDURE, Second Edition, approximately 1000 pages, 1993. (Text)

KANE'S CIVIL PROCEDURE IN A NUTSHELL, Third Edition, 303 pages, 1991. Softcover. (Text)

SIEGEL'S HORNBOOK ON NEW YORK PRACTICE, Second Edition, Student Edition, 1068 pages, 1991. Softcover. (Text) 1993–94 Supplement.

SLOMANSON AND WINGATE'S CALIFORNIA CIVIL PROCEDURE IN A NUTSHELL, 230 pages, 1992. Softcover. (Text)

Commercial Law

BAILEY AND HAGEDORN'S SECURED TRANSACTIONS IN A NUTSHELL, Third Edition, 390 pages, 1988. Softcover. (Text)

HENSON'S HORNBOOK ON SECURED TRANSACTIONS UNDER THE U.C.C., Second Edition, 504 pages, 1979, with 1979 pocket part. (Text)

MEYER AND SPEIDEL'S BLACK LETTER ON SALES AND LEASES OF GOODS, 317 pages, 1993. Softcover. (Review)

NICKLES' BLACK LETTER ON NEGOTIABLE INSTRUMENTS (AND OTHER RELATED COMMERCIAL PA-

Commercial Law—Continued

PER), Second Edition, 574 pages, 1993. Softcover. (Review)

SPEIDEL AND NICKLES' NEGOTIABLE INSTRUMENTS AND CHECK COLLECTION IN A NUTSHELL, Fourth Edition, 544 pages, 1993. Softcover. (Text)

STOCKTON AND MILLER'S SALES AND LEASES OF GOODS IN A NUTSHELL, Third Edition, 441 pages, 1992. Softcover. (Text)

STONE'S UNIFORM COMMERCIAL CODE IN A NUTSHELL, Third Edition, 580 pages, 1989. Softcover. (Text)

WHITE AND SUMMERS' HORNBOOK ON THE UNIFORM COMMERCIAL CODE, Third Edition, Student Edition, 1386 pages, 1988 with 1993 pocket part (covering Rev. Arts. 3, 4, new 2A, 4A). (Text)

Community Property

MENNELL AND BOYKOFF'S COMMUNITY PROPERTY IN A NUTSHELL, Second Edition, 432 pages, 1988. Softcover. (Text)

Comparative Law

GLENDON, GORDON AND OSAKWE'S COMPARATIVE LEGAL TRADITIONS IN A NUTSHELL. 402 pages, 1982. Softcover. (Text)

Conflict of Laws

HAY'S BLACK LETTER ON CONFLICT OF LAWS, 330 pages, 1989.

Softcover. (Review)

SCOLES AND HAY'S HORNBOOK ON CONFLICT OF LAWS, Student Edition, 1160 pages, 1992. (Text)

SIEGEL'S CONFLICTS IN A NUTSHELL, 470 pages, 1982. Softcover. (Text)

Constitutional Law—Civil Rights

BARRON AND DIENES' BLACK LETTER ON CONSTITUTIONAL LAW, Third Edition, 440 pages, 1991. Softcover. (Review)

BARRON AND DIENES' CONSTITUTIONAL LAW IN A NUTSHELL, Second Edition, 483 pages, 1991. Softcover. (Text)

ENGDAHL'S CONSTITUTIONAL FEDERALISM IN A NUTSHELL, Second Edition, 411 pages, 1987. Softcover. (Text)

MARKS AND COOPER'S STATE CONSTITUTIONAL LAW IN A NUTSHELL, 329 pages, 1988. Softcover. (Text)

NOWAK AND ROTUNDA'S HORNBOOK ON CONSTITUTIONAL LAW, Fourth Edition, 1357 pages, 1991. (Text)

VIEIRA'S CONSTITUTIONAL CIVIL RIGHTS IN A NUTSHELL, Second Edition, 322 pages, 1990. Softcover. (Text)

WILLIAMS' CONSTITUTIONAL ANALYSIS IN A NUTSHELL, 388 pages, 1979. Softcover. (Text)

[III]

Consumer Law—see also Commercial Law

EPSTEIN AND NICKLES' CONSUMER LAW IN A NUTSHELL, Second Edition, 418 pages, 1981. Softcover. (Text)

Contracts

CALAMARI AND PERILLO'S BLACK LETTER ON CONTRACTS, Second Edition, 462 pages, 1990. Softcover. (Review)

CALAMARI AND PERILLO'S HORNBOOK ON CONTRACTS, Third Edition, 1049 pages, 1987. (Text)

CORBIN'S TEXT ON CONTRACTS, One Volume Student Edition, 1224 pages, 1952. (Text)

FRIEDMAN'S CONTRACT REMEDIES IN A NUTSHELL, 323 pages, 1981. Softcover. (Text)

KEYES' GOVERNMENT CONTRACTS IN A NUTSHELL, Second Edition, 557 pages, 1990. Softcover. (Text)

SCHABER AND ROHWER'S CONTRACTS IN A NUTSHELL, Third Edition, 457 pages, 1990. Softcover. (Text)

Copyright—see Intellectual Property

Corporations

HAMILTON'S BLACK LETTER ON CORPORATIONS, Third Edition, 732 pages, 1992. Softcover. (Review)

HAMILTON'S THE LAW OF CORPO-RATIONS IN A NUTSHELL, Third Edition, 518 pages, 1991. Softcover. (Text)

HENN AND ALEXANDER'S HORNBOOK ON LAWS OF CORPORATIONS, Third Edition, Student Edition, 1371 pages, 1983, with 1986 pocket part. (Text)

Corrections

KRANTZ' THE LAW OF CORRECTIONS AND PRISONERS' RIGHTS IN A NUTSHELL, Third Edition, 407 pages, 1988. Softcover. (Text)

Creditors' Rights

EPSTEIN'S DEBTOR–CREDITOR LAW IN A NUTSHELL, Fourth Edition, 401 pages, 1991. Softcover. (Text)

EPSTEIN, NICKLES AND WHITE'S HORNBOOK ON BANKRUPTCY, 1077 pages, 1992. (Text)

NICKLES AND EPSTEIN'S BLACK LETTER ON CREDITORS' RIGHTS AND BANKRUPTCY, 576 pages, 1989. (Review)

Criminal Law and Criminal Procedure—see also Corrections, Juvenile Justice

ISRAEL AND LaFAVE'S CRIMINAL PROCEDURE—CONSTITUTIONAL LIMITATIONS IN A NUTSHELL, Fifth Edition, 475 pages, 1993. Softcover. (Text)

LaFAVE AND ISRAEL'S HORNBOOK ON CRIMINAL PROCEDURE, Second Edition, 1309 pages, 1992 with 1992 pocket part. (Text)

[IV]

Criminal Law and Criminal Procedure—Continued

LAFAVE AND SCOTT'S HORNBOOK ON CRIMINAL LAW, Second Edition, 918 pages, 1986 with 1993 pocket part. (Text)

LOEWY'S CRIMINAL LAW IN A NUTSHELL, Second Edition, 321 pages, 1987. Softcover. (Text)

LOW'S BLACK LETTER ON CRIMINAL LAW, Revised First Edition, 443 pages, 1990. Softcover. (Review)

PODGOR'S WHITE COLLAR CRIME IN A NUTSHELL, Approximately 300 pages, 1993. Softcover. (Text)

SUBIN, MIRSKY AND WEINSTEIN'S THE CRIMINAL PROCESS: PROSECUTION AND DEFENSE FUNCTIONS, 470 pages, 1993. Softcover. Teacher's Manual available. (Text)

Domestic Relations

CLARK'S HORNBOOK ON DOMESTIC RELATIONS, Second Edition, Student Edition, 1050 pages, 1988. (Text)

KRAUSE'S BLACK LETTER ON FAMILY LAW, 314 pages, 1988. Softcover. (Review)

KRAUSE'S FAMILY LAW IN A NUTSHELL, Second Edition, 444 pages, 1986. Softcover. (Text)

MALLOY'S LAW AND ECONOMICS: A COMPARATIVE APPROACH TO THEORY AND PRACTICE, 166 pages, 1990. Softcover. (Text)

Education Law

ALEXANDER AND ALEXANDER'S THE LAW OF SCHOOLS, STUDENTS AND TEACHERS IN A NUTSHELL, 409 pages, 1984. Softcover. (Text)

Employment Discrimination—see also Gender Discrimination

PLAYER'S FEDERAL LAW OF EMPLOYMENT DISCRIMINATION IN A NUTSHELL, Third Edition, 338 pages, 1992. Softcover. (Text)

PLAYER'S HORNBOOK ON EMPLOYMENT DISCRIMINATION LAW, Student Edition, 708 pages, 1988. (Text)

Energy and Natural Resources Law—see also Oil and Gas

LAITOS AND TOMAIN'S ENERGY AND NATURAL RESOURCES LAW IN A NUTSHELL, 554 pages, 1992. Softcover. (Text)

Environmental Law—see also Energy and Natural Resources Law; Sea, Law of

CAMPBELL–MOHN, BREEN AND FUTRELL'S ENVIRONMENTAL LAW: FROM RESOURCES TO RECOVERY, (Environmental Law Institute) Approximately 975 pages, 1993. (Text)

FINDLEY AND FARBER'S ENVIRONMENTAL LAW IN A NUTSHELL, Third Edition, 355 pages, 1992.

Environmental Law—Continued
Softcover. (Text)

RODGERS' HORNBOOK ON ENVIRONMENTAL LAW, 956 pages, 1977, with 1984 pocket part. (Text)

Equity—see Remedies

Estate Planning—see also Trusts and Estates; Taxation—Estate and Gift

LYNN'S INTRODUCTION TO ESTATE PLANNING IN A NUTSHELL, Fourth Edition, 352 pages, 1992. Softcover. (Text)

Evidence

BROUN AND BLAKEY'S BLACK LETTER ON EVIDENCE, 269 pages, 1984. Softcover. (Review)

GRAHAM'S FEDERAL RULES OF EVIDENCE IN A NUTSHELL, Third Edition, 486 pages, 1992. Softcover. (Text)

LILLY'S AN INTRODUCTION TO THE LAW OF EVIDENCE, Second Edition, 585 pages, 1987. (Text)

MCCORMICK'S HORNBOOK ON EVIDENCE, Fourth Edition, Student Edition, 672 pages, 1992. (Text)

ROTHSTEIN'S EVIDENCE IN A NUTSHELL: STATE AND FEDERAL RULES, Second Edition, 514 pages, 1981. Softcover. (Text)

Federal Jurisdiction and Procedure

CURRIE'S FEDERAL JURISDICTION IN A NUTSHELL, Third Edition, 242 pages, 1990. Softcover. (Text)

REDISH'S BLACK LETTER ON FEDERAL JURISDICTION, Second Edition, 234 pages, 1991. Softcover. (Review)

WRIGHT'S HORNBOOK ON FEDERAL COURTS, Fourth Edition, Student Edition, 870 pages, 1983. (Text)

First Amendment

BARRON AND DIENES' FIRST AMENDMENT LAW IN A NUTSHELL, Approximately 450 pages, September, 1993 pub. Softcover. (Text)

GARVEY AND SCHAUER'S THE FIRST AMENDMENT: A READER, 527 pages, 1992. Softcover. (Reader)

Future Interests—see Trusts and Estates

Gender Discrimination—see also Employment Discrimination

THOMAS' SEX DISCRIMINATION IN A NUTSHELL, Second Edition, 395 pages, 1991. Softcover. (Text)

Health Law—see Medicine, Law and

Human Rights—see International Law

Immigration Law

WEISSBRODT'S IMMIGRATION LAW AND PROCEDURE IN A NUTSHELL,

Immigration Law—Continued Third Edition, 497 pages, 1992. Softcover. (Text)

Indian Law—see American Indian Law

Insurance Law

DOBBYN'S INSURANCE LAW IN A NUTSHELL, Second Edition, 316 pages, 1989. Softcover. (Text)

KEETON AND WIDISS' INSURANCE LAW, Student Edition, 1359 pages, 1988. (Text)

Intellectual Property Law—see also Trade Regulation

MILLER AND DAVIS' INTELLECTUAL PROPERTY—PATENTS, TRADEMARKS AND COPYRIGHT IN A NUTSHELL, Second Edition, 437 pages, 1990. Softcover. (Text)

International Law—see also Sea, Law of

BUERGENTHAL'S INTERNATIONAL HUMAN RIGHTS IN A NUTSHELL, 283 pages, 1988. Softcover. (Text)

BUERGENTHAL AND MAIER'S PUBLIC INTERNATIONAL LAW IN A NUTSHELL, Second Edition, 275 pages, 1990. Softcover. (Text)

FOLSOM'S EUROPEAN COMMUNITY LAW IN A NUTSHELL, 423 pages, 1992. Softcover. (Text)

FOLSOM, GORDON AND SPANOGLE'S INTERNATIONAL BUSINESS TRANSACTIONS IN A NUTSHELL, Fourth Edition, 548 pages, 1992. Softcover. (Text)

Interviewing and Counseling

SHAFFER AND ELKINS' LEGAL INTERVIEWING AND COUNSELING IN A NUTSHELL, Second Edition, 487 pages, 1987. Softcover. (Text)

Introduction to Law—see Legal Method and Legal System

Introduction to Law Study

HEGLAND'S INTRODUCTION TO THE STUDY AND PRACTICE OF LAW IN A NUTSHELL, 418 pages, 1983. Softcover. (Text)

KINYON'S INTRODUCTION TO LAW STUDY AND LAW EXAMINATIONS IN A NUTSHELL, 389 pages, 1971. Softcover. (Text)

Judicial Process—see Legal Method and Legal System

SINHA'S JURISPRUDENCE (LEGAL PHILOSOPHY) IN A NUTSHELL. 379 pages, 1993. Softcover. (Text)

Juvenile Justice

FOX'S JUVENILE COURTS IN A NUTSHELL, Third Edition, 291 pages, 1984. Softcover. (Text)

Labor and Employment Law—see also Employment Discrimination, Workers' Compensation

CONISON'S EMPLOYEE BENEFIT PLANS IN A NUTSHELL, Approximately 465 pages, 1993. Softcover. (Text)

Labor and Employment Law—Continued

LESLIE'S LABOR LAW IN A NUT-SHELL, Third Edition, 388 pages, 1992. Softcover. (Text)

NOLAN'S LABOR ARBITRATION LAW AND PRACTICE IN A NUT-SHELL, 358 pages, 1979. Softcover. (Text)

Land Finance—Property Security—see Real Estate Transactions

Land Use

HAGMAN AND JUERGENSMEYER'S HORNBOOK ON URBAN PLANNING AND LAND DEVELOPMENT CONTROL LAW, Second Edition, Student Edition, 680 pages, 1986. (Text)

WRIGHT AND WRIGHT'S LAND USE IN A NUTSHELL, Second Edition, 356 pages, 1985. Softcover. (Text)

Legal History—see also Legal Method and Legal System

Legal Method and Legal System—see also Legal Research, Legal Writing

KEMPIN'S HISTORICAL INTRODUCTION TO ANGLO-AMERICAN LAW IN A NUTSHELL, Third Edition, 323 pages, 1990. Softcover. (Text)

REYNOLDS' JUDICIAL PROCESS IN A NUTSHELL, Second Edition, 308 pages, 1991. Softcover. (Text)

Legal Research

COHEN AND OLSON'S LEGAL RESEARCH IN A NUTSHELL, Fifth Edition, 370 pages, 1992. Softcover. (Text)

COHEN, BERRING AND OLSON'S HORNBOOK ON HOW TO FIND THE LAW, Ninth Edition, 716 pages, 1989. (Text)

HAZELTON'S COMPUTER–ASSISTED LEGAL RESEARCH: THE BASICS, Approximately 70 pages, 1993. Softcover. (Coursebook)

Legal Writing and Drafting

MELLINKOFF'S DICTIONARY OF AMERICAN LEGAL USAGE, 703 pages, 1992. Softcover. (Text)

SQUIRES AND ROMBAUER'S LEGAL WRITING IN A NUTSHELL, 294 pages, 1982. Softcover. (Text)

Legislation—see also Legal Writing and Drafting

DAVIES' LEGISLATIVE LAW AND PROCESS IN A NUTSHELL, Second Edition, 346 pages, 1986. Softcover. (Text)

Local Government

MCCARTHY'S LOCAL GOVERNMENT LAW IN A NUTSHELL, Third Edition, 435 pages, 1990. Softcover. (Text)

REYNOLDS' HORNBOOK ON LOCAL GOVERNMENT LAW, 860 pages, 1982 with 1993 pocket part. (Text)

Mass Communication Law

ZUCKMAN, GAYNES, CARTER AND DEE'S MASS COMMUNICATIONS LAW IN A NUTSHELL, Third Edition, 538 pages, 1988. Softcover. (Text)

Medicine, Law and

HALL AND ELLMAN'S HEALTH CARE LAW AND ETHICS IN A NUTSHELL, 401 pages, 1990. Softcover (Text)

JARVIS, CLOSEN, HERMANN AND LEONARD'S AIDS LAW IN A NUTSHELL, 349 pages, 1991. Softcover. (Text)

KING'S THE LAW OF MEDICAL MALPRACTICE IN A NUTSHELL, Second Edition, 342 pages, 1986. Softcover. (Text)

Mining Law—see Energy and Natural Resources Law

Mortgages—see Real Estate Transactions

Natural Resources Law—see Energy and Natural Resources Law, Environmental Law

TEPLY'S LEGAL NEGOTIATION IN A NUTSHELL, 282 pages, 1992. Softcover. (Text)

Office Practice—see also Computers and Law, Interviewing and Counseling, Negotiation

Oil and Gas—see also Energy and Natural Resources Law

HEMINGWAY'S HORNBOOK ON THE LAW OF OIL AND GAS, Third Edition, Student Edition, 711 pages, 1992. (Text)

LOWE'S OIL AND GAS LAW IN A NUTSHELL, Second Edition, 465 pages, 1988. Softcover. (Text)

Patents—see Intellectual Property

Partnership—see Agency—Partnership

Products Liability

PHILLIPS' PRODUCTS LIABILITY IN A NUTSHELL, Fourth Edition, approximately 325 pages, 1993. Softcover. (Text)

Professional Responsibility

ARONSON AND WECKSTEIN'S PROFESSIONAL RESPONSIBILITY IN A NUTSHELL, Second Edition, 514 pages, 1991. Softcover. (Text)

LESNICK'S BEING A LAWYER: INDIVIDUAL CHOICE AND RESPONSIBILITY IN THE PRACTICE OF LAW, 422 pages, 1992. Softcover. Teacher's Manual available. (Coursebook)

ROTUNDA'S BLACK LETTER ON PROFESSIONAL RESPONSIBILITY, Third Edition, 492 pages, 1992. Softcover. (Review)

WOLFRAM'S HORNBOOK ON MODERN LEGAL ETHICS, Student Edition, 1120 pages, 1986. (Text)

WYDICK AND PERSCHBACHER'S CALIFORNIA LEGAL ETHICS, 439 pages, 1992. Softcover.

Professional Responsibility—
Continued
(Coursebook)

Property—see also Real Estate Transactions, Land Use, Trusts and Estates

BERNHARDT'S BLACK LETTER ON PROPERTY, Second Edition, 388 pages, 1991. Softcover. (Review)

BERNHARDT'S REAL PROPERTY IN A NUTSHELL, Third Edition, 475 pages, 1993. Softcover. (Text)

BOYER, HOVENKAMP AND KURTZ' THE LAW OF PROPERTY, AN INTRODUCTORY SURVEY, Fourth Edition, 696 pages, 1991. (Text)

BURKE'S PERSONAL PROPERTY IN A NUTSHELL, Second Edition, 399 pages, 1993. Softcover. (Text)

CUNNINGHAM, STOEBUCK AND WHITMAN'S HORNBOOK ON THE LAW OF PROPERTY, Second Edition, approximately 900 pages, 1993. (Text)

HILL'S LANDLORD AND TENANT LAW IN A NUTSHELL, Second Edition, 311 pages, 1986. Softcover. (Text)

Real Estate Transactions

BRUCE'S REAL ESTATE FINANCE IN A NUTSHELL, Third Edition, 287 pages, 1991. Softcover. (Text)

NELSON AND WHITMAN'S BLACK LETTER ON LAND TRANSACTIONS AND FINANCE, Second Edition, 466 pages, 1988. Softcover. (Review)

NELSON AND WHITMAN'S HORNBOOK ON REAL ESTATE FINANCE LAW, Second Edition, 941 pages, 1985 with 1989 pocket part. (Text)

Regulated Industries—see also Mass Communication Law, Banking Law

GELLHORN AND PIERCE'S REGULATED INDUSTRIES IN A NUTSHELL, Second Edition, 389 pages, 1987. Softcover. (Text)

Remedies

DOBBS' HORNBOOK ON REMEDIES, Second Edition, approximately 900 pages, 1993. (Text)

DOBBYN'S INJUNCTIONS IN A NUTSHELL, 264 pages, 1974. Softcover. (Text)

FRIEDMAN'S CONTRACT REMEDIES IN A NUTSHELL, 323 pages, 1981. Softcover. (Text)

O'CONNELL'S REMEDIES IN A NUTSHELL, Second Edition, 320 pages, 1985. Softcover. (Text)

Sea, Law of

SOHN AND GUSTAFSON'S THE LAW OF THE SEA IN A NUTSHELL, 264 pages, 1984. Softcover. (Text)

Securities Regulation

HAZEN'S HORNBOOK ON THE LAW

Securities Regulation—Continued

OF SECURITIES REGULATION, Second Edition, Student Edition, 1082 pages, 1990. (Text)

RATNER'S SECURITIES REGULATION IN A NUTSHELL, Fourth Edition, 320 pages, 1992. Softcover. (Text)

Sports Law

CHAMPION'S SPORTS LAW IN A NUTSHELL. 325 pages, 1993. Softcover. (Text)

SCHUBERT, SMITH AND TRENTADUE'S SPORTS LAW, 395 pages, 1986. (Text)

Tax Policy

DODGE'S THE LOGIC OF TAX, 343 pages, 1989. Softcover. (Text)

UTZ' TAX POLICY: AN INTRODUCTION AND SURVEY OF THE PRINCIPAL DEBATES, 260 pages, 1993. Softcover. Teacher's Manual available. (Coursebook)

Tax Practice and Procedure

MORGAN'S TAX PROCEDURE AND TAX FRAUD IN A NUTSHELL, 400 pages, 1990. Softcover. (Text)

Taxation—Corporate

SCHWARZ AND LATHROPE'S BLACK LETTER ON CORPORATE AND PARTNERSHIP TAXATION, 537 pages, 1991. Softcover. (Review)

WEIDENBRUCH AND BURKE'S FEDERAL INCOME TAXATION OF CORPORATIONS AND STOCKHOLDERS IN

A NUTSHELL, Third Edition, 309 pages, 1989. Softcover. (Text)

Taxation—Estate & Gift—see also Estate Planning, Trusts and Estates

MCNULTY'S FEDERAL ESTATE AND GIFT TAXATION IN A NUTSHELL, Fourth Edition, 496 pages, 1989. Softcover. (Text)

PEAT AND WILLBANKS' FEDERAL ESTATE AND GIFT TAXATION: AN ANALYSIS AND CRITIQUE, 265 pages, 1991. Softcover. (Text)

Taxation—Individual

HUDSON AND LIND'S BLACK LETTER ON FEDERAL INCOME TAXATION, Fourth Edition, 410 pages, 1992. Softcover. (Review)

MCNULTY'S FEDERAL INCOME TAXATION OF INDIVIDUALS IN A NUTSHELL, Fourth Edition, 503 pages, 1988. Softcover. (Text)

POSIN'S FEDERAL INCOME TAXATION, Second Edition, approximately 550 pages, 1993. Softcover. (Text)

ROSE AND CHOMMIE'S HORNBOOK ON FEDERAL INCOME TAXATION, Third Edition, 923 pages, 1988, with 1991 pocket part. (Text)

Taxation—International

DOERNBERG'S INTERNATIONAL TAXATION IN A NUTSHELL, Second Edition, approximately 375 pages, 1993. Softcover. (Text)

BISHOP AND BROOKS' FEDERAL

Taxation—International—Continued

PARTNERSHIP TAXATION: A GUIDE TO THE LEADING CASES, STATUTES, AND REGULATIONS, 545 pages, 1990. Softcover. (Text)

BURKE'S FEDERAL INCOME TAXATION OF PARTNERSHIPS IN A NUTSHELL, 356 pages, 1992. Softcover. (Text)

SCHWARZ AND LATHROPE'S BLACK LETTER ON CORPORATE AND PARTNERSHIP TAXATION, 537 pages, 1991. Softcover. (Review)

Taxation—State & Local

GELFAND AND SALSICH'S STATE AND LOCAL TAXATION AND FINANCE IN A NUTSHELL, 309 pages, 1986. Softcover. (Text)

Torts—see also Products Liability

KIONKA'S BLACK LETTER ON TORTS, Second Edition, approximately 350 pages, 1993. Softcover. (Review)

KIONKA'S TORTS IN A NUTSHELL, Second Edition, 449 pages, 1992. Softcover. (Text)

PROSSER AND KEETON'S HORNBOOK ON TORTS, Fifth Edition, Student Edition, 1286 pages, 1984 with 1988 pocket part. (Text)

Trade Regulation—see also Antitrust, Regulated Industries

MCMANIS' UNFAIR TRADE PRACTICES IN A NUTSHELL, Third Edition, 471 pages, 1993. Softcover. (Text)

SCHECHTER'S BLACK LETTER ON UNFAIR TRADE PRACTICES AND INTELLECTUAL PROPERTY, Second Edition, approximately 300 pages, 1993. Softcover. (Review)

Trial and Appellate Advocacy—see also Civil Procedure

BERGMAN'S TRIAL ADVOCACY IN A NUTSHELL, Second Edition, 354 pages, 1989. Softcover. (Text)

CLARY'S PRIMER ON THE ANALYSIS AND PRESENTATION OF LEGAL ARGUMENT, 106 pages, 1992. Softcover. (Text)

DESSEM'S PRETRIAL LITIGATION IN A NUTSHELL, 382 pages, 1992. Softcover. (Text)

GOLDBERG'S THE FIRST TRIAL (WHERE DO I SIT? WHAT DO I SAY?) IN A NUTSHELL, 396 pages, 1982. Softcover. (Text)

HEGLAND'S TRIAL AND PRACTICE SKILLS IN A NUTSHELL, 346 pages, 1978. Softcover. (Text)

HORNSTEIN'S APPELLATE ADVOCACY IN A NUTSHELL, 325 pages, 1984. Softcover. (Text)

JEANS' TRIAL ADVOCACY, Second Edition, approximately 575

Trial and Appellate Advocacy—
Continued
pages, 1993. Softcover. (Text)

Trusts and Estates

ATKINSON'S HORNBOOK ON WILLS, Second Edition, 975 pages, 1953. (Text)

AVERILL'S UNIFORM PROBATE CODE IN A NUTSHELL, Third Edition, approximately 450 pages, 1993. Softcover. (Text)

BOGERT'S HORNBOOK ON TRUSTS, Sixth Edition, Student Edition, 794 pages, 1987. (Text)

McGOVERN, KURTZ AND REIN'S HORNBOOK ON WILLS, TRUSTS AND ESTATES–INCLUDING TAXATION AND FUTURE INTERESTS, 996 pages, 1988. (Text)

MENNELL'S WILLS AND TRUSTS IN A NUTSHELL, 392 pages, 1979. Softcover. (Text)

SIMES' HORNBOOK ON FUTURE INTERESTS, Second Edition, 355 pages, 1966. (Text)

TURANO AND RADIGAN'S HORNBOOK ON NEW YORK ESTATE ADMINISTRATION, 676 pages, 1986 with 1991 pocket part. (Text)

WAGGONER'S FUTURE INTERESTS IN A NUTSHELL, 361 pages, 1981. Softcover. (Text)

Water Law—see also Environmental Law

GETCHES' WATER LAW IN A NUTSHELL, Second Edition, 459 pages, 1990. Softcover. (Text)

Wills—see Trusts and Estates

Workers' Compensation

HOOD, HARDY AND LEWIS' WORKERS' COMPENSATION AND EMPLOYEE PROTECTION LAWS IN A NUTSHELL, Second Edition, 361 pages, 1990. Softcover. (Text)

Advisory Board

[XIV]

UNIFORM PROBATE CODE

IN A NUTSHELL

THIRD EDITION

By

LAWRENCE H. AVERILL, JR.
Professor of Law
University of Arkansas at Little Rock

ST. PAUL, MINN.
WEST PUBLISHING CO.
1993

Nutshell Series, In a Nutshell, the Nutshell Logo and the WP symbol are registered trademarks of West Publishing Co. Registered in the U.S. Patent and Trademark Office.

COPYRIGHT © 1978, 1987 WEST PUBLISHING CO.
COPYRIGHT © 1993 By WEST PUBLISHING CO.
                          610 Opperman Drive
                          P.O. Box 64526
                          St. Paul, MN 55164–0526
                          1–800–328–9352

Library of Congress Cataloging-in-Publication Data
Averill, Lawrence H.
    Uniform probate code in a nutshell / by Lawrence H. Averill, Jr.
—3rd ed.
        p.   cm. — (Nutshell series)
    Includes index.
    ISBN 0–314–02476–X
    1. Probate law and practice—United States—States.   I. Title.
II. Series.
KF765.Z95A94   1993
346.7305'2—dc20
[347.30652]
                                                    93–31236
                                                    CIP

ISBN 0–314–02476–X

To Suzanne,
Larry, and Liz

*

III

PREFACE

The Uniform Probate Code, in its official 1992 text with comments, as published by the West Publishing Company, is a very impressive document. This volume contains four hundred and eighty-six pages of the Code's text, two hundred and five pages of appendices and a one hundred and seventy page index. It contains three hundred and eighty two sections plus several alternates. Numerous separate and related Uniform Acts are incorporated into the Code. In total, it constitutes the second largest Code approved by the National Conference of Commissioners on the Uniform State Laws and by the American Bar Association that has been given the title of "Uniform." A Code of this magnitude, complexity, and subtlety is not capable of being comprehensively explained and analyzed in the Nutshell format. A Nutshell on this Code must have a different format and serve a different purpose.

The goal of this Nutshell is to provide the reader with a basic understanding of the provisions and concepts of the Uniform Probate Code. The style of writing is designed to explain the Code, not to quote it. Hopefully the reader will find the text easy to read and easy to comprehend.

Because the organization within the Code itself is excellent, the Nutshell follows this organization with a few exceptions. Consequently, the Nutshell is broken down into seven parts which correspond with the first seven articles of the Code itself. Deviating from the Code format, the Nutshell is then broken down into consecutive chapters each of which cover a smaller area of the Code. Within each chapter, there are titled subheadings designated as sections and symbolized in the following manner: § 0.00. Cross reference to such a section in the Nutshell will appear in this form: [§ 0.00].

Because most of the cross references in this Nutshell will be to various parts of the Code, the reference format is of importance. As part of the text, a section of the Code will be cited "Section 0–000" and a Comment of the Code will be cited "Comment to Section 0–000." As a reference to the text, a section will be cited [0–000] and a Comment will be cited [0–000, Comment].

Several additional research aids are included in this Nutshell. First, the "Outline," which immediately follows this Preface, is comprehensive and serves as a useful outline of the Code and its major subject matter divisions. Second, there is a "Table of Uniform Probate Code Sections" that will make reference to the appropriate page in which each cited Section and Comment is discussed or cited in the Nutshell. Third, an alphabetical list, with full citations, is included in the "Table of Cases." Fourth, for purposes of assisting the reader in further study of the subject, a selective collection of "Collateral Authorities" is provided, with full citations, and referred to throughout the text. Finally, an "Index" is included which emphasizes key words and phrases for easy access to particular subject matter.

Several persons deserve special recognition for the preparation of this Nutshell. First, Thomas Federico, a third year student at the University of Arkansas at Little Rock School of Law, was very

PREFACE

helpful in gathering materials, verifying citations, providing editorial support and preparing preliminary drafts of several subdivisions. Second, my secretary, Juaniece Ammons, provided excellent support in typing the new copy. To these people and others who took part in this endeavor, I offer my sincerest gratitude.

Modern word processing capabilities provided by the personal computer has made this task of preparing new edition much more efficient and accurate. In this regard West Publishing Company deserves special mention for providing me with a WordPerfect copy of the Second Edition of this Nutshell. This action greatly reduced the retyping that goes into the preparation of a new edition.

LAWRENCE H. AVERILL, JR.

Little Rock, Arkansas
June 4, 1993

*

OUTLINE

	Page
PREFACE	V
TABLE OF CASES	XXVII
TABLE OF COLLATERAL AUTHORITIES	XXXI
TABLE OF UNIFORM PROBATE CODE SECTIONS	XXXIX
TABLE OF STATUTES	LXXIX

Chapter 1. General Introduction and History 1

§ 1.01	General Introduction	1
§ 1.02	History	2
§ 1.03	Promulgation and Maintenance of the Code	6
§ 1.04	Influence of the Uniform Probate Code	9
§ 1.05	Outline and Overview	10

PART ONE. GENERAL PROVISIONS, DEFINITIONS AND PROBATE JURISDICTION OF THE COURT

Chapter 2. Purposes, Rule of Construction, Policies and Definitions 15

§ 2.01	Purposes and Rule of Construction	15
§ 2.02	Overriding Policies and Provisions	16
	A. Fraud	16
	B. Perjury for Falsified Documents	17
	C. Proof of Death or Status	18
	D. Definitions	20

IX

Page

Chapter 3. Jurisdiction, Venue and Courts ------ 22

§ 3.01 Jurisdiction and Multiple Venues ---- 22

§ 3.02 The Court and Registrar -------------- 23

Chapter 4. Notice and Virtual Representation ------------------------- 25

§ 4.01 Notice ------------------------------- 25

§ 4.02 Virtual Representation ---------------- 26

PART TWO. INTESTATE SUCCESSION, WILLS AND DONATIVE TRANSFERS

Chapter 5. Intestate Succession ----------- 29

§ 5.01 Introduction ------------------------- 29

§ 5.02 General Pattern --------------------- 31

§ 5.03 Shares of the Surviving Spouse, Descendants and Other Relations ---- 37

    A. Shares of the Surviving Spouse and Descendants ------------------ 37

    B. Shares of Other Relatives -------- 39

    C. Factual Illustrations --------------- 41

§ 5.04 Descendants and Representation ----- 44

§ 5.05 Determination of Status ------------- 53

    A. Introduction to Status ----------- 53

    B. Adopted Persons --------------- 54

    C. Half-Blooded Persons ------------ 59

    D. Afterborn (posthumous) Persons 59

    E. Nonmarital Issue ----------------- 59

    F. Relationships by Affinity --------- 60

    G. Aliens or Noncitizens ------------ 61

		Page
§ 5.06	Survivorship and Simultaneous Death	62
§ 5.07	Prior Gifts and Transactions	64
	A. Advancements	64
	B. Factual Illustrations	70
	C. Debtor Heirs	71
§ 5.08	Negative Testacy Provision	71

Chapter 6. Elective Share of Surviving Spouse and the Augmented Estate Concept 73

§ 6.01	Introduction to Spousal Protections	73
§ 6.02	Elective Share of the Surviving Spouse	78
§ 6.03	The Augmented Estate Calculation	84
	A. Definition of the Augmented Estate	84
	B. Segment 1 of the Augmented Estate	85
	C. Segment 2 of the Augmented Estate	85
	D. Segment 3 of the Augmented Estate	92
	E. Segment 4 of the Augmented Estate	93
	F. Summary of the Augmented Estate	94
§ 6.04	Exclusions From the Augmented Estate	95
§ 6.05	Funding the Elective Share	98
§ 6.06	The Election Procedure	102
§ 6.07	Representative Illustration of the Elective Share	105

Page

Chapter 7. Pretermitted Spouses and Children 113

§ 7.01   Pretermitted Spouse 113
§ 7.02   Pretermitted Children 116

Chapter 8. The Family Protections 121
§ 8.01   Introduction 121
§ 8.02   Protective Amounts and Their Bene-
          ficiaries 123
          A.   Homestead Allowance 123
          B.   Family Allowance 123
          C.   Exempt Property Allowance 124
§ 8.03   Procedural Provisions 124

Chapter 9. Wills and Related Doctrines 126
§ 9.01   Introduction 126
          A.   The Statute of Wills 126
          B.   Code Policy and Devices 127
          C.   Formality Analysis and the Sub-
                stantial Compliance Doctrine 128
§ 9.02   Execution Requirements 132
          A.   Testator's Capacity 132
          B.   The Ordinary Witnessed Will ... 133
          C.   The Holographic Will 137
          D.   The Foreign and International
                Will 139
          E.   The Self–Proved Will 144
§ 9.03   Revocation of Wills 146
          A.   General Revocation Principles .. 146
          B.   Revocation by Physical Act 147
          C.   Revocation by Subsequent Instru-
                ment 149

		Page
§ 9.03	Revocation of Wills—Continued	
	D. Revocation by Operation of Law	151
	E. The Lost or Destroyed Will	151
§ 9.04	Revival of Revoked Wills	153
§ 9.05	Supersession, Revocation and Revival Compared	158
§ 9.06	Incorporation by Reference	160
§ 9.07	Testamentary Additions to Trusts	163
§ 9.08	Events of Independent Significance	165
§ 9.09	References to Separate Writings	166
§ 9.10	Succession Contracts	168
§ 9.11	Confidential Public Depository	171
§ 9.12	Will Custodians	172
§ 9.13	No Contest or Claim Clauses	173

Chapter 10. Rules of Construction Applicable to Wills Only 174

§ 10.01	Introduction to Rules of Construction for Wills	174
§ 10.02	Devisee Lapse	176
	A. Introduction	176
	B. Scope and Limitations of the Antilapse Protection	178
	C. Application to Relevant Lapse Problems	181
	D. Testator's Expressed Contrary Intention	184
	E. Factual Illustrations	186
§ 10.03	Accessions Regarding Devises of Securities	191
§ 10.04	Ademption and Nonademption by Extinction	195

Page

§ 10.05 Ademption by Satisfaction 201
§ 10.06 Miscellaneous Rules of Construction 206
    A. After–Acquired Property 207
    B. Right Of Nonexoneration 207

Chapter 11. Rules of Construction Applicable to Wills and to Other Governing Instruments 208

§ 11.01 Introduction to Rules of Construction for All Governing Instruments 208
§ 11.02 Survivorship Duration Determinations 209
§ 11.03 Antilapse of Beneficiary Designations in Nominative Instruments 210
§ 11.04 Relational Terminology for Dispositive Purposes 212
    A. Beneficiary Status 212
    B. Multiple Generation Class Gifts 216
    C. Determination of Representation 217
§ 11.05 Constructional Rules for Future Interests 218
    A. Introduction to Future Interests 218
    B. Future Interests in Trust 219
        1. Survivorship 219
        2. Antilapse 221
    C. Worthier Title 223
    D. Definition of "Heirs" 224
§ 11.06 Choice of Law 224

Chapter 12. General Miscellaneous Provisions and Topics 227

§ 12.01 Introduction to Miscellaneous Matters 227
§ 12.02 Disclaimer of Property Interests 228

		Page
§ 12.03	Termination of Marital Status	233
	A. Introduction	233
	B. Definition of a Surviving Spouse	233
	C. Revocation of Interests and Powers by Operation of Law	235
§ 12.04	Effect of Homicide	237
§ 12.05	Protection of Payors and Third Parties	242
§ 12.06	Powers of Appointment	246
	A. Introduction and Definitions	246
	B. Exercise of Power of Appointment	249
	C. Virtual Representation and General Powers of Appointment	252

Chapter 13. Uniform Statutory Rule Against Perpetuities 255

§ 13.01	Introduction	255
§ 13.02	Statutory Rule Against Perpetuities	259
§ 13.03	Date of Creation of Interest	262
§ 13.04	Reformation	263
§ 13.05	Exclusions from the Rule	266
§ 13.06	Date of Application	268
§ 13.07	Illustrations Using the USRAP	268
§ 13.08	Honorary Trusts	271

PART THREE. PROBATE OF WILLS AND ADMINISTRATION

Chapter 14. Introduction to the Flexible System of Administration 275

§ 14.01	Introduction	275

Page

§ 14.02 Illustrative Techniques 280

    A. Estate Valued at Less Than $5,000 280

    B. Estate Valued at Less Than Family Protections and Expenses 281

        1. Intestacy 282

        2. Testacy 285

    C. Estates Valued in Excess of Family Protections and Expenses . 287

        1. Intestacy 287

        2. Testacy 290

    D. Protective Devices 291

        1. Demand for Notice 292

        2. Formal Proceedings 292

        3. Supervised Administration .. 293

        4. Other Protective Devices 294

        5. Bond 295

        6. Improper Distribution 295

        7. Fraud and Perjury 296

        8. Continuing Jurisdiction over Personal Representatives and Applicants 296

    E. Will Contests 297

Chapter 15. General Provisions on Probate of Wills and Administration 301

§ 15.01 Devolution of Decedents' Estates and the Necessity of Probate and Administration 301

§ 15.02 Time Limitations on Probate and Administration 303

Page

§ 15.03 Jurisdiction, Venue and Related Matters for Probate and Administration 305

A. Jurisdiction over the Subject Matter 305

B. Jurisdiction over the Person and Notice 306

C. Venue 308

D. Independent Proceedings and Joinder 310

E. Demand for Notice 311

F. Decedent's Causes of Action 312

Chapter 16. Procedures for Succession Without Administration .. 314

§ 16.01 The Passive and Affidavit Procedures for Small Estates 314

§ 16.02 The Summary Procedure for Small Estates 316

§ 16.03 Universal Succession 318

A. Purpose and Effect of Universal Succession 318

B. Contents of Application for Universal Succession 321

C. Registrar's Responsibilities and Findings in Universal Succession 322

D. Powers and Liabilities of Universal Successors 324

E. Creditors' Rights under Universal Succession 325

F. Responsibility among Universal Successors 328

Page

Chapter 17. Informal and Formal Appointment Proceedings ... 330

§ 17.01 Introduction 330
§ 17.02 Informal Appointment 331
   A. Initiation and Scope 331
   B. Contents of Application 332
   C. Registrar's Responsibilities and Findings 335
§ 17.03 Formal Appointment 337

Chapter 18. Informal Probate and Formal Testacy Proceedings 340

§ 18.01 Informal Probate 340
   A. Initiation and Scope 340
   B. Contents of Application 341
   C. Registrar's Responsibilities and Findings 343
   D. Special Notice Requirement 347
§ 18.02 Formal Testacy 347
   A. Purpose and Effect 347
   B. Contents of Petition 349
   C. Pre–Hearing Notice 351
   D. Court Responsibilities and Content of Order 352
   E. The Uncontested Case 353
   F. The Contested Case 355
   G. Effect of Order 357
   H. Formal Testacy and the Missing Person 359

Chapter 19. Supervised Administration 361

§ 19.01 Supervised Administration 361

Page

**Chapter 20.   The Personal Representa-
tive** ----------------------------------- 366

§ 20.01   Introduction to the Personal Representative ----------------------------------- 366

§ 20.02   Priority and Disqualification for Appointment ----------------------------------- 368

§ 20.03   Appointment, Bonding and Control - 373

    A.   Appointment ----------------------------- 373

    B.   Bonding ----------------------------------- 374

    C.   Control Procedures ----------------- 377

§ 20.04   Duties, Powers and Liabilities -------- 379

    A.   Introduction to Duties, Powers
and Liabilities ---------------------- 379

    B.   Duties ----------------------------------- 380

    C.   Powers ----------------------------------- 385

    D.   Liabilities and the Exculpatory
Provision ----------------------------- 386

§ 20.05   Liability of Third Persons ------------- 387

§ 20.06   Successor and Co-personal Representatives ----------------------------------- 389

§ 20.07   Compensation and Expenses of the
Personal Representative and Other
Agents ----------------------------------- 390

§ 20.08   The Personal Representative's Liability to Third Persons ------------------- 392

§ 20.09   Termination and Removal ------------- 393

Chapter 21.   The Special Administrator 397

§ 21.01   The Special Administrator ------------- 397

Chapter 22.   Creditors' Claims -------------- 401

§ 22.01   Introduction to Creditors' Claims ---- 401

§ 22.02   Notice and Nonclaim Limitations ---- 402

Page

§ 22.03 Presentation, Allowance and Rejection of Claims 407

§ 22.04 Payment of Claims 409

§ 22.05 Secured Claims and Encumbered Assets 411

Chapter 23. Special Distribution Provisions 413

§ 23.01 General Distribution Rules 413

§ 23.02 Distribution in Kind 419

§ 23.03 Apportionment of Estate Taxes 422

Chapter 24. Closing Estates 426

§ 24.01 Informal Closing Procedure 426

§ 24.02 Distributee Liability 428

§ 24.03 Formal Closing Proceedings 429

§ 24.04 Discharge of Security for Fiduciary Performance 434

§ 24.05 Subsequent Administration 434

Chapter 25. Settlement Agreements 436

§ 25.01 Settlement Agreements 436

PART FOUR. FOREIGN PERSONAL REPRESENTATIVE AND ANCILLARY ADMINISTRATION

Chapter 26. Foreign Personal Representative and Ancillary Administration 441

§ 26.01 The Multi–State Estate 441

§ 26.02 the Domiciliary Foreign Personal Representative 443

Page

§ 26.03 Jurisdiction over the Foreign Personal Representative 446

§ 26.04 Coordination of Domiciliary and Ancillary Proceedings 447

PART FIVE. THE PROTECTION OF PERSONS UNDER DISABILITY AND THEIR PROPERTY

Chapter 27. Introduction to Guardianship and Conservatorship 451

§ 27.01 Introduction 451

§ 27.02 Overview and Policies of the Code .. 453

Chapter 28. General Provisions on Guardianship and Conservatorship 457

§ 28.01 Organization, Interrelationships, and Definitions 457

§ 28.02 Jurisdiction and Venue for Guardianship and Protective Proceedings .. 460

    A. Jurisdiction over the Subject Matter 460

    B. Jurisdiction over the Person 462

    C. Venue 463

    D. Request for Notice 463

Chapter 29. Avoidance Devices and Durable Powers of Attorney 465

§ 29.01 Miscellaneous Avoidance Devices 465

§ 29.02 Durable Powers of Attorney 467

Chapter 30. The Guardian of a Minor .. 471

§ 30.01 The Guardian of a Minor 471

Page

**Chapter 31. The Guardian of an Incapac-
itated Person** 476

§ 31.01 The Guardian of an Incapacitated Per-
son 476

**Chapter 32. Protective Proceedings and
the Conservator** 484

§ 32.01 Protective Proceedings and the Conservator 484

A. Generally 484

B. Selection and Bonding of the Conservator 488

C. Powers of the Court 490

D. Powers, Duties and Liabilities of
the Conservator 492

E. The Conservator's Title 498

F. Liability of Third Persons 500

G. Creditors' Claims 500

H. The Conservator's Liability to
Third Persons 502

I. Duration, Termination and Removal of the Conservator 502

§ 32.02 The Foreign Conservator 504

PART SIX. NONPROBATE TRANSFERS

**Chapter 33. Nontestamentary Contractu-
al Arrangements** 507

§ 33.01 Nontestamentary Contractual Arrangements 507

Page

Chapter 34. Multiple–Party Accounts ···· 511

§ 34.01 Introduction to Multiple-Party Accounts ··· 511

§ 34.02 Definitions and General Provisions for Multiple–Party Accounts ········· 513

§ 34.03 Multiple–Party Account Forms for Financial Institutions ···················· 516

§ 34.04 Ownership During Lifetime of Multiple–Party Accounts ···················· 518

§ 34.05 Rights at Death for Multiple–Party Accounts ································· 519

§ 34.06 Rights of Creditors in Multiple–Party Accounts ··························· 520

§ 34.07 Protection for Financial Institution Using Multiple–Party Accounts ········· 523

Chapter 35. Uniform TOD Security Registration Act ······················· 526

§ 35.01 Introduction to Securities Registered in Beneficiary Form ···················· 526

§ 35.02 Definitions for Securities Registered in Beneficiary Form ···················· 526

§ 35.03 Ownership During Lifetime of the Owner of Securities Registered in Beneficiary Form ···························· 528

§ 35.04 Ownership on the Death of the Owner of Securities Registered in Beneficiary Form ···························· 531

§ 35.05 Protection for Registering Entities Using Security Registration in Beneficiary Form ···························· 532

PART SEVEN. TRUST ADMINISTRATION

Page

Chapter 36. Introduction ---------------------- 533
§ 36.01 Introduction ------------------------------ 533
§ 36.02 Definitions ------------------------------- 534

Chapter 37. Trust Registration ------------ 536
§ 37.01 Trust Registration ----------------------- 536

Chapter 38. Jurisdiction, Venue and Other Court Procedures for Trusts --------------------------- 540
§ 38.01 General Purpose for Trust Provisions 540
§ 38.02 Jurisdiction and Venue over Trusts 541
    A. Jurisdiction over the Subject Matter ------------------------------ 541
    B. Jurisdiction over the Person ----- 541
    C. Venue --------------------------- 542
§ 38.03 Forum Non Conveniens in Trust Litigation ------------------------------- 543
§ 38.04 Virtual Representation in Trust Litigation ------------------------------- 543

Chapter 39. Trustee's Duties, Liabilities, Protections and Powers -- 545
§ 39.01 Duties of a Trustee --------------------- 545
§ 39.02 The Trustee's Liability to Third Persons --------------------------------- 547
§ 39.03 The Trustee's Accounts ---------------- 548
§ 39.04 Powers of a Trustee --------------------- 549

Page

Chapter 40. The Foreign Trustee 551

§ 40.01   The Foreign Trustee 551

Index 555

*

TABLE OF CASES

References are to Pages

Arrowsmith v. Mercantile Safe Deposit & Trust Co., 313 Md. 334, 545 A.2d 674 (1988), *270*

Atwood v. Rhode Island Hospital Trust Co, 275 F. 513 (1st Cir.1921), *164*

Bradshaw v. McBride, 649 P.2d 74 (Utah 1982), *406*

Brewington, In re Estate of, 173 Mont. 458, 568 P.2d 133 (Mont.1977), *61*

Bucci's Will, Matter of, 57 Misc.2d 1001, 293 N.Y.S.2d 994 (N.Y.Sur.1968), *62*

Chapp v. High School Dist. No. 1 of Pima County, 118 Ariz. 25, 574 P.2d 493 (Ariz.App.1978), *467*

Christensen, Estate of v. Christensen, 655 P.2d 646 (Utah 1982), *116*

Colorado State Board of Agriculture v. First Nat'l Bank, 39 Colo.App. 506, 567 P.2d 820 (Colo.App.1977), *392*

Columbia Union Nat. Bank and Trust Co. v. Bundschu, 641 S.W.2d 864 (Mo.App.1982), *438*

Corbett's Estate, In re, 203 Neb. 392, 279 N.W.2d 89 (Neb.1979), *359*

Craig v. Rider, 651 P.2d 397 (Colo.1982), *358*

Cunningham v. Taggart, 95 N.M. 117, 619 P.2d 562 (N.M.App. 1980), *116*

Daigle, Estate of, 634 P.2d 71 (Colo.1981), *406*

Dandrea v. McCarty, 40 Colo.App. 547, 577 P.2d 1112 (Colo.App. 1978), *125*

Erickson, Estate of, 806 P.2d 1186 (Utah 1991), *138*

Estate of (see name of party)

Evans, In re Guardianship of, 179 Mont. 438, 587 P.2d 372 (Mont.1978), *458*

First Church of Christ, Scientist v. Watson, 286 Ala. 270, 239 So.2d 194 (Ala.1970), *10*

First Nat. Bank in Minot v. Bloom, 264 N.W.2d 208 (N.D.1978), *510*

Fitzgerald, Estate of, 738 P.2d 236 (Utah App.1987), *138*

Fox's Will, In re, 214 N.Y.S.2d 405, 174 N.E.2d 499 (N.Y.1961), *152*

Ganier, Estate of v. Estate of Ganier, 418 So.2d 256 (Fla.1982), *116*

Girod, In re Estate of, 64 Haw. 580, 645 P.2d 871 (Hawaii 1982), *438*

Guardianship of (see name of party)

Hartman, In re Estate of, 172 Mont. 225, 563 P.2d 569 (Mont. 1977), *153*

Havel, In re Estate of, 156 Minn. 253, 194 N.W. 633 (Minn. 1923), *152*

Hollingsworth v. Hollingsworth, 240 Ark. 582, 401 S.W.2d 555 (Ark.1966), *130*

Hutchinson, In re Estate of, 577 P.2d 1074 (Alaska 1978), *122*

In re (see name of party)

Jurek, Estate of v. State, 170 Mich.App. 778, 428 N.W.2d 774 (Mich.App.1988), *41*

Lemayne v. Stanley, 3 Lev. 1 (1691), *130*

Lopata v. Metzel, 641 P.2d 952 (Colo.1982), *95*

Matter of (see name of party)

McFayden, Estate of v. Sample, 235 Neb. 214, 454 N.W.2d 676 (Neb.1990), *203*

McGurrin v. Scoggin, 113 Idaho 341, 743 P.2d 994 (Idaho App. 1987), *134*

McKellar, Estate of, 380 So.2d 1273 (Miss.1980), *130*

Merrill v. Wimmer, 481 N.E.2d 1294 (Ind.1985), *269*

Muder, Estate of v. Muder, 159 Ariz. 173, 765 P.2d 997 (Ariz. 1988), *138*

O'Brien, Estate of v. Robinson, 109 Wash.2d 913, 749 P.2d 154 (Wash.1988), *510*

Oney v. Odom, 95 N.M. 640, 624 P.2d 1037 (N.M.App.1981), *406*

Orlando v. Prewett, 218 Mont. 5, 705 P.2d 593 (Mont.1985), *170*

Royal, Estate of, 826 P.2d 1236 (Colo.1992), *134*

Russell v. Estate of Russell, 216 Kan. 730, 534 P.2d 261 (Kan. 1975), *10*

Schmitt v. Pierce, 344 S.W.2d 120 (Mo.1961), *62*

Smith v. Smith, 519 S.W.2d 152 (Tex.Civ.App. 5 Dist.1974), *10*

Strong Bros. Enterprises, Inc. v. Estate of Strong, 666 P.2d 1109 (Colo.App.1983), *407*

Swett v. Estate of Wakem, 490 A.2d 679 (Me.1985), *408*

Taylor v. Estate of Taylor, 770 P.2d 163 (Utah App.1989), *130*

Thompson v. Potts, 66 Ohio St.2d 433, 423 N.E.2d 90, 20 O.O.3d 371 (Ohio 1981), *10*

Thompson v. Royall, 163 Va. 492, 175 S.E. 748 (Va.1934), *148*

Truman v. Estate of Collins, 162 Ariz. 367, 783 P.2d 813 (Ariz. App.1989), *309*

Tulsa Professional Collection Services, Inc. v. Pope, 485 U.S. 478, 108 S.Ct. 1340, 99 L.Ed.2d 565 (1988), *402*

Vadlamudi's Estate, In re, 183 N.J.Super. 342, 443 A.2d 1113 (N.J.Super.L.1982), *242*

Wilkins v. Fireman's Fund American Life Ins. Co., 107 Idaho 1006, 695 P.2d 391 (Idaho 1985), *238*

Young v. Hitz, 235 Neb. 939, 458 N.W.2d 221 (Neb.1990), *356*

*

TABLE OF COLLATERAL AUTHORITIES

Treatises and Law Review Articles	Citation, Page References
AMERICAN LAW INSTITUTE, RESTATEMENT (SECOND) OF CONFLICT OF LAWS (1971)	Restatement (Second) of Conflict of Laws, 226
AMERICAN LAW INSTITUTE, RESTATEMENT (SECOND) OF PROPERTY (1986)	Restatement (Second) of Property, 217, 224, 246, 247
AMERICAN LAW INSTITUTE, RESTATEMENT (SECOND) OF TRUSTS (1959)	Restatement (Second) of Trusts, 271, 272, 545
AMERICAN LAW INSTITUTE–AMERICAN BAR ASSOCIATION, UNIFORM PROBATE CODE PRACTICE MANUAL (Wright ed. 1972)	UPC Practice Manual (1972), 5, 6
AMERICAN LAW INSTITUTE–AMERICAN BAR ASSOCIATION, UNIFORM PROBATE CODE PRACTICE MANUAL (2d ed. 1977) (2 vols.)	UPC Practice Manual (1977), 6, 307, 362, 365, 382, 384, 398, 402, 415, 421, 428, 431, 432, 442, 452, 460, 474, 476, 490, 492, 493, 498, 499, 511
Roger W. Andersen, *The Influence of the Uniform Probate Code in Nonadopting States*, 8 U. PUGET SOUND L.REV. 599 (1985)	Andersen, Influence of the Uniform Probate Code, 9
Thomas E. Atkinson, *Wanted—A Model Probate Code*, 23 J.AM.JUR.SOC'Y 183 (1940)	Atkinson, Model Probate Code, 4

XXXI

Treatises and Law Review Articles

Citation, Page References

THOMAS E. ATKINSON, WILLS (2d ed. 153)

Atkinson, Wills, 1, 55, 59, 64, 66, 71, 74, 77, 134, 137, 146, 151, 152, 157, 165, 176, 195, 201, 224, 235, 237, 330, 366, 368, 369, 397, 414, 443, 508

Lawrence H. Averill, Jr., *Administering Decedents' Estates Under the Uniform Probate Code*, RIA's SUCCESSFUL ESTATE PLANNING: IDEAS AND METHODS ¶ 4,121 (Res Inst. Am.1993)

Averill, Administering Decedents' Estates, 280

Lawrence H. Averill, Jr., *An Eclectic History and Analysis of the 1990 Uniform Probate Code*, 55 ALBANY L.REV. 891 (1992)

Averill, An Eclectic History and Analysis, 2, 6

Ira Mark Bloom, *Perpetuities Refinement: There is an Alternative*, 62 WASH.L.REV. 23 (1987)].

Bloom, Perpetuities Refinement, 257

G.T. BOGERT, TRUSTS (6th edition 1987)

Bogert, Trusts, 271

BLACK'S LAW DICTIONARY (Nolan–Haley rev. 4th ed., 1968)

Black's Law Dictionary, 1

FRANCIS J. COLLIN, ALBERT L. MOSES, & JOHN J. LOMBARD, JR., DRAFTING THE DURABLE POWER OF ATTORNEY: A SYSTEMS APPROACH

Collin, Moses & Lombard, Drafting the Durable Power of Attorney, 467

Jesse Dukeminier, *The Uniform Statutory Rule Against Perpetuities: Ninety Years in Limbo*, 34 U.C.L.A.L.REV. 1023 (1987)

Dukeminier, *Ninety Years in Limbo*, 257

Richard W. Effland, *Caring for the Elderly Under the Uniform Probate Code*, 17 ARIZ. L.REV. 373 (1975)

Effland, Caring for the Elderly, 453, 459

**Treatises and Law
Review Articles**

**Citation,
Page References**

Mary Louise Fellows, *Testing
Perpetuity Reforms: A Study
of Perpetuity Cases 1984–89,*
25 REAL PROPERTY, PROBATE
AND TRUST JOURNAL 597 (1991)

Fellows, Testing Perpetuity
Reforms, 257, 261

WILLIAM FRATCHER, PROBATE CAN
BE QUICK AND CHEAP: TRUSTS
AND ESTATES IN ENGLAND (1968)

Fratcher, Probate Can Be
Quick and Cheap, 3

Susan F. French, Application
of Antilapse Statutes to Appointments Made by Will, 53
WASH.L.REV. 405 (1978)

French, Application of Antilapse Statutes, 180

J. GRAY, THE RULE AGAINST PER-
PETUITIES (4th ed. 1942)

Gray, Rule Against Perpetuities, 255

Ashbel G. Gulliver & Cather-
ine J. Tilson, *Classification
of Gratuitous Transfers,* 51
YALE L.J. 1 (1941)

Gulliver & Tilson, Gratuitous
Transfers, 128

Sheldon F. Kurtz, *Powers of
Appointment Under the 1990
Uniform Probate Code:
What Was Done—What Re-
mains to Be Done,* 55 ALB.
L.REV. 1151 (1992)

Kurtz, Powers of Appoint-
ment, 254

Sheldon F. Kurtz, *The Augmented Estate Concept Un-
der the Uniform Probate
Code: In Search of an Equitable Elective Share,* 62 IOWA
L.REV. 981 (1971)

Kurtz, The Augmented Estate,
77

John H. Langbein, *Substantial
Compliance with the Wills
Act,* 88 HARV.L.REV. 489
(1975)

Langbein, Substantial Compliance, 128, 130

John H. Langbein, *The Nonprobate Revolution and the
Future of the Law of Succession,* 97 HARV.L.REV. 1108
(1984)

Langbein, The Nonprobate
Revolution, 3

XXXIII

COLLATERAL AUTHORITIES

Treatises and Law Review Articles	Citation, Page References
John H. Langbein & Lawrence W. Waggoner, *Reforming the Law of Gratuitous Transfers: The New Uniform Probate Code,* 55 ALB.L.REV. 871 (1992)	Langbein & Waggoner, New Uniform Probate Code, 97, 154, 158
W. Barton Leach, *Perpetuities in Perspective, Ending the Rule's Reign of Terror,* 65 HARV.L.REV. 722 (1952)	Leach, Perpetuities in Perspective, 256
James Lingren, *The Fall of Formalism,* 55 ALB.L.REV. 1009 (1992)	Lingren, Fall of Formalism, 131
ROBERT J. LYNN, THE MODERN RULE AGAINST PERPETUITIES (1966)	Lynn, Modern Rule Against Perpetuities, 255
John H. Martin, *Justice and Efficiency Under a Model of Estate Settlement,* 66 VA. L.REV. 727 (1980)	Martin, Model of Estate Settlement, 318
S. Alan Medlin, *An Examination of Disclaimers Under UPC Section 2–801,* 55 ALBANY L.REV. 1233 (1992)	Medlin, Examination of Disclaimers, 233
PAGE ON THE LAW OF WILLS (Bowe–Parker rev. ed., 1960) (8 vols.)	Page, Wills, 126, 161, 165, 168, 169, 176, 512
PROBLEMS IN PROBATE LAW—A MODEL PROBATE CODE (1946)	Model Probate Code, 4, 152, 360, 362, 452
Eugene F. Scoles, *Succession Without Administration: Past and Future,* 48 MO. L.REV. 371 (1983)	Scoles, Succession Without Administration, 314, 319
AUSTIN W. SCOTT, THE LAW OF TRUSTS (3d ed. 1967) (6 vols.)	Scott, Trusts, 388, 511
LEWIS M. SIMES, LAW OF FUTURE INTERESTS (2d ed. 1966)	Simes, Future Interests, 213, 246

Treatises and Law Review Articles	Citation, Page References
UNIFORM PROBATE CODE, OFFICIAL 1992 TEXT WITH COMMENTS, (West Pub.Co.1993)	UPC, i
UNIFORM PROBATE CODE NOTES (Joint Editorial Board for the Uniform Probate Code)	UPC Notes, 18
Lawrence W. Waggoner, *Drafting Under the Uniform Statutory Rule Against Perpetuities and Related Generation–Skipping Tax Grandfathering Considerations*, 17 ACTEC NOTES 245 (1992)	Waggoner, Drafting Under the USRAP, 262
Lawrence W. Waggoner, *Perpetuity Reform*, 81 MICH. L.REV. 1718 (1983)	Waggoner, Perpetuity Reform, 256
Lawrence W. Waggoner, *The Uniform Statutory Rule Against Perpetuities: Oregon Joins Up*, 26 WILLAMETTE L.REV. 259	Waggoner, USRAP in Oregon, 271
WEBSTER'S THIRD NEW INT'L DICTIONARY (1981)	Webster's Third New Int'l Dictionary, 162
JOHN GABRIEL WOERNER, AMERICAN LAW OF GUARDIANSHIP OF MINORS AND PERSONS OF UNSOUND MIND (1897)	Woerner, Law of Guardianship, 451

Uniform Laws	Citation, Page References
UNIF. COMMERCIAL CODE, 1 TO 5 U.L.A.—UNIF. COMMERCIAL CODE (1968)	Uniform Commercial Code, 527
UNIF. CUSTODIAL TRUST ACT, 7A U.L.A.—BUSINESS AND FINANCE LAWS 7–28 (Supp.1993)	Uniform Custodial Trust Act, 104
UNIF. DETERMINATION OF DEATH ACT (1980), 12 U.L.A.—CIVIL PROCEDURE AND REMEDIAL LAWS 384–88 (Supp.1993)	Uniform Determination of Death Act, 18

Uniform Laws

**Citation,
Page References**

UNIF. DISCLAIMER OF PROPERTY IN-
TERESTS ACT, 8A U.L.A.—ES-
TATE, PROBATE AND RELATED
LAWS 85–91 (1983)

Uniform Disclaimer of Property Interest Act, 228–33

UNIF. DISCLAIMER OF TRANSFERS
BY WILL, INTESTACY OR APPOINT-
MENT ACT, 8A U.L.A.—ESTATE,
PROBATE AND RELATED LAWS
93–109 (1983)

Uniform Disclaimer Transfers
by Will, Intestacy or Ap-
pointment Act, 228

UNIF. DURABLE POWER OF ATTOR-
NEY ACT, 8A U.L.A.—ESTATE,
PROBATE AND RELATED LAWS
275–286 (1983); 104–08
(Supp.1993)

Uniform Durable Power of Attorney Act, 8, 467–70

UNIF. ESTATE TAX APPORTION-
MENT ACT OF 1958, 8A
U.L.A.—ESTATE, PROBATE AND
RELATED LAWS 287–301 (1983)

Uniform Estate Tax Appor-
tionment Act, 422–25

UNIF. GUARDIANSHIP AND PROTEC-
TIVE PROCEEDINGS ACT, 8A
U.L.A.—ESTATE, PROBATE AND
RELATED LAWS 437–519 (1983);
129–48 (Supp.1993)

Uniform Guardianship and
Protective Proceedings Act,
8, 453–505

UNIF.INT'L WILLS ACT, UNIF. PRO-
BATE CODE §§ 2–1001 TO 1010, 8
U.L.A.—ESTATE, PROBATE AND
RELATED LAWS 178–211 (1983)

Uniform International Wills
Act, 8, 127, 139–44, 172

UNIF. INTESTACY, WILLS, AND DO-
NATIVE TRANSFERS ACT, 8A
U.L.A.—ESTATE, PROBATE AND
RELATED LAWS 154–270 (Supp.
1993)

Uniform Intestacy, Wills, and
Donative Transfers Act, 8

UNIF. MULTIPLE-PERSON AC-
COUNTS ACT, 8A U.L.A.— ES-
TATE, PROBATE AND RELATED
LAWS 271–87 (Supp.1993)

Uniform Multiple–Person Accounts Act, 8

Uniform Laws

Citation, Page References

UNIF. NONPROBATE TRANSFERS AT DEATH ACT, 8A U.L.A.— ESTATE, PROBATE AND RELATED LAWS 288–319 (Supp.1993)

Uniform Nonprobate Transfers at Death Act, 8

UNIF. PARENTAGE ACT, 9 U.L.A.—MATRIMONIAL, FAMILY AND HEALTH LAWS 587–622 (1979)

Uniform Parentage Act, 60

UNIF. PROBATE CODE, 8 U.L.A.— ESTATE, PROBATE AND RELATED LAWS (1983, Supp.1993)

Code [See Table of Code References]

UNIF. SIMULTANEOUS DEATH ACT, 8A U.L.A.—ESTATE, PROBATE AND RELATED LAWS 561–589 (1983)

Uniform Simultaneous Death Act (1940), 62

UNIF. SIMULTANEOUS DEATH ACT (1991), 8A U.L.A.—ESTATE, PROBATE AND RELATED LAWS 322–29 (Supp.1993)

Uniform Simultaneous Death Act (1991), 8, 64, 210

UNIF. STATUTORY RULE AGAINST PERPETUITIES ACT, 8A U.L.A.— ESTATE, PROBATE AND RELATED LAWS 348–89 (Supp.1993)

USRAP, 8, 210, 257–71

UNIF. SUCCESSION WITHOUT ADMINISTRATION ACT, 8A U.L.A.— ESTATE, PROBATE AND RELATED LAWS 409–224 (1993 Supp.)

Uniform Succession Without Admin. Act, 8

UNIF. TESTAMENTARY ADDITIONS TO TRUSTS ACT, 8A U.L.A.— ESTATE, PROBATE AND RELATED LAWS 603–616 (1983)

Uniform Testamentary Additions to Trusts Act, 170–72

UNIF. TESTAMENTARY ADDITIONS TO TRUSTS ACT (1991), 8A U.L.A.—ESTATE, PROBATE AND

Uniform Testamentary Additions to Trusts Act (1991), 165

Uniform Laws	Citation, Page References
RELATED LAWS 426–31 (Supp. 1993)	
UNIF. TOD SEC. REGISTRATION ACT, 8A U.L.A.—ESTATE, PROBATE AND RELATED LAWS 436–45 (Supp.1993)	Uniform TOD Security Registration Act, 8, 526–32
UNIF. TRANSFERS TO MINORS ACT (1983), 8A U.L.A.—ESTATE, PROBATE AND RELATED LAWS 446–89 (Supp.1993)	Uniform Transfers to Minors Act, 524
UNIF. TRUSTEES' POWERS ACT, 7B U.L.A.—BUSINESS AND FINANCIAL LAWS 743–761 (1985)	Uniform Trustees' Powers Act, 550

TABLE OF UNIFORM
PROBATE CODE SECTIONS

**[References to Uniform Probate Code Sections
and Comments]**

Sec.	This Work Page
Art. I	11
	15
	16
1–102(a)	15
1–102(b)	15
1–102(b)(1)—1–102(b)(5)	16
1–103	16
1–104	16
1–105	16
1–106	16
	296
	308
	428
	433
	447
	549
1–106, Comment	17
1–107	18
1–107(1)	19
1–107(2)	19
1–107(3)	19
1–107(5)	19
1–107(6)	20
1–108	27
	252
	253
	537
1–108, Comment	252
1–201	20

Sec.	This Work Page
1–201(4)	211
1–201(4a)	278
1–201(5)	61
1–201(6)	85
	406
1–201(9)	61
1–201(11)	553
1–201(13)	364
	417
	421
1–201(18)	277
1–201(19)	32
	208
	209
1–201(21)	66
1–201(23)	277
1–201(24)	25
	336
	338
	432
1–201(32)	529
1–201(33)	61
1–201(35)	529
	535
1–201(36)	367
	398
1–201(39)	34
1–201(43)	192
1–201(45)	398
	534
1–201(47)	398
1–201(50)	531
1–201(54)	535
1–201, Comment	21
	534
1–301	22
	442
1–302(a)	22
1–302(b)	22
1–302(c)	460
1–303	463
1–303(a)	23
1–303(b)	23

Sec.	This Work Page
1–303(c)	23
1–304	298
	357
	548
1–304 to 1–306	24
1–306	298
1–307	24
1–308	24
	357
1–309	24
1–310	17
	296
	308
1–401	25
	28
	307
	312
	334
	343
	351
	363
	402
	478
	486
	542
1–401(a)	25
1–401(a)(1)—1–401(a)(2)	25
1–401(a)(3)	26
1–401(b)	26
1–401(c)	26
1–402	26
1–403	27
	438
1–403(1)	27
1–403(2)(i)	27
	252
	253
1–403(2)(ii)	27
	544
1–403(2)(iii)	28
	437
1–403(3)(i)	28
1–403(3)(ii)	28

Sec.	This Work Page
1–403(4)	28
1–403, Comment	253
Art. II	4
	7
	8
	9
	11
	21
	139
	271
Art. II, Pts. 1–4	233
2–101(a)	29
2–101(b)	72
2–101, Comment	72
2–102	32
2–102, Comment	32
2–103	32
	40
2–104	20
	63
	121
	209
	210
	302
	531
2–105	34
	40
	105
2–106	49
	178
	179
	217
2–106, Comment	51
	217
2–107	59
2–108	59
2–109	65
	68
2–109(a)	65
2–109(c)	67
	68
2–109, Comment	68
2–110(a)	66

Sec.	This Work Page
2–110, Comment	66
2–111	71
2–113	62
	79
2–114	237
2–114(a)	60
2–114(b)	55
	57
2–114(c)	57
Art. II, Pt. 2	225
Art. II, Pt. 2, General Comment	79
Art. II, Pt. 2, App. VII, General Comment	77
2–201 to 2–207	521
2–201(a)	79
2–201(c)	79
	93
2–201(d)	79
2–202	21
	82
	84
	523
2–202(a)(1)(i)	85
2–202(a)(1)(iv)	90
2–202(a)(1)(v)	88
2–202(a)(1)(vi)	86
2–202(a)(1)(vii)	85
	97
2–202(a)(1)(ix)	89
2–202(a)(2)	91
2–202(b)(1)	85
2–202(b)(2)	85
2–202(b)(2)(i)—2–207(b)(iii)	96
2–202(b)(2)(i)(A)	86
	96
2–202(b)(2)(i)(B)	87
2–202(b)(2)(i)(C)	87
	523
2–202(b)(2)(i)(D)	88
2–202(b)(2)(ii)(A)	89
2–202(b)(2)(ii)(B)	90
2–202(b)(2)(iii)(A)	91
	100
	101
2–202(b)(2)(iii)(B)	92
	101

Sec.	This Work Page
2–202(b)(2)(iii)(C)	92
	96
	100
2–202(b)(3)	92
	523
2–202(b)(4)	85
	93
	97
	523
2–202(c)	95
2–202(d)	94
	102
2–202(e)	84
2–202, Comment	85
	86
	87
	89
	103
2–203	84
2–203(a)	100
2–203(b)	83
	100
	101
2–203(b)(c)	85
2–203(c)	83
	101
2–204	122
	415
2–204(a)	101
2–204(b)	243
2–205(a)	102
	103
2–205(c)	103
2–205(d)	101
	103
2–206(a)	103
2–206(b)	104
	125
2–206(c)(1)	105
2–206(c)(2)	104
2–206(c)(3)	105
2–206, Comment	105
2–207	234
	237

	This Work
Sec.	**Page**
2–207(a)	95
2–207(b)	95
2–207(b)(2)(i)—2–207(b)(2)(iii)	95
2–207(c)	96
2–207(d)	96
2–208	98
	243
2–301(a)	113
2–301(b)	116
2–301, Comment	114
	115
2–302(b)	117
	120
2–302(c)	120
2–302(d)	118
2–302, Comment	120
Art. II, Pt. 4	122
	225
Art. II, Pt. 4, General Comment	121
2–401	121
2–402	121
	123
	419
2–402A	123
2–403	121
	124
2–404	121
	123
	285
2–405	124
2–405(a)	125
2–405(b)	125
2–501	132
2–502	133
	156
	346
2–502(a)	127
2–502(b)	127
	137
	138
2–502, Comment	137
	138
2–503	130
	156
	157

Sec.	This Work Page
2–503 (Cont'd)	168
	346
2–504	127
	144
	298
2–504(a)	145
2–504(b)	145
2–504, Comment	145
2–505(a)	11
	136
2–505(b)	136
2–505, Comment	136
2–506	127
	139
	140
	346
2–507	126
	146
2–507(a)(1)	149
2–507(a)(2)	147
2–507(b)—2–507(d)	149
2–507(c)	150
2–507(d)	150
2–507, Comment	147
	158
2–508	151
	236
2–509	153
	157
	159
2–509(a)	153
	154
2–509(b)	154
2–509(c)	155
2–510	155
	161
	162
2–511	164
2–511, Comment	165
2–512	166
2–513	166
2–513, Comment	167
	168
2–514	170
	171

Sec.	This Work Page
2–514, Comment	170
2–515	171
2–516	172
2–517	173
	416
Art. II, Pt. 6	175
2–601	174
	175
	184
	207
	251
	302
2–601(3)	516
2–602	126
	207
2–602(c)(3)(i)	182
2–602, Comment	207
2–603	21
	34
	114
	177
	178
	184
	203
	210
	212
	217
	222
	223
2–603(a)(3)	180
2–603(a)(4)	180
2–603(a)(4)(ii)	179
2–603(b)	180
2–603(b)(1)	179
2–603(b)(2)	179
2–603(b)(2)	179
2–603(b)(3)	184
2–603(b)(4)	182
2–603(c)	182
2–603(c)(1)	182
2–603(c)(3)(ii)	182
2–603(c)(3)(iii)	183
2–603(c)(3)(iv)	183

Sec.	This Work Page
2–603, Comment	177
	181
	184
2–604	114
	177
	203
	210
	223
2–604(a)	183
2–604(b)	183
2–605	192
2–605(a)	192
2–605(a)(1)—2–605(a)(3)	193
2–605(b)	193
2–605, Comment	192
	193
2–606	197
2–606(a)	197
2–606(a)(1)—2–606(a)(5)	197
2–606(a)(6)	198
2–606(b)—2–606(e)	198
2–607	207
2–608	250
2–608, Comment	251
2–609	67
	202
	412
2–609(a)	202
2–609(c)	203
	204
2–609, Comment	203
2–701	208
	223
	252
2–702	8
	20
	63
	179
	209
	217
	218
	220
	531

Sec.	This Work Page
2–702(d)	209
2–702(e)	243
2–702(f)	243
2–703	225
2–704	251
2–705	214
2–705(a)	214
2–705(b)	214
	216
2–705(c)	214
	216
2–705, Comment	216
2–706	21
	211
	217
2–706(a)(2)	211
2–706(d)	243
2–706(d)—2–706(e)	212
2–706(e)	243
2–706, Comment	211
2–707	21
	217
	220
	222
2–707(b)	220
2–707(e)(1)	221
2–707(e)(2)	221
2–707, Comment	220
	223
2–708	216
2–709	21
	217
2–709(a)(1)	217
2–709(a)(2)	218
2–709(a)(3)	218
2–709(b)	217
2–709(c)	217
2–709, Comment	217
2–710	223
2–711	105
	224
	273
Art. II, Pt. 8	227
2–801	228

| | This Work |
Sec.	Page
2–801(a)	229
2–801(b)(1)—2–801(b)(2)	230
2–801(b)(2)	230
2–801(b)(4)	230
2–801(c)	230
2–801(d)	179
2–801(d)(1)	68
	231
2–801(d)(2)	231
2–801(d)(3)	231
2–801(e)	231
2–801(f)	232
2–801(g)	232
2–801, Comment	229
	232
2–801, Comments, (App. VII)	229
2–801, App. VII	228
2–802	60
	233
2–802(a)	234
2–802(b)	233
	236
2–802(b)(1)	234
2–802(b)(2)	234
2–802(b)(3)	234
2–803	21
	179
	235
	238
2–803(a)(1)	326
2–803(a)(3)	239
2–803(b)	238
	239
2–803(c)	238
2–803(c)(1)	239
2–803(c)(2)	240
2–803(d)	240
	242
2–803(e)	240
2–803(f)	238
2–803(g)	241
2–803(h)	242
	243

Sec.	This Work Page
2–803(i)	242
	243
2–803, Comment	241
2–804	21
	179
	233
	235
2–804(a)(2)	237
2–804(b)	157
	236
	237
2–804(d)	157
	236
2–804(e)	237
2–804(f)	235
2–804(g)	243
2–804(h)	243
2–804, Comment	246
Art. II, Pt. 9	8
	257
2–901	210
	259
2–901(a)	260
2–901(b)	260
2–901(c)	260
2–901(d)	261
2–901(e)	261
2–901, Comment	261
	262
2–902(a)	262
2–902(b)	263
2–902(c)	263
2–903	263
	264
	265
2–903(2)	264
2–903(3)	265
2–903, Comment	264
	265
2–904	266
2–904(1)	266
2–904(2)	267
2–904(3)	267

	This Work
Sec.	Page
2–904(4)	267
2–904(5)	267
2–904(6)	267
2–905	268
2–905(b)	268
2–907(a)	271
	272
2–907(b)	272
2–907(c)(1)	273
2–907(c)(2)	273
2–907(c)(4)	273
2–907(c)(6)	273
2–907(c)(7)	273
Art. II, Pt. 10	8
	127
	141
2–1001	21
	449
2–1001(2)	143
2–1002(a)	141
2–1002(b)	142
2–1003—2–1005	346
2–1003(a)	142
2–1003(b)	142
2–1003(c)	142
2–1003(d)	142
2–1003(e)	142
2–1004(a)	143
2–1004(b)	143
2–1004(c)	143
2–1004(d)	143
2–1005	143
	144
2–1005, Comment	144
2–1006	144
	144
2–1006, Comment	144
2–1007	144
2–1009	143
2–1010	172
Art. III	8
	12
	21

Sec.	This Work Page
Art. III (Cont'd)	23
	24
	233
	444
	446
	463
	472
	502
	548
Art. III, General Comment	311
3–101	301
	331
	383
	401
3–101(3)	444
3–101A	301
3–102	290
	302
	315
	445
3–103	302
	331
	373
3–104	296
	302
	406
	411
3–105	24
	306
	392
3–106	26
	306
	307
3–106, Comment	306
3–107	278
	303
	310
	341
3–107, Comment	279
3–108	286
	289
	291

	This Work
Sec.	**Page**
3–108 (Cont'd)	297
	299
	303
	305
	318
	333
	341
	352
	362
	363
	403
	431
	432
	445
3–109	313
3–201(a)(1)	308
3–201(a)(2)	309
3–201(c)	23
3–201(d)	309
3–202	309
	447
3–202, Comment	309
3–203	233
	286
	339
	368
3–203(a)	368
3–203(b)	370
	371
3–203(b)(1)	372
3–203(b)(1)—3–203(b)(2)	371
3–203(b)(2)	371
3–203(c)	370
	372
3–203(d)	372
3–203(e)	371
	372
3–203(f)	369
3–203(g)	309
	373
	445
3–203(h)	368
3–204	26

Sec.	This Work Page
3–204 (Cont'd)	292
	311
	322
	334
	335
	337
	343
	345
	351
	365
	382
	401
	463
	495
Art. III, Pt. 3	282
	318
3–301	318
	331
	332
	341
3–301(a)	290
	334
	343
3–301(a)(1)	283
	286
	288
	321
	338
	350
3–301(a)(1)(i)—3–301(a)(1)(v)	333
3–301(a)(1)(i)—3–301(a)(1)(vi)	342
3–301(a)(1)(vi)	286
3–301(a)(2)	286
	321
3–301(a)(2)(i)—3–301(a)(2)(iii)	343
3–301(a)(3)	334
3–301(a)(4)	283
	288
	350
3–301(a)(4)(i)	321
3–301(a)(4)(i)—3–301(a)(4)(ii)	333
3–301(a)(4)(ii)	351
3–301(a)(5)	334

Sec.	This Work Page
3–301(a)(6)	334
3–301(b)	297
	308
3–301, Comment	308
3–302	291
	294
	318
	341
	343
3–303 to 3–311	24
3–303(a)(1)—3–303(a)(4)	345
3–303(a)(5)—3–303(a)(6)	337
	345
3–303(a)(7)	345
3–303(b)	346
	445
3–303(c)	346
3–303(d)	346
3–304	168
	345
3–305	323
	340
	344
3–305, Comment	344
3–306(b)	347
3–306[*]	343
3–307	290
3–307(a)	283
	288
	294
	335
	369
3–307(b)	283
	288
	317
	335
3–308(a)(1)—3–308(a)(4)	336
3–308(a)(6)	334
3–308(a)(7)	336
	370
3–308(b)	337
	445
3–309	332

Sec.	This Work Page
3–309 (Cont'd)	336
	338
	370
3–309, Comment	336
3–310	334
3–311	337
3–312	320
	324
3–312 to 3–322	8
	282
	318
3–312, Comment	320
	321
3–313	282
	286
	287
	290
	321
	322
3–313(a)	321
3–314	282
3–314(a)	322
3–314(a)(5)	286
	323
3–314(b)	311
	323
3–314(c)	323
3–314, Comment	323
3–315	282
	294
	323
	324
3–316	283
3–316(1)	324
	328
3–316(2)	324
3–316(3)	325
3–317(a)	325
3–317(b)	328
3–317(d)	329
3–317(e)	329
3–317, Comment	283
	326

	This Work
Sec.	**Page**
3–318(a)	297
	308
	328
3–319	328
	329
3–320	327
3–321	325
3–321, Comment	325
3–322	326
3–401	289
	292
	297
	298
	311
	347
	378
	401
	434
3–402	338
3–402	363
3–402(a)	152
	289
	350
3–402(b)	289
	351
3–403	26
	289
	293
	363
3–403(a)	352
3–403(b)	359
3–403, Comment	352
3–404	356
3–404, Comment	356
3–405	354
3–406	355
3–406(a)	298
	355
3–406(b)	145
	298
	355
3–406, Comment	145
3–407	298

Sec.	This Work Page
3–407 (Cont'd)	355
3–408	309
	354
	447
3–409	353
	354
	360
3–409, Comment	360
3–410	353
3–410, Comment	353
3–411	353
3–412	289
	298
	353
	357
	429
3–412(1)	298
	357
3–412(1)—3–412(2)	298
3–412(2)	358
3–412(3)	358
3–412(3)(i)—3–412(3)(ii)	298
3–412(3)(iii)	298
3–412(4)	358
3–412(5)	360
3–413	289
	358
3–414	26
	292
	293
	298
	311
	338
	363
	401
3–414(b)	339
3–414, Comment	339
3–501	293
	361
	362
	418
3–502	26
	293

Sec.	This Work Page
3–502 (Cont'd)	294
	362
	363
	401
3–503	293
	364
3–503(a)	364
3–503(b)	364
3–503(c)	364
3–504	293
	364
	365
	388
3–505	293
	362
	365
3–601	335
	373
3–602	296
	307
	373
	446
3–603	295
	375
	398
3–604	295
	375
	376
3–604 to 3–606	547
3–605	295
	323
	327
	375
	401
3–606	490
3–606(a)(1)—3–606(a)(5)	377
3–606(b)	377
3–607	294
	364
	378
	395
	401
3–607(a)	378

Sec.	This Work Page
3–607(b)	378
3–607, Comment	378
3–608	384
	393
	394
	434
3–609	394
	399
3–610(a)	394
	426
3–610(b)	395
3–610(c)	337
	395
3–611	294
	339
	395
3–611(a)	395
3–611(b)	382
	395
	396
	445
3–612	337
	396
3–613	389
3–614(1)	399
3–614(2)	399
3–614, Comment	397
3–615(a)	399
3–615(b)	399
3–616	399
3–617	400
3–618	400
3–701	291
	374
3–702	374
3–703(a)	380
	380
3–703(b)	387
3–703(c)	443
3–704	283
	380
3–705	23
	284

	This Work
Sec.	**Page**
3–705 (Cont'd)	347
	381
3–706	85
	382
	383
3–706, Comment	382
3–707	382
3–708	383
3–709	383
	384
3–710	385
3–711	291
	385
	401
3–712	386
	498
3–713	386
3–714	283
	291
	388
3–715	380
	385
	386
3–715(1)—3–715(27)	494
3–715(7)	385
3–715(14)	385
3–715(16)	385
3–715(18)	385
	391
3–715(21)	385
	391
	397
3–715(22)	442
3–715(25)	386
3–716	389
3–717	389
3–718	390
3–719	391
3–720	391
3–721	391
3–721, Comment	392
Art. III, Pt. 8, General Comment	407
3–801	23

Sec.	This Work Page
3–801 (Cont'd)	25
	285
	380
	402
	404
3–801(a)	403
3–801(b)	403
	404
3–801, Comment	381
	405
3–802	313
	408
3–802(b)	326
	408
3–802, Comment	409
3–803(a)	408
	426
3–803(a)—3–803(b)	405
3–803(a)(1)	282
	305
	403
	404
	409
3–803(a)(2)	285
	403
	404
3–803(b)	405
	448
3–803(c)	405
3–803(d)(1)	406
	411
3–803(d)(2)	406
3–803, Comment	403
	406
3–804(1)	407
3–804(2)	406
	407
3–804(3)	408
3–804, Comment	407
3–805	122
3–805(a)	410
3–805(b)	410
3–806(a)	407

	This Work
Sec.	**Page**
3–806(a) (Cont'd)	408
	408
3–806(b)	408
3–806(d)	408
3–806(e)	409
3–807	34
3–807(a)	409
3–807(b)	409
3–808	393
	406
	502
	548
3–808(a)	393
3–808(b)	393
3–808(c)	393
3–808(d)	393
3–808, Comment	392
	548
3–809	406
	411
3–809(1)	412
3–809(2)	412
3–810(a)	410
3–810(b)	410
3–811	411
3–812	409
3–813	411
3–814	412
3–815(a)	448
3–815(b)—3–815(c)	448
3–816	448
3–901	124
	301
	315
3–902	116
	118
	328
3–902(a)	198
	414
	415
3–902(b)	414
	415
3–902(c)	416

Sec.	This Work Page
3–902A(c)	416
3–903	71
	416
3–904	416
3–904, Comment	416
3–905	173
	416
3–906	419
3–906(a)(1)	124
	419
3–906(a)(2)	285
	419
3–906(a)(2)(i)	419
3–906(a)(2)(ii)	420
3–906(a)(2)(iii)	125
	419
3–906(a)(3)	420
3–906(a)(4)	420
3–906(b)	413
3–907	420
3–908	329
	420
3–909	327
	329
	402
	421
3–910	291
	329
	422
3–911	422
3–912	328
	436
3–913	417
	546
	553
3–914(a)	417
3–914(b)	417
3–914, Comment	417
3–915	418
	466
3–915(b)	418
3–915(c)	418
	419

Sec.	This Work Page
3–916	21
	415
	422
3–916(b)	423
3–916(c)(1)	423
3–916(c)(2)	423
3–916(c)(3)	424
3–916(c)(4)	424
3–916(d)(1)	424
3–916(e)(1)	423
3–916(e)(2)	423
	424
3–916(e)(5)	423
3–916(f)	424
3–916(g)	425
3–916(h)	425
	444
3–916, Comment	423
3–1001	26
	290
	293
	300
	311
	365
	395
	405
	415
	429
	430
	431
3–1001(a)	288
	289
	291
	292
3–1001(b)	433
3–1002	292
	311
	395
	405
	415
	429
	430
	447

Sec.	This Work Page
3–1003	285
	295
	307
	394
	405
	426
3–1003(a)(1)—3–1003(a)(3)	426
3–1003(a)(2)	426
3–1003(b)	284
	285
	426
3–1003, Comment	394
3–1004	296
	302
	402
	429
3–1004, Comment	429
3–1005	284
	285
	302
	318
	426
3–1006	327
	421
	428
3–1006, Comment	428
3–1007	434
3–1007, Comment	434
3–1008	434
3–1101	300
	436
	437
	447
3–1102	300
	436
	437
3–1102(1)	437
3–1102(2)	437
3–1102(3)	438
	439
3–1102, Comment	438
	439
Art. III, Pt. 12, General Comment	314
3–1201	302

Sec.	This Work Page
3–1201 (Cont'd)	315
3–1201(a)	281
	315
3–1201(b)	281
	315
3–1202	281
	316
3–1202, Comment	315
3–1203	123
	284
	317
3–1204	123
	284
	317
3–1204(a)	317
3–1204(b)	318
3–1204(b)—3–1204(c)	284
3–1204(c)	318
Art. IV	12
	21
	374
	505
4–101	21
4–101(1)—4–101(2)	444
4–201	309
	443
	504
4–202	443
4–203	443
4–204	309
	444
4–205	444
4–206	444
4–207	445
	505
4–301	446
	505
4–302	446
4–303(a)	446
4–303(b)	447
4–401	447
Art. V	12
	21

	This Work
Sec.	**Page**
Art. V (Cont'd)	23
	229
	453
	456
	457
Art. V, Pt. 1	8
	453
	457
Art. V, Pts. 1–4	459
5–101	465
5–101, Comment	466
5–102	466
5–102(b)	460
5–102, Comment	467
5–103	21
5–103(1)—5–103(22)	459
5–103(3)	459
5–103(6)	458
5–103(7)	476
5–103(21)	479
5–104	463
Art. V, Pt. 2	8
	453
	457
	458
5–201	474
5–201 to 5–212	458
	471
5–202	472
5–202(a)	472
5–202(b)	471
	472
5–202(c)	472
5–202(d)	472
5–203	472
5–204	472
5–204 to 5–206	472
5–204(a)	471
5–204(b)	473
5–205	463
5–206	485
5–206(b)	26
5–207	472

Sec.	This Work Page
5–208	462
5–209	458
5–209(a)	473
5–209(b)	473
5–209(b)(1)	473
5–209(c)	473
5–209(c)(2)	474
	482
5–209(d)	473
5–209(e)	473
5–209, Comment	473
5–210	474
5–211	461
5–212	471
5–212(a)	474
5–212(b)	475
5–212(c)	475
5–212(d)	475
5–247(c)	501
Art. V, Pt. 3	8
	453
	457
	458
5–301	476
	480
5–301 to 5–312	458
5–301(a)	477
5–301(b)	477
5–301(c)	477
5–301(d)	477
5–301, Comment	477
5–302	463
5–303(a)	478
5–303(b)	479
5–303(c)	479
5–304	478
	485
5–304(a)(1)	478
5–304(a)(2)	478
5–304(a)(3)	478
5–304(c)	26
	478
5–305(a)	479

Sec.	This Work Page
5–305(b)	479
	480
5–305(c)	480
5–306(a)	480
5–306(b)	480
5–306(c)	480
5–306(d)	480
5–306, Comment	481
5–307	462
5–308	481
5–308(a)	481
5–308(b)	481
5–309	458
	476
	481
	482
5–310	482
5–311(a)	482
5–311(b)	482
5–311(c)	483
5–311, Comment	483
5–312	461
Art. V, Pt. 4	8
	453
	457
	458
5–401	484
5–401 to 5–431	458
5–401(a)	485
5–401(b)	485
5–401(c)	19
	485
5–402(1)	461
5–402(2)	461
5–402(3)	462
5–403(1)	463
5–403(1)—5–403(2)	463
5–404(a)	485
5–405	26
5–405(a)	485
5–406(a)	486
5–406(b)	486
5–406(c)	486

Sec.	This Work Page
5–406(d)	486
	487
5–406(e)	486
5–406(f)	487
5–407	491
	492
	500
5–407(a)	487
5–407(a)(1)	491
5–407(a)(2)	491
5–407(b)(3)	103
	229
	491
5–407(c)	229
	492
5–407(d)	492
	500
5–408	487
5–408(a)	487
5–408(a)—5–408(b)	488
5–408(b)	488
5–408(c)	488
5–409(a)	489
5–409(a)(1)	505
5–409(a)(1)—5–409(a)(7)	489
5–409(b)	490
5–410	490
5–411	490
5–412	462
5–414	503
5–415(a)	462
	497
5–415(a)(4)	503
5–415(b)	462
	498
5–415(c)	497
5–416	496
5–417	496
	497
5–418	497
	502
	503
5–419	498

Sec.	This Work Page
5–419(b)	499
5–419(c)	499
5–420(a)	499
5–420(b)	499
5–421	498
5–422	500
5–423	459
	493
5–423(a)	493
	496
5–423(b)	493
5–423(c)	493
5–423(c)(1)—5–423(c)(26)	494
5–423(c)(25)	505
5–424(a)	494
5–424(a)(1)	494
5–424(a)(2)	494
5–424(a)(3)	494
5–424(a)(4)	495
5–424(b)	495
5–424(c)—5–424(d)	495
	502
5–424(e)	495
5–425	492
	500
5–426	492
	497
5–427	501
5–427(a)	501
5–427(b)	501
5–427(c)	502
5–427(d)	502
5–428	502
5–429	462
	503
5–430	504
5–431	504
Art. V, Pt. 5	8
	467
5–501	21
	468
5–501 to 5–503	468
5–501 to 5–505	467

Sec.	This Work Page
5–502	468
	469
5–503(a)	469
5–503(b)	470
5–504	467
5–505	468
Art. VI	8
	13
	21
	513
	514
6–101	508
6–101(a)(1)—6–101(a)(3)	508
6–101(b)	509
6–101, Comment	509
Art. VI, Pt. 2	512
6–201	21
	513
6–201(2)	516
6–201(4)	523
6–201(6)	514
6–201(8)	515
6–201(10)	515
	524
6–201(11)	519
6–201, Comment	514
	515
6–202	514
6–203	516
6–204(a)	516
6–204(b)	516
6–204, Comment	516
6–205(a)	516
6–206	513
6–206(b)	518
6–211	519
6–211(a)	519
6–211(b)	518
	519
6–211(c)	518
6–211(d)	516
	518
6–211, Comment	518

Sec.	This Work Page
6–211, Comment (Cont'd)	519
6–212(a)	519
	519
6–212(b)(1)	520
6–212(b)(2)	520
6–212(c)	516
	520
6–212(d)	521
6–212, Comment	519
6–213(a)	521
6–213(b)	521
6–214	521
6–214, Comment	521
6–215	521
6–215(a)	522
6–215(b)	522
6–215(d)	522
6–221	523
	524
6–222(1)	524
6–222(2)	524
6–223	524
6–224	524
6–225	524
6–226	516
	524
6–226(b)	525
6–227	525
Art. VI, Pt. 3	526
6–301	21
	526
	529
6–301(1)	528
6–301(2)	528
6–301(3)	530
6–301(4)	527
6–301(5)	527
6–301, Comment	527
	528
6–302	529
6–302, Comment	529
6–303	530
6–303, Comment	529

Sec.	This Work Page
6–304	528
6–305	528
6–306	530
6–306, Comment	531
6–307	531
6–308(a)	532
6–308(c)	532
6–308(d)	532
6–308, Comment	532
6–309	526
6–310	532
Art. VII	13
	23
	533
Art. VII, General Comment	534
Art. VII, Pt. 1, General Comment	536
	538
7–101	535
	537
	538
	552
7–102	536
7–103	538
7–103(a)	542
	552
7–103(b)	542
7–104	537
7–104, Comment	537
7–105	535
	552
	553
7–105, Comment	551
7–201	538
	542
7–201(a)	541
7–201(a)(2)	548
7–201(b)	538
	541
7–202	542
7–203	543
7–204	542
7–205	541
7–206	26

Sec.	This Work Page
7–206 (Cont'd)	541
7–301	545
7–302	380
	496
	545
	546
7–302 to 7–307	545
7–302, Comment	546
7–303	546
7–303(a)—7–303(c)	546
7–303, Comment	546
7–304	546
7–305	547
7–306	547
7–306(a)	548
7–306(b)	548
7–306(c)	548
7–306(d)	548
7–307	549
Art. VII, Pt. 4	549
Art. VIII	14
Art. X, Pt. 2	172

*

TABLE OF STATUTES

References are to Pages

UNITED STATES CODE ANNOTATED
26 U.S.C.A.—Internal Revenue Code

Sec.	This Work Page
2503(b)	69
2518	232

INHERITANCE (PROVISION FOR FAMILY AND DECENDANTS) ACT OF 1975

Sec.	This Work Page
Ch. 63	75

UNIFORM TESTAMENTARY ADDITIONS TO TRUST ACT

Sec.	This Work Page
1	165

STATE STATUTES

ARIZONA REVISED STATUTES

Sec.	This Work Page
14–3971	316

TABLE OF STATUTES

ARKANSAS CODE ANNOTATED

	This Work
Sec.	Page
28–9–211	61
28–9–215	30
28–11–301—28–11–305	39

WEST'S ANNOTATED CALIFORNIA PROBATE CODE

	This Work
Sec.	Page
2(b)	10
6111	136
	138
6111(b)(1)	138
6111(b)(2)	139
6408	61
6408, Comment	61

IDAHO CODE

	This Work
Sec.	Page
15–1–101 to 15–7–401	6

IOWA CODE ANNOTATED

	This Work
Sec.	Page
633.211	39

MINNESOTA STATUTES ANNOTATED

	This Work
Sec.	Page
524.2–102	39
524.2–102(1)	39

NEW MEXICO STATUTES ANNOTATED

	This Work
Sec.	Page
45–3–1201	316

LXXX

TABLE OF STATUTES

WYOMING STATUTES

Sec.	This Work Page
2–4–101(a)(ii)	39

TREASURY REGULATIONS

Reg.	This Work Page
20.2031–8	89

*

UNIFORM
PROBATE CODE
IN A NUTSHELL

THIRD EDITION

*

CHAPTER 1

GENERAL INTRODUCTION AND HISTORY

§ 1.01 General Introduction

The word "probate" in the English language has had a variety of meanings throughout the history of Anglo–American jurisprudence. Technically, the term "probate" refers to the process of proving and deciding the validity of a will before a court having competent jurisdiction; more generally, it refers to all matters appropriately before the probate courts. [Black's Law Dictionary]. Similarly, "probate courts" in the United States are granted jurisdiction not only over the probate of wills, but also the entire process of the administration of decedents' estates including their initiation, the collection of assets, the settling of creditors' claims and their closing and distribution. Some probate courts also have jurisdiction over the affairs and property of persons under a disability, such as minors and other incapacitated persons. Adding to this complexity several jurisdictions call probate courts "orphans' courts," "surrogate's courts," "courts of ordinary" or by the name of the court in the jurisdiction which has general or some other subject matter jurisdiction. [Atkinson, Wills § 4].

The Uniform Probate Code [Code] adopts a very broad meaning and application to the word "pro-

1

bate." It not only includes law dealing with the affairs and estates of decedents and persons under a disability but also includes law dealing with specified nontestamentary transfers, contracts and bank deposits and with certain procedural and substantive rules of trusts and their administration. The theory of the Code is that there is a close interrelationship between these various areas of law and that they are all in need of unification, modernization, clarification and uniformity.

Unquestionably the Code's content pertains to a cornerstone of our society. It is readily clear that the law dealing with the distribution and management of wealth at death or during disability is of profound concern and importance to our society. With the inevitability of death at some time and the inevitability of disability during minority and its reasonable possibility during the later years of life coupled with the present ability for people to possess or accumulate property the law dealing with these matters needs substantive rules which are relevant to modern societal needs and procedural rules which are efficient in time, cost and understanding. The Code addresses itself to these principles.

§ 1.02 History

Necessarily, no attempt will be made to trace the history of all of the areas of law dealt with by the Code. [See Averill, Eclectic History and Analysis, at 893–901]. Suffice it to say that many of the concepts of this area of law in this country are traceable to the English law system. Paradoxically, whereas when states first enacted probate laws they removed many of the archaic and undesirable elements of the English laws, the English probate law has now surpassed and excels over the law of most of the states today. Actually, many of the modern and improved rules and procedures presently existing under English law greatly influenced the draftsmen of the Uniform Probate Code. [Fratcher, Probate Can Be Quick and Cheap].

In recent years, the word "probate" unfortunately symbolizes in the minds of some people the evils of graft, waste and delay. The resultant cry has been "avoid probate." Professor Langbein contends that this is what is happening. [See Langbein, The Nonprobate Revolution]. Several successful commercial enterprises have been launched from this conceptual pad and they accuse the legal profession of perpetuating and perpetrating this undesirable situation.

The source of much of the present dissatisfaction is in the laws themselves. First, there is insufficient uniformity between the laws of the fifty states. This fact may cause not only unjust results but also an inherent confusion and distrust among a very mobile lay populace. Second, some of the relevant laws in this area in many states are not contemporary; consequently, they do not take into account the material changes which have occurred in our society. Not only have we changed from a primarily rural to primarily urban society but also from one with a primary emphasis directed to ownership of real estate to one directed toward ownership of personal property and other contractual relationships. Furthermore, our society continues to progress from one educationally and sociologically provincial to one nationally and even internationally cognizant. In addition, the continued increase in the number of person who have had multiple marriages and children with more than a single spouse creates a social phenomenon that much current succession law does not adequately address. This trend is one of the themes set out as one of the principal reasons for the substantial alteration to Article II made in the 1990 Code. [Art. 2, prefatory note]. Many of the present laws on these matters, therefore, do not adequately deal with the primary problems posed by the average person in regard to lifetime transfer and succession at death of wealth or in the management of that person's property during disability.

These deficiencies are not only obvious today but were obvious to some over fifty years ago. In 1940, Professor Atkinson suggested to the American Bar Association Section of Real Property, Probate and Trust Law [hereinafter referred to as the Probate Section] that this organization prepare a Model Probate Code. [Atkinson, Model Probate Code, at 189]. This idea resulted in the publication of a Model Probate Code and accompanying studies in 1946. [Model Probate Code].

Although the Model Probate Code had a direct influence and effect on revisions in several states, it had neither the comprehensiveness nor the impetus to influence a majority of states to adopt it. Therefore, in 1962, the Probate Section and the National Conference of Commissioners on Uniform State Laws [hereinafter referred to as the National Conference] accepted a suggestion made by J. Pennington Straus of the Philadelphia Bar to revise and consolidate the Model Probate Code and other related and relevant uniform laws into a uniform probate law. In response, each organization formed a separate committee and Professor William F. Fratcher of the University of Missouri School of Law was appointed Research Director to conduct preliminary studies during 1963–64. Thereafter a Reporting Staff was recruited to draft the Uniform Probate Code under the supervision of the two committees. Professor Richard V. Wellman then of the University of Michigan and now of the University of Georgia became the Reporting Staff's Chief Reporter.

After six drafts, six years of extensive research, consultation, and discussion, an official text was approved in August, 1969, by the National Conference and by the House of Delegates of the American Bar Association. Although inspired and initiated as a project to redraft and update the Model Probate Code, the eventual finished product turned out to be much more. It not only is more comprehensive in coverage but also exhibits greater innovation and imagination. In addition, many of its basic philosophies are different. Consequently, the Code offers a more viable package for influencing and affecting modern probate legislation.

Naturally, through the last twenty years the Code has been the subject of a great deal of legal commentary. A significant portion of it is cited throughout this Nutshell. One of the most important works publications was the *Uniform Probate Code Manual* published by the Association of Continuing Legal Education Administrators in 1972

and edited by Professor Robert R. Wright. [UPC
Practice Manual (1972)]. It contained a series of
articles by recognized authorities on all parts of
the Code. Professor Wellman, as editor, updated
and expanded this manual in a second edition
published in 1977. [UPC Practice Manual (1977)].
Since that edition, the manual has not been updated.

In March of 1971 Idaho [Idaho Code §§ 15–1–101
to 15–7–401 (Effective July 1, 1972)] became the
first state to adopt the Code substantially in whole.
Since that time, more than thirty percent of the
fifty states have enacted laws that substantially
conform to the Code or major parts of it. Pro-
motion and enactment of the Code have not been
easy in the states and have had varying degrees of
success. Its primary detractors include what
would appear to be bonding companies, loosely
organized groups of older bar members and occasionally newspaper publishers. In some situations,
these opponents have proved to be formidable ad-
versaries and have shown considerable influence in
the state legislature.

§ 1.03 Promulgation and Maintenance of the Code

For the purpose of promulgating the Uniform
Probate Code, a Joint Editorial Board for the Uniform Probate Code was established in 1970. [See
Averill, Eclectic History and Analysis, at 893–901].
Its membership consists of five persons nominated
by the National Conference and five nominated by
the Probate Section. Its responsibilities are: (a) to
monitor literature dealing with the Code; (b) to
watch for problems that develop in the Code itself

and that arise in states which have enacted or are considering enacting it; (c) to educate the Bar and public about the Code; and, (d) to reevaluate, alter and edit the Code's text for the purpose of removing imperfections and improving content, both substantially and editorially. Professor Wellman was named the Board's first Educational Director.

With all of this supervision and support, the Code is continually being updated and improved. During 1975–76, the National Conference and the House of Delegates of the American Bar Association approved significant amendments called the "1975 Technical Amendments" promulgated by the Joint Editorial Board. Many of these amendments included suggestions and improvements made by various bar committees which have studied the Code for enactment in their respective states. Other alterations were made in 1977, 1979, 1982, 1984, 1987, 1988, 1989, 1990, 1991 and 1993. [See UPC, at ix]. The 1990 revision substantially rewrote Article II. The process never stops, however. In 1993, significant Technical Amendments were introduced that substantially reorganized and reconstituted the Code's elective share provisions that had been rewritten in the 1990 revision.

When the initial enthusiasm and national effort to enact the Uniform Probate Code as a comprehensive code lost much of its original momentum, the National Conference altered its promotional approach regarding several new and old matters. In relevant, and appropriately separable, areas of probate law, the National Conference developed freestanding acts from similar provisions integrated into the Code as it existed at the relevant time.

The reverse chronology also occurred. Some separate Uniform Acts have been subsequently integrated into the Code in order to broaden its coverage. These techniques permitted the provisions to become law either as part of the whole Uniform Probate Code or as a separable and possibly more palatable distinct uniform act.

Accordingly, the Uniform Durable Power of Attorney Act was approved in 1979 and modified Part 5 of Article V; the Uniform Guardianship and Protective Proceedings Act was approved in 1982 and altered Parts 1, 2, 3, and 4 of Article V; the Uniform International Wills Act was approved in 1977 and added part 10 to Article 2; and the Uniform Succession Without Administration Act was approved in 1983 from sections 3–312 to 3–322 which had been added to Article III of the Code in 1982.

The trend to offer both an integrated text and freestanding acts has intensified during the last few years. The 1990 UPC contains several of them. The Uniform Statutory Rule Against Perpetuities Act, called USRAP, was promulgated separately in 1986 and was incorporated as Part 9 of the new Article II. The Uniform Nonprobate Transfers at Death Act which includes the Uniform Multiple–Person Accounts Act and the Uniform TOD Security Registration Act was promulgated in 1989 and mirrors Article VI of the 1990 UPC. The new Article II has been separately promulgated as the Uniform Intestacy, Wills, and Donative Transfers Act in 1991. Finally, section 2–702 of the 1990 UPC was promulgated as the new Uniform Simultaneous Death Act in 1991.

The existence of freestanding acts makes the Code a more dynamic document. It permits those who advocate probate and related law reform to select the most palatable part for passage in their jurisdiction. This should increase the influence of the Code on the law and motivate more jurisdictions to adopt its reform proposals.

§ 1.04   Influence of the Uniform Probate Code

The influence and the use of the Code is growing in a variety of ways. [See Anderson, Influence of the Uniform Probate Code]. The laws of nearly all if not all states have been affected by the Code. The primary vehicles of influence are as follows:

(1) Enactment as a Code in full with some amendments. Fourteen states fall into this category: Alaska, Arizona, Colorado, Florida, Hawaii, Idaho, Maine, Michigan, Minnesota, Montana, Nebraska, New Mexico, North Dakota, and Utah. [Code, at p. 1 (Supp.1992).

(2) Piece-meal enactment of segments or sections of the Code for inclusion into another probate code or law. Nearly all the other states have enacted some part or section of the Code. Sections of article II have been particularly popular. For example, California incorporated many provisions, in whole or in part, of the Code into its recent revision of its probate code. In order to assure proper judicial construction of these Code provisions, the new law requires that any portion of the California code which is derived "in substance" from the Uniform Probate Code, must be "construed as to effectuate the

general purpose to make uniform the laws of those states which enact" provisions of the Uniform Probate Code. [West's Ann.Cal.Prob.Code § 2(b)].

(3) Referred to as a model of modern policy by a court interpreting its own non Code provision. [See, e.g., First Church of Christ, Scientist v. Watson (1970)].

(4) Referred to as secondary or persuasive authority for determining proper rules of construction for the common law. [See, e.g., Russell v. Estate of Russell (1975); Thompson v. Potts (1981); Smith v. Smith (1974)].

Even if comprehensive enactment does not continue, the Code's influence over the law of probate and related matters will continue to increase.

§ 1.05 Outline and Overview

When one attempts to study and understand a body of law as complex and comprehensive as the Code is, one commonly, and possibly justifiably, has feelings of despair. In order to dispel these feelings, it is helpful for the reader or student to obtain an understanding of the document's organization and general content. Actually, one of the Code's most beneficial features is its functionally efficient organization. Its numbering system is the familiar one number hyphen three numbers [0–000] approach with which most are familiar from other Uniform Laws such as the Uniform Commercial Code. Organizationally, it is broken into eight articles within which numerous parts are included. This numbering system constitutes a part of the outline of the Code's content. Consequently, for every section of the Code the initial single number indicates the article within which this section is included, the first number of the group of three numbers indicates the part of the article within which it is found and the last two numbers indicate, of course, the particular section of the article and part cited. Each section in turn is frequently also divided into lettered subparts which greatly aid in identification and reference. For example, Section 2–505(a) indicates the following matters: (1) the initial "2" means it is part of Article II concerned with "Intestate Succession and Wills;" (2) the first "5" indicates that the section is in Part 5 of this Article and concerns "Wills"; (3) the "05" indicates the particular section number within this Part and Article entitled "Who May Witness" and (4) the "(a)" indicates the particular subparagraph in the section cited. This type of organization pervades the whole Code. With a little experience, one will know a substantial amount about the content of a section merely by knowing the entire section number.

In order to get a proper perspective of the Code, a brief summary of its content is appropriate. Article I contains what might be called the Code's housekeeping and foundational provisions. A few examples include sections dealing with the Code's purposes and rule of construction, important pervasive definitions, the court's subject matter jurisdiction and an inclusive method for and time of notice provision.

Article II contains twenty-three percent of the sections in the Code which makes it the second largest article. It includes the substantive core of what is referred to as the law of wills, intestate succession, and donative transfers. In addition to provisions dealing with how to execute a will and with distribution under intestacy, it also includes provisions concerning the surviving spouse's elective share, family protections, rules of construction for wills and other donative instruments, disclaimers, the safekeeping of wills, the Rule Against Perpetuities, and other related matters.

Article III is the largest article in the Code containing almost thirty-six percent of the sections. It consists of a comprehensive and flexible system for the probate of wills and the administration of decedents' estates. It includes, for example, provisions that: set a statute of limitations on probate and administration; create an administration system of multiple techniques for accomplishing the various desired actions; deal comprehensively with the status, function and activities of the personal representative; determine and settle creditors' claims; deal with distributions, closings and the compromising of controversies concerning estates; and, provide several special procedures to deal with the very small estate. Article IV is interrelated with Article III and deals with foreign personal representatives and ancillary administration.

Article V contains the third largest number of sections in the Code comprising approximately seventeen percent. It comprehensively covers the area of law concerned both with the protection of persons who are disabled either because of incapacity, disappearance or minority and with the protection of their property. Significantly, it also includes several escape devices so that elaborate formal procedures need not be used. The inclusion of guardianship provisions in a probate code is consistent with current jurisdictional concepts of probate courts under many court systems. In addition, because the fiduciary relationships and administrative functions of a guardian and a conservator are substantially similar to that of a personal representative, it is logical to include provisions on these matters in the Code.

The next two articles of the Code are not as obviously relevant to what would normally be conceived as probate matters. Article VI deals with non-probate transfers including durable powers of attorney, multiple-party bank accounts, transfer on death security registrations and other types of documents that relate to the effect of death on property. It is beneficial to include provisions on these matters in the Code due to the extreme state of confusion and lack of uniformity in the current law in most states and because they concern the succession of property at death. In addition, their validity and effect have a direct relationship to a personal representative's administration of a decedent's estate.

Finally, in Article VII the Code includes provisions concerned with the administration of both inter vivos and testamentary trusts. Article VII is divided into three parts which include trust registration, jurisdiction of the Court concerning trusts and the duties and liabilities of the trustee. These provisions were included in the Code for several reasons: (1) uniformity is needed as much in the area of trust administration law as it is in the area of decedents' estates law; (2) an obvious similarity exists between the relationship of a trustee to its beneficiaries and a personal representative to its beneficiaries; and (3) the full power Court concept of the Code, made it logical to include trustees under the jurisdiction of this Court.

Article VIII contains provisions concerned only with the Code's effective date and repealer and therefore needs no further discussion in this Nutshell.

PART ONE

GENERAL PROVISIONS, DEFINITIONS AND PROBATE JURISDICTION OF THE COURT

CHAPTER 2

PURPOSES, RULE OF CONSTRUCTION, POLICIES AND DEFINITIONS

§ 2.01 Purposes and Rule of Construction

Article I of the Code includes introductory provisions that generally define its purposes and rule of construction in conformance with the rules of good statutory draftsmanship. As is customary with uniform laws, it requests that courts liberally construe and apply the Code in a manner which will best carry out and promote its underlying purposes and policies. [1–102(a)]. In their broadest sense, the most obvious purposes of the Code are to make uniform and to improve the areas of law and procedure with which it is concerned among the several jurisdictions in the United States. [1–

102(b)]. Hallmark principles for accomplishing this meritorious reform include simplification, clarification, efficacy, efficiency and serviceability. [See 1–102(b)(1)–(5)]. Only time and experience with the Code's provisions will prove whether it can achieve its goals.

The Code also includes the other housekeeping provisions typically found in modern statutes. These provide that general principles of law and equity are to supplement the Code's own provisions [1–103], that provisions held to be invalid are to be severed from those which are valid and effective [1–104], and that if reasonably avoidable, subsequent legislation shall not impliedly repeal Code provisions in whole or in part. [1–105].

§ 2.02 Overriding Policies and Provisions

Article I of the Code includes several provisions that have pervasive and overriding application.

A. FRAUD

Any person, who is injured by another's fraud perpetrated in connection with any proceeding or filing under the Code, with the intent of circumventing the Code's provisions or purposes, may seek and obtain appropriate relief from the perpetrator or may seek and obtain restitution from any person, innocent or otherwise, who benefitted from the fraud. [1–106]. Bona fide purchasers are expressly exempt from such liability, however. When an action is permitted under this provision, a special statute of limitations is substituted for all other statutes of limitation ordinarily applicable. This time limitation period requires that the proceeding be commenced within two years after the discovery of the fraud but if against one who was not a perpetrator of the fraud, no later than five years after the commission of the fraud. Frauds perpetrated against the decedent during the decedent's lifetime are not included within the scope of this provision.

The effect of this provision prevents the Code's other limitation periods from protecting the fraud perpetrator or gratuitous beneficiaries. [1–106, Comment]. It also creates a remedy that is available directly against the perpetrator and other beneficiaries and that is supplemental to all of the other remedies and protections given under the Code. An important limitation on the scope of this section is that if there are formal proceedings with notice and hearing before the Court, res judicata may prevent persons who were properly before the Court and subject to the jurisdiction of those proceedings from instituting any actions under it.

B. PERJURY FOR FALSIFIED DOCUMENTS

In order to discourage misuse of the various Code's procedures, the penalties of perjury are applicable to any deliberate falsification of any document filed with the Court. [1–310]. The mere filing of an application, petition or demand for notice is deemed to include a verification of its veracity. The threat of perjury prosecution under this provision has broad application. Although perjury penalties will in all likelihood never be strictly or conscientiously enforced, the provision will serve as a psychological bar against misuse of the Code's procedures.

Significantly, verifications are apparently deemed to be a part of every filing even though the verification itself is absent from the document. This might mean, therefore, that the verification need not even be on the document thereby eliminating the need for notarization of documents filed with the Court. [See 18 Uniform Probate Code Notes (Joint Editorial Board for the Uniform Probate Code) 15 (Hereinafter cited as UPC Notes)].

C. PROOF OF DEATH OR STATUS

The Code establishes rules relating to the fact of death or of other status, such as one being missing or detained, because their determination can be a very important question arising during the course of proceedings under the Code. [1–107]. Generally, the rules of evidence used in the court of general jurisdiction are applicable to determine death in a judicial proceeding. [1–107]. In addition the Code contains the following specific provisions concerning evidence of death. First, the Code defines the meaning of death as that determined either (1) by the Uniform Determination of Death Act, or (2) if the enacting state does not have that Act, by a determination in accordance with accepted medical standards that there is an irreversible cessation of all functions of either (a) circulatory and respiratory function, or (b) the entire brain, including the brain stem. [1–107(1)]. Second, a certified or authenticated copy of a death certificate establishes prima facie proof of death, the place, date and time of death and the identity of the decedent provided the certificate appears to have been issued by an official or agency of the purported place of death. [1–107(2)]. Third, a certified or authenticated copy of any record or report of either a domestic or foreign governmental agency establishes prima facie evidence that a person is missing, detained, dead, or alive and of the dates, circumstances, and places disclosed in the document. [1–107(3)]. Fourth, if the prima facie evidence of either the second or the third rules is not available, evidence of death may be proof by any evidence including circumstantial evidence if proof satisfies the clear and convincing evidence standard of proof.

Fifth, when the previous rules do not apply, a person is presumed to be dead if a person has been absent for a continuous period of five years. [1–107(5)]. This presumption applies only if during that time the absent person was not heard from and after diligent search or inquiry no satisfactory explanation is available to explain the absence. Unless evidence can prove that death occurred earlier, the date of death is presumed to be at the end of the five-year period. The question of status concerning whether someone is "missing" is important, for example, when determining whether a conservator or other protective order can be issued to protect that missing person's property. [See 5–401(c)].

Finally, if a certificate that constitutes prima facie evidence under either the second or the third rules mentioned above states a time of death, that time is evidence of the determination whether a person survived another person by 120 hours. [1-107(6); see 2-104 and 2-702; §§ 5.06, 11.02]. If it shows the person survived by the required 120 hours, the time on the certificate is clear and convincing evidence of that survivorship. The timing of death of the person whose death must be survived may be determined by any of the above rules.

D. DEFINITIONS

The Code contains a large number of definitions that are applicable throughout its content. [1-201]. These definitions are extremely important to an understanding of the Code and any student of the Code must gain a working knowledge of them. For the sake of clarity, comprehension and brevity, the meaning of each word will be provided only when the definition is relevant to the discussion in this text. For informational and overview purposes, Chart 2-1 lists them in alphabetical order.

CHART 2–1

General Definitions

Agent
Application
Beneficiary
Beneficiary designation
Child
Claims
Community property *
Conservator
Court
Descendant
Devise
Devisee
Disability
Distributee
Estate
Exempt property
Fiduciary
Foreign personal representative
Formal proceedings
Governing instrument
Guardian
Heirs
Incapacitated person
Informal proceedings
Interested person
Issue
Joint tenants with the right of survivorship
Lease
Letters

Minor
Mortgage
Nonresident decedent
Organization
Parent
Payor
Person
Personal representative
Petition
Proceeding
Property
Protected person
Protective proceeding
Registrar
Security
Separate property *
Settlement
Special Administrator
State
Successor personal representative
Successors
Supervised Administration
Survive
Testacy proceeding
Testator
Trust
Trustee
Ward
Will

* Definitions for community property states, only.

Articles II, III, IV, V and VI also include separate definitions that control in particular sections, parts or articles. [See 2–202, 2–603, 2–706, 2–707, 2–709, 2–803, 2–804, 2–1001, 3–916, 4–101, 5–103, 5–501, 6–201, 6–301; see also 1–201, Comment].

CHAPTER 3

JURISDICTION, VENUE AND COURTS

§ 3.01 Jurisdiction and Multiple Venues

The Court under the Code is given subject matter jurisdiction over all subjects with which the Code deals including the administration of the decedents' estates, interpretation of wills, determination of heirs and successors, the estates of protected or disabled persons, the protection of disabled persons and trusts. [1–302(a)]. The Court is also empowered to take all "necessary and proper" action for the purpose of administering justice in any matters properly before it. [1–302(b)]. The territorial reach of the Court's jurisdiction is based on one of the following factors: (1) the relevant person was domiciled in the state, (2) the relevant property of a non-domiciliary is located in the state, (3) the relevant property is under the control of a fiduciary who is subject to the laws of the state, or (4) the person, contractual device or fiduciary relationship is within the state. [1–301]. The latter relationships to the state refer respectively to minors or incapacitated persons residing within the state, to the existence of multiple party accounts and security registrations located in the state and to trusts being subject to administration in the state.

22

The Code includes a detailed set of provisions dealing with the problems caused by the existence of multiple venues. When two or more courts are appropriate venues, the Court within which the proceeding was first commenced has exclusive right to continue its jurisdiction. [1–303(a)]. Furthermore, any issue concerning the venue must be determined by this Court and must be held in abeyance by any other court. [1–303(b)]. When the Court determines that in the interest of justice venue should be in another court, it may transfer the proceedings to another court of the same state. [1–303(c); see also 3–201(c)]. Although the parties do not need to re-initiate the proceeding when it is transferred under this provision, they will presumably be required to repeat some of the notices. [See 3–705, 3–801].

In addition to the above general provisions on jurisdiction and venue, the Code includes special subject matter jurisdiction, personal jurisdiction and venue rules for the probate of wills and administration of decedents' estates under Article III [see § 15.03], for the protection of persons under disability and their property under Article V [see § 28.02] and for the administration of trusts under Article VII. [See § 38.02].

§ 3.02   The Court and Registrar

With respect to matters concerning the courts and practice before them, the Code is extremely flexible and is designed to work within the framework of the state in which it is adopted. Generally, only two features appear to be essential: (1) the Court must be able to render binding adjudications in any civil litigation to which the fiduciary may be a party and (2) appeals from the Court must go to the same court to which appeals from courts of general jurisdiction go. [See 1–308, 1–309]. In other respects the Code conforms to the practice and procedure rules of the court of general jurisdiction in the state. [See 1–304 to 1–306].

The Code creates a new position or office in the Court. This position is called the "Registrar" and the person who holds this title will handle the informal proceedings to establish wills and to appoint personal representatives under Article III. [1–307; see 3–105, 3–303 to 3–311]. The Registrar's functions must be performed either by a judge of the Court or by a person so designated by a court order which must be filed and recorded in the office of the Court.

CHAPTER 4

NOTICE AND VIRTUAL REPRESENTATION

§ 4.01 Notice

Although several provisions contain their own special notice procedures [see, e.g., 3–801 (Notice to Creditors)], the principal method and time for giving notice for a formal proceeding under the Court's exclusive subject matter jurisdiction is contained in the Code in one inclusive provision. [1–401]. When notice of the time and place of a hearing on a petition for any hearing is necessary under this provision, it must be given to all interested persons or when appropriate to their attorneys. [1–401(a)]. The term "interested person" is broadly defined and basically includes any person with an interest in or against the estate involved in the proceeding. [1–201(24)]. The particular persons, who are considered interested and who require notice, may vary depending on the nature of each proceeding.

Three methods of giving notice of a hearing are provided and any one will, depending on the circumstances, satisfy the notice requirement. If the address and location of the person to be notified is known, then notice may be given either by registered or ordinary first class mail or by personal service. [1–401(a)(1)–(2)]. The mailing or the delivery of the notice must be accomplished at least fourteen days before the hearing date. If the address or identity of any person is unknown, notice must be made by publication once a week for three consecutive weeks in a county newspaper having general circulation. [1–401(a)(3)]. The last published notice must appear at least ten days before the hearing date. When good cause is shown, the Court is given the discretion to provide for a different method or time of giving notice for the hearing. [1–401(b)]. Petitioners must prove on or before the hearing that the appropriate notice was given and must file such proof in the proceeding. [1–401(c)]. Any person, including fiduciaries, may waive the required notice by filing a signed written waiver in the proceeding. [1–402]. Numerous provisions throughout the Code either expressly or impliedly require use of this notice provision, including those concerned with decedents' estates, guardianships and protective proceedings and trusts. [See, e.g., 3–106, 3–204, 3–403, 3–414, 3–502, 3–1001, 5–206(b), 5–304(c), 5–405, 7–206].

§ 4.02 Virtual Representation

When formal judicial proceedings arise involving trusts and estates, it is common to have a large number of persons whose interests may be affected by the proceedings. Frequently these persons are not only numerous but also unknown, unborn or unascertainable. Notwithstanding, their interests need to be protected. It is desirable, therefore, to have some rules that permit certain persons of a large group with a common interest to represent other persons with the same interest. This is referred to as the doctrine of virtual representation.

The Code includes a comprehensive provision explaining the scope and application of the virtual representation doctrine in Code proceedings. [1–403]. First, the doctrine applies solely to formal judicial proceedings involving trusts or estates and supervised settlements that are subject to the Code's subject matter jurisdiction. [1–403]. Second, in order for the representation rule to apply, it is required that the pleadings describe the interests affected and give reasonable information to their owners either by name or class or by reference to the instrument creating the interests or in some "other appropriate manner." [1–403(1)]. Third, if the above two requirements are satisfied, the following virtual representation rules are applicable.

1. Court orders that bind the sole holders or all co-holders of a general power of appointment or power of revocation bind all other persons to the extent that their interests are subject to these powers. [1–403(2)(i); see 1–108; § 12.-06(C)].

2. When no conflict of interest exists between a fiduciary and the persons for whom the fiduciary acts, Court orders binding the fiduciary may under some circumstances bind the person whose estate it controls. [1–403(2)(ii)]. This binding effect may occur between all of the fiduciary relationships dealt with in the Code, including the conservator-ward, guardian-ward, trustee-beneficiary (in specified situations) [see § 38.04],

the personal representative-persons interested in the decedent's undistributed estate, and sometimes even in the parent-child relationships.

3. An unrepresented, unborn or unascertained person is bound by court orders to the extent that person's interest was adequately represented by another participating person who had a substantially identical interest in the proceeding. [1–403(2)(iii)].

The final requirement in order for the above virtual representation rules to take effect is that notice must be given according to Section 1–401 to every interested person, to one of the specifically named persons who can bind other interested persons [1–403(3)(i)], or to all known persons who have interests substantially identical to those of the unborn or unascertained persons and who are not otherwise bound above. [1–403(3)(ii)].

If the Court determines that representation of an interest under the above rules would be inadequate, it has the discretion at any point in the proceedings to appoint a guardian ad litem to represent the interests of any person who is a minor, incapacitated, unborn, unascertained, or whose identity or address is unknown. [1–403(4)]. One guardian ad litem may be appointed to represent several persons or interests if these persons or interests do not between themselves raise conflicts of interests. When the Court exercises its discretion, the reasons for making an appointment of a guardian ad litem must become a part of the record of the proceedings.

PART TWO

INTESTATE SUCCESSION, WILLS AND DONATIVE TRANSFERS

CHAPTER 5

INTESTATE SUCCESSION

§ 5.01 Introduction

Studies indicate that a substantial percentage of persons who have accumulated wealth during their lifetime die without creating effective or totally effective inter vivos arrangements and without making effective testamentary instruments for the disposition of their property. When this happens, decedent's property passes by intestate succession according to a statutory estate plan. [See 2–101(a)].

The theoretical purpose of intestate succession statutes is to distribute a decedent's wealth in a pattern that represents a close facsimile to that which an average person would have designed had that person's desires been properly manifested. Obviously, to accomplish this task on a general basis legislatures have developed objective rather than subjective programs that are necessarily subject to debate. Furthermore, any legislation on this matter naturally reflects the attitudes of the legislature of that moment under its contemporary societal ideals and policies. Attitudes change, of course, as these ideas and policies change.

When it comes to an estate planned by operation of law, the state has many options. The extreme systems might run from a system of no inheritance and confiscation of the entire estate by the state to a complex regulatory system that distributes the estate to designated relatives on the basis of need. England has a form of the latter model creating a statutory trust of the inheritable estate for the benefit of certain close relatives including the surviving spouse and minor children. No state in this country, however, has adopted either of these systems.

Intestate inheritance is recognized by all fifty states and territories at least for the benefit of certain relatives. The standard intestacy statute specifically apportions the intestate's property among a list of prioritized relatives. The surviving spouse, descendants and parents of the intestate are the standard preferred beneficiaries. In varying degrees, other ancestors and collateral relations are also protected after the preferred relations. Except for the surviving spouse, inheritance is usually limited to consanguine relations. Occasionally, the surviving spouse's consanguine relations may take if the decedent's consanguine relations cannot. [See Ark. Code Ann. § 28–9–215] The relational range of consanguinity necessary in order to take in intestacy varies among the states.

Most intestacy statutes protect consanguine relations through grandparents and their descendants. Some even make no express relational cutoff point and if the specified relations in the statute cannot take, pass the intestate's estate to the determinable nearest of kin. All states recognized that the property escheats to the state if no one qualified under the intestacy provisions can take.

In recent times when intestacy statutes have been the subject of legislative reform, several policy disputes have arisen. For example, a policy controversy usually arises over the share of the surviving spouse. This controversy usually relates to the share that the surviving spouse takes when there are surviving descendants of the intestate and when there are no surviving descendants of the intestate but other consanguine relatives of the decedent survive. Many persons have urged that the share of the surviving spouse be enlarged from the share usually provided at common law and in many states, today. The 1969 version of the Code adopted this approach and the 1990 Code expands it further. Another common policy issue concerns the inheritance rights of nonmarital children and their natural parents. The common law was very restrictive of such rights and the current trend is to eliminate restrictions and to base inheritance on maternity and paternity determinations.

§ 5.02   General Pattern

As with the vast majority of intestacy statutes, the Code distributes the net intestate estate among decedent's relatives according to a set of contingencies. These contingencies divide the relatives into classes which are in turn scaled on a specific priority list. Except as will be explained under the concept of "representation," relatives included in a relational class of persons which is closer to the decedent, take to the exclusion of those in a relational class which is more distant from the decedent. The specific classes of relatives whose members are entitled to take as distributees under the Code include the decedent's "surviving spouse," "descendants," "parents," "descendants of decedent's parents," "grandparents" and "descendants of grandparents." [2–102, 2–103]. The Code uses the term descendant instead of the term issue. In that the term "issue" has biological connotations, the term "descendant" is more appropriate because the Code recognizes inheritance rights beyond biological relations, i.e., adoption. [2–102, Comment].

A key term in many of the classes of relatives described as taking a share is the word "descendant." [2–103]. This word is defined to include all of a person's lineal descendants at all generations. [1–201(9)]. Consequently, when the Code refers to a decedent's descendants, it means the decedent's children, grandchildren, great grandchildren, etc. When it refers to the descendants of the decedent's parents, it means the decedent's siblings (i.e., brothers and sisters), nephews and nieces, grandnephews and grandnieces, etc. [See Chart 5–1]. A reference to the descendants of grandparents, of course, means the decedent's uncles and aunts, first cousins, first cousins once removed in the descendancy, etc.

CHART 5–1

Relationship Diagram

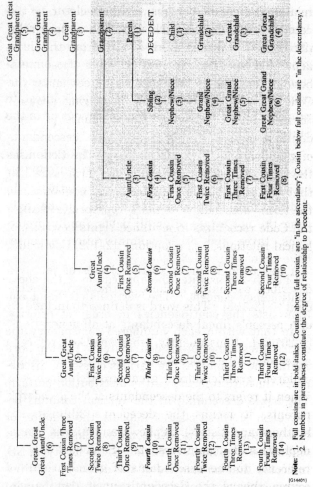

Note: 1. Full cousins are in bold italics. Cousins above full cousin are "in the ascendancy"; Cousin below full cousins are "in the descendancy."
2. Numbers in parentheses constitute the degree of relationship to Decedent.

[G14401]

Chart 5–1 diagrams a decedent's family tree. The shaded area emphasizes the Code's relational umbrella of covered relations. This protective umbrella has greater significance under the Code than merely to take in intestacy. [See, e.g., the Code's antilapse provision, 2–603; § 10.05].

If none of the above named classes of relatives include one or more persons qualified to take the estate, the Code provides that the property escheats to the State. [2–105]. This latter contingency means that no matter what the circumstances are when a person dies, the contingencies will adjust and will eventually pass one's intestate property either to some person or persons or to the State.

Significantly, the Code makes no distinction between real and personal property [1–201(39)] or between the sex of the surviving relatives. In addition, intestate distributions are made only from the net estate after all debts, family protections, taxes and other administration expenses have been paid. [3–807].

Chart 5–2 illustrates the application of the above contingency concept. The vertical left hand column lists the contingencies in order of priority. Note that within each numbered contingency the entire intestate estate is distributed. The top horizontal line designates the various classes of distributees that are relevant in the distribution pattern. The boxes descending in the vertical columns below each of these classes indicate the fraction or amount that persons who come within the classes will share or divide. In each box, the logotype, NS, indicates that no relative of the decedent qualifies within this class of distributees at the moment when the distribution shares are determined, and the logotype, 00, indicates that persons within this class would not take a share even if some of them qualified at the moment when distribution is made.

CHART 5–2

General Pattern of Intestate Succession Under the Uniform Probate Code (1990)

CONTINGENCIES	Spouse [2-102, 2-102A]	Descendants [2-102(1)(i), (3), (4), 2-103(1)]	Parents [2-102(2), 2-103(3)]	Parents' Descendants by Representation [2-103(3)]	Grandparents or their Descendants by Representation [2-103(4), 2-108(e)] Paternal	Grandparents or their Descendants by Representation [2-103(4), 2-108(e)] Maternal	State [2-105]
1-A	All	00*	∞	∞	∞	∞	∞
1-B	[$150,000] and ½ remainder	½ remainder**	∞	∞	∞	∞	∞
1-C	[$100,000] and ½ remainder	½ remainder***	∞	∞	∞	∞	∞
AND	All Community Property	00	∞	∞	∞	∞	∞
2	[$200,000] and ¾ Remainder	NS	¼ remainder	∞	∞	∞	∞
3	All	NS	NS	∞	∞	∞	∞
4	NS	All	∞	∞	∞	∞	∞
5	NS	NS	All	∞	∞	∞	∞
6	NS	NS	NS	All	∞	∞	∞
7	NS	NS	NS	NS	½	½	∞
8	NS	NS	NS	NS	All	NS	∞
9	NS	NS	NS	NS	NS	All	∞
10	NS	NS	NS	NS	NS	NS	Escheat

Header span: UNIFORM PROBATE CODE §§ 2-102, 2-102A, 2-103

LEGEND: NS indicates that no relative of the decedent qualifies within this class of distributees at the time when distribution is determined;
00 indicates that persons within this class can not take a share even if some of them qualify within this class when distribution is made

* If all of decedent's descendants are also the surviving spouse's descendants and no other descendants of the surviving spouse survives the decedent.

** If all of the decedent's surviving descendants are also descendants of the surviving spouse and the surviving spouse has one or more surviving descendants who are not descendants of the decedent.

*** If one or more of the decedent's surviving descendants are not descendants of the surviving spouse.

[G14402]

§ 5.03 Shares of the Surviving Spouse, Descendants and Other Relations

A. SHARES OF THE SURVIVING SPOUSE AND DESCENDANTS

Under the Code, depending upon the existence of specified relations to the decedent, a surviving spouse is accorded substantial shares if the decedent dies intestate. [See Chart 5–2]. The maximum share that a surviving spouse will take equals the total net intestate estate and the minimum share equals the first $100,000 of the net estate plus ½ anything exceeding that amount in the estate.

The surviving spouse takes all the intestate estate in two situations. First, the surviving spouse takes all the estate if the decedent is also survived by children who are all children of the decedent and the spouse. This is a new provision and is derived from several studies that indicate testators usually follow this approach in their wills. Because intestacy portions should closely track the distribution patterns of the typical testator, the findings were incorporated into the Code. Second, the surviving spouse takes all the estate if the decedent is not survived by descendants and parents notwithstanding other blood relations of the decedent survive. This is in line with the 1969 Code and the law in many state intestacy statutes.

Between the above two situations lie three special familial circumstances. If parents survive but no descendants survive, a surviving spouse takes the first $200,000 of the net estate plus ¾ of anything exceeding that amount in the estate. The large monetary prioritized amount insures that surviving spouses will take the entire estate in most cases.

Addressing the phenomenon of growing numbers of multi-relationship children, the Code reduces the share of a surviving spouse in order to provide for descendants who are not the surviving spouse's descendants. Notwithstanding the reduction, the share of the surviving spouse is substantial. If the decedent is survived by one or more descendants who are also descendants of the surviving spouse and by descendants who are not descendants of the surviving spouse, the surviving spouse takes the first $150,000 of the net estate plus ½ of anything exceeding that amount remaining in the estate. If decedent is not survived by one or more descendants who are also descendant of the surviving spouse but is survived by one or more descendants who are not descendants of the surviving spouse, the surviving spouse takes the first $100,000 of the net estate plus ½ of anything exceeding that amount in the estate. Both these provision give limited protection in relatively large estates to decedent's descendants of relationships other than the one existing at death.

When it is realized that the above share of the surviving spouse is in addition to the family protection [see § 8.02] and other nonprobate assets that pass to the spouse, it is clear that the Code will pass all of an intestate's estate in the predominant number of cases.

Recent legislation in several states has produced some variations on protecting the surviving spouse in intestacy. For example, in Minnesota the surviving spouse takes the first seventy thousand dollars plus one half of the balance of the intestate estate. [Minn.Stat.Ann. § 524.2–102]. In the same situation in Iowa, the surviving spouse of a decedent takes all of the property of the estate if the decedent left no issue or left issue all of whom are issue of the surviving spouse. [Iowa Code Ann. § 633.211]. Another common provision in this regard is that if there are no issue, the surviving spouse takes all of the intestate estate. [Iowa Code Ann. § 663.211; Minn.Stat.Ann. § 524.2–102(1); Wyo.Stat. 1977, § 2–4–101(a)(ii)]. Increasing the inheritance share to surviving spouses is in accord with current concepts of the needs of surviving spouses and with the typical distribution patterns of married persons who die with wills. On the other hand, there are states that still only provide the surviving spouse with one-third or less if issue survive. [See, e.g., Ark. Code Ann. §§ 28–11–301, –305].

B. SHARES OF OTHER RELATIVES

If an intestate dies and is not survived by a spouse or descendants, the entire net estate passes to the decedent's parents equally or if only one survives, to the survivor. If both parents fail to survive, the estate passes to their descendants by representation. If an intestate dies and is not survived by a spouse, descendants, decedent's parents or their descendants, the entire net estate passes to the decedent's grandparents or their descendants by representation. Grandparental shares are divided into maternal and paternal categories if one of more appropriate persons in both categories survive decedent. One-half passes to the maternal grandparents or their descendants by representation and the other one-half passes to the paternal grandparents or their descendants by representation. All surviving grandparents share equally the share passing in the appropriate category. Any surviving grandparent in either category takes to the exclusion of any surviving descendants of either grandparent in that category. If no grandparent survives in one category, the share of that category passes to the descendants of either grandparent in that category. If neither grandparent nor any of their descendants survive in one category, the share for that category passes in a similar manner to the grandparents or their descendants by representation in the other category.

An important variation between the Code and the law in many non-Code states concerns the issue of distant relatives and their intestate inheritance rights. The Code provides that the property will escheat to the State if there are no takers who qualify under its specific intestacy pattern. [2–105]. Consequently, decedent's grandparents and their descendants are the most distant relatives who can inherit under the Code. [2–103]. [See highlighted portion of Chart 5–1]. This feature is designed not only to simplify proof of relationship but also to cut off so-called "laughing heirs" who, as very distant relatives, are far beyond the normal confines of the modern family unit and the probable donative intent of the decedent. It probably does not conform to the desires of the typical person because most persons, if they think about the issue, do not want property to pass to the state. Of course, a person is able to benefit such distant relatives if that person so provides in a valid will or will substitute. The relational limitation on inheritance has been held valid against an equal protection contention by an intestate's second cousin and closest heir. [Estate of Jurek v. State (1988)].

C.   FACTUAL ILLUSTRATIONS

CHART 5–3
The Stairs of Inheritance

Assumption: In all of the following hypotheticals assume decedent, D, died intestate and the problem is to determine the respective shares of the named surviving persons. In all hypotheticals only D's closest relations are mentioned.

Hypothetical 1: Decedent is survived by spouse, S, and two children, A and B, who are children of both D and S.

Answer: S takes the entire estate.

Hypothetical 2: Decedent is survived by spouse, S, and two grandchildren, G1 and G2, who are descendants of both D and S.

Answer: S takes the entire estate.

Hypothetical 3: Decedent is survived by spouse, S, and two children, A and B; A is D's child by a prior relationship and B is a child of both D and S.

Answer: S takes the first [$100,000] and ½ of the balance of the estate;

A and B share equally the other ½ balance of the estate.

Hypothetical 4:   Decedent is survived by spouse, S, and two grandchildren, G1 and G2.   G1 is D's grandchild by a prior relationship and G2 is D's grandchild of both D and S.

Answer: S takes the first [$100,000] and ½ of the balance of the estate;

G1 and G2 share equally the other ½ balance of the estate by representation.

Hypothetical 5:   Decedent is survived by spouse, S, and two children, A and B, who are children of both D and S; D is also survived by C who is S' child from a prior relationship.

Answer: S takes the first [$150,000] and ½ of the balance of the estate;

A and B share equally the other ½ balance of the estate.

C takes nothing directly from D's estate.

Hypothetical 6:   Decedent is survived by spouse, S, and one or both parents but no descendants.

Answer: S takes the first [$200,000] and ¾ of the balance of the estate;

D's surviving parents share equally, or if only one survived the survivor takes, the ¼ balance of the estate.

Hypothetical 7:   Decedent is survived by one or more descendants and one or more parents; no spouse survived.

Answer: D's surviving descendants take the entire estate by representation.*

D's surviving parents take nothing from the estate.

Hypothetical 8:   Decedent is survived by one or more parents and one or more descendants of D's parents.

Answer: D's surviving parents share equally, or if only one survived the survivor takes, the entire estate;

The descendants of D's parents take nothing from D's estate.

Additional Assumption: The following hypotheticals assume that no spouse, descendants or parents of the decedent survived.

* The concept of representation is defined in the Code. [2–106; see § 5.04].

Hypothetical 9: Decedent is survived by one or more descendants of D's parents.

Answer: The descendants of D's parents take by representation.

Hypothetical 10: Decedent is survived by one or more maternal grandparents and one or more paternal grandparents and one or more descendants of both maternal and paternal grandparents.

Answer: D's surviving maternal grandparents share equally, or if only one survived the survivor takes, $\frac{1}{2}$ the estate;

D's surviving paternal grandparents share equally, or if only one survived the survivor takes, $\frac{1}{2}$ the estate;

None of the descendants of the grandparents take from the estate.

Hypothetical 11: Decedent is survived by one or more maternal grandparents, one or more descendants of maternal grandparents, and one or more descendants of paternal grandparents but no paternal grandparent survived.

Answer: D's surviving maternal grandparents share equally, or if only one survived the survivor takes, $\frac{1}{2}$ the estate;

The descendants of paternal grandparents take $\frac{1}{2}$ of the estate by representation;

None of the descendants of maternal grandparents take from the estate.

Hypothetical 12: Decedent is survived by one of more descendants of both the maternal and the paternal grandparents but no maternal or paternal grandparent survived.

Answer: Descendants of the maternal grandparents take $\frac{1}{2}$ the estate by representation;

Descendants of the maternal grandparents take $\frac{1}{2}$ the estate by representation.

Hypothetical 13: Decedent is survived by one or more maternal grandparents but no paternal grandparents or descendants of paternal grandparents survived.

Answer: D's surviving maternal grandparents
                    share equally, or if only one survived the
                    survivor takes, the entire estate;

Hypothetical 14: Decedent is survived by one or more de-
                    scendants of maternal grandparents but
                    no maternal grandparents and no paternal
                    grandparents or descendants of paternal
                    grandparents survived.

Answer: D's surviving descendants of the maternal
                    grandparents take the entire estate by
                    representation.

Hypothetical 15: Decedent is survived by one or more de-
                    scendants of paternal grandparents but no
                    paternal grandparents and no maternal
                    grandparents or descendants of maternal
                    grandparents survived.

Answer: D's surviving descendants of the paternal
                    grandparents take the entire estate by
                    representation.

Hypothetical 16: Decedent is survived by great-grandpar-
                    ents or descendants of great-grandparents
                    or both.

Answer: The estate escheats to the state.

§ 5.04   Descendants and Representation

When the Code designates the descendants of a
class of relatives as the takers in intestacy, it is
frequently necessary to reclassify these descendants into two sub-classifications which further
describe their relationship to the decedent. These
subclassifications can be visualized schematically
on vertical and horizontal graphic formats. The
vertical classification refers to a descendant's family tree or stocks of lineal ancestors and descendants. The horizontal classification refers to a
descendant's degree of relationship to the decedent.
Each degree of relationship is a separate generation. These sub-classifications can be better understood by examining Charts 5–4 and 5–5.

CHART 5–4

Stocks Identification

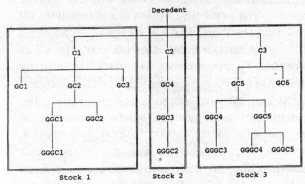

[LEGEND: C = Children; GC = Grandchildren; GGC = Great Grandchildren;
GGGC = Great Great Grandchildren]   [G14404]

CHART 5–5

Generation Identification

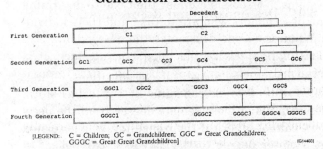

[LEGEND: C = Children; GC = Grandchildren; GGC = Great Grandchildren;
GGGC = Great Great Grandchildren]   [G14403]

Because these charts deal with a decedent's own
descendants, the starting point for examining the
vertical-horizontal sub-classifications is with the
decedent's three children. As Chart 5–4 indicates
vertically, each child constitutes a separate stock
within which that child's own descendant are listed

and graphed on a generation by generation basis. Child C1, grandchildren GC1, GC2, GC3, and their more remote descendants constitute one stock. (Stock 1). The same description is applicable to C2 and C3 and their respective descendants. (Stocks 2 and 3). As Chart 5–5 indicates horizontally, all of the decedent's descendants are classified also by degree or generation. Under this sub-classification the children constitute a separate generation, the grandchildren another and each generation of more remote descendants other generations. Therefore, C1, C2 and C3 are all in the same horizontal class, i.e., the First Generation. All the grandchildren would also constitute a horizontal class of their own, i.e., the Second Generation. The same type of vertical and horizontal analysis is also relevant to decedent's collateral relatives. [See Chart 5–1]. By using these two classification systems, it is possible under the Code to determine the descendants who are to take and their individual shares.

Two general principles are important in the application of the above sub-classifications. First, with respect to descendants in the same stock, descendants of more remote degree from the decedent cannot inherit if their ancestor, who is related in a closer degree to the decedent, can take. In other words, using Chart 5–4 again as an example, GC1 will not be able to take anything by intestacy if C1 can take. The same rule would apply to the other grandchildren if their respective ancestor is able to take. Second, descendants of more remote degree from the decedent can inherit if their ancestor, who is related in a closer degree, cannot take even though there are other descendants of closer degree. In other words, using Chart 5–4 again as an example, GC1 will be able to take by intestacy if C1 can not take. GC1 can take even if C2 and C3 can take because GC1 is allowed to represent GC1's ancestor. This is basically the application of the doctrine of "representation."

The concept of representation is recognized in some form or another in all common law jurisdictions. As indicated, it permits persons who are of more remote degree of kinship to an intestate to take some share from the estate even though there are relatives of closer degree of kinship to the intestate. Unfortunately, understanding the basic concept does not adequately explain what share each relative will take. Neither the commonly used terms of "per capita" and "per stirpes," nor the many statutory variations have adequately or consistently explained the meaning of the concept. The most common problem has been the determination of the generation which is to be considered the root generation for purposes of setting the stock shares of the more remote relatives who are able to represent their ancestors. For example, under a common but not uniform interpretation of the words "per stirpes," this root generation was always the generation closest in degree of relationship to the decedent even if none of those in the closest degree were able to take.

The antithesis of representation is a system of pure per capita with no representation. This system provides that all persons of the same degree of relationship who are in the closest degree relationship take an equal share. Descendants of the relation are not allowed to represent the ancestor. A pure per capita without representation system is not applicable in any state to resolve intestate inheritance issues of descendants of the decedent but has been used in some states to resolve inheritance issues in regard to distant collateral relations.

With the caveat that there are many variations, the concept of representation has been defined in three basic ways. For convenience, they will be call per stirpes, per capita with per capita representation, and per capita at each generation.

Per stirpes: Under a per stirpes system, the initial division of the estate is made at the generation nearest to the decedent, regardless of whether there are any members of that generation who are alive. The number of primary shares is the number of living persons in that nearest generation plus the number of deceased persons who themselves have living descendants. The latter are permitted to represent their ancestor

Per capita with per capita representation: Under a per capita with per capita representation, the initial division of the estate is made at the first generation which left a living member. Representation is recognized for living descendants of that generation. The same approach is taken in dividing the share of each deceased member of that generation who leaves descendants surviving. This was the system adopted in the 1969 Code.

Per capita at each generation: Under a per capita at each generation system, the estate is divided into primary shares at the first generation which contains one or more living members. Representation is recognized for living descendants of this generation. After the living members are allocated their shares, the remaining shares are combined and divided among the next generation which contains any living members in the same way, and so on. The Code now officially adopts this system. [2–106].

Using Chart 5–4, the following example contrasts the three approaches. If C2 and C3 are alive, C1 is deceased and all grandchildren are alive, all three systems will distribute among the descendants in the same manner: the portion that the descendants receive will be divided into three stocks with C2 and C3 each receiving one-third and the grandchildren of C1 dividing their ancestor's one-third stock share equally. Accordingly, GC1, GC2 and GC3 will each receive one-third of one-third or one-ninth. None of the grandchildren (C2 and C3's children) will share in the estate because their respective ancestors, C2 or C3, survived and took their shares.

If all of the children (C1, C2 and C3) are dead, however, the per stirpes system will divide it differently from the other two systems. Here, per stirpes continues to designate the children as the root generation; consequently, the portion will be divided into three stocks again and the grandchildren of each child would divide their one-third stock equally. GC4 will obviously receive more than the others because there is no one else with whom to divide the one-third stock share. Under per capita with per capita representation and per capita at each generation, the distributable portion will be divided equally to each grandchild. Because all takers are of the same degree of relationship to the decedent, these system ignore the stocks involved and distributes the estate on a per capita basis.

There are circumstances where per capita with per capita representation will operate in the same way as per stirpes, but per capita at each generation will be different. Generally, this will occur when there are three or more persons in a generation, of which one or more survived the decedent but two or more failed to survive leaving representatives.

Using Chart 5–4, presume that C3 survived but that C1 and C2 are deceased. As explained above under both the per stirpes and per capita with per capita representation systems, the distributable portion will be divided into three stock shares. C3 receives a full one-third, and the children of each deceased child (C1 and C2) divide their ancestor's one-third stock share. GC1, GC2 and GC3 take one-third of one-third or one-ninth and GC4 takes a full one-third. If the per capita at each generation method applied, the distributable portion is also divided into thirds and C3 would receive the one-third. The remaining two stock shares, however, are combined together and the children of the deceased children, C1 and C2, each share equally in the remaining two-thirds of the estate. In other words, rather than retaining the stock shares and dividing these shares depending on how many children each represented ancestor had, all of the persons in the same generation always receive an equal share. In our example, each grandchild representing an ancestor receives one-fourth of two-thirds or one-sixth. If several of these grandchildren are also unable to take and if they left surviving descendants, the same procedure is followed again by combining all of the shares for the deceased grandchildren into one share and then by dividing it equally among all of the great grandchildren who represent their ancestors.

The foundation for using the per capita at each generation system, lies in the belief that most decedents, if they thought about it, desire to divide the estate equally among living relatives of equal degree but to favor a living relative of a closer degree. [See 2–106, Comment]. The importance of the matter is relevant only when the descendants are of unequal degree. A notable feature of the per capita at each generation method is that it never allows a person of more remote degree to inherit more than a person of closer degree. In addition, the Code carefully avoids the problem of share manipulation through the use of disclaimers. For example, in the last hypothetical, if C3 had three or more children or descendants of children, could C3, by disclaiming the share, cause a larger share to pass to C3's descendants than C3 would take directly? The Code prohibits this because takers from disclaimant only receive the share the disclaimant would have received. [See § 12.02].

Chart 5–6 provides another hypothetical and its resolution under the most common representation methods including the ones discussed above.

It is important to emphasize that although the examples discussed were concerned with the decedent's own descendants, the Code's methods are equally applicable to representation determinations concerning the descendants of decedent's parents or grandparents.

CHART 5–6

Representation Hypothetical and Resolution

A.   Graphic Problem

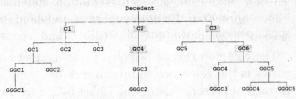

[LEGEND: C = Children;   GC = Grandchildren;   GGC = Great Grandchildren;
GGGC = Great Great Grandchildren;   ▓▓▓ = Deceased]

B.   Assumptions and Problem

1.   Decedent is predeceased by the following: C1, C2, C3, GC4, and GC6. Assume the net estate is valued at $108,000. Of the surviving descendants, who, in what fractions and amounts, will take under:
   a.   Per stirpes;
   b.   Per capita without representation;
   c.   Per capita with per capita representation; and,
   d.   Per capita at each generation. [2-106].

C.   Problem Resolutions

Answers in Fractions	GC1	GC2	GC3	GC5	GGC3	GGC4	GGC5
1. Per Stirpes	1/9	1/9	1/9	1/6	1/3	1/12	1/12
2. Per Capita without representation	1/4	1/4	1/4	1/4	-0-	-0-	-0-
3. Per capita with per capita representation	1/6	1/6	1/6	1/6	1/6	1/12	1/12
4. Per Capita at each generation [2-106]	1/6	1/6	1/6	1/6	1/9	1/9	1/9

D.   Fractions converted to Dollars
1.   1/3   = $36,000
2.   1/4   = $27,000
3.   1/6   = $18,000
4.   1/9   = $12,000
5.   1/12   = $9,000

[G14405]

§ 5.05   Determination of Status

A.   INTRODUCTION TO STATUS

The Code describes its intestate succession beneficiaries in terms of relational classification including "parent," "grandparent," "descendant," "heirs" and "surviving spouse." For distribution calculation purposes, it is necessary to identify the person or persons who qualify as members of these classifications. This determination is a problem of status. Because of the importance of this problem for intestate succession and other related purposes, the Code contains several specific provisions concerning the status of step-descendants, step-ancestors, half-bloods, posthumous heirs, adopted persons, persons born out of wedlock and spouses.

The common thread between these distinct categories is the reference to inheritance by, from and through a person. Using the Chart 5–7, if by, from and through inheritance is applicable, there is inheritance by C from P and through P from P's other descendants and P's ancestors and collateral relations: conversely, there is inheritance by P from C and through C from C's descendants.

CHART 5–7

By, From and Through

```
                          PR
                           |
            From P   P   By P      |  Through P
              ↓             ↑
Through C  |  By C    C   From C    |
                           |
                          CD
```

Legend: C = Child with Status Concern; CD = Child's Descendants, P = Parents; PR = Parents' Relations (including P's other descendants, P's ancestors and collaterals)   [G14406]

B. ADOPTED PERSONS

One's classification as a member of a relational classification may be based upon adoption. The issue of the consequences of an adoption has been a common subject of inheritance legislation. The legislation throughout the fifty-plus jurisdictions in this country varies in scope and content. The Code includes a provision for adopted persons that attempts to deal with the primary issues faced from an inheritance standpoint. [2–114(b)]. The Code does not define what adopted means. Assumably, it refers to a court proceeding set out in other statutes of enacting jurisdiction. The question whether relationships of persons in the nature of adopted relationships will satisfy this provision is also unanswered by the Code. Concepts of equitable adoption and other similar remedial inheritance devices would have to be developed by the courts aside from the specific terms of the Code. [See, e.g., Atkinson, Wills § 23, at pp. 91–92].

The Code recognizes that there are two primary types of adoption circumstances. For purposes of convenience these types might be called the "new family adoption," and the "family realignment adoption." They will be discussed separately.

New Family Adoption: The "new family adoption," concerns the situation where a natural parent or both natural parents voluntarily put their child up for adoption and an entirely new family, usually a husband and wife, adopt this child. In this situation, the Code adopts the policy of severing the relationship of the adopted child from that child's natural parents: it grafts a new relationship between the adopted child and the adopting parents for inheritance purposes. [See Chart 5–8]. Under this analysis, the adopted person inherits by, from and through that person's adopting parents and vice-versa. [2–114(b)]. On the other hand, no by, from or through inheritance rights continue between the adopted child and the natural parents or vice-versa. [2–114(b)]. A total severance of the inheritance relationship is accomplished.

Using Chart 5–8 for reference, if any of AC's adopted family died intestate and AC was entitled to a share, AC, or AC's descendants if AC did not survive, inherit from AC's adopting parents, APS, and from the adopting parents' relations through APS if APS did not survive. The reverse is also applicable. If AC or AC's descendants died, AP would inherit from AC and from AC's descendants through AC if AC did not survive. In addition AP's other relations would inherit from AC through AP if AP did not survive. In the new family adoption situation, however, inheritance rights between AC and AC's natural parents, NP, are severed. AC will not inherit from or through NP and NP will not inherit from or through AC.

CHART 5–8

Adopted Person's Family Tree

New Family Adoption

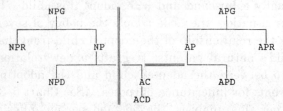

Legend: AC = Adopted Child; AP = Adopted Parents; NP = Natural Parents; _D = Descendants; _G = Ancestors; _R = Collateral Relations; | = Adoption wall; — = Adoption bridge   [G14407]

Family Realignment Adoption: The "family realignment adoption" is a more complex situation and requires greater elaboration from an inheritance standpoint. This type of adoption concerns the situation where one of the natural parents continues as a normal custodial parent of the child, a new adopting parent or non-natural parent adopts this child, and the other natural parent continues in a noncustodial relationship. [See Chart 5–9]. In this situation, the Code does not automatically sever inheritance possibilities between the child and either of the child's natural parents. [2–114(b)]. The child is permitted to inherit by, from and through both natural parents and the adopting parent. The adopting parent inherits by, from and through the child. Either natural parent may also inherit by, from and through the child if that natural parent has openly treated the child as that person's child and has not refused to support the child during the child's years when support is legally mandated. [2–114(c)].

CHART 5–9

Adopted Person's Family Tree
Family Realignment Adoption

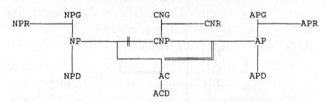

Legend: AC = Adopted Child; CNP = Custodial Natural Parent; NP = Noncustodial Natural Parent; _D = Descendant; _G = Ancestors; N_ = Natural Relationship; _P = Parent; _R = Collateral Relations; | = Adoption wall; — = Adoption bridge   [G14408]

This provision permits an adopted person, AC, who has been adopted by a new spouse, to inherit from three parents: the two natural parents, CNP and NP, and the adopting parent, AP. AC is capable of inheriting from relatives of any of the three parents through the parent if any or all of these parents failed to survive. The adopting parent, AP, will inherit from AC, but the natural parents, CNP and NP, individually inherit from AC only if each openly treated AC as a child and willingly supported AC. Considered through the viewpoint of the adopted child, these provisions seem reasonable. It may be totally contrary to the desires of the custodial natural parent to think that the child's property might go to the noncustodial natural parent or that parent's relatives, but it is not the custodial natural parent's concerns or interests that are important.

Using Chart 5–9 for reference, if any of AC's adopted family died intestate and AC was entitled to a share, AC, or AC's descendants if AC did not survive, would inherit from AC's adopting parent, AP, and through this adopting parent from the adopting parent's relations if AP did not survive. The reverse is also applicable. If AC died, AP would inherit from AC and from AC's descendants through AC if AC did not survive. In addition AP's other relations would inherit from AC through AP if AP did not survive. As contrasted to the "new family adoption" situation, inheritance rights are not totally severed from the AC's natural parents: AC will inherit from CNP and NP and through CNP and NP. Neither CNP nor NP will inherit from AC, however, unless each openly treated AC as his or her own and did not refuse to support AC. The same by, from and through analysis applies also to AC's descendants.

C. HALF–BLOODED PERSONS

Half-blooded relatives are decedent's collateral relatives who share one common ancestor with that of the decedent but not both common ancestors. Descendants of parents and grandparents who are only "relatives" of the half-blood to the decedents inherit the same as they would if they were whole-blooded relatives. [2–107].

D. AFTERBORN (POSTHUMOUS) PERSONS

Individuals who were conceived before the decedent's death but born after it, inherit the same as if they had been born during the decedent's lifetime. [2–108]. These persons must live 120 hours or more after their birth in order to qualify. The only relatives who might be able to fall within this category would be either decedent's descendants, parents' descendants or grandparents' descendants.

E. NONMARITAL ISSUE

States have typically had special statutes dealing with the status of persons born out of wedlock or, using current terminology, nonmarital persons. [Atkinson, Wills § 22]. Although these statutes vary greatly in scope and context, generally they deal with inheritance by, from and through the person born out of wedlock. Recent judicial decisions have caused many states to review their present law.

The Code is no exception to this transition. The Code provides that the marital status of parents as far as their children are concerned is irrelevant for inheritance purposes. [2–114(a)]. In other words, within the meaning of the intestacy laws for purposes of determining succession, a nonmarital child inherits by, through, and from natural parents so long as the parent and child relationship can be established. Inheritance by or from the child by natural parents, however, occurs only if the parent openly treated the child as the parent's child and did not refuse to support the child while the parent had a legal obligation to provide support. The parent-child relationship or parentage may be established under the relevant state law, such as the Uniform Parentage Act which was approved by the National Conference in 1973. [Uniform Parentage Act].

F. RELATIONSHIPS BY AFFINITY

Under the Code the most important relationship by affinity is the spousal relationship. This not only has importance in dealing with distribution in intestacy but also with elective share rights, the revocation of wills, the family protections and in priority for appointment as personal representative. Although the Code leaves the requirements for a marriage to the law of domestic relations, it specifically explains how, what and when legal proceedings sever the relationship. [2–802]. An explanation of this provision is provided below. [See § 12.03].

Except for the inheritance rights of the surviving spouse, relatives who are related to the decedent solely by affinity do not inherit under the Code. [See In re Estate of Brewington (1977)]. When the Code uses the relational terminology parents, grandparents or descendants, persons classifiable in those groups as step or foster relations are excluded from these classes of persons. [1–201(5), (9), (33)]. California, however, now treats the relationship between a person and the person's foster stepparent the same as if it were an adoptive relationship under two conditions. The conditions are (1) that the relationship began while the stepchild was a minor and continued through the parties' joint lifetimes, and (2) clear and convincing evidence establishes that the foster or stepparent would have adopted the person except for a legal barrier. [West's Ann. Cal. Prob. Code § 6408]. The comment to the section observes that the typical example satisfying the second condition would be where the parent of the foster or stepchild refused to consent to the adoption by the foster or stepparent. [West's Ann. Cal. Prob. Code § 6408, Comment].

G. ALIENS OR NONCITIZENS

Despite their unconstitutionality, reciprocity or "Iron Curtain" acts still exist in some states. [E.g., Ark. Code Ann. § 28–9–211]. These statutes usually state that a noncitizen heir cannot inherit from a domiciled decedent unless a domiciled heir may inherit from a decedent in the noncitizen's state or country. Under the Code, persons who are aliens or noncitizen are not disqualified merely because of their alienage. [2–113].

§ 5.06 Survivorship and Simultaneous Death

In order to inherit, an heir must survive the intestate. The general common law rule holds, however, that survival need not be for any specific length of time: any measurable length of time such as one minute or theoretically one second is sufficient. When the question of one's survival materially affects the distribution of the intestate's estate, the timing of death becomes an extremely disrupting and litigable issue. Many states have attempted to alleviate the problem by enacting the original Uniform Simultaneous Death Act. [Uniform Simultaneous Death Act (1940)]. Section 1 of this Act provides that in an intestacy situation when "there is no sufficient evidence that the persons have died otherwise than simultaneously, the property of each person shall be disposed of as if he had survived. * * * " Unfortunately, this solution is only a partial one. It clearly implies that if there is adequate proof of the actual sequence of death in measurable time, the presumption does not apply and the "surviving" heir, no matter for how short a period of time, will be entitled to inherit that heir's intestate share from the intestate's estate. This issue alone has caused litigation over who survived, and unnecessary expense by requiring multiple administrations of the same property. [See, e.g., Matter of Bucci (1968); Schmitt v. Pierce (1961)].

The Code's survivorship provision for inheritance in intestacy eliminates these problems in the vast majority of situations. Drawing upon a frequently employed estate planning device, the Code requires that in order to qualify as an heir, a person must survive the decedent for 120 hours. [2–104]. Furthermore, the burden of proving the heir's survivorship for the stated length of time is put on those who claim through the heir. All failures of such proof are conclusively presumed to show failure to survive. [See § 2.02(c)]. The only exception to this rule is that the survival time requirement does not apply if the decedent's property would escheat to the state because of a death of the only heir or heirs during this time period. In this situation, the common law's mere survivorship rule applies.

Although questions of the time of death might still present a problem, this provision will substantially reduce litigation over who has survived and avoid multiple administration of the same property where it is totally unnecessary. On the other hand, the provision could have an adverse tax consequence in a very large intestate estate, if the federal or other estate tax marital deduction is lost because a surviving spouse dies within the 120 hour period. Large estates of this nature, however, generally have received proper estate planning advice and consequently should include a will, which contains its own simultaneous death and survivorship requirements.

The Code adopts as a default rule of construction the same durational survivorship technique for all types of gratuitous transfers including wills and all other governing instruments. [See 2–702; § 11.-02]. The 120 hour survivorship requirement is now part of the 1991 version of the Uniform Simultaneous Death Act. [Uniform Simultaneous Death Act (1991)].

§ 5.07 Prior Gifts and Transactions

A. ADVANCEMENTS

At common law an heir's intestate share would be affected if the heir received an advancement from the intestate during the latter's lifetime. By common law definition, an advancement meant an irrevocable inter vivos gift of money or property, real or personal, to a child by a parent that enables the child to anticipate the child's inheritance from the parent to the extent of the gift. [Atkinson, Wills § 129]. If a child who received an advancement subjected the advancement to the "hotchpot,"[1] its value was added to the estate for calculation purposes only, and the child's distribution directly from the intestate's estate equaled the excess of the child's share over the value of the advancement received. If the value of the child's advancement exceeded the child's intestate share, the child would neither participate in the hotchpot nor receive an intestate share from the estate. The child, of course, kept the advancement. The theory of this doctrine is to bring about a degree of equality between the children of a decedent. Some states have extended the doctrine to other heirs in addition to the intestate's children.

1. A hotchpot is a fictional estate that is determined for calculation purposes only. It does not ever actually exist but is used to determine the proper distribution amount from estates that do exist.

The principal question raised when there has been an inter vivos gift by a donor to a prospective heir is whether the gift is intended as an advancement. Because the intent of the donor at the time of the gift is the determinative factor, not all such gifts are so characterized. Seldom, however, does one find that a donor has clearly indicated that intent. The transferring document, if there even is one, will seldom specifically indicate one way or the other. The result has been that the question of what constitutes proof of this intent has caused a substantial amount of litigation.

The relevant Code provision clarifies, expands, and restricts the application of the advancement doctrine. [2–109]. A gift is an advancement only if any one of several formalities is satisfied. A gift is a formal advancement if either the donor "declared in a contemporaneous writing" or the heir "acknowledged in writing" that the gift is an advancement. [2–109(a)]. The required writing may, rather than declaring the gift is an advancement, merely indicate that the gift must be taken into account in computing the division or distribution of decedent's intestate estate. No words of art such as "advancement" must be used by the donor. The gist of the declaration must indicate that the donor intended that the gift constitutes what lawyers call advancements. There is also no specific requirement that the written declaration of intent to make a formal advancement has to be communicated to the donee at the time of the gift. It could be a contemporaneous written note or indication that the gift is a formal advancement which is included with the donor's personal records. Of course, the writing must be available or provable after the donor's death when distribution decisions are made.

The Code extends the application of the advancement concept to any individual who is an heir. This is a major extension of the doctrine from many state statutes that limit the doctrine solely to gifts to decedent's children or descendants. [Atkinson, Wills § 129, at p. 722]. In the Code, the word "heirs" is defined to include all those who would be entitled to take by intestate succession the decedent's property including the surviving spouse. [1–201(21)]. Consequently, formal advancements may be made to collateral relatives and even to the surviving spouse and affect their intestate shares.

Although under the 1969 Code, the advancee had to be both a "prospective heir" at the time of the gift and an heir at the decedent's death to cause a formal advancement to affect advancee's intestate's share, the 1990 Code requires only that the advancee be an heir at decedent's death. [2–110(a) and Comment]. The scenario mentioned in the Comment concerns a written advancement to a grandchild at the time the grandchild's parent (the decedent's child) is still alive. If the donor dies and the child and grandchild survive, the child takes a full share and the advancement is of no consequence because the grandchild does not take anything in intestacy due to the survivorship of the grandchild's ancestor. If on the other hand the child died between the date of the gift and donor's death, the formal advancement now causes the grandchild to have his or her intestacy share reduced by the amount of the advancement.

Whereas the common law limited advancements to decedents who died totally intestate, the Code applies its doctrine of advancement to decedents who die either totally or partially intestate. This is an extension of the doctrine and reverses the common law presumption that a testator who died with a will that passed a portion of the estate had revoked all advancements. This extension is justified considering the Code's formality requirement and the interrelationship and consistency of the concept of advancement with the Code's provision dealing with the related testacy doctrine of ademption by satisfaction. [See 2–609; § 10.05].

The Code specifically provides that where a donee of a formal advancement fails to survive the donor, the formal advancement does not affect the shares that the donee's descendants take from the donor's intestate estate unless the donor's contemporaneous writing expressly provides that the gift affects the descendants' shares. [2–109(c)]. A donee's written acknowledgement that the gift affects the donee's descendants is not sufficient and will not rebut the statutory presumption. The latter limitation is a change from the 1969 Code, which allowed either the donor's writing or donee's acknowledgement to bind the donee's descendants. The Code prevents an advancee, however, from disclaiming his or her intestate share for the purpose of having a full intestate share pass to his or her descendants. This is accomplished through the disclaimer section which provides that only the disclaimant's interest not the share devolves to the disclaimant's descendants. [2–801(d)(1)]. The result is that the advancee's descendants take only the advancee's share from the decedent's estate less the value of the formal advancement if relevant to the issue.

The Comment states that a formal advancement need not necessarily be an outright gift. [2–109, Comment]. If the formality requirements are met, other will substitutes such as life insurance payable to the advancee could constitute an advancement under the Code.

If a formal advancement exists, the provision's Comment explains how to adjust for it in distributing the decedent's intestate estate. [2–109, Comment]. [See also § 5.07(B)]. Valuation of a formal advancement is determined as of the time of the donee's possession or enjoyment or as of the donor's death, whichever occurs first. [2–109(c)].

Although the formality requirements probably coincide with modern estate planning practice and theory, because most gifts today are not thought of as transfers in anticipation of an inheritance, there are still pluses and minuses to consider. On the positive side, the rules alleviate the evidentiary problem of proving intent by requiring that the intent be in writing. Frequent litigation attempting to discover decedent's intent is precluded by the irrebuttable presumption. On the negative side, the provision precludes proof of intent unless a proper writing is present even where decedent clearly expressed intent in forms other than in writing. For example, the Code's formality requirement may deny proof of decedent's clearly expressed oral intent. If the gifts are of a small nature, little real harm is done and the policy recognized by the Code is meritoriously carried out. If, however, large gifts were made to an heir that were intended to be advancements, no amount of evidence showing that intent is admissible unless the statutory formality is satisfied.

It may be unrealistic to expect a person to put advancement intent in a proper writing when we know that person died intestate and probably did not seek legal counsel for his or her financial matters. It would not be unreasonable to assume that most persons would consider large gifts of $10,000 or more to have strings attached. Generally, most people desire equality among equals and the extra windfall of large gifts made to one and not to others during the intestate's lifetime is not consistent with that principle.

In a perfect society, persons would not make large gifts without advice of counsel, but we know this is not the case. It seems that a middle ground might have been created that applies the writing requirement to gifts under $10,000 [2] but for gifts above $10,000 applies a presumption, either for or against, an advancement construction with the qualification that relevant extrinsic information, including declarations by the decedent, would be admissible to determine the intent.

2. The federal gift tax law says that gifts of $10,000 or less per person per year are exempt from gift and estate tax consequences. I.R.C. § 2503(b). Therefore, similar to the Code's no-advancement rule, gifts of that nature have no subsequent consequences. The reverse is true of gifts above the amount: they do have gift and estate tax consequences.

B. FACTUAL ILLUSTRATIONS

CHART 5–10

Advancement Calculations

Hypothetical   In all of the following hypotheticals assume decedent, D, made gifts to the named donees and these gifts were declared in a proper writing to be an advancement to the donee. Assume that D died intestate and D was survived by a spouse, S, two children, C1 and C2, and a grandchild, G1. G1 was C3's child; C3 did not survive D. C1 is D's child by a previous relationship. The problem is to determine the respective distributive intestate shares of the takers from D's estate.

Assumption 1:   D made advancements of $20,000 to C2, $50,000 to C3, and $30,000 to G1. D's total distributable estate equals $350,000.

Answer:

Hotchpot	Amount	
Distributable Estate*	$350,000	
C2's Advancement	$ 20,000	
G1's Advancement	$ 30,000	
Total of Hotchpot	$400,000	

Distribution		
S's share equals		$250,000
Remaining estate	$150,000	
C1's ⅓ Share		$ 50,000
C2's ⅓ Share	$50,000–$20,000	$ 30,000
G1's ⅓ Share	$50,000–$30,000	$ 20,000
Total Distributed from Estate*		$350,000

Comment: Because C3 did not survive D and does not take from D's estate, C3's advancement is ignored. C1, C2 and G1 shares equal the balance of the estate after the surviving spouse share is deducted. The advancements received are deducted from the heirs who received them in order to equalize the gratuitous transfers to the heirs. Because C3's advancement did not specifically include G1, it does not affect G1's share from D's estate. The advancement directly to G1 affects G1's share even if G1 was not an heir at the time of the advancement because G1 is an heir at the time of D's death.

Assumption 2:   D made advancements of $20,000 to C2 and $50,000 to G1. D's total distributable estate equals $210,000.

Answer:

Hotchpot # 1	Amount	
Distributable Estate*	$210,000	
C2's Advancement	$ 20,000	
G1's Advancement	$ 50,000	
Total of Hotchpot	$280,000	

Distribution		
S's share equals		$190,000
Remaining estate	$90,000	
C1's ⅓ Share		$30,000
C2's ⅓ Share	$30,000–$20,000	$10,000
G1's ⅓ Share	$30,000–$50,000	($20,000)

Comment: Because G1 owes $20,000 to the estate if G1 participates in the hotchpot, G1 will not participate.

* The Distributable Estate and the Total Distributed from Estate amounts must be identical; otherwise, an error in calculation has occurred.

A second hotchpot must be completed.

Answer:	Hotchpot # 2	Amount	
	Distributable Estate*	$210,000	
	C2's Advancement	$20,000	
	Total of Hotchpot	$230,000	
	Distribution		
	S's share equals		$165,000
	Remaining estate	$65,000	
	C1's ⅓ Share		$ 32,500
	C2's ⅓ Share	$32,500–$20,000	$ 12,500
	Total Distributed from Estate*		$210,000

Comment: Because G1 did not participate, C1's and C2's intestate shares equal ½ of the balance of the estate after the surviving spouse share is deducted. G1 does not take the normal intestacy share but G1 also does not have to return the advancement.

* The Distributable Estate and the Total Distributed from Estate amounts must be identical; otherwise, an error in calculation has occurred.

C. DEBTOR HEIRS

Although the Code permits the debt owed to the estate by a debtor-heir to be charged against the heir's intestate share, it does not permit that debt to be charged against the share of the debtor-heir's descendants if the debtor-heir fails to survive the decedent. [2–111; see also 3–903; § 23.01].

§ 5.08 Negative Testacy Provision

The common law generally stated that one could not disinherit an heir by fiat. [Atkinson, Wills § 36, at p. 145]. Consequently, if a person executed a will that disinherited the person's heir but for whatever reason that will did not pass all of decedent's property, the heir would still be able to share. For example, if T wrote a will that stated "I give all my property to X. I intentionally disinherit my son C and do not want my son to take anything from this estate" C would be disinherited if X is capable of taking at T's death. But if X died prior to T and did not leave someone who could take in his or her place according to the law of lapse or antilapse, C would be able to take.

The Code includes a provision recognizing what might be considered the negative will as far as intestacy is concerned. It provides that if a decedent has excluded or limited the right of an heir to succeed to that person's intestate property, the exclusion or limit is binding even if the decedent dies intestate. For example, using the above example, C would not take even if X's devise lapsed. The share of the disinherited heir passes as if the heir disclaimed the interest. [2–101(b)]. There may be situations where it is difficult to determine whether the decedent intentionally disinherited an heir. For example, mere omission from the will would probably not be considered the expressed disinheritance required under this section. On the other hand, a will that states that an heir is disinherited or that an heir shall only receive a certain amount from the estate and no more, would constitute the type of disinheritance for which this section would operate. As mentioned, the disinherited heir's share in intestacy passes as if that heir had disclaimed the interest. This means that the disinherited heir's descendants may take by representation but only the share the heir would have received. [2–101, Comment].

CHAPTER 6

ELECTIVE SHARE OF SURVIV-
ING SPOUSE AND THE AUG-
MENTED ESTATE CONCEPT

§ 6.01   Introduction to Spousal Protections

If one were to build a spousal protection statute
from the beginning, many difficult decisions would
have to be made. The threshold question would be
whether a spousal protection statute is needed at
all. Studies indicate that the vast majority of
married persons pass substantial portions of their
estates to their surviving spouses and that spousal
disinheritance is not a major problem. The problem, however, is that some circumstances and cases
have arisen where people have attempted to disinherit their surviving spouses. Marital discord and
other difficulties sometimes cause married persons
to act like non-married persons. Consequently, it
is worthwhile for the law to provide a safety net so
that those who are unfairly disinherited will be
able to protect their merited interest in the decedent's estate. On the other hand, its limited utility indicates that caution should be taken to limit
protective provisions to situations deserving control and not to extend protection beyond its purpose and to cause interference with legitimate
property allocations.

Assuming a spousal protection statute is desirable, there are numerous types of protection devices that might be selected. Anglo–American common law initially selected the dower/curtesy concept to protect spouses from disinheritance. This was primarily a real property protection device and typically was limited to a one-third life interest. Many states have expanded the concept to include personal property and have often enlarged the fractional interest in the estate from a life estate to one in fee.

The forced share is another common protection device enacted in many states. With wide variations, a typical forced share statute provides that if a decedent spouse does not pass a minimum arbitrary percentage, usually running from one-third to one-half, of that person's probate estate to the surviving spouse, the surviving spouse may elect to take that share under a spousal protection right. [Atkinson, Wills § 33]. The electing spouse takes the share in fee.

A third device, called community property, is found in nine states. This is a combined accrual and accumulation technique providing that property gained during a marriage is owned equally by each spouse. Community property goes beyond the typical spousal protection provisions that are found in common law states because it establishes a lifetime division of the property as well as a method for dividing an estate upon death of a spouse. It is actually a property division system among married persons and not merely a post-death safety-net minimum protection technique. Each spouse is treated in a sense as a tenant in common of the property earned by both spouses during the marriage. Community property operates as a protection from inter vivos disposition as well as testamentary disinheritance. States that have community property do not ordinarily need other spousal protection statutes although some have them to deal with noncommunity property acquired by the spouses before and during marriage.

A fourth device is a judicial share determined after death by some tribunal on the basis of set criteria. The financial needs of the surviving spouse and children are the primary considerations. The process empowers the appropriate judicial tribunal, usually a probate court, with the authority to entrust assets of the decedent's estate into a type of statutory trust for the benefit of the surviving spouse and other dependent persons. It springs from an assumed legal obligation on the part of the decedent to provide support for certain designated relatives. It suffers from indefiniteness as to application and result. A system of this nature prevails in England and other commonwealth countries. [See, e.g., Inheritance (Provision for Family and Dependents) Act 1975, c. 63].

Aside from the share, another consideration for a spousal protection provision concerns the coverage of the safety net. Dower and forced share have generally been limited to providing protection from the assets that are a part of the decedent's estate. Inter vivos transfers to others and the surviving spouse have, with a few exceptional circumstances, been excluded from the protective device. Other concepts developed to prevent this,

such as permitting the surviving spouse to recover
from intent to defraud transfers, or illusory transfers, have not operated satisfactorily and have not
provided the necessary predictability for planning
purposes. In addition, seldom did the law take
into account assets the surviving spouse may have
received by other devices. Consequently, there
was frequently the potential for over-protection for
the surviving spouse. If the spousal protection is a
safety net, this is as much an evil of the law as the
disinheritance technique constituted.

Another concern relates to the scope of the protected beneficiaries. Most current devices only
protect the surviving spouse. There are certainly
arguments for the protection of dependent children
and dependent relatives or companions. With the
exception of protection for certain descendants in
Louisiana, the protection statutes have not gone
beyond the surviving spouse.

Assuming an identifiable sum or share is protected for the surviving spouse, it is necessary to
determine the method by which the share will be
satisfied. Most protective devices favor the lump
sum, distribute outright, approach. Periodic payments offer another alternative. This method
would be particularly applicable if need were the
primary determinant of the share. If periodic payments are made on the basis of need, the question
of their duration arises.

Other factors might be relevant. Should the
length of the marriage be a significant factor to the
amount of the safety net protection? Should certain types of misconduct on the part of the surviv-

ing spouse cause a loss of the safety net? And finally, should the safety net be applied to the appropriate family unit regardless of the marital status of the persons.

With rare exceptions, states have enacted statutes which in some manner or other protect the surviving spouse from disinheritance by the decedent spouse. These statutes can be generally and broadly categorized into three types: statutory dower, forced share and community property. Within each category there is a large variety of methods and combinations. [Atkinson, Wills § 33]. The fractional interest among these categories range from one-third to one-half or is sometimes tied into the surviving spouse's intestate share. Depending upon the type, the shares are sometimes exempt from the decedent's creditors' claims and sometimes not exempt. They may also differ as to whether the surviving spouse must make an election against the will to obtain a share or must renounce the share in order to take under decedent's estate plan.

Although the Code accepts the spousal protection concept and includes an elective share device, its provisions differ significantly in scope and procedure from anything existent in non-Code states today. [See Kurtz, Augmented Estate]. Significantly, the Code's spousal protection provisions are intended only for common law jurisdictions which enact the Code and not for community property states. [App. VII, Art. II, Pt. 2, General Comment].

The Code's decipherable purposes for its spousal protection system are eclectic. They include de-

sires: (1) to confer upon married persons broad
freedom of disposition; (2) to provide a protective
monetary safety net against spousal disinheritance; (3) to give recognition to the economic partnership of marriage by increasing the protective
share for longer marriages than for shorter ones;
(4) to adjust for the dispositional problems raised
by multiple marriages and multi-family descendants; (5) to prevent will substitutes from defeat-
ing the prior purposes; (6) to prevent the surviving
spouse from electing the forced share when decedent's estate plan adequately provides for the
spouse or when the spouse's personal wealth compares to decedent's wealth; (7) to ease administration of the protective share processes; and (8) to
provide predictability for persons who adequately
plan their estates. It is clear that these purposes
will not be consistently achievable in all circumstances. Because of potential conflict between
them under specific circumstances, they point toward theoretical aspirations and not to subjective
particular results.

§ 6.02 Elective Share of the Surviving Spouse

The 1990 Code made significant alterations to
the elective share provisions of the 1969 version.
In most respects, the new provisions built upon the
1969 version. Although the 1990 Code includes
the augmented estate concept, it drastically alters
the method and amount of protection accorded the
surviving spouse and requires significant alterations in the composition and funding of the augmented estate. 1993 Technical Amendments reorganized and renumbered the 1990 version and

made several significant substantive changes. The following discussion refers to the 1993 version.

Under the Code, dower and curtesy are abolished. [2–113]. In addition, the Code's election applies only if the decedent was domiciled at death in the Code state; otherwise the spousal protection laws of the decedent's domicile control those rights. [2–201(d)]. If the domicile requirement is met, then the surviving spouse may elect to take a sliding scaled percentage of the "augmented estate." [2–201(a)]. Significantly, the surviving spouse is entitled to the family protection in addition to the elective share protection. [See §§ 8.01–02]. This means that a surviving spouse will be able to take the entire probate estate or $43,000 of it, whichever is less, as satisfaction of the family protection. The elective share protection is additional to this protection. [2–201(c)].

The opportunity to take this elective share exists whether the decedent died intestate, testate with a will which disinherits the surviving spouse, or testate with a will which gives all or part of the estate to the surviving spouse. The decision to elect depends upon three determinations: (1) the elective share amount; (2) the determination of the augmented estate; and (3) the satisfaction of the elective share amount.

Whereas the elective share in the 1969 version of the Code adopted an absolute one-third share of the augmented estate as the foundational protection for the surviving spouse, the Code now adopts an accrual-type elective share. [Art. II, Pt. 2, Elective Share of Surviving Spouse, Gen. Comment]. The method of accrual employs a rational but arbitrary rising percentage scale based upon the length of the marriage. The elective share percentage ascends from a low of three percent of the augmented estate after the first year of marriage to a high of fifty percent of the augmented estate after fifteen years of marriage. The Code's incremental percentage accrues at the rate of three percent per year for the first ten years and then four percent per year for the next five years. At the end of fifteen years, each spouse has earned a fifty percent interest at death in each of the other's entire estate. [See Chart 6–1]. In addition, the Code includes a supplemental or minimum safety-net monetary amount for a surviving spouse below which the elective share cannot equal regardless of the length of the marriage. Accordingly, any surviving spouse is entitled to a minimum elective share of $50,000. The amount of the minimum amount is suggested and subject to alteration by an enacting state.

CHART 6–1

Elective Share Percentage

Length of Marriage	Elective Share Percentage
Less than 1 year	Supplemental amount only
1 year but less than 2 years	3% of the augmented estate
2 years but less than 3 years	6% of the augmented estate
3 years but less than 4 years	9% of the augmented estate
4 years but less than 5 years	12% of the augmented estate
5 years but less than 6 years	15% of the augmented estate
6 years but less than 7 years	18% of the augmented estate
7 years but less than 8 years	21% of the augmented estate
8 years but less than 9 years	24% of the augmented estate
9 years but less than 10 years	27% of the augmented estate

Length of Marriage	Elective Share Percentage
10 years but less than 11 years	30% of the augmented estate
11 years but less than 12 years	34% of the augmented estate
12 years but less than 13 years	38% of the augmented estate
13 years but less than 14 years	42% of the augmented estate
14 years but less than 15 years	46% of the augmented estate
15 years or more	50% of the augmented estate

The accrual approach theorizes that marriages are similar to economic partnerships and thus the partnership interest of one spouse should increase in the other spouse's assets as the marriage endures. At the moment persons are married, little of their property has been earned as a result of the marriage in an economic partnership sense. The Code provides that as the marriage continues each spouse earns an increasing percentage interest in the estate of the other spouse. This percentage constitutes the share that may be elected at the death of a spouse by the surviving spouse. This reciprocal maturing interest attaches to all of the assets of both spouses not merely the assets acquired during the marriage. This pervasive accrual approach differs significantly from community property states where the automatic one-half interest attaches only to assets earned during the marriage and not to "separate property" obtained prior to marriage or derived from third persons by inheritance or gratuitous transfer during marriage. Administrative efficiency is promoted because there need not be any tracing of assets to determine their source. It also roughly accords with the ways that married persons treat their assets: few distinguish separate from marital property when making gifts or devises to spouses.

After determining the appropriate elective share, it is necessary to identify an estate against which the elective share will be computed and funded. As indicated, the Code calls this estate the "augmented estate." [2–202; § 6.03]. It starts with the decedent's estate that is subject to administration through a decedent's estate and that passes at decedent's death either by intestacy or by testacy. To be fully effective, however, the spousal protection statute must take into account certain inter vivos transfers of the decedent spouse. Consequently, the Code includes in the augmented estate what it calls the decedent's non probate estate. If this strategy is not effected, persons determined to disinherit their spouses could easily transfer their assets to third persons through the use of relatively frail inter vivos transactions or of probate estate purging transfers on their deathbed or in near deathbed situations. A law that permits easy and unburdensome avoidance establishes too vast a loophole and encourages disinheritance even in the most undesirable situation.

Concomitantly, the Code prevents the surviving spouse from receiving more than the circumstances merit. Thus, the surviving spouse must include in the augmented estate both the assets derivable from the decedent as a result of the latter's death and all of the surviving spouse's personal assets including the surviving spouse's comparable nonprobate transfers to others. These latter inclusions discourage elections by surviving spouses in marriages of short duration and where the surviving spouse has substantial personal assets.

Finally, recognizing an underlying philosophy of freedom of disposition and clarity of title and ownership, the Code excludes several categories of nonmarital interests and completed lifetime transfers made by either spouse.

The sum of the value of decedent's controllable estate plus the value of the surviving spouse's controllable estate less the value of nonmarital interests and completed transfers equal the augmented estate. [§ 6.03].

For added protection from disinheritance, the Code includes a monetary minimum for all surviving spouses. Equal to a suggested $50,000, this provision guarantees that the surviving spouse will not take less than this amount from the augmented estate. If after funding the surviving spouse's elective share amount, the spouse takes less than $50,000, the spouse is entitled to take from the nonspousal beneficiaries of the augmented estate the difference between what the spouse took under the elective share and $50,000. The difference is satisfied from the nonspousal portions of the augmented estate in the same order as the elective share is satisfied. [2–203(b), (c); § 6.05]. This supplemental amount is calculated by subtracting from $50,000 the amounts that the surviving spouse receives from the elective share process. Funding of this amount is discussed below. [See § 6.05].

In summary, the Code's elective share recognizes the importance of the length of the marriage, adopts an efficient mechanical calculation technique, includes the appropriate parts of the assets from both the decedent and surviving spouse's estate plans, excludes completed transactions that should not be disturbed because of the death of a prior owner, and provides a fixed dollar minimum amount for support protection.

§ 6.03 The Augmented Estate Calculation

A. DEFINITION OF THE AUGMENTED ESTATE

The augmented estate concept is the most complex part of the Code's elective share device and a thorough understanding of its meaning and scope is essential. [2–202]. The augmented estate is a hotchpot estate in that it does not really exist as a cohesive estate. [See § 5.07]. It is created for purposes of calculating the value of the elective share. Similar but separate concepts deal with the funding of the elective share amount. [2–203; see § 6.05].

Generally, the augmented estate includes all assets less liabilities owned or controlled by the decedent and by the decedent's surviving spouse plus certain gratuitous transfers made by either spouse to third persons. More specifically, it is composed of four distinct segments. [2–202]. If the same property or interest is includable in more than one segment, it is includable in the segment that would yield the highest value; however, the value for the same interest may only be included in one segment. [2–202(e)].

B. SEGMENT 1 OF THE AUGMENTED ESTATE

The first segment (hereinafter called Segment 1) includes what normally is thought of as the decedent's gross probate estate less enforceable claims, funeral and administration expenses, and the family protections. [2–202(b)(1)]. The probate estate is composed of all the property that passes by intestacy if a person had died intestate. [2–202(a)(1)(vii)]. Claims include all of decedent's liabilities at death but do not include estate and inheritance taxes or title disputes over probate estate property. [2–202, Comment; see 1–201(6) (Claims)]. The valuation of Segment 1 property is determined at the date of death [2–202(b)(1); see also 3–706].

C. SEGMENT 2 OF THE AUGMENTED ESTATE

The second segment (hereinafter called Segment 2) includes all properties over which decedent immediately prior to death retained certain interests, powers or relationships. [2–202(b)(2)]. The Code refers to Segment 2 properties as the "decedent's nonprobate transfers to others." [2–202(a)(1)(i)]. Although transfers of this nature pass outside the probate estate, they may be subject to reclaim if they are required to contribute to the funding of the surviving spouse's elective share amount. [2–202(b)(2); see 2–203(b)(c); see also § 6.05]. Properties that have comparable relationships to the surviving spouse are includable in the augmented estate under Segment 4. [2–202(b)(4)].

The following interests are included as Segment 2 property:

(1) The value of all nonprobate transfers to others (third persons), including all types of property interests, no matter where situated but not including property included in Segment 1, in which decedent retained at the time of death a particular interest or power. The following transfers are included:

(A) Property over which decedent retained a personal, unshared, presently exercisable general power of appointment. [2–202(b)(2)(i)(A)]. A presently exercisable general power of appointment is defined as a power exercisable in favor of the decedent, decedent's creditors or creditors of decedent's estate and includes a power to revoke or invade the principal of the interest. [2–202(a)(1)(vi)]. It makes no difference whether (1) decedent or someone else created the power, [2–202, Comment]; (2) the interest was created before or after the marriage to the surviving spouse; or, (3) at the time in question, the decedent had capacity to exercise the power. [2–202(a)(1)(vi)]. A typical example of a property interest includable under this provision is property in a trust which the decedent may unilaterally revoke. This provision prevents the revocable inter vivos trust and other forms of revocable property transfers from being effective spousal protection avoidance devices. A power of this nature is equivalent to full ownership; therefore, its inclusion in the augmented estate is reasonable.

(B) Property in which decedent held a fractional interest in joint tenancy with right of survivorship with one or more third persons. [2–202(b)(2)(i)(B)]. It makes no difference whether (1) decedent personally or someone else created the fractional interest in decedent, [Cf. 2–202, Comment]; or (2) the interest was created before or after the marriage to the surviving spouse. It applies to all joint tenancies with right of survivorship interests even if the decedent does not hold a unilateral power to sever the joint tenancy but merely holds an equal voice in such decision. [2–202, Comment]. It is the fractional interest coupled with the right of survivorship that triggers the inclusion of these interests. A joint interest in a survivorship interest is equivalent to full ownership as to the fractional part. The value of the includable property equals the value of the fractional interest to the extent it passed by right of survivorship.

(C) Property in which decedent held an ownership interest in any property, account or registration held in POD, TOD, or co-ownership with right of survivorship. [2–202(b)(2)(i)(C)]. It makes no difference whether the interest was created before or after the marriage to the surviving spouse. It applies to all types of financial arrangements in which decedent held accounts or other financial devices in decedent's own name with a survivorship interest in one or more third persons. The value of the includable interest is the extent of the decedent's ownership interest that passed at death to or for the third persons named on the account. Typical examples of property interests includable under this provision consist of multiple-party financial and security TOD registration accounts. [See §§ 34.01, 35.01] An ownership interest in one of these account is equivalent to full ownership; therefore, its inclusion in the augmented estate is reasonable.

(D) The proceeds of any type of life insurance policy on decedent's life that decedent owned immediately prior to death or over which decedent retained a personal, unshared, presently exercisable general power of appointment over the policy or its proceeds. [2–202(b)(2)(i)(D)]. Ownership is not defined but probably includes any incident of ownership such as a power to change the beneficiary. A power includes the power to designate the beneficiary of the policy. [2–202(a)(1)(v)]. Life insurance is broadly defined to include accidental death insurance. It makes no difference who originally purchased the policy or whether the policy was purchased before or after the marriage to the surviving spouse so long as the decedent owns the policy or holds a presently exercisable power of appointment over it. The value of the includable amount equals the value of the proceeds to the extent they passes to third persons at decedent's death. As part of the surviving spouse's nonprobate transfers to others, however, policies on and controlled by the surviving spouse are valued at their adjusted interpolated terminal reserve value as of decedent's date of death. [2–202, Comment; see Treas. Reg. § 20.2031–8]. The control over a life insurance policy required by this provision is equivalent to full ownership of the policy.

It is important to note that Segment 2 does not specifically include other types of policy arrangements such as annuities and retirement agreements. [See 2–202(b)(2)(ii)(A)]. It also does not include the life insurance owned by the decedent on others' lives. To the extent these policies have value, they will be valued as part of the decedent's probate (Segment 1) estate.

(2) The value of property that the decedent gratuitously transferred to third persons during marriage to the surviving spouse but in which the decedent retained specified interests or powers. The following transfers are included:

(A) Property irrevocably transferred by decedent to the extent the decedent retained a right to possession or enjoyment of or the income from the property at the time of decedent's death. [2–202(b)(2)(ii)(A)]. A right to income includes payments under annuity and other similar contractual arrangements. [2–202(a)(1)(ix)]. When this provision applies, the value includable in the augmented estate is the value of whatever portion of the property to which decedent's retained interest related. It is important to distinguish the situation covered by this provision from the situation where decedent holds or retains only a life interest in an interest created by someone else or transferred by decedent prior to the marriage to the surviving spouse. In the latter situation, no portion of the value of the property is included in decedent's augmented estate because decedent did not transfer the interest and retain a life interest during the marriage.

(B) Property transferred by decedent to the extent the income or principal of the property remained at the time of the decedent's death subject to a power exercisable either by decedent alone or in conjunction with any other person, or by a nonadverse party, for the benefit of decedent, decedent's creditors or creditors of decedent's estate. [2–202(b)(2)(ii)(B)]. The scope of this inclusion is different from the inclusion of the property subject to an unshared presently exercisable power of appointment. The power covered by this provision includes only powers created or retained in regard to decedent's transfers. It includes, however, not only unshared powers retained by decedent but also powers decedent shared with others and even powers exercisable by nonadverse person. A nonadverse person is one who does not have a substantial beneficial interest in the property. [2–202(a)(1)(iv)]. In addition, the property is included whether the power extends over the property's principal or the income or both. The value of the includable property equals the value of the property subject to the power to the extent (1) the power was exercisable at decedent' death to or for the benefit of any third person, or (2) the property subject to the power passed at decedent's death by exercise, release, lapse, in default, or otherwise to or for the benefit of any third person.

(3) The value of property irrevocably transferred to third persons by decedent during marriage to the surviving spouse and within a two year period preceding decedent's date of death that would otherwise have been included within Segment 2 if it had not been transferred or that exceeds a certain amount. The following transfers are included:

(A) Property that passes as a result of the termination of a right or interest in or power over any property that would have been included in Segment 2 of the augmented estate under (1)(A), (B), and (C) or (2)(A), above, if the right, interest, or power had not terminated before the decedent's death. [2–202(b)(2)(iii)(A)]. A termination means the right or interest was (a) terminated by the terms of the governing instrument, or (b) transferred or relinquished by decedent. [2–202(a)(2)]. A power terminates when it is exercised, released, lapsed, defaulted or otherwise but a presently exercisable general power of appointment terminates only when exercised or released and not merely by lapse, default or otherwise. The value of the includable property under this provision equals the same value that the property would have had if the transfer had not occurred except that the valuation date is the time of the termination of decedent's power or interest and that the value is limited only to the extent the property passed upon termination to or for the benefit of any third person.

(B) Any transfer of insurance on the decedent's life if the proceeds would have been included under (1)(D) had the transfer not occurred. [2–202(b)(2)(iii)(B)]. The value of the includable amount equals the value of the proceeds to the extent they passed at decedent's death to or for the benefit of any third person.

(C) Property irrevocably transferred to or for the benefit of third persons but only to the extent the aggregate value of all transfers to any donee exceeds $10,000 in either year. [2–202(b)(2)(iii)(C)]. This provision protects the surviving spouse against large near death gifts but recognizes a significant small gift exclusion. Irrevocable transfers prior to the two years before death are excluded in total and regardless of value.

D. SEGMENT 3 OF THE AUGMENTED ESTATE

The third segment (hereinafter called Segment 3) includes all of decedent's nonprobate property which the surviving spouse gratuitously received or derived from the decedent by reason of the latter's death. [2–202(b)(3)] This includes property received by the surviving spouse from decedent by way of survivorship, appointment, benefits of life insurance on decedent's life, benefits from retirement plans in which decedent participated and of any other property that would have been included as parts (1) and (2) of Segment 2, described above, had it passed to a third person. Social security system survivorship benefits are, however, specifically exempt. Segment 3 also does not include any Segment 1 properties received from the decedent's estate or the value of the spouse's family protections. [2–201(c); see § 8.02].

E. SEGMENT 4 OF THE AUGMENTED ESTATE

The fourth segment (hereinafter called Segment 4) includes (1) all of the surviving spouse's individual property and (2) the surviving spouse's Segment 2 property (the spouse's nonprobate transfers to others) as if that spouse predeceased decedent, to the extent these properties are not included in Segments 1 and 3. [2–202(b)(4)]. This Segment is all inclusive and supplemental to the other segments. It includes not only assets earned during the marriage but also assets acquired prior to marriage and assets derived gratuitously from the decedent and other persons. It also includes the spouse's fractional interests in survivorship property, the ownership interests in financial accounts and security registrations and property passing to the spouse by reason of the decedent's death. In addition, it includes the commuted value of income and other future interests. Property included under Segment 4 is valued at the decedent's death except that the value of spouse's fractional and ownership interests in survivorship property and in financial accounts and security registrations are valued immediately before decedent's death. The value of enforceable claims against any property or against the spouse are deducted from the value of the property included. Life insurance on the spouse's life that is includable in Segment 4 is valued at its present value and not its value as of the surviving spouse's death. Segment 4 guarantees that surviving spouses will have to account for their own estate and estate plan in opting for the elective share.

F. SUMMARY OF THE AUGMENTED ESTATE

The sum of the value of these four segments equals the augmented estate and the surviving spouse's elective share equals the elective share percentage times the augmented estate. Using a hypothetical, Chart 6–2 graphically outlines the parts of the augmented estate and the necessary calculations. [See § 6.07].

For income and other partial interests includable under Segment 3 and Segment 4, value equals the commuted value of any amounts payable to the surviving spouse either currently or after decedent's death under trusts, life insurance settlement options, annuity contracts, public or private pensions, and disability compensation arrangements. [2–202(d)]. This means that the date of death value must be determined for serial payments of income to the surviving spouse in the future. The method of determining such value is not specified and will be part of the advocative process when an elective share is sought and will have to be determined by the court under the particular circumstances of the case. [See Langbein & Waggoner, The New Uniform Probate Code, at 883].

§ 6.04   Exclusions From the Augmented Estate

Several qualifications and exclusions to the augmented estate deserve special mention. Because the nonprobate transfers to others of both spouses concerns gratuitous transactions by the spouse, transfers for which either spouse received adequate and full consideration in money or money's worth are excluded from the augmented estate. [2–202(c)]. The augmented estate also excludes all irrevocable transfers, and exercises or releases of powers of appointment made with the written consent or joinder of the other spouse.

Antenuptial and postnuptial contracts, agreements and waivers of a right of election of a surviving spouse are also specifically recognized so long as they are (a) in writing, (b) voluntary, and (c) not unconscionable. [2–207(a)]. The family protection allowances may similarly be waived. The surviving spouse who contests a waiver has the burden of showing that the waiver was not executed voluntarily or it was unconscionable when executed and lacked fair disclosure prior to execution. [2–207(b); see, e.g., Lopata v. Metzel (1982)]. Fair disclosure is explained. It must be either (a) a "fair and reasonable disclosure" of the decedent's assets and liabilities, (b) a voluntary and express waiver of any disclosure, or (c) knowledge of the decedent's assets and liabilities was possessed or reasonably available. [2–207(b)(2)(i)–(iii)]. Unconscionability is a question of law and is not a jury question. [2–207(c)].

If the relevant agreement waives "all rights" or contains equivalent language, each spouse waives all rights to elective share and the family protections in the other spouse's estate and renounces all interests passing from the other spouse by intestacy or by a will executed before the agreement. [2–207(d)].

In addition, certain gratuitous transfers by the spouses are excluded. First, transfers made prior to the marriage with the other spouse are excluded even if interests are retained so long as the retained interests are not characterizable as certain types of segment 2 powers. [2–202(b)(2)(i)–(iii); see § 6.03]. Examples of common interests that might be retained in pre-marriage transfers and not cause inclusion include life interests and nongeneral powers of appointment. An example of a retained interest that would cause inclusion in the augmented estate, include an unrestricted, unshared power to revoke held at death. [2–202(b)(2)(i)(A)]. Second, irrevocable and outright gifts to third persons up to $10,000 per donee per year are excluded whenever they are made. [2–202(b)(2)(iii)(C)]. The first exclusion assists in clearing titles and reduces disruption to finalized gratuitous transfers that an elected share petition can cause. The second exclusion protects normal donative transfers from elective share attack. Both exclusions may be occasionally abused by spouses and might propel a court to ignore the literal application of the Code and apply inherent equitable powers over abusive spousal share avoidance transfers. [See Langbein & Waggoner, The New Uniform Probate Code, at 881 n.12].

Finally, the Code permits third persons, e.g., parents, grandparents and other relatives, to transfer property in trust for the benefit of a person who is married or may get married and still protect the property from the elective share of the person's surviving spouse. Unless the trust beneficiary holds a unilateral presently exercisable power to appointment, a fractional share held in joint tenancy with right of survivorship, or the remainder of the trust estate passes as part of the beneficiary's probate estate at death, the trust assets will not be part of the augmented estate if the beneficiary's surviving spouse seeks an elective share against the beneficiary's estate. This trust is exempt even if the beneficiary holds any one or more of the following interests: a life interest, an inter vivos or testamentary nongeneral power of appointment, and a presently exercisable general power of appointment if the latter power is limited by an ascertainable standard or is exercisable only with the consent of an adverse or nonadverse person. The exclusion from the augmented estate of interests in trusts that are created by third persons protects family estate plans from the disruption of elective share petitions by surviving spouses. If the property were transferred outright to the beneficiary, however, the property would be part of the augmented estate. If these same interests are held by the surviving spouse, they must be included in Segment 4 of the augmented estate as "property owned" by that spouse. [2–202(b)(4); see 2–202 (a)(1)(vii)]. In this situation, the interests would be valued at their commuted valued. This distinction between the inclusion in the augmented estate for interests held by the decedent as compared with those held by the surviving spouses may impose an unequal economic burden on the surviving spouse.

The Code includes provisions protecting payors, and other third persons who dealt with a beneficiary prior to notice that the surviving spouse intends to file or has filed a petition for the elective share. [2–208; see § 12.05].

§ 6.05   Funding the Elective Share

The third step in analyzing the elective share processes is the matter of funding the elective share amount or the supplemental elective share. Once the elective share percentage and the augmented estate are determined, a monetary amount is set by multiplying the elective share percentage times the augmented estate. For example, if the spouses have been married 11½ years, the elective share equals 34%, and if the augmented estate equals $500,000, the elective share amount equals $170,000. How that amount is going to be funded is the subject of this section.

For funding purposes, the Code divides the augmented estate into three separate hotchpots or funds. Each fund is composed of property interests that are included in the augmented estate depending on certain characterization decisions that will be explained. The ultimate goal is to fully fund the elective share amount. To accomplish this goal and to allocate the necessary contribution from each fund, the funds are arranged in an order of priority. Fund 1 interests must contribute first to satisfy the elective share amount and must be exhausted before seeking contribution from Fund 2 interests. Fund 3 interests are required to contribute if the previous two funds do not fully satisfy the elective share amount. Chart 6–2 graphically outlines the process of satisfying the augmented estate amount and the necessary calculations. [See § 6.07].

Fund 1 is composed of the amounts of the augmented estate that are received or attributable to the surviving spouse * and includes the following amounts:

---

* The 1992 Technical Amendments eliminated the provision that required the surviving spouse to deduct interests in the augmented estate that passed to the spouse but were disclaimed. Although the removal of this provision is defended as further recognition of the economic partnership of marriage, it may cause the Code's elective share system to have much greater application. It alters the emphasis of the Code's elective share provisions from protection from disinheritance to a form of community property ownership. The change means that adequate provision for the surviving spouse is not enough, it must be adequate ownership in fee. Under the change, trusts, such as the QTIP trust, for the surviving spouse will be at risk of full or partial destruction if the surviving spouse elective ownership share is not otherwise satisfied by the estate plan. In the multi-family situations, the destruction of these types of trusts, in whole or in part, may fuel the litigation fires between surviving spouses and decedent's surviving descendants of a prior marriage. It was this type of litigation that the Code intends to avoid. Notwithstanding the increased litigation, removal of the disclaimer limitation will increase the number of estates where the surviving spouse might seek the elective share because the surviving spouse finds it desirable to take decedent's augmented estate in fee rather than in trust. Concomitantly, it will impose the complexity of the elective share

1. The intestate and testate portions of Segment 1 that pass to the surviving spouse from the decedent;

2. The amounts included in Segment 3;

3. Twice the elective share percentage ** times the amounts of Segment 4 of the augmented estate.

[2–203(a)]. If after deducting the value of the surviving spouse's share, the elective share amount is satisfied, this is the end of the process and thus the surviving spouse will take nothing further.

If there remains an elective share deficiency, Fund 2 must be calculated and it includes the following amounts: (1) the amounts of the non-spousal portions of Segment 1; and (2) the amount of Segment 2 of the augmented estate less the value of certain irrevocable transfers made by decedent within the two year period prior to death. [2–203(b); 2–202(b)(2)(iii)(A) and (C); see § 6.03]. The third person beneficiaries of these included amounts must contribute to the funding of the elective share deficiency. All contributions from these beneficiaries are made on a pro rata basis. A pro rata share equals the value of the recipient's

procedure, and thus higher costs of administration, on a larger number of estates.

** In order to properly calculate the value of the surviving spouse's portion of segment 4 assets, it is necessary to double the elective share percentage. In the economic sharing concept, the surviving spouse's personal assets are shared as well by the decedent. Therefore, if the elective share percentage is 34% and the surviving spouse's personal estate equals $1,000, 68% of this amount or $680 is attributable to the marriage: the 34% share of the surviving spouse and 34% contributed by the decedent.

interest divided by total value of Fund 2. Fund 2 transfers must be fully exhausted before proceeding to Fund 3.

If interests in Fund 2 assets are exhausted and the elective share amount still remains unsatisfied, Fund 3 must be calculated. It includes the irrevocable transfers made by decedent within the two year period prior to death that are included in Segment 2 except for life insurance proceeds of policies irrevocably transferred by decedent during this period of time. [2–203(c); 2–202(b)(2)(iii)(A) and (C)]. The insurance proceeds are included in Fund 2. [2–203(b); 2–202(b)(2)(iii)(B)]. The recipients of Fund 3 must contribute to the remaining unsatisfied portion of elective share amount. All contributors of Fund 3 contribute on a pro rata basis. A pro rata share equals the value of recipient's interest divided by the value of Fund 3. The elective share amount should be fully funded after the three contribution steps are completed.

Only the original recipients and their gratuitous donees are liable for contribution. [2–204(a)]. In addition, a recipient may either pay the value of the amount of contribution due or give up the proportional part of the nonprobate reclaimable asset received. No recipient or gratuitous donee of a recipient is required to contribute more than the pro rata portion as determined through the above funding process even though the elective share amount is not fully satisfied because some recipients are unable to contribute or are jurisdictionally unavailable. [2–205(d); see also 2–203(b) and (c)]. For example, if a recipient of Fund 2 interests is unable or unavailable to pay the pro rata portion, the other recipients of Fund 2 amounts do not have to make up the difference. Fund 3 recipients must contribute only if Fund 2 is insufficient to satisfy assuming all recipients in Fund 2 contributed their full pro rata portion. These limitations on funding mean that some surviving spouses will not be able to collect their full elective share amount.

The funding procedures require valuation determination similar to those required for the augmented estate procedure. [See § 6.03]. A difference may apply in regard to determining the value of Fund 1. If the surviving spouse takes a partial or future interest from the decedent spouse's will, these interests will be valued at their commuted value. [2–202(d); § 6.03]. A life interest, e.g., a QTIP trust, for the benefit of the surviving spouse in a trust in the will of the decedent spouse is a common example of such an interest. Otherwise the valuation determinations are the same.

§ 6.06   the Election Procedure

In order to take the elective share, the surviving spouse must file in court and mail to the personal representative a petition for such share within nine months after the date of death or within six months after decedent's will is probated, whichever limitation last expires. [2–205(a)]. Notwithstanding these overall limitation periods, Segment 2 assets will only be included in the augmented estate if the petition is filed within nine months after the date of death. For good cause shown and if requested before the nine month limitation expires, the surviving spouse may seek and obtain an extension of the time for election from the Court. If the petition if filed within the time set for the extension, the Segment 2 assets are included.

The elective share procedure under the Code requires that there be full notice and a hearing. Notice of time and place of the hearing must be given by the surviving spouse to all persons interested in the estate and to Segment 1 distributees and Segment 2 recipients whose interests will be adversely affected by the elective share petition. [2–205(a)]. The Court, then, has the responsibility for determining the elective share, its satisfaction and the liability of recipients for contribution. [2–205(d)].

A petition demanding the elective share may be withdrawn by the surviving spouse any time before entry of a final determination. [2–205(c)]. In addition, the right of election is personal to the surviving spouse and cannot be exercised by anyone else before or after the surviving spouse's death; however, it may be exercised on behalf of the surviving spouse by a conservator, guardian or agent under a power of attorney. [2–206(a); see 5–407(b)(3)].

The Code's provisions attempt to strike a balance between encouraging and restricting a surviving spouse from petitioning for the election. [2–202, Comment]. In addition, they definitely will encourage persons concerned about potential election problems to seek counseling. Because many of these questions cannot be determined within filing limitation periods, and because an election petition may be withdrawn without adverse consequences,

petitioning for the elective share as a matter of
course in uncertain cases might be advisable in
order to protect the surviving spouse's elective
option. On the other hand, retention of the assets
received by the recipients until the limitation period expires might be desirable because it puts a
ceiling upon their contribution. If a will exists,
Segment 1 recipients will definitely want to start
the six-month statute of limitations running by
probating it.

If the surviving spouse is incapacitated and the
election is exercised by a proper person representing the spouse, amounts received by the fiduciary
in satisfaction of the elective share amount from
Segment 1 and Segment 2 must be placed in a
custodial trust under the Uniform Custodial Trust
Act or, if the enacting state does not have that Act,
under the terms of a custodial trust established in
the Code. [2–206(b)]. Under the statutory custodial trust, the fiduciary electing for the surviving
spouse is the trustee, the surviving spouse is the
beneficiary, the decedent spouse is the settlor, and
the date of the trust is the date of the decedent's
death.

The trustee is required to administer the trust
for the benefit of the beneficiary. [2–206(c)(2)].
The trustee has discretion to expend trust property
for the use and benefit of the beneficiary and
others who were supported by the beneficiary
when the incapacity occurred or who are legally
entitled support from the beneficiary. The trustee
may without court order determine when, how and
what is expended. The trustee must, however,

take into account the beneficiaries' other support, income and property including government benefits such as social security and medicare. [2–206, Comment]. If the enacting state provides, the trust may have to consider need qualification limits set for other government assistance programs such as medicaid.

Unless the incapacitated surviving spouse regains capacity and terminates the trust, no one including the incapacitated spouse may terminate the trust. [2–206(c)(1)]. The trust automatically terminates on the death of the incapacitated spouse. On termination at the surviving spouse's death, the remaining trust property passes according to the estate plan, if any, of the predeceased spouse against whose estate the surviving spouse had elected the elective share. The property passes as if the predeceased spouse died immediately after the surviving spouse rather than before. If the predeceased spouse had a will, the will controls if it effectively disposes of the estate. If the will fails to dispose of the property or there is no will, the property passes to the predeceased spouse's heirs determined at the time of the surviving spouse's death. [2–206(c)(3), 2–711, 2–105; §§ 11.-05(D), 5.03].

§ 6.07 Representative Illustration of the Elective Share

The following Chart 6–2 analyzes a representative scenario where the Code's Elective Share would be applied. The calculation forms comprehensively outline the many categories of transactions that need to be characterized when a surviving spouse makes an election. The hypothetical is merely an illustration of the process and does not cover all possibilities and issues. As is readily apparent, the process can be quite complex.

CHART 6–2

AN ELECTIVE SHARE ILLUSTRATION

Hypothetical: D died on July 1, 1993. D is survived by a spouse, S, D's two adult children by a previous marriage, C and E, and S's seventeen year old child by a previous marriage, F. D and S were married on December 1, 1980. D's valid will devises all personal effects to S and the residue to C and E, equally. W, X, Y and Z are tax exempt and otherwise recognized charitable entities. S has properly filed the necessary petitions requesting the elective share. The Uniform Probate Code of 1990, as amended in 1993, is in effect in D's domicile.

Assumptions: (1) The following outlines D's financial situation and transactions prior to and at death. Except as specifically noted, D paid for all property and made all contributions with personal funds, and made all transfers gratuitously.

Item	Relevant Financial Transactions	Date *	Value **
1.	Gross probate estate	07/01/93	$500,000
2.	Estimated administration expenses	07/01/93	$32,000
3.	Funeral expenses	07/01/93	$4,000
4.	Enforceable claims	07/01/93	$6,000
5.	Homestead, exemptions, and allowances	07/01/93	$43,000
6.	Personal effects	07/01/93	$10,000
7.	Multiple-party bank account in names of D and S, S made contributions of 10%	07/01/93	$20,000
8.	Automobile held in D and F's names as joint owners with right of survivorship	07/01/93	$10,000
9.	Securities held in the name of D, "TOD" Charity Y	07/01/93	$20,000
10.	Life insurance on D's life, premiums paid by D, E named beneficiary	07/01/93	$50,000
11.	Life insurance on D's life, premiums paid by D, S named beneficiary	07/01/93	$110,000
12.	Securities held by tenancy by the entireties with S	07/01/93	$24,000
13.	Irrevocable gift of securities to Charity X	12/26/91	*$20,000*
14.	Irrevocable gift of securities to Charity Z	12/26/90	*$20,000*
15.	Gift of residence to C, D reserved life estate	06/01/90	$50,000
16.	Gift of securities in trust for C and E, D reserved power to revoke	12/01/80	$200,000
17.	Remainder of apartment building to C and E, D reserved life estate	12/01/80	*$200,000*

(2) The following outlines S's financial situation and transactions prior to and at D's death.

---

* Date of death is used for all transactions that take effect at D's death: other dates concern transactions that were completed prior to death.

** Values indicated are those applicable to the Augmented Estate. Those in italics are the values on the date of the transaction. All other values are as of the date of death.

Item	Relevant Financial Transactions	Date*	Value**
18.	Investments purchased with S's earnings during marriage to D	03/01/93	$10,000
19.	Irrevocable cash gift to Charity W	12/26/91	*$20,000*
20.	Irrevocable cash gift in trust to F	12/26/90	*$30,000*
21.	Wedding present from D to S	12/01/80	$8,000
22.	Inherited securities from S's father	07/01/79	$58,000

Problem: Using the above assumptions, calculate S's Elective Share including the augmented estate and the allocatable contributions.

A.	Computation of the Augmented Estate and Elective Share		
1.	**Item**	**Segment 1: Value of Decedent's Net Probate Estate [2–202(b)(1)]**	**Amounts**
a.	1.	Gross probate estate	$500,000
b.	2.	Administration expenses, debts and losses	$37,000
c.	3.	Funeral expenses	$4,000
d.	4.	Enforceable claims [1–201(6)]	$6,000
e.	5.	Homestead, exemptions, and allowances [2–402, 2–403, 2–404]1	$43,000
f.		Total Deductions from Probate Estate [Add A.1.b.—A.1.e. amounts]	$90,000
g.		Value of Segment 1 Net Estate [Subtract A.1.f. from A.1.a.]	$410,000
h.		Surviving spouse's portion of distributable estate [Item 6.]	$10,000
i.		Nonspousal beneficiaries' portion of distributable estate	$400,000
j.		Distributable estate [Add A.1.h. and A.1.i.]	$410,000
2.	**Item**	**Segment 2: Decedent's Reclaimable Estate [2–202(b)(2)]**	**Amounts**
a.		Property Subject to Decedent's Presently Exercisable General Power of Appointment [2–202(b)(2)(i)(A)]	
	16.	Gift of securities in trust for C and E, D reserved power to revoke 2	$200,000
b.		Decedent's Fractional Interest in Joint Tenancy with Right of Survivorship Property [2–202(b)(2)(i)(B)]	
	8.	Automobile registered in D and F's names as joint owners with right of survivorship	$10,000

* Date of death is used for all transactions that take effect at D's death: other dates concern transactions that were completed prior to death.

** Values indicated are those applicable to the Augmented Estate. Those in italics are the values on the date of the transaction. All other values are as of the date of death.

1. The value used equals the total value of the family protections.

2. Although this gift was made before marriage, D retained a power to revoke and thus it is includable in the augmented estate at its date of death value.

2.	Item	Segment 2: Decedent's Reclaimable Estate [2–202(b)(2)]	Amounts
c.		Decedent's Ownership interest in any property, account or registration held in POD, TOD, or co-ownership with right of survivorship. [2–202(b)(2)(i)(C)].	
	9.	Securities registered in the name of D, "TOD" Y Charity	$20,000
d.		Life Insurance Proceeds From Decedent's Owned or Controlled Policies on Own Life [2–202(b)(2)(i)(D)]	
	10.	Life insurance on D's life, premiums paid by D, E named beneficiary	$50,000
e.		Property Decedent Irrevocably Transferred but Retained Possession, Enjoyment or Income Interest [2–202(b)(2)(ii)(A)]	
	15.	Gift of residence to C, D reserved life estate **3**	$50,000
f.		Property Decedent Transferred subject to Decedent's Retained (Shared or Unshared) Power of Appointment to Benefit Decedent or Decedent's Creditors, Estate, or Creditor's of the Estate [2–202(b)(2)(ii)(B)]	
			$0
g.		Property Decedent Transferred subject to a Nonadverse Party's Power of Appointment to Benefit Decedent or Decedent's Creditors, Estate, or Creditor's of the Estate [2–202(b)(2)(ii)(B)]	
			$0
h.		Total Segment 2 Interests Held at Decedent's Death [Add A.2.a.–A.2.g. Interests]	$330,000
		[Interests Transferred Within Two Years of Death]	
i.		Property That Had Been Subject to Decedent's Presently Exercisable General Power of Appointment [2–202(b)(2)(iii)(A); see 2–202(b)(2)(i)(A)]	
			$0
j.		Property In Which Decedent Had Held a Fractional Interest in Joint Tenancy with Right of Survivorship Property [2–202(b)(2)(iii)(A); see 2–202(b)(2)(i)(B)]	
			$0
k.		Property In Which Decedent Had Held an Ownership interest in any property, account or registration held in POD, TOD, or co-ownership with right of survivorship. [2–202(b)(2)(iii)(A); see 2–202(b)(2)(i)(C)]	
			$0
l.		Property Decedent Irrevocably Transferred but in Which Decedent Had Retained Possession, Enjoyment or Income Interest [2–202(b)(2)(iii)(A); see 2–202(b)(2)(ii)(A)]	
			$0
m.		Property Decedent Transferred Had Been Subject to Decedent's Retained (Shared or Unshared) Power of Appointment to Benefit Decedent or Decedent's Creditors, Estate, or Creditor's of the Estate [2–202(b)(2)(iii)(A); see 2–202(b)(2)(ii)(B)]	
			$0
n.		Property Decedent Transferred subject to a Nonadverse Party's Power of Appointment to Benefit Decedent or Decedent's Creditors, Estate, or Creditor's of the Estate [2–202(b)(2)(iii)(A); see 2–202(b)(2)(ii)(B)]	
			$0

3. Item 15 is included in the Augmented Estate because D retained an income interest and the gift was made during the marriage to S. Item 16, the gift of the

2.	Item	Segment 2: Decedent's Reclaimable Estate [2–202(b)(2)]	Amounts
o.		Life Insurance Proceeds That Decedent Had Owned or Controlled Policies on Own Life [2–202(b)(2)(iii)(B); see 2–202(b)(2)(i)(D)]	
			$0
p.		Property Irrevocably Transferred to Third Persons To the Extent Transfers Exceeds $10,000 Per Donee Per Year [2–202(b)(2)(iii)(C)]	
	13.	Irrevocable gift of securities to Charity X4	$10,000
q.		Total Segment 2 Interests Transferred within Two Years of Decedent's death [Add A.2.i.–A.2.p. Interests]	$10,000
r.		Total Value of Segment 2 Transfers Included [Add A.2.h. and A.2.q.]	$340,000
3.	Item	Segment 3: Value of Decedent's Property Passing to Surviving Spouse by Reason of Decedent's Death [2–202(b)(3)]	Amounts
a.		Value of Decedent's Property Passing to Surviving Spouse by Reason of Decedent's Death [2–202(b)(3)]	
	6.	Personal effects	$10,000
	7.	Multiple-party bank account in names of D and S, S made contributions of 10% 5	$18,000
	10.	Life insurance on D's life, premiums paid by D, S named beneficiary	$110,000
	11.	Securities held by tenancy by the entireties with S 6	$12,000
b.		Total Value of Segment 3 Transfers Included [Add A.3.a. Interests]	$150,000
4.	Item	Segment 4: Spouse Assets and Reclaimable Assets at Decedent's Death [2–202(b)(4)]	Amounts
a.		Property Owned by Surviving Spouse at Decedent's Death	
	7.	Multiple-party bank account in names of D and S, S made contributions of 10% 7	$2,000
	11.	Securities held by tenancy by the entireties with S 8	$12,000
	18.	Inherited securities from S's father	$58,000
	19.	Wedding present from D to S	$8,000
	21.	Investments purchased with S's earnings during marriage	$10,000
b.		Total Value of Property Owned by Surviving Spouse at Decedent's Death [Add A.4.a. Interests]	$90,000

apartment building to C and E, is not included even though D retained an income interest up to the time of death because this gift was made prior to the marriage to S.

4. This gift, although irrevocable, was made within two years preceding D's death and therefore is included to the extent it exceeds $10,000 in a single year to a single donee. The value of the inclusion is the value of the gift at the date of the gift less $10,000. No part of Item 14, the $20,000 gift to Charity Z, is included because it was irrevocable and made more than two years before D's death.

5. The value of this transaction in Segment 3 equals D's ownership interest at date of death or ninety percent of the account: the other ten percent is included in Segment 4.

6. The value of this transaction in Segment 3 equals only one-half the value of the property: the other half is included in Segment 4.

7. The value of this transaction in Segment 4 equals S's ownership interest at date of death or ten percent of the account: the other ninety percent is included in Segment 3.

8. See footnote 6.

4.	Item	Segment 4: Spouse Assets and Reclaimable Assets at Decedent's Death [2–202(b)(4)]	Amounts
c.		Property Reclaimable If Surviving Spouse Predeceased Decedent	
	20.	Irrevocable gift of securities to W 9	$10,000
d.		Total Value of Property Reclaimable If Surviving Spouse Predeceased Decedent [Add A.3.c. Interests]	$10,000
e.		Total Value of Segment 4 Transfers Included [Add A.4.b. and A.4.d.]	$100,000

5.	Recapitalization and Calculation of Elective Share	Amounts
a.	Segment 1 [enter A.1.g. from above]	$410,000
b.	Segment 2 [enter A.2.r. from above]	$340,000
c.	Segment 3 [enter A.3.b. from above]	$150,000
d.	Segment 4 [enter A.4.e. from above]	$100,000
e.	Value of Augmented Estate [Add A.5.a.–A.5.d.]	$1,000,000
f.	The Elective Share Percentage [See Chart 6–1, § 6.02; 2–201(a)] 2–Years of Marriage 13	42%
g.	Elective Share Amount of the Augmented Estate [Multiply A.5.e. times A.5.f.]	$420,000

B.	Funding the Elective Share	
1.	Calculation of Fund 1—Surviving Spouse's Share of Elective Share [2–203(a)]	Amounts
a.	Elective Share Amount [Enter A.5.g.]	$420,000
b.	Amounts Passing to Surviving Spouses from Segment 1 [Enter A.1.h.]	$10,000
c.	Amounts Passing to Surviving Spouses from Segment 3 [Enter A.5.c.]	$150,000
d.	Amount Equal to Twice the Elective Share of Segment 4 Assets [A.5.d. times A.5.f. times 2]	$84,000
e.	Value of Surviving Spouse's Interests Charged Against Share [Add B.1.b. through B.1.d.]	$244,000
f.	Value of Elective Share Deficiency [Subtract B.1.e. from B.1.a.]	$176,000
	[Complete B.2, below, only if B.1.f. is greater than 0.]	

2.	Calculation of Fund 2—Remainder of the Augmented Estate Less Irrevocable Transfers [2–203(b)]	Amounts
a.	Amounts Passing to Third Persons from Segment 1 [A.1.i.]	$400,000
b.	Total Segment 2 Interests Held at Decedent's Death [A.2.h.]	$330,000
c.	Life Insurance Proceeds That Decedent Had Owned or Controlled Policies on Own Life [A.2.0 interests]	$0
d.	Remainder of the Augmented Estate [Add B.2.a.—B.2.a.—B.2.c. interests]	$730,000

9. This gift, although irrevocable, was made within two years preceding D's death and therefore is included to the extent it exceeds $10,000 in a single year to a single donee. The value of the inclusion is the value of the gift at the date of the gift less $10,000. No part of Item 20, the $30,000 gift to F, is included because it was irrevocable and made more than two years before D's death.

B.	Funding the Elective Share				
3.	Calculate Pro Rata Proportion for Contribution of Segments 1 and 2 Recipients Who Did not Receive an Irrevocable Transfer Within two years of Decedent's Death				
	a.	b.	c.	d.	e.
Item	Recipient	Recipient's Share	Pro Rata Portion 10	Value of Elective Share Deficiency [B.1.f.]	Total Contribution [B.3.c. * B.3.d.] 11
	C	$350,000	47.95%	$176,000	$84,384
	E	$350,000	47.95%	$176,000	$84,384
	D	$ 10,000	1.37%	$176,000	$2,411
	Y ·	$ 20,000	2.74%	$176,000	$4,822
f.	Value of Elective Share Deficiency			$176,000	
g.	Total Contributions		100.00%		$176,000
h.	Balance				$0
	[Complete B.4., below, only if the B.3.h. Balance is greater than 0.]				
4.	Calculation of Fund 3—Segment 2 Irrevocable Transfers [2–203(c)]				Amounts
a.	Total Segment 2 Interests Transferred within Two Years of Decedent's death [A.2.q.]				$10,000
b.	Life Insurance Proceeds That Decedent Had Owned or Controlled Policies on Own Life [A.2.p. interests]				$0
c.	Balance of Irrevocable Segment 2 Transfers [Subtract B.4.b. from B.4.a.]				$10,000
5.	Calculate Pro Rata Proportion for Contribution of Recipients of Irrevocable Segment 2 Transfers				
	a.	b.	c.	d.	e.
	Recipient	Recipient's Share	Pro Rata Portion12	Balance of Irrevocable Transfers [B.4.c.]	Total Contribution [B.5.c. * B.5.d.]
	Charity X13	$10,000	0.00%	$0	$0
f.	Value of Elective Share Deficiency			$0	
g.	Total Pro Rata Contributions		0.00%		$0
h.	Balance			—	$0

10. Divide the Recipient's Share, B.3.b., by the Remainder of the Augmented Estate, B.2.d.

11. The lesser of the B.3.c. times B.3.d. or the Recipient's share.

12. Divide the Recipient's Share, B.4.b., by the Value of Irrevocable Transfers within Two years of Death.

13. No contribution is due from Charity X for the gift it received because the interests included in Fund 2 fully satisfied the Elective Share.

CHAPTER 7

PRETERMITTED SPOUSES
AND CHILDREN

§ 7.01 Pretermitted Spouse

A situation related to disinheritance of a spouse
concerns the spouse who is not provided for as a
spouse in the will because the marriage to testator
occurred after the execution of the will. Most
states do not specifically protect the spouse but
rely on their spousal protection provisions against
disinheritance. The Code contains a special remedy for this situation.

Under the Code, if a surviving spouse is a pretermitted spouse, the spouse is entitled to a spouse's
intestate share valued at no less than the value the
spouse would have received if the testator had died
intestate. [2–301(a)]. The provision's application
is dependent only upon the fact that the marriage
occurred after the will was executed. This is not
an election on the part of the surviving spouse but
an intestacy right. It is not avoided merely because the spouse was a devisee under the will.
The only consequence of the spouse being a devisee
is that the spouse must deduct the devise from the
intestacy share required by the statute. This
intestate share is limited, however, to the portion
of the testator's estate that is not devised to one or
more children of the testator who were born before

113

the marriage to the surviving spouse and who are not children of the surviving spouse. Devises to children or descendants of the child who take under the antilapse provisions of Section 2–603 or 2–604 are also exempt from this share.

The Code recognizes several important exceptions to this intestacy share right. First, there is no intestacy right if the will or other evidence indicates it was made in contemplation of the testator's marriage to the surviving spouse. Second, the testator may express an intention that the will is effective notwithstanding subsequent marriage or marriages. Third, the share does not apply if the testator provided for the surviving spouse by way of transfers outside the will and these transfers were intended in lieu of a testamentary provision. The latter intent may be shown by statements of the testator or from reasonable inferences from the nature of the transfer or other evidence. The burden of proof of satisfying any or all of the exceptions is placed upon the moving party urging the application of one or more of the exceptions. [2–301, Comment].

It is not clear whether transfers outside the will act as advancements and therefore as deductions from the intestacy share or whether they must be only in total substitution for the share. For example, consider the situation where the calculated intestacy share equals $100,000. How would a life insurance policy in favor of the surviving spouse for $50,000 be treated? Does the testator's intent to make the transfer in lieu of a testamentary provision relate only to a full satisfaction, i.e., the $50,000 is in place of the $100,000, or might the surviving spouse have to treat the $50,000 as an advancement and bring it into the hotchpot for subsequent recalculation? The latter approach would seem to be a more equitable approach both in terms of a share of the surviving spouse and in terms of the consequences of this intestate's share coming out of gifts to other persons.

The justification for this provision is that it attempts to do what most testators probably would want to do had they contemplated the prior will and the changed marital circumstances. [2–301, Comment]. In addition, it may reduce the number of elections against the estate under the elective share provisions. With the stated liberal extrinsic evidence rules and relatively complete elaboration of differing situations, the Code exceptions should provide sufficient barriers to the application of this section where it was not intended. On the other hand, although the provision attempts to address the variables and to protect against misuse of the provision, it does not contain the explicit limitations and procedures imposed by the elective share provisions designed to address these problems.

In calculating the surviving spouse's share it is necessary to create an internal hotchpot in the estate. First, the net distributable estate is calculated and the devises to the qualified children or descendants of children are subtracted from that estate. The spouse's intestate share then would be calculated against the remaining amount. Abatement, therefore, is suffered only by the beneficiaries of the will who are not in the preferred class of children or descendants of children. The general abatement provision of the Code is applicable to abatement of these devises caused by the application of this provision. [2–301(b); 3–902; § 23.01].

Under the 1969 provision, several courts dealt with the issue of intentional omission. [See, e.g., Cunningham v. Taggart (1980); Estate of Christensen v. Christensen (1982); Estate of Ganier v. Estate of Ganier (1982)].

§ 7.02 Pretermitted Children

Except in the State of Louisiana, no other jurisdiction within the United States has an effective forced kinship provision in favor of descendants and other heirs; consequently, if one desires, one may disinherit one's children. [Atkinson, § Wills 36]. Although this disinheritance power may be partially altered by the statutory family protections [see § 8.02], the closest and most common facsimile to forced kinship provisions is one that protects pretermitted descendants. The general rationale behind such provisions is that it is presumed the testator did not intend to disinherit the descendant who is omitted in the testator's will. Among the states which have such provisions, their contents vary greatly as to who, when and how they are to be applied.

Because pretermitted heir statutes are intended and designed to prevent injustice and reduce will contests when unintentionally omitted heirs survive a testator, the statute should be designed to accomplish these goals. Unfortunately, some statutes that exist in non-Code states have actually produced the opposite results. Accordingly, the Code's provision contains very precise prerequisites and limitations that are designed to reduce this litigation and judicial misinterpretation.

The Code establishes conditional thresholds against which each applicable situation must be tested. First, the protection is limited to pretermitted children and does not protect disinheritance of other descendants and relatives. Second, the child must be born or adopted after the execution of the will that disinherits the child. Third, intent to disinherit must not appears on the "face of the will." Fourth, the disinherited or omitted child must not have been provided for by transfers outside the will intended to be in lieu of testamentary provision. [2–302(b)] A liberal admissibility of extrinsic evidence rule is adopted in regard to proof of intent to use nontestamentary transfers in lieu of testamentary transfers. Extrinsic evidence may include the testator's declarations, the value of the transfer vis à vis the estate and "other evidence" that is relevant to proof of intent.

If the threshold requirements are satisfied, the omitted child must then test the sections protection against two circumstances. The first standard applies to situations where the testator had no children living when the will was executed. The second standard applies where the testator had one or more children living when the will was executed. In the first situation the omitted child takes an intestate share from the estate unless the natural or adopted child's parent is "devised all or substantially all" of the estate, survives the testator and is entitled to take under the will. The last condition concerns whether the will might have been revoked by other law. Several matters are left unanswered. Assumably, the child's parent does not have to be the spouse of the decedent: marriage between the decedent and that child's other parent would not seem to be necessary.

The general abatement provision of the Code is applicable to abatement of devises caused by the application of this provision. [2–302(d); 3–902; § 23.01].

If testator had one or more children living when the will was executed, the pretermitted child takes only if one or more of those existing children at the time of the will's execution received a legal or equitable interest in the estate from the will. If pre-will children take, the pretermitted child takes a represented pro rata share from the total value of the interests devised to the pre-existing children. The interest of the pre-existing children's devises abate pro rata according to their respective interests. The nature of the interest accorded, e.g., legal, equitable, present, future, to the omitted child must conform to the extent possible to the character to the devises to the pre-existing children. In general, the character of the estate plan must be preserved to the maximum degree possible. In other words, the pretermitted child does not take a separate share from the estate but is a forced devisee among the gifts given to the pre-existing children. Chart 7–1 uses a hypothetical to illustrate the process.

CHART 7–1

Computation of a Pretermitted Child's Share

Hypothetical 1: Testator has two living children, A and B, when will was executed. Will provides noth-

ing for A and B. Subsequent to will execution, C is born. Testator dies.

Answer: Under the pretermitted children section of the Code,
the pretermitted child C would not be entitled to
take anything from the estate because pre-existing
children of the testator were not devised property
under the will. This provision is included to provide
equality among children who are born before and
after a will is executed. Some pretermitted heir
statutes in the states would give C a share although
A and B would take nothing. The Code is trying to
treat equals equally.

Hypothetical 2: Testator has two children A and B when will
is executed. The will gives $9,000 to A and
$9,000 to B. Subsequent to the will execu-
tion, C is born.

Answer: C will be entitled to share a portion of the devises to
A and B. C will not be able to take from other assets
in the estate. In this example, C would be entitled to
take $6,000. This is an equal portion with the other
two children, A and B, from the total of the property
passed to A and B in the will. A and B would each
take $6,000 also and their gifts would be abated
$3,000 apiece.

Hypothetical 3: Assuming the same condition as hypothetical
2 except that the will gives A $6,000 and B
$12,000. Testator dies.

Answer: C would be able to take a pro rata share of the total
of the gifts to A and B. As one of the three children,
C would be able to take one-third of the total gifts to
A and B. This equals one-third of $18,000 or $6,000.
In other words, C will take 6,000 of the total gifts to
A and B. Since B received two-thirds of the total of
those gifts, two-thirds of the $6,000 will come from
B's share. Concomitantly, one-third of the forced
share of C will come from A's devise. This means
that A's interest will be abated by $2,000 and B's
interest will be abated by $4,000. The final distribu-
tion of these gifts will be A will take $4,000, B will
take $8,000 and C will take $6,000. Although this
solution does not result in perfect equality, it addresses the pretermitted heir problem, it attempts to
address the presumed intent of the testator due to
the pretermission, and it attempts to provide basic
equality among those who do take. Although A now
takes less than C, the loss was a pro rata portion of
the abatement. In addition, the satisfaction of the

pretermitted child's forced share has no effect on the
other devises made in the will. Consequently, the
total estate plan suffers minimal disruption and
abatement problems are greatly diminished.

The Code also incorporates a specific exception
to the general exclusionary evidence rule concerned with mistake in the inducement. This provision allots an intestate share for a child living
when the will was executed who is omitted because
the testator believed the child to be dead. [2–
302(c)]. The admissibility and sufficiency of evidence concerning such a belief are controlled by
the general rules of evidence and burden of proof
of the Code state. [See 2–601, Comment]. The
provision does not protect the omitted child if the
child would have been omitted had the child been
alive, or if the child had been provided for by
transfers outside the will intended to be in lieu of
testamentary provision. [2–302(b), and Comment]

CHAPTER 8

THE FAMILY PROTECTIONS

§ 8.01 Introduction

It is common for states to have statutes that attempt to financially protect a decedent's family unit. These statutes typically provide specified surviving family members of a decedent with a minimal amount of protection both from the decedent's creditors and from the decedent's own intentional disinheritance. Although these statutes come in a variety of kinds and names, they are commonly broken down into three categories: (1) homesteads, (2) exemptions and (3) allowances. The Code contains a representative for all three categories of the above family protections.

Although the Code's provisions on homestead [2–402], exemptions [2–403] and allowance [2–404] differ in many respects, there is a significant degree of similarity and a definite interrelationship between all of them. Significantly, all three limit their benefits only for relatives of a decedent who died domiciled in the Code state. [2–401]. To qualify under any of the categories the protected beneficiaries must survive the decedent by 120 hours. [Art. II, Pt. 4, General Comment; see 2–104]. Although all benefits received under all three provisions are ordinarily in addition to any share passing to the beneficiaries by intestacy, by elective share of the surviving spouse and by will, a testator may specifically in his will make devises to these beneficiaries in lieu of any or all family protection benefits.   For example, the will might state "This devise to my [surviving spouse or children] is expressly in lieu of [his, her or their] right to the homestead allowance, exempt property and the family allowance; any acceptance of such benefits shall be charged against this devise."   Although a decedent in a will may thus limit devises to the protected beneficiaries to an amount no greater than the amount provided by these family protections, the decedent cannot by will take away or limit these amounts below the statutory minimum without a prior waiver. [See 2–204].   Consequently, the Code's family protections preclude disinheritance to the extent of their monetary limitations.

These provisions also provide their beneficiaries with protection against a decedent's unsecured creditors: they are all expressly exempt from, and are in priority to, all unsecured claims against the estate.   The family protections have priority even over expenses of administration.   [Compare Art. II, Pt. 4 with 3–805; see In re Estate of Hutchinson (1978)].   If the estate is not sufficient even to satisfy all of the family protections, the Code interrelates these three protective devices so that an order of priority of payment is established.   The homestead allowance is satisfied first, followed by the family allowance which under these circumstances may not last for more than one year, and finally followed by satisfaction of the exempt property allowance.   Finally, the monetary value of these family protection provisions is the benchmark for application of the Code's summary administration procedures for the small estate. [See 3–1203, 3–1204; § 16.02].

§ 8.02   Protective Amounts and Their Beneficiaries

A.   HOMESTEAD ALLOWANCE

The Code provides for a specific monetary homestead allowance either for the surviving spouse or, if there is no surviving spouse, an equal share of the allowance for each minor child and each dependent child of the deceased. [2–402]. The suggested amount, which is alterable by enacting legislatures, is $15,000. The Code also includes an optional provision that coordinates its homestead allowance with any existing state constitutional homestead right tied to the family home, i.e., the value of the family home is charged against the Code's monetary homestead allowance. [2–402A].

B.   FAMILY ALLOWANCE

For purposes of support and maintenance during the period of administration, the Code provides for the payment from the estate of a reasonable monetary allowance for the benefit of the surviving spouse, minor legal dependents and other actually dependent children. [2–404]. The allowance may be paid either to the surviving spouse or, if there is no surviving spouse, to the children or dependents or their guardians. When a child or dependent does not live with the surviving spouse, however, the allowance may be apportioned between the surviving spouse and the child or other dependent as their respective needs require. Any allowance may be paid in a lump sum or in periodic installments. A protected person's right to the family allowance terminates upon his death including even approved unpaid amounts. If the estate is insolvent, an allowance cannot continue for more than one year from the decedent's death.

C. EXEMPT PROPERTY ALLOWANCE

The Code also provides a $10,000 exempt property allowance in favor of either the surviving spouse or the decedent's children if there is no surviving spouse. [2–403]. Significantly, the children need not be minors or dependents of the decedent. The exempt property allowances will ordinarily first be charged against household furniture, automobiles, furnishings, appliances and personal effects. [3–906(a)(1)]. If the value of these assets, less security interest held by third parties against them, does not equal the specified monetary amount, however, the protected beneficiaries are entitled to other assets of the estate to the extent necessary to make up the difference.

§ 8.03 Procedural Provisions

Ordinarily, the determination and distribution of the family protection rights will be accomplished informally by the personal representative and the protected persons without the need of court proceedings or supervision. [2–405; see 3–901]. The

Court is empowered to give appropriate relief, however, when a personal representative or any aggrieved person requests such by petition. For example, whether a family allowance should be extended is a matter within the discretion of the trial court. [Dandrea v. McCarty (1978)].

Several important limitations are imposed upon the personal representative and the determination of the family protections. [2–405(a)]. First, the homestead and the exempt property allowance may not be satisfied with property specifically devised when other assets of the estate are otherwise sufficient. Second, the personal representative, without court order, may not set and distribute a family allowance which exceeds a lump sum of more than $18,000 or periodic payments of more than $1,500 per month for one year. Third, the homestead and the family allowance cannot be satisfied in kind with assets out of the residue that a residuary devisee requests remain in the estate. [3–906(a)(2)(iii)].

If the surviving spouse is incapacitated and the spouse's representative elects to exercise the elective share, unexpended portions of the three family protection provisions may be added to the custodial trust created under the elective share procedure. [2–405(b); see 2–206(b); § 6.06].

CHAPTER 9

WILLS AND RELATED DOCTRINES

§ 9.01 Introduction

A. THE STATUTE OF WILLS

A fundamental device for distributing wealth upon death is the will. Presently, a will is a creature of statute. To constitute a valid will, these statutory provisions customarily require that a will must: (1) be voluntarily executed; (2) be executed by a competent person; (3) appear in a written or other specifically approved form; (4) be intended to take effect only after the testator's death; and (5) dispose of property, or make other directions, or both. [See 1 Page, Wills § 1.2]. Wills are also characteristically ambulatory and revocable. They are ambulatory in the sense that they apply to the situation that exists at the testator's death rather than that which was present at the time of the execution. [See 2–602]. Wills are also revocable by a competent testator who follows the proper revocation procedure. [See 2–507; § 9.03]. Although all jurisdictions by statute provide methods for making and revoking wills, execution requirements unfortunately vary greatly between them. This lack of uniformity results in a serious lack of predictability for persons whose estates cross state lines or who change domiciles during their lives.

B.   CODE POLICY AND DEVICES

The Code's will provisions have three primary objectives: (1) to make uniform among the jurisdictions the execution requirements for wills; (2) to reduce execution requirements to their indispensable minimum; and (3) to validate as often as possible instruments purporting to be wills.

For basic validity, the Code recognizes four separate and alternative will execution techniques, the successful satisfaction of any one of which produces a probatable will in the Code state. For convenience, the four techniques result in four types of wills called the ordinary witnessed will [2–502(a)], the holographic or handwritten will [2–502(b)], the foreign will [2–506], and the international will. [Art. II, Pt. 10, Uniform International Wills Act]. The Code also includes a special procedure for executing a fifth kind of will called the self-proved will, which although not essential for basic validity is useful to follow for purposes of easing proof of execution requirements in contested will cases. [2–504]. Significantly, the Code does not include recognized procedures for nuncupative or other types of special wills.

C. FORMALITY ANALYSIS AND THE SUBSTANTIAL COMPLIANCE DOCTRINE

Legal scholarship is rife with discussions of the merits, demerits and proper utility for formalities. [See, e.g., Gulliver & Tilson, Gratuitous Transfers; Langbein, Substantial Compliance]. Several purposes have been identified including purposes to protect and safeguard the testator, to provide reliable proof and evidence, to provide an event that emphasizes the finality of intent and of the act of execution, to result in a document that will receive the anticipated legal response and recognition and to provide administrative judicial efficiency. The purposes present a good case for requiring certain formalities to take place before one should be said to have satisfied the requirements. Considering the solemnness, importance, and finality of a will, it has been common for states to set out elaborate formalities necessary to be followed in order to satisfy and to produce a recognizable and valid will.

Generally, a will is an intent enforcing type of document. The goal of the instrument is to identify and explain the desires of the testator. It is assumed that if these desires and intent are adequately expressed, they will be obeyed. The difficulty is that they have no effect and are a nullity unless the instrument can be proven and thereby probated. To probate one must satisfy the execution formalities set out in the statute that recognizes a will as a transfer device. The dilemma created by legal formalities is that if a formality is not obeyed and it is considered a crucial formality, the failure to satisfy the formality may cause the instrument to fail and thus cause an intent denying rather than intent enforcing result.

Because the validity or invalidity of an instrument such as a will may be so important in terms of the distribution of an estate, the determination of validity has been a highly litigated issue. Opponents of wills will offer any reason to deny probate. Consequently, the formalities of the execution statute have been fertile fodder for these arguments. Courts that face this litigation are put in a policy bind. On the one hand, the court is conscious and respectful of legislative intent as expressed in the appropriate wills statute. If the legislature has set out a particular formality to follow, it is not for the court to ignore. On the other hand, the finding of invalidity of a will on a failure on the part of the testator to conform to a technical formality may appear extremely picayune and callous when the result dashes what is clearly expressed and finalized intent of the testator. Recently, significant efforts have been taken to reduce the necessary formalities for the execution of wills. This is in part in response to some very technical decisions applying a strict construction concept.

Generally, the courts have followed the concept of strict construction: i.e., an instrument must satisfy all the formalities set out in the statute. Consequently, when analyzing the validity of the instrument, one has to dissect the statute word by word to see if and what formalities are satisfied. In an effort that the policy of strict construction be kept within its legitimate domain, courts have adopted the doctrine that formalities not included in the statute will not be added. Generally, one must only satisfy the formalities required and no more. [See, e.g., Lemayne v. Stanley (1691) but cf. Estate of McKeller (1980)]. In addition, courts do not object to greater formalization than the statute requires.

Even where strict construction is the court's philosophy, some have been willing to ignore or to generously interpret some incidental formalities in the statutes. For example, a statute might require the testator to "request" the witnesses to witness the will. The word "request" may be liberally interpreted to mean the circumstances must indicate that the testator wanted the witnesses to witness the will. The testator need not have actually verbally requested the witnesses to do so. [See, e.g., Hollingsworth v. Hollingsworth (1966)]. This might be referred to as a reasonable compliance standard for these incidental formalities.

It is difficult, however, to distinguish between a formality that is going to receive a strict construction versus one that will receive a reasonable construction. Advocates of more liberal analyses of will formalities have determined that courts will not, on their own, adopt a more reasonable approach with regards to most formalities set out in will statutes. [Langbein, Substantial Compliance; see also Taylor v. Estate of Taylor (1989)]. Consequently, it is urged that a statutory substantial compliance or dispensing power be included. The Code now includes such a provision in Section 2–503.

Basically this provision permits a court to dispense with one or more of statutory formalities even if they have not been followed so long as the proponents of the document or writing establish by clear and convincing evidence that the testator intended the document to constitute the decedent's will or other will related instructions. An example of this would be a will that requires two witnesses but the testator only had one witness. If the standard of proof could be met, a court could dispense with the second witness and permit the will to be probated. This provision does not encourage testators to disregard the letter of the execution statutes: it merely provides a remedy in those cases where a rejection of the will causes significant intent denying results to occur notwithstanding the available proof of that intent. In addition, it is not designed to convert incomplete plans into finalized plans. Its purpose is to convert ineffective attempts at finalized intent into effective, finalized plans if the standard of evidence can be satisfied.

The provision is unspecific as to which formalities may be dispensed. With the exception that there must be a document or a writing added upon a document, all other formalities are subject to the dispensing remedy. Considering the uniqueness of wills validity situations, the dispensing power will be exercised on a case by case basis. Decisions on this issue will generally be too factually restrictive and therefore not provide precedent for later cases.

Some have argued that the law should abolish major formalities other than the merest physical evidence of the instrument. [See, e.g., Lingren,

Fall of Formalism (urges abolition of attestation requirement)]. The sole question should be an evidentiary matter concerning testamentary intent. Advocates of this approach would add a suggested model that follows a more precise formality. The point is the model would not be required but would be preferred planning and practice technique.

The Code adopts a middle ground approach to these issues. First, the Code includes several types of formal wills and has pared the actual formalities for each type down to minimum levels. Most instruments that are executed as wills will satisfy one or more of the types of formalities. Second, the Code provides an escape device in that the court is accorded a dispensing authority for formalities not followed so long as the standard of proof is met. This will cover the occasional case where clear unfairness will occur if the will is not recognized. Third, the Code provides a model form to follow. This is the self-proved will and it has its own attributes and advantages if proper practice follows its formalities to the letter.

§ 9.02 Execution Requirements

A. TESTATOR'S CAPACITY

A pervasive execution requirement under the Code for all recognized types of wills is that the testator must possess testamentary capacity. This capacity means that the testator must be of a certain age and possess the necessary mental ability. [2–501]. For uniformity purposes, the Code sets the age of eighteen or more years as the age a person must be in order to be able to execute a valid will. This age conforms to the age for will execution in the vast majority of states in this country and a single uniform age for will execution is desirable. The Code also continues the universal rule that a testator must be of sound mind in order to make a probatable will. Although the term "sound mind" is not defined in the Code, prior law is well developed in this area and should provide a definition.

B. THE ORDINARY WITNESSED WILL

Consistent with its purpose to keep execution requirements as simple as possible, the Code requires that only the bare essentials be satisfied in order to execute the ordinary witnessed will. Chart 9–1 compares the Code's execution requirements with other common requirements found in various wills statutes. In addition to the age and sound mind requirements discussed above, the Code requires the following: (1) a writing; (2) the testator's signature or a proxy signature in testator's presence and by testator's direction; (3) two witnesses; (4) the witnesses must be competent at the time of witnessing; (5) the witnesses must sign the will; and (6) the witnesses must witness either the signing process or the testator's acknowledgment of that signature or the testator's acknowledgment of the will. [2–502].

The Code does not require: (1) a signing at the end of the will; (2) the witnesses to sign in the

testator's presence; (3) the witnesses to sign in
each other's presence; and (4) a statement in all
cases by the testator that testator publishes the
document as testator's will. Mention of these non-
requirements is important because although strict
compliance with the stated formalities required by
a will statute is mandatory, generally no additional
ones are required. [Atkinson, Wills § 62; see
§ 9.01]. On the other hand, although the Code is
silent on when a witness must sign the will as
witness, several decisions have refused to probate
wills where the witnesses signed outside the normal execution process. In one case after the testator signed the will in the hospital, it was taken to a
residence where the necessary witnesses signed the
will. This was held to be ineffective. [Estate of
McGurrin v. Scoggin (1987)]. In another case, it
has held that necessary witnesses must sign prior
to the testator's death. [Estate of Royal (1992)].

Because wills under the Code are valid even if
one follows these extra requirements, or in other
words over-executes the will, it will be common for
many attorneys in Code states to continue their old
practice of having their clients over-execute their
wills.

CHART 9–1

Ordinary Wills Execution Requirements
Comparison With the Uniform Probate
Code Requirements

List of Common Execution Requirements	UPC Requirements [Reference].
A. Testator—age of majority— varies (18 yrs. to 21 yrs.)	"Any person 18 or more years of age" [2–501, and 2–501, Comment (Uniform age advocated)].

List of Common Execution Requirements	UPC Requirements [Reference].
B. Testator—of sound mind at time of execution	"of sound mind" [2–501].
C. A writing or some permanent record	"in writing" [2–502(a)(1)].
D. Signed by testator—the intended signature or proxy in his presence and by his direction	"signed by testator or in testator's name by some other individual in the testator's conscious presence and by the testator's direction" [2–502(a)(2)].
E. Signed (signature) at the "logical" end of the will	[No similar requirement—may be signed anywhere on will]
F. Witnesses—number:	
1. Two	"two individuals" [2–502(a)(3)].
2. Three	[Not applicable]
G. Witnesses—competent at time of execution	"An individual generally competent" [2–505(a)].
H. Witnesses—disinterested—no direct pecuniary benefit	[No disinterested requirement] "The signing of a will by an interested witness does not invalidate the will or any provision of it." [2–505(b)].
1. Will invalid, or	[Not applicable]
2. Interest taken away	[Not applicable]
I. Witnesses—attestation—authentication:	
1. The testator signing, or	[See I.4., below]
2. The testator's acknowledgment of the signature, and/or	[See I.4., below]
3. The testator's publication of the will, or	[Not applicable]
4. Any of the above	"witnessed either the signing of the will ... or the testator's acknowledgment of the signature or of the will" [2–502(a)(3)].
J. Witnesses—must [be requested to]:	[No "request" required]
1. Prove (no signing)	[Not applicable]
2. Sign anywhere	"signed by" [2–502(a)(3)].
3. Subscribe (at end)	[Not applicable]
K. Witnesses—sign in testator's presence:	[Not applicable]
1. "Conscious presence" test, or	
2. Within the same room test.	
L. Witnesses—sign, attest or subscribe or both in each others' presence	[Not applicable]
M. Executed by testator with testamentary intent (The instru-	[Presumed; see 3–407 (the burden of proving lack of testamentary ca-

List of Common Execution Requirements	UPC Requirements [Reference].
ment usually states it is a will)	pacity is on the contestants)].

The Code also specifically defines who is eligible
and competent to be a witness to a will. Under
this provision, the test of competence is whether at
the time of witnessing the witness of the will was
generally competent to testify as a witness in
court. [2–505(a)]. Significantly, the Code completely eliminates the prohibition or penalty imposed under non-Code law on persons witnessing a
will who receive an interest from the will. [2–
505(b)]. Consequently, a will is valid even if an
essential witness is interested and the interested
witness can also take any devise provided in the
will regardless of any rights of the witness to take
an intestate share. The Code leaves all underlying
questions of undue influence to a direct attack in a
will contest. It is important to emphasize, however, that by this rule the Code is not intended to
encourage the use of either minors or devisees as
witnesses but is designed to prevent injustices that
have occurred under the contrary current law.
For example, the Code's rule will not invalidate a
will because a witness, unknown to the testator,
was under the age of majority or take away or
reduce the interest of a devisee under a will because the innocent and unknowing devisee signed
as witness. [2–505, Comment]. In order to further
discourage volitional witnessing by a devisee, California added to its similar provision a clause tha
creates a presumption of undue influence against
the devisee-witness with regard to that devisee's
share. [West's Ann.Cal.Prob.Code § 6111]. Evi-

dence the witness did not know of the devise in the will should be relevant and admissible to rebut the presumption.

C. THE HOLOGRAPHIC WILL

The Code also includes a provision giving recognition to holographic wills. [2–502(b)]. Approximately one-half of the states have provisions authorizing holographic wills. Such recognition is consistent with modern will policies which generally are to increase recognition and to reduce the number of denials of probate. In addition, many of the old fears with regard to fraud and undue influence have either not materialized or are not relevant today because the holographic procedure satisfactorily protects a person from these dangers.

The Code's holographic execution procedure has only two requirements: (1) the instrument must be signed by the hand of the testator and (2) its material provisions must be in the testator's handwriting. [2–502(b)]. The Code's "material provisions" terminology must be compared to the "entirely written" terminology found in most holographic statutes today. The Code's terminology is specifically intended to counteract a strict statutory construction applied by some courts to the words "entirely written." [2–502, Comment; see Atkinson, Wills § 75]. These courts have held holographic wills invalid if they contain any printed matter on their faces provided that the testators intended the printed matter to be a part of the wills. By contrast, the "material provisions" ter-

minology should permit a holding of validity for a
holographic will executed on a printed will form if
the printed portions can be eliminated and if the
handwritten portions still adequately describe the
testator's testamentary scheme. [2–502(b), Comment; see Estate of Fitzgerald (1987)]. Although
testamentary intent might not be present from the
handwritten portion, it should be provable by the
admission of extrinsic evidence provided by the
printed portion. [Estate of Muder v. Muder
(1988)].

Significantly, the Code neither requires that a
holographic will be dated nor prescribes the location of the testator's signature. The primary question arising when there is no date or when the
signature is in an unusual place, or when both of
these facts are present, is whether the person intended the instrument to be a will or nothing more
than a statement of what would be done if executed as a will. This is, of course, an evidentiary
problem dealing with testamentary intent and
properly is not an execution formality problem.
[See Estate of Erickson (1991)].

California, which adopted the Code's "material
provisions" language, adopted two limitations if
the holographic will is not dated. [West's Ann.Cal.
Prob.Code § 6111]. First, if the provisions of an
undated holographic will are inconsistent with
those of another will, the holographic will is considered invalid unless it can be established that the
holographic will was executed after the other will
[West's Ann.Cal.Prob.Code § 6111(b)(1)]. Second,
the will is also invalid if it is established that the
testator lacked testamentary capacity during any

period of time when the undated holographic will might have been executed unless it can be established that the holographic will was executed while the testator had testamentary capacity. [West's Ann.Cal.Prob.Code § 6111(b)(2)].

D. THE FOREIGN AND INTERNATIONAL WILL

In our modern mobile society, the question of the validity of wills executed according to the wills execution laws of other states or countries is an important consideration. The principal problem is how to protect a person's reasonable expectations concerning an instrument that the person believes to be a valid will. The Code includes two statutory devices to deal with this problem. The first is a special choice of law rule with regard to the probate of foreign wills properly executed according to the wills' execution laws of other states or countries. [2–506]. The second establishes a special execution procedure for executing a will that will be valid in all jurisdictions that join an international convention or that enact the appropriate act. The latter procedure is incorporated in Part 10 of Article II of the Code and also constitutes the provisions for the freestanding Uniform International Wills Act (Hereinafter referred to as the International Wills Act).

Based upon the existence of any specific contact between the testator and the foreign jurisdiction the Code adopts a broad choice of law rule as to execution. [2–506]. In addition to recognizing the validity of any foreign instrument that happens to be executed according to the above described Code's techniques, a will is also valid if executed in compliance with the law of any of the following jurisdictions: (1) the place of execution; (2) the testator's domicile at the time of execution; (3) the testator's place of abode at the time of execution; (4) the place of the testator's nationality at the time of execution; (5) the testator's domicile at the time of death; (6) the testator's place of abode at the time of death; or (7) the testator's nationality at the time of death. [2–506]. If an instrument is a valid will under the laws of any of these jurisdictions, then the will is valid and may be probated in a Code state.

In effect, if a relevant contact is satisfied, the Code literally incorporates by reference the execution statute of the relevant jurisdictions. Consequently, the execution procedures of these other jurisdictions represent additional methods of executing a proper will. In addition, the reference to the laws of these other jurisdictions presumably includes all aspects of the actual execution process. The only expressed limitation placed by the provision on this reference to the execution laws of other jurisdictions is that the will must be "written"; consequently, nuncupative wills will not be recognized in the Code state even if recognized by the law of the jurisdiction having a relevant contact. It is not clear whether the reference to the other jurisdiction's law includes its rules with regard to the testator's and witnesses' capacities.

It is important to emphasize that the terms of this provision apply to wills being offered for probate for the first time and are not restricted to wills that have been previously probated in the foreign jurisdiction. This provision anticipates probate of the foreign executed will in the testator's domicile. Ancillary procedures are separately dealt with in the Code. [See § 26.04].

The distinction between the International Wills Act and the choice of law provision is significant. Whereas the choice of law rule attempts to validate wills executed under the laws of other jurisdictions, the Act anticipates an execution intended to be valid in jurisdictions that recognize it. By following the Act, the testator selected a procedure that anticipates probate in different jurisdictions. The expectation that this execution process will be valid for probate of the will wherever necessary is greater than the expectation of the testator who, at death, happens to have an estate requiring probate in several jurisdictions. Enactment of the International Wills Act is crucial to the protection of these expectations. Unless the federal government adopts the Act in the form of an international will convention, it will be up to each state individually to approve this legislation. [Art. II, Pt. 10. International Wills Act, Prefatory Note, 88–89]. At least eight states have enacted the free standing uniform act. [See 8 U.L.A., at 189 (Supp.1993)].

The application of the International Wills Act is not dependent upon the place of execution, the location of assets or the nationality, domicile or residence of the testator. [2–1002(a)]. Its procedures are independent of that status. If the proper execution procedure is followed, the will is presumed to be valid under the Act. On the other hand, the fact that a will is not validly executed under the Act does not affect its formal validity under other will statutes and acts. [2–1002(b)]. Nor would execution under the Act preclude the probate of such will under other wills acts or provisions including the choice of law provision.

The basic requirements of an international will are as follows:

(1) The will must be in writing. [2–1003(a)]. This writing requirement covers any form of expression made by recognizable signs on a durable substance. Any language can be used.

(2) The testator must declare that the document is testator's will and that testator knows its contents in the presence of three people, i.e., two witnesses and another "authorized person." [2–1003(b)]. The contents of the will need not be revealed to these persons.

(3) The testator must sign the will or acknowledge testator's signature if testator had previously signed it in the presence of these three persons. [2–1003(c)].

(4) If the testator indicates a reason for testator's inability to sign, any other person may sign as proxy for the testator if the authorized proxy signs the testator's name at the latter's direction and makes note of this on the will. [2–1003(d)].

(5) The witnesses and the authorized person must attest the will by signing it in the presence of the testator. [2–1003(e)].

An "authorized person" is defined as a person who has been admitted to practice law before the courts of the state and who is in good standing as an active law practitioner in the state [2–1009], or as a person who is empowered to supervise the execution of international wills according to the laws of the United States. [2–1001(2)].

Several other points of form are set out in the Act but the failure to comply with them will not cause the will to be invalid. [2–1004(d)]. These requirements include:

(1) All signatures must be placed at the end of the will; [2–1004(a)]

(2) On multiple page wills, each sheet must be signed by the testator or proxy and must be numbered; [Id.]

(3) The date of the execution of the will must be noted at the end of the will by the authorized person; [2–1004(b)] and

(4) The authorized person must ask the testator whether testator desires to make a declaration concerning the safekeeping of the will, and that expressed desire must be mentioned in the certificate attached to the will. [2–1004(c)].

The International Wills Act sets out a form of a certificate that must be signed by the authorized person and that recites the requirements under the Act for valid execution of an international will. [2–1005]. Similar to an attestation clause, or self-proved will affidavit [see § 9.02(E)], the certificate contains all of the elements necessary for the identification of the parties to the execution process including the testator, the witnesses and the authorized person and expressly outlines the necessary formalities to obtain the protection and recognition under the act. Three copies of this certificate must be executed.

Probate of the will with a certificate attached should be immediate since the certificate is conclusive of the formal validity of the instrument as a will. [2–1006]. Of course, such a will can be contested under formal testacy proceedings on the grounds of lack of capacity, fraud, undue influence, revocation, substantive ineffectiveness, and even forgery and genuineness. [2–1005, Comment; 2–1007; 2–1006; 2–1006 Comment]. The authorized person must retain one of the executed copies of the certificate, deliver another to the testator and attach the third to the will itself. [2–1005]. This multi-certificate execution process is touted to provide a reminder to the authorized person of the terms of its content, a document that may be found with testator's papers to inform interested persons of the existence of the will and its location, and to protect against unauthorized alterations to the certificate. [2–1005, Comment].

E. THE SELF–PROVED WILL

The Code adds a new execution technique for a special will called the "self-proved will." [2–504]. Basically, it is similar to the procedure for an ordinary witnessed will but includes a notarized affidavit executed by the testator and the witnesses. It also adds to the ordinary witnessed will execution process the following three execution formalities: (1) the testator must declare to the witnesses that the will is testator's last will; (2) the witnesses must sign as witness to testator's will; and (3) the witnesses must sign in the testator's presence and hearing.

The forms for two alternative affidavits are included in the Code. In a manner similar to the technique of the attestation clauses typically included in wills today, the affidavits describe the formalities and facts that were followed and observed in execution. Because they are affidavits, however, they both must be notarized. The first affidavit form permits the self-proved will affidavit to be a part of the will itself and actually constitutes the execution thereof. [2–504(a)]. In using this form, the testator and the witnesses execute the affidavit and the will simultaneously. [2–504, Comment]. The second affidavit form is to be executed separately from and subsequently to the execution of the ordinary witnessed will. [2–504(b)]. When using this form, the testator and the witnesses execute the will separately and then subsequently in a separate or continuous proceeding complete and sign the affidavit.

The effect of executing a self-proved will is not very significant. In most respects, when a self-proved will is offered for probate, it is subject to the same treatment as any other validly executed will. Its principal distinguishing feature is to permit the will to be admitted to probate in a formal testacy proceeding without the necessity of testimony of one of the subscribing witnesses. [3–406(b)]. The will, however, still is subject to contest for grounds such as revocation, undue influence, lack of testamentary capacity, fraud and even forgery. [3–406, Comment; see § 18.02(F)]. Notwithstanding its limited significance, use of one or the other of these forms should become standard practice for attorneys who draft and supervise the execution of wills.

§ 9.03   Revocation of Wills

A.   GENERAL REVOCATION PRINCIPLES

An inherent characteristic of a will is the power of the testator to revoke it. [2–507]. Just as statutes specifically prescribe the procedure by which wills must be executed, statutes typically prescribe the procedure by which wills must be revoked. The three generally accepted revocation methods are: (1) by physical act; (2) by subsequent instrument; and (3) by operation of law due to changed circumstances. [Atkinson, Wills § 84]. The first two methods require three principal elements that must occur concurrently: (1) an authorized act or instrument; (2) an intent on the part of the testator to revoke; and (3) a testator possessing legal capacity. Revocation by operation of law springs not from intentional acts on the document or subsequent testamentary documents but from changed circumstances between the date of the will's execution and the date of the testator's death. It springs automatically from the happening of these events. The Code recognizes and defines all three of these methods.

Each revocation method creates a formalit ˈ against which testator's intent must be evaluatec and compared. If the conditions of these methods of revocations are not obeyed, the will will not be revoked and the identifiable intent of the testator defeated. The best example would be a testator who has verbally expressed to many, including non-interested persons, that the testator presently revokes a previous will but the testator performs neither a physical act nor executes a subsequent revocatory instrument. Although it may be argued that since no physical act or subsequent instrument was executed the testator's intent was merely formative and not determinative, one may also conclude that the testator's intent was not followed. Consequently, just as with execution formalities, revocation formalities must be limited to the minimum degree necessary to protect the purposes of the formalities.

B.   REVOCATION BY PHYSICAL ACT

The Code permits a testator to revoke a will or any part of a will by performing certain revocatory acts on the will. These acts must be performed with the intent and for the purpose of revoking the will or a part of it. The revocatory act may be performed by another person if that person performs the act in the testator's conscious presence and by the testator's direction. A "conscious presence" test was specifically adopted in order to eliminate a line of sight test some courts have applied when "in the presence" is required by the statute. [2–507, Comment].

A revocatory act includes the typical laundry list of physical acts. [2–507(a)(2)]. The list includes burning, tearing, canceling, obliterating, and destroying. Usually, revocation statutes do not explain the degree to which each act must be performed on the will. This statutory omission causes interpretative problems for courts when the physical act performed by the testator fails to clearly match the statutory list of revocatory physical acts. On occasion, courts have refused to recognize a revocation when testator's act did not technically fit the court's definition of what is necessary to constitute a revocatory act. [See, e.g., Thompson v. Royall (1934)]. The Code attempts to prevent restrictive interpretations of the revocatory acts by providing specifically that a burning, tearing, or canceling is a revocatory act notwithstanding the burning, tearing, or canceling does not touch actual words of the will. Assumedly, this means that although some form of physical evidence of revocation must appear on the will itself, front or back, the act need not deface the printed words on the instrument.

Revocation of a will by physical act may raise greater risks of fraud than execution raises because the appearance of revocatory acts on a will is inherently ambiguous as far as the testator's actual intent is concerned. Consequently, courts must be cautious about claims of physical revocation and should require adequate proof with extrinsic evidence, including the testator's statements, if any, that the testator intended a revocatory act to constitute a physical revocation.

C. REVOCATION BY SUBSEQUENT INSTRUMENT

Revocation by subsequent instrument is also recognized by the Code when accomplished by an instrument executed with the same formalities as any valid will. [2–507(a)(1); see § 9.02]. Revocation of any prior will by this method may also be accomplished in whole or in part.

One of the most litigated situations concerning the revocation by subsequent instrument is when a testator executes a subsequent will which is inconsistent in whole or in part with a prior will, but which does not specifically revoke the prior will. The relevant issue which arises is whether the subsequent inconsistencies revoke the prior will or its provisions, or whether the prior will or its provisions are merely superseded by the subsequent inconsistent will or its provisions. Of course, if both wills are probated after the testator's death, the provisions and terms of the subsequent will prevail. If, however, the subsequent will is revoked before the testator's death, the determination of the issue whether the prior will was revoked or merely superseded is important. If the subsequent will merely superseded the prior will, revocation of the subsequent inconsistent will or its provisions reinstates the prior will or its provisions. If the prior will is held to have been revoked, however, that will or its provisions will be effective again only if reexecuted or the doctrine of revival is applicable. [See § 9.04].

The Code attempts to give some meaning to the concept of revocation by inconsistency. [2–507(b)–

(d)]. It begins with the general proposition that a previous will is revoked by inconsistency if the testator intended the subsequent will to replace rather than supplement the previous will. Clearly, an expression of such intent in the subsequent will would be effective to do this. Unfortunately, an expressed intent does not always appear in the subsequent will and courts may be faced with the responsibility of evaluating extrinsic evidence, if any, or to employ relevant evidentiary presumptions.

The Code deals directly with these evidentiary problems. First, the Code recognizes the general admissibility of extrinsic evidence to prove this intent. It then sets certain presumptions depending on the circumstances of the two or more wills. A testator is presumed to have intended revocation rather than supplementation of the previous will if the subsequent will makes a complete disposition of the testator's estate. [2–507(c)]. On the other hand, the testator is presumed to have intended a subsequent will to be merely a supplemental rather than revocatory of a previous will if the second subsequent will does not make a complete disposition the testator's estate. [2–507(d)]. Either presumption may be rebutted on a clear and convincing standard by extrinsic evidence. If not rebutted, the presumption stands. If a subsequent will entirely disposes of testator's estate, the burden of overcoming the presumption falls on those who wish to argue that the subsequent will is merely supplemental. On the other side, if the will is merely inconsistent in part, the burden of proving that the subsequent will revoked the prior will falls on those who want to argue revocation.

The application of the presumption may be important to the operations of the revival provision.

D. REVOCATION BY OPERATION OF LAW

At common law, revocation by operation of law was recognized in two situations: a single woman's will was revoked when she subsequently married, and a single man's will was revoked after his marriage and birth of an issue. [Atkinson, Wills § 85]. No other change of circumstances would revoke a will by operation of law.

The Code characterizes the issue as one of changed circumstances. [2–508]. It limits the revocatory effect of changed circumstances on wills to divorce by a spouse and to the testator's homicide by a devisee. The scope and application of these particular circumstances are discussed separately. [See §§ 12.03, 12.04]. No other change of circumstances shall be deemed to revoke a will by operation of law.

E. THE LOST OR DESTROYED WILL

Another problem related to revocation concerns the effect of a lost or unintentionally destroyed will. The general rule has been that in the absence of statutory provisions to the contrary, the lost or destroyed will may be admitted to probate upon adequate proof of its content and due execution. [Atkinson, Wills § 97]. If such proof cannot be maintained or if a statute restricts the proof of such wills, the lost or destroyed will has been in a sense revoked. Many non-Code states have statutes that specifically apply to the probate of such wills. A typical provision which is found in some of these statutes is that the lost or destroyed will cannot be probated unless it is "proved to be in existence at the time of the death of the testator, or is shown to have been fraudulently destroyed in the lifetime of the testator." [Atkinson, Wills § 97]. The quoted phrase has caused litigation where the will was lost or destroyed during the testator's lifetime but not by testator's action or authority and not fraudulently by another person. According to the literal language of the quoted phrase, such a will cannot be probated and has thereby in effect been revoked by a means not approved by the revocation statute. Several courts have circumvented this result by giving the key words, "existence" or "fraudulently" unusual meanings. [See, e.g., In re Fox's Will (1961); In re Estate of Havel (1923)].

The Code contains no special limitation on the probate of a lost or destroyed will other than to require that such will be probated in a "Formal Testacy" proceeding. [3–402(a); see § 18.02]. The apparent rationale is that specific guidelines either create a rigidity which prevents appropriate adaptation in all cases or cause interpretations of the statutes which are direct affronts to the literal meaning of the language. [See Model Probate Code, at 20]. The Code avoids these problems by leaving this matter to the rules of procedure and evidence of the probate proceeding itself. Legal presumptions concerning lost wills may also be relevant. For example, some jurisdictions have a presumption that if a will is traced to the testator decedent and cannot be found, there is a presumption of revocation. This rule may be applicable under the Code as well. [In re Estate of Hartman (1977)]. Of course, the rules concerning overcoming the presumption would also be applicable. [Id.].

§ 9.04   Revival of Revoked Wills

The revival of revoked wills provision originally promulgated in the Code has been significantly reworked in the 1990 version. Similar to the approach taken in the revocation by subsequent instrument provision, the Code adopts separate rules depending upon whether the subsequent will wholly revokes the previous will or merely partly revokes the previous will. [2–509]. In regard to revival of the previous will if the subsequent will is physically revoked, the Code creates different evidentiary requirements to prove revival. If a physically revoked subsequent will wholly revokes the previous will, revival occurs only when those who seek revival present evidence that the testator intended the previous will to be revived. [2–509(a)]. This puts the burden on those seeking revival of the previous will. The Code permits extrinsic evidence including statements by the testator to be admissible to prove intent. Assumedly, if no evidence is introduced or if the evidence is inconclusive, the prior will will not be revived. For example, if T executed Will 1 and wholly revokes it by express terms in Will 2, T's physical revocation of Will 2 is presumed not to revive Will 1 unless adequate proof of T's intent to revive is admitted into evidence. [2–509(a)]. Extrinsic evidence including statements by T is admissible to determine T's intent. Revival intent means an intent that the previous will will take affect as executed. Information concerning the testator's knowledge of the contents of the previous will is relevant evidence. [See Langbein & Waggoner, New Uniform Probate Code, at 886–87].

With regard to a physically revoked subsequent will that only partly revokes the previous will, the Code adopts the rule that revival is presumed unless those who contend that no revival occurred introduce evidence showing the testator did not intend revival of the prior instrument. [2–509(b)]. This puts the burden on those seeking nonrevival of the previous will. The Code permits extrinsic evidence including statements by the testator to be admissible to prove intent. Assumedly, if no evidence is introduced or if the evidence is inconclusive, the prior will will be revived. For example, if T executed Will 1 and only partially revoked it by express terms in Will 2, T's physical revocation of Will 2 will presumably revive Will 1 unless the person, who contends that T did not intend to revive the prior will, introduces evidence of that contrary intent. Again extrinsic evidence including statements by T is admissible to determine T's intent.

From the above examples, it is crucial to determine whether the subsequent will wholly or partially revokes the prior will. [See § 9.05]. In litigation on these types of issues, it is common that the party who must rebut the presumption loses because the extrinsic evidence is inadequate or inconsistent.

The Code's revival provision does not apply to the situation where the prior will has also been physically revoked by the testator. For example, if T executed Will 1 and revoked it by physical act and by the express terms in Will 2, T's physical revocation of Will 2 will not revive Will 1. No extrinsic evidence, including statements by T, is admissible to determine T's intent. Revival of Will 1 will occur only if the testator reexecutes Will 1 or executes Will 3 that incorporates by reference Will 1 into Will 3. [See 2–510; § 9.06].

Revival is also limited if the subsequent revoking will is in turn revoked by a later will. In this situation it makes no difference whether the subsequent will wholly or partially revokes the prior will. In either case, the revoked portions of the prior will are revived only if testator's intent to revive them appears from the terms of the latest will. [2–509(c)]. For example, if T properly executed Will 1 but partially revoked it by properly executed Will 2, the revocation of Will 2 by properly executed Will 3 will not revive the portions of Will 1 revoked by Will 2 unless the revival of the revoked portion appears for the terms of the Will 3. Evidence of intent is limited to the words on the face of the will unless some other evidence admissibility rule applies. Assumably, statements by T regarding revival are also inadmissible.

Although conditions for revival may not be present, one must not forget the potential application of the dispensing power concept in regard to execution, revocation, alteration and revival of wills. [2–503; § 9.01(C)]. A document, writing or even interlineation on a will might be treated as executed in compliance with the Code's will statute, if proponents of the document, writing or interlineation prove by clear and convincing evidence that the testator desired it to constitute a revival of a prior revoked clause or will. Because the full range of this provision has not been explored by the drafters in the comments or by the courts, it is difficult to craft an example that will definitely apply the principal. For purposes of further reflection consider the following example:

T properly executed Will 1 that is partially revoked by properly executed Will 2. As indicated above, the revocation of Will 2 by Will 3 will not revive the portions of Will 1 revoked by Will 2 unless the revival of the revoked portion of Will 1 appears for the terms of the Will 3. Evidence of intent will be limited to the face of the will and statements by T regarding revival are assumably inadmissible. If T wrote a personal letter to a beneficiary of Will 1 expressing the belief that Will 1 was revived because Will 2 had been revoked by Will 3, the holographic letter may satisfy the dispensing power requirements, i.e., it is a writing and it expresses the intent to revive the prior will. This letter may not qualify as a valid will under section 2–502 because it is not signed or is not witnessed or lacks testamentary intent. If the letter and other relevant extrinsic evidence constitutes sufficient clear and convincing proof that the testator intended the revival, the letter might be admitted to probate the same as a properly executed will would be and it would be given the effect it exhibits.

Treating this writing as the equivalent of a will is not inconsistent with the exclusion of extrinsic rule as applicable if revival is the basis of the revival. In this situation, the dispensing power under section 2–503 is being used not the revival concept under section 2–509. These are separate concepts each to be applied under its own scope and limitations.

As indicated, the Code provides for the automatic revocation of provisions in favor of a spouse who the decedent divorced and in favor of the spouse's relatives. [2–804(b); see § 12.03]. If decedent remarries the prior spouse or the divorce is nullified, the provisions for spouse or relatives are automatically revived by operation of law. [2–804(d)].

When a testator physically revokes a will or a part thereof with the immediate present intent of making a new will or of substituting a new partial alteration and when the will or alteration is not made or is ineffective for any reason, many courts under the "dependent relative revocation" doctrine have presumed that the testator would prefer to die testate than intestate. Consequently, the revoked will or its provisions, if the contents can be ascertained, have been admitted to probate in the absence of evidence overcoming this presumption. [Atkinson, Wills § 58]. The Code takes no official position on the scope and extent of this doctrine.

It merely makes an affirmative reference to the doctrine in the Comment to Section 2–507 and leaves the doctrine's recognition and development to the courts. There may be occasional situations where this doctrine would produce the better result than revocation or revival would. [See Langbein & Waggoner, New Uniform Probate Code, at 887].

§ 9.05 Supersession, Revocation and Revival Compared

The Code is relatively precise in its coverage of the procedural interrelationship of the will doctrines of supersession, revocation, and revival. [See §§ 9.03, 9.04]. Supersession deals with the situation where a subsequent testamentary clause or instrument suspends the effectiveness of a prior testamentary clause or instrument if all instruments and circumstances remained the same until testator's death. If relevant matters remain the same at the death of the testator, the subsequent or superseding provision will control and the prior disposition is effectively revoked. A supersession characterization is important, however, if, for some reason or event, the subsequent clause or instrument fails, the removal of the superseding disposition automatically reinstates the superseded disposition's effectiveness if possible under the circumstances. On the other hand, if a subsequent clause or will is characterized as revoking rather than superseding the prior clause or will, the removal or ineffectiveness of the subsequent clause or will does not reinstate the prior disposition unless the prior disposition is revived under the Code's revival provision. The Code's revival provision has its own presumptions concerning this matter. [2–509; § 9.04].

The interrelationship of the above concepts may create a progression of procedural issues to resolve in some situations. Consider the following problems:

CHART 9–2

Supersession, Revocation and Revival Compared

Assumption 1:
1. T properly executes Will 1 that provides: "The grandfather's clock to A, $10,000 to B, and the residue to C."
2. T later properly executes Will 2 that has no revocation clause and only provides, "The grandfather's clock to D."
3. T subsequently physically revokes Will 2.
4. A wants the grandfather clock; C contends it is part of the residuary.

Analysis: If a prior clause or will is only partially altered by inconsistency, two presumptions under the Code are potentially applicable. First, the subsequent inconsistent provision is presumed merely to supersede the former: both provisions are in effect at death unless otherwise revoked. If the subsequent provision is revoked or becomes ineffective, the former provision is automatically effective. This presumption of supersession, however, may be rebutted by clear and convincing evidence. This means that those contending revocation rather than supersession may prove by the appropriate standard of proof that the testator intended revocation rather than supersession. Second, notwithstanding revocation of the prior clause or instrument, those desiring effectiveness for the prior clause or instrument can still argue and prove revival. Under the revival provision when the previous will or clause is only partially revoked by inconsistency, revival is presumed if the subsequent will or clause is revoked by physical act. [See § 9.04]. This presumption is rebuttable by a preponderance of evidence propounded by those who argue no revival. Consequently, the person seeking effectiveness for the prior clause can use both affirmative presumptions. An intent to revoke is not the same as an intent not to revive because these intent issues concern the testator's state of mind at different times. The person contending revocation of the prior clause by the subsequent clause or will and nonrevival of the prior clause upon physical revocation of the subsequent clause is faced with a double burden of proof.

Assumption 2: A. T properly executes Will 1 that provides: "The grandfather's clock to A, $10,000 to B, and the residue to C."

  B. T later properly executes Will 2 that has no revocation clause and provides, "The grandfather's clock to D. $10,000 to B, and the residue to C."

  C. T subsequently physically revokes Will 2.

  D. A wants the grandfather clock; C contends it is part of the residuary.

Analysis: When the inconsistencies are characterized as revocation, the presumptions are reversed. Because the second will makes a complete disposition of the testator's estate, it is presumed that the testator intended revocation rather than supplementation of the previous will unless the revocation is rebutted by clear and convincing evidence. If rebutted, the previous terms prevail automatically as indicated in the previous illustration. Even where the subsequent clause or will is presumed to have revoked the prior will, however, A may submit evidence that the revoked will was revived. The standard of proof is by a preponderance of evidence standard. If this proof is met, the former instrument will be revived and the former gift will prevail. This assumes a revocation of the subsequent instrument or clause by physical act. [See § 9.03].

The above two examples and analyses clearly indicate that the Code is very favorable to reinstatement under supersession or revival of prior provisions. This is often justified because otherwise testator will die intestate.

§ 9.06 Incorporation by Reference

The overwhelming majority of American courts recognize the doctrine of "incorporation by refer-

ence." [Atkinson, Wills § 80]. Generally, this doctrine holds that an unexecuted document or instrument may be incorporated for specific purposes
into a validly executed will. [2 Page, § 19.17]. In
order to avoid obvious possibilities of fraud, generally six prerequisites must be satisfied in order for
the doctrine to apply. They include: (1) a validly
executed will; (2) a distinct reference to the unexecuted document in the will itself; (3) a showing or
statement in the will that the document is in
existence at the time the will is executed; (4) proof
that the document was actually in existence at the
time of execution; (5) a showing of intent on the
part of the testator to incorporate the document
into the will; and (6) a showing that the document
offered is the one referred to in the will. The
courts have not adhered to the above requirements
consistently. For example, requirements 1 and 4
have been strictly adhered to whereas 2 and 5 have
sometimes been liberally applied. If a document is
held to have been incorporated by reference into a
will, it is treated as part of the will for the specific
purpose it is to serve and as if it had been fully
recited in the will itself. [2 Page, § 19.32].

The Code substantially codifies the doctrine of
incorporation by reference as described above. [2–
510]. The one exception is that requirement 3 is
not a prerequisite. Consequently, so long as there
is proof that the document was actually in existence at the time of execution (requirement 4), the
Code does not require that there be a showing or
statement in the will that the document is in
existence at the time that the will is executed.

The essence of the doctrine is the determination that the testator intended to incorporate the document into the will. The Code requires that the language of the will "manifest" this intent. The key word "manifest" when used as a verb means "to show plainly: make palpably evident or certain by showing or displaying." [Webster's Third New Int'l Dictionary 1375]. This means that although there must be some indication of an intent to incorporate by reference another document on the face of the will, it is not necessary that precise language be used such as "I intend to incorporate" as a means of showing this intent. The intent can be derived from the total meaning of the relevant clauses in the will. For example, under this provision, it would be feasible to find that a testator intended to incorporate a previously improperly executed "will" into a subsequent codicil merely by reference to the previous instrument. This would be true even though technically, the testator did not intend to incorporate the previous document into the codicil but intended merely to modify it.

Contrary to interpretations in some states, the Code permits a valid holographic will to incorporate a non-holographic instrument into it. [2–510]. The problem posed is whether the incorporation of a non-holographic instrument, which provides the primary information concerning the testator's estate plan, into the holographic will constitute an infringement upon the requirement that the "material portions of the document" must be in the testator's handwriting. Although the Code does not specifically state the theory underlying its incorporation by reference provision, it may be assumed in this situation that the incorporation is for purposes of admissible evidence and not for purposes of integrating the instrument into the incorporating will. Because a holographic will is capable of being interpreted by extrinsic evidence, it follows that a non-holographic instrument incorporated into the holographic will which qualifies under the incorporation by reference provision should be a proper form of admissible evidence.

§ 9.07   Testamentary Additions to Trusts

For purposes of drafting and administrative convenience and for the benefit of future flexibility, it is a common estate planning technique to include a devise in a client's will that passes property from the estate to a trustee of a trust for the benefit of beneficiaries named in the trust. This type of clause is called a "pour-over" clause. Before statutes were enacted to validate these devises, a question might arise whether the beneficiaries had been adequately identified in the will when their identity is found only in the trust. If the trust existed when the will was executed and remained unchanged at testator's death, the devise usually satisfied the requirements of incorporation by reference. [§ 9.06]. Even if the trust had been changed, if it possessed substantial assets or corpus, the doctrine of independent significance could be used to validate the devise. [§ 9.08]. Estate planning techniques, however, have become much more sophisticated and reliance upon a trust not being changed or a trust actually possessing a corpus is too restrictive and might cause some pour-over devises which do not satisfy either cir-

cumstance to fail. [See, e.g., Atwood v. Rhode
Island Hospital Trust Co. (1921)]. This is a very
undesirable possibility where planning and expectations are involved.

The Code protects these planning and expectation factors. [2–511]. Its provision not only validates the simple pour-over devise into an existing
trust, but also addresses the validity issues concerning more sophisticated techniques. In regard
to the threshold question, the devise is not invalid
because the trust is amendable or revocable or
even if it is actually amended after the execution
of the will or the testator's death. Second, the
devise is valid notwithstanding the existence, size
or character of the corpus of the trust during the
testator's lifetime. The pour-over trust may be
established in either of two methods: The trust can
be established during the testator's lifetime either
by the testator, or by the testator and some other
person, or by some other person. Second, the trust
can be established at testator's death if the trust is
identified in the testator's will and the trust's
terms are (a) recited in a non-testamentary written
instrument that was executed at any time before,
with or after the testator executed the will or (b)
recited in the will of another individual who has
predeceased the testator. If the trust is created
during the testator's lifetime, it may be a funded or
unfunded life insurance trust even if the trustor
has reserved all rights of ownership in the insurance contracts.

The testator is given the option whether to treat
the trust as a testamentary trust under the testator's will or to allow it to be governed by the terms

of the trust and by its terms and provisions including amendments made to the trust before or after the testator's death. The presumption is that unless the testator's will indicates otherwise, the property devised will be administered under the terms and conditions of the trust and not as a new testamentary trust. If the trust is revoked or terminated before the testator's death, the pourover devise lapses unless the testator's will provides that it does not lapse.

The Code's provisions have been converted into Section 1 of the Uniform Testamentary Additions to Trusts Act. [2–511, Comment].

§ 9.08   Events of Independent Significance

One doctrine of the law of wills that is typically not codified but which is absolutely essential to its proper functioning is the doctrine of "events of independent significance." Basically, this doctrine permits certain evidence outside the will to be admitted in order to determine who receives and what property passes under the testator's will. [2 Page, § 19.34]. A statement of its principle is that if a fact, be it an act or event, has significance other than to pass property at death, this significance entitles that fact to control and to determine the disposition of the property. Significantly, the above principle applies regardless of whether the testator or third persons can affect the act or event subsequent to the will's execution. [Atkinson, Wills § 81]. Typical examples of the application of the doctrine are the common use in wills of such terms as "children," "cousins," "brothers and sisters," the "residue" and "all my property." In order to determine the meaning of each of these words or phrases, it is necessary to look at facts outside the face of the will; however, because these words have obvious significance other than to pass property at death, extrinsic evidence is admitted to show their meaning.

Apparently for uniformity and clarity purposes, the Code includes a provision that codifies a broad statement of the common law rule. [2–512]. This provision is applicable to acts or events that occur not only before or after the execution of the will but also that occur after the testator's death. Under its test, testamentary dispositions may be controlled by these acts and events only if the latter "have significance apart from their effect upon the dispositions made by the will." Although the Code generally leaves to the Court the determination of what comes within its test, it does expressly state that under the test the execution or revocation of another's will constitutes such an event. This separate and specific rule permits a testator to dispose of testator's property according to the terms of another's will notwithstanding that the other's will was executed before or after the testator's will.

§ 9.09 References to Separate Writings

The Code permits, under limited circumstances and with explicit restrictions, a separate writing to dispose of certain tangible personal property notwithstanding that the writing does not satisfy any will execution procedure, the incorporation by reference doctrine or the events of independent significance doctrine. [2–513]. The requirements for such a writing are as follows:

(1) The writing must be signed by the testator;

(2) The items disposed of and the devisees must be described with reasonable certainty;

(3) The items disposed of must be tangible personal property;

(4) The tangible personal property items disposed of must not otherwise be specifically disposed of by the testator's will; and

(5) There must be a reference to this writing in a properly executed will of the testator.

If these requirements are satisfied, it makes no difference whether the writing comes into existence before or after the execution of the will, whether the writing is actually altered by the testator after the execution of the will, or whether the writing has significance other than its effect on the dispositions made in the will.

One important limitation on the use of this type of transfer device is that it is limited to the disposition of tangible personal property. The provision specifically prohibits the use of this device for the disposition of money. This limitation on type of property disposable using the device inferentially also bars its use to dispose of evidences of indebtedness, documents of title, securities, and property used in trade or business under this device. [2–513, Comment].

The writing and signature formalities put a relatively high burden on users of this device. Unsigned holographic writings do not qualify. To be effective, the latter instruments would have to be probatable under the Code's formality dispensing provision. [2–513, Comment; see 2–503; § 9.01(C)]. Although the absence of a dating requirement removes a barrier to validity for these devices, the possibility that undated and partially or wholly conflicting signed writings may be found among a decedent's records after death may cause serious construction problems. A disadvantage from such misuse of the device might cause the underlying will to be denied informal probate. [See 3–304].

On the whole, the recognition of such a device is justified on the grounds that it is in line with the policies of giving effect to the testator's intent and of relaxing execution formalities. [2–513, Comment; see § 9.01]. Considering the limitation placed upon the type and extent of property that may be disposed of in this manner, problems of fraud, duress and undue influence are not serious considerations. One of the most beneficial aspects of this provision is to provide a convenient and simple device for persons who desire to change their wills frequently with respect to devises of tangible personal property and effects. This new device appears to be popular both with laymen and with practicing attorneys.

§ 9.10 Succession Contracts

Contracts concerned with the succession of property have generally been held to be valid and enforceable. [1 Page, § 10.1]. In their broadest general categories, these contracts include contracts to make a will or to devise, contracts not to revoke a will or devise, and contracts to revoke a will or to die intestate or both. The substantive requirements for such contracts are determined by the law of contracts, not by the law of succession. Contract law, therefore, determines such issues as offer and acceptance, certainty of terms, consideration, capacity, and any formality requirement such as the Statute of Frauds. The formality requirement issue, however, raises significant interrelationship concerns between the law of contracts and the law of succession. Obviously, succession contracts may effect the determination of who succeeds to the property after the death of the deceased promisor.

One of the most common problems concerning succession contracts is whether oral succession contracts may be proved. [1 Page, §§ 10.10–10.11]. Because the Statute of Wills is not applicable, in most states the basic question has been the applicability of the Statute of Frauds. Unless the state has a specific provision dealing with succession contracts that adequately limits the proof of oral succession contracts, the Statute of Frauds constitutes no significant limitation on the proof of these oral contracts. Even where the Statute of Frauds' provision relating to the sale of real estate applies to a succession contract dealing with transfers of real estate, the courts commonly apply exceptions to the statute such as part performance and other presumptions to circumvent the Statute's proof restriction and permit the oral contracts to be proved. Depending upon one's viewpoint toward formality requirements, this circumvention of the Statute of Frauds may or may not be beneficial. Notwithstanding this value judgment, the ineffectiveness of the Statute of Frauds as a bar to proof of succession contract has significantly encouraged litigation over these matters.

In order to reduce the uncertainties and litigation caused by oral succession contracts, the Code tightens the proof requirements for all three categories of succession contracts. [2–514]. It provides that a succession contract can be established against a decedent's estate only if (1) material provisions of the contract are stated in the decedent's will, or (2) an express reference in the will is made to such a contract that is supplemented by other admissible extrinsic evidence proving the terms of the contract, or (3) evidence of the contract appears in a writing signed by the decedent. In addition, the Code specifically provides that no presumption of a contract not to revoke a will can be created by the mere execution of a joint will or mutual wills. Otherwise, this provision is not intended to alter the rules of evidence with regard to the proof of such contracts. [2–514, Comment].

Clearly, this provision intentionally limits the proof of succession contracts and washes away all of the authority and decisions dealing with the application of the Statute of Frauds and its exceptions. [Orlando v. Prewett (1985)]. As with the adoption of any new formalistic requirement, the expectations of some persons will be destroyed. [See § 9.01(C)]. Considering that one of the parties to the contract is no longer available to testify, however, it would appear to be good public policy to require some form of written evidence that the contract actually exists. In addition, the limitations themselves leave adequate room for the courts to develop reasonable interpretation of the requirements so that harm will not be caused to a substantial number of persons. The terms "material provisions" and "evidencing" and the admissibility of extrinsic evidence where the will makes reference to the contract are three concepts in the provision that give the courts adequate interpretive flexibility.

Significantly, the Code makes no attempt to restrict or delineate what otherwise is necessary to prove succession contracts; nor does it attempt in any way to deal with the problem of the appropriate remedy when such contracts are proved. In addition, so that these new formalities do not interfere with pre-existing rights, this provision specifically applies only to succession contracts made after the effective date of the Code. [2–514]. Pre-existing succession contracts will be tested by the previously applicable formality requirement, if any.

§ 9.11 Confidential Public Depository

Under rules to be established by each court, the Code provides that a testator or testator's agent may deposit a will with any court for purposes of protective preservation. [2–515]. So that as much confidentiality as is feasible is maintained, the Code provides that only the testator or the agent, authorized in writing, may obtain repossession of the will. Although the testator's conservator may also be allowed to examine the will, the Court is to set strict procedures designed to maintain the confidentiality of the will. Under such procedures, for example, the conservator is not to be given possession of the will but only to be permitted to examine it. Upon the completion of this examination, the will must be resealed and left on deposit.

When the Court is informed of the testator's death, it is to notify any person who is designated to receive the will and to deliver the will to that person on request. In the alternative, the Court may deliver the will to the appropriate court.

Under the Uniform International Wills Act reproduced in Part 10 of the Code, a registry system is created for the international will. [2–1010]. The system provides a location where authorized persons can file for safekeeping specific information concerning the international will. The information filed, which will be preserved in confidence until death, is limited to the name, social security and any other individual identifying number established by law, address, and date and place of birth of the testator, and the intended place of deposit or safekeeping of the international will. The official, which the Code suggests be the Secretary of State, may make this information available only to persons who present a death certificate of the testator or satisfactory evidence of the testator's death to the central information center.

§ 9.12 Will Custodians

A custodian of a will of a testator who has died is on request of an interested person under a duty to deliver with reasonable promptness any will of the testator either to a person who is able to secure its probate or to an appropriate Court if no such person is known. [2–516]. Willful failure to deliver a will causes the custodian to be liable to any person who suffers damages as a consequence of that failure. A custodian may also be subject to the penalty of contempt of court if the custodian willfully refuses or fails to deliver a will, although required to do so by a court order issued as a result of a proceeding specifically brought to compel delivery.

§ 9.13   No Contest or Claim Clauses

The Code also codifies the rule in many states that an anti-contest or anti-claim clause in a will is unenforceable against an interested person if that person had probable cause to institute the proceeding. [3–905; replicated in 2–517]. For example, under the probable cause standard, this clause protects devisees in a will from automatic forfeiture of the devise for instituting a contest proceeding against the will. Since the devisee obviously lost the contest it is usually difficult to establish probable cause. The provision is unclear on how the probable cause standard applies to a devisee who is a creditor of the estate and who submits a claim against the estate despite the forfeiture provision in the will. If the devisee succeeds on the claim, does this constitute probable cause and permit the devisee to take a devise also? Is this not what the testator might have desired to prohibit? How this provision resolves the above questions and other similar ones will have to wait for court decisions. Fortunately, litigation over forfeiture clauses is not common. At best this provision provides a residual remedy to prevent injustice.

CHAPTER 10

RULES OF CONSTRUCTION APPLICABLE TO WILLS ONLY

§ 10.01 Introduction to Rules of Construction for Wills

Inherently, a will is nothing more than words structured so as to communicate the testator's desires. In order to carry out the will's purposes and effects, it is necessary to ascribe a meaning to the words. When determining the meaning of words used in a will, the cardinal principle is that the subjective intent of the testator, as expressed in testator's will and if not against public policy, controls the legal effect of the will's dispositions. [Cf. 2–601]. Consequently, a testator may ascribe a meaning to a word different from the ordinary meaning. If the testator's own meaning can be determined it should control. When the testator's meaning cannot be determined or is inadequately expressed, the interpreters must seek the meaning of the word from other sources.

As with any area of law, there are frequently used words of art or common recurring situations. Because of the frequency of the use of these words or of the occurrence of the situation, the law must develop uniform and set definitions and interpretations. These definitions and interpretations serve two purposes: (1) they provide a rule of construction for wills where the testator's expressed intent is inadequate or lacking; and, (2) they provide a set of uniform rules that drafters of wills may incorporate by reference either explicitly or implicitly. The Code not only includes a long list of general definitions that are useful for these purposes, [see § 2.02(E)] but also incorporates rules of construction for many of the most common problems concerning will interpretation and construction. [Art. II, Pt. 6]. Presumably, these rules of construction are based upon what the drafters determined the typical testator would desire if the testator had expressly indicated that intent. Significantly, they do not apply if evidence indicates testator had a contrary intention. [2–601].

Because many of the rules of construction in this chapter and in other parts of the Code are applicable only to particular types of testamentary gifts, definitions of the various classes of testamentary gifts are important. Due to the absence of definitions of these terms in the Code, the common law definitions are relevant. Generally, testamentary gifts are classified into four different categories, i.e., specific, general, demonstrative and residuary devises. A specific devise is a gift of a specific item or portion of the estate. A general devise is a gift of a set value or generally described property which is to be charged against the whole estate and not a specific portion. A demonstrative devise is a gift payable out of the whole estate but which is in the first instance charged against certain parts of the estate. A residuary devise is a gift of the remainder of the estate. [See 6 Page, Wills §§ 48.1–.10].

§ 10.02 Devisee Lapse

A. INTRODUCTION

Common law holds that when a devisee (including a legatee) died between the execution of the will and the death of the testator, the devise to that person lapses. [6 Page, Wills § 50.20]. If a devisee died before the execution of the will, the devise is void. [6 Page, Wills § 50.22]. These characterizations generate a constructional presumption providing that neither the dead devisee nor that devisee's estate can take the devise. A lapsed or void devise passes to others according to a set of other presumptions. [Atkinson, Wills § 140]. First, the devise passes to one or more devisees named as alternative devisees including survivors of survivorship type devises such as class gifts. If no alternative devisee is named, the devise passes to the residuary devisee, if any. If no residuary devisee is named, or if the residuary devise becomes void or lapses, the devise passes by intestacy. All of these presumptions yield to a testator's expressions of contrary intent.

The following methods are commonly used by testators to avert or resolve these problems: (1) a testator makes the devise to several persons as joint tenants expecting the survivorship of one or more of the joint tenants to prevent lapse; (2) a testator specifically provides for alternative devises to other persons until the likelihood of total failure of the devise is negligible; or, (3) a testator uses class gifts with their built in survivorship presumptions.

Because lapse occurs more often than many testators have anticipated and because lapse causes disinheritance of the devisee and the devisee's relational stock, the vast majority of jurisdictions in this country have enacted what are commonly referred to as "antilapse statutes." Although called "antilapse statutes," they do not prevent lapse but actually create a statutory substitute devise to the devisee's descendants. [2–603, Comment]. Generally, these statutes permit the descendants of certain classes of dead devisees to stand in their ancestor's place for purposes of taking under a testator's will. They create a rule of construction that may be altered by the testator. If a testator intends that lapse occurs, it will occur and the devise will fail. None of the statutes apply to all testamentary gifts and they vary greatly as to their scope.

Cognizant that the lapse and voidness of devises are common, unanticipated occurrences in wills, the Code contains a comprehensive, although restricted, set of constructional rules concerned with lapse and its related problems. [2–603, 2–604]. Due to the multiplicity of issues that concern lapse, the Code's provisions are relatively complex. Three levels of concern must be digested for a proper understanding of these provisions: one must determine (1) the scope and limitations of the provisions; (2) the application to relevant lapse problems; and, (3) how a testator may override their application.

B. SCOPE AND LIMITATIONS OF THE ANTILAPSE PROTECTION

As with other similar statutes, the Code's substitute devise protection does not apply to all devisees. This protection is only provided for (1) devisees who come within the relational classification of being a testator's grandparent or a lineal descendant of a grandparent [See the Code's relational umbrella of covered relations highlighted in Chart 5–2, § 5.02] and (2) devisees who are stepchildren of the testator or of the donor of a power of appointment exercised by the testator's will. If a devisee is not a person who comes within the relational umbrella or a step-child, the common law rule of lapse applies and there is no substitute devise. For example, descendants of devisees who are uncovered relatives related by marriage or who are legal strangers would not be protected by this provision. When testator's spouse is a devisee, the spouse's descendants also are not protected by the provision. This situation is to be compared to the case when the spouse's child, a step child of testator, is the devisee. When the step-child is a devisee, the step-child's descendants are protected by the provision but if a devise is made to a surviving spouse and no one else, the spouse's descendants, including a possible step-child, are not protected under the provision.

If a devisee is a qualified devisee and the devise lapses, a substitute devise is created for the devisee's surviving descendants. [2–603; see also 2–106, § 5.03]. Descendants who take the substitute devise share only the interest the devisee would have taken if the devisee had survived the testator and whatever they take, they take by representation. [2–603(b)(1), (2); see also 2–106 (Representation defined)]. Significantly, only the devisee's descendants receive this substituted devise; other relatives of the devisee, such as ancestors and collaterals, are not accorded a substitute devise under the provision. Furthermore, in order for the substitute descendants of deceased devisees to take under the provision, they must survive the testator by 120 hours although they need not survive the deceased devisee by any specific length of time. [See § 2–702; § 11.02]. If descendants of a qualified devisee fail to survive, the common law rule of lapse applies and there is no substitute devise.

The Code's antilapse provision is expansive in regard to the timing of the lapse and to the types of devises covered. Its rules apply to all types of devises including specific, general, demonstrative and residuary. It applies notwithstanding that the qualified devisee died before the testator's will was executed or died between the execution date and the testator's death. [2–603(a)(4)(ii)]. Beyond actual death of a devisee, the provision applies in all circumstances where the devisee is deemed under the Code to have predeceased the testator. [See 2–702, 2–801(d), 2–803, 2–804]. The antilapse provision also specifically applies to descendants of devisees of class gifts regardless whether the common law treats the devise as lapsed or void. [2–603(b)(2)]. Class gifts include, for example, devises to one's children, siblings, cousins and similar single generation relational groups. Because of an inherent substitute devise effect, the Code's provision does not apply to class devises such as devises to one's issue, descendants, heirs, next of kin and other multi-generational relational groups.

In a significant clarification of the law of lapse, the Code specifically applies its substitute gift protection to the exercise of powers of appointment. [See § 12.06; see also, e.g., French, Application of Antilapse Statutes]. Under the Code, the exercise of a testamentary power of appointment is a devise and an appointee of an exercised testamentary power of appointment is a devisee. [2–603(a)(3), (4)]. Exercised testamentary powers are protected by the substitute gift presumption if the appointee either comes within the class of being a grandparent or a lineal descendant of a grandparent [See the Code's relational umbrella of covered relations highlighted in Chart 5–2, § 5.02] or is a stepchild of the donor of a power of appointment exercised by the testator's will or of the testator who is donee of the power. [2–603(b)]. For example, if D devised or deeded property "to T for life, remainder to G's children as T shall appoint," and T exercised the power in favor of A but A predeceased T leaving surviving descendants, A's surviving descendants would take a substitute devise if A is a member of the covered relations of either D or T. It makes no difference whether the power of appointment is a general or special power so long as the appointee's relational threshold requirement is met. The exercise may be to an individual or a class. If the substitute gift presumption applies, it does not matter that the substitute taker is not a member of the class of permissible appointees so long as the appointee is a permissible appointee and meets the relational threshold requirement.

C. APPLICATION TO RELEVANT LAPSE PROBLEMS

Beyond the threshold determination of substantive relevance, one is faced with a range of application problems that run from simple to complex. The Comment to section 2–603 contains excellent illustrations explaining the operation of this provision. In the simple case the answers are easy. For example, if T devised property to A and A died before T or did not survive T by 120 hours or more, A's surviving descendants, if any, will take the devise as substitute devisees if A falls with the relational umbrella protected by the Code and if a contrary intent is not established. Another simple example would be the will that makes a devise to A's children, where at T's death, two of A's children survived and one predeceased T but left descendants who survived T. The descendants of the predeceased child collectively receive a substitute devise equal to the shares of A's two children who survived T. These descendants share the devise among themselves by representation. In both examples, it makes no difference to the result whether the nonsurviving devisee died before or after the will was written.

More complex problems concern wills in which the testator has created alternative devises. For example, who takes if T devised property "to A, but if A does not survive T, to B" and assuming A does not survive T but leaves descendants who do?

Under the Code, B will take because the alternative devise prevails. Taking the same example further, who takes if B also predeceases T but leaves no descendants who survived T? In this situation A's surviving descendants will take a substitute devise because the alternative devise failed and the substitute devise presumption prevails. [2–603(b)(4)]. Continuing one step further, who takes if B also predeceased T and like A left descendants who do? Again, the Code provides that A's descendants will take a substitute devise to the exclusion of B's descendants because A's descendants were the primary substitute gift as A held the primary devise. [2–603(c)(1), 2–603(c)(3)(ii)]. The primary devise is the one that will be effective if all nonsurviving devisees had survived the testator which in this example will always be A. [2–603(c)(3)(i)].

A third group of circumstances that cause lapse problems are the devises that include an alternative gift to the person or persons who would have been the substitute taker under the antilapse provision. [2–603(c)]. For example, consider the lapse problem raised when T devised property "to A, but if A does not survive T, to A's children" and assuming A does not survive T but leaves a child, B, who survived T and two grandchildren, F and G, who survived T but whose parent, C, predeceased T. The devise to the children, B and C, is a "younger generation devise" because it is to a descendant of the primary devise, A, it is an alternative devise to the primary devise, it is one for which a substitute gift is created and it would have gone into effect if all deceased devisees had survived except for the primary devisee, A, who predeceased the testator. [2–603(c)(3)(iii)]. In this situation the "younger-generation substitute gift" to F and G takes precedence over the primary substitute gift to B and C; consequently, F and G, collectively, take one half of the estate and B takes the other half. [2–603(c)(3)(iv)]. If this priority of substitute gifts did not apply, it would be possible to conclude that B takes one-half of the devise plus one half of the devise to A and F and G would share only the one-half of one half rather than one-half of the whole devise. The Code's approach to this matter conforms to the probable intention of most testators.

If a devise lapses and the substitute devise provisions are inapplicable, the Code has a special provision designating to whom the lapsed devise passes. Significantly, the following rules apply to all lapsed devises regardless of who the devisee is. All lapsed devises other than the residuary devise become part of the residue and pass to the residuary devisees. [2–604(a)]. When the residue is devised to two or more devisees and one share fails for any reason, that devisee's share passes to the other residuary devisee or devisees. [2–604(b)]. This is a meritorious rule of construction because it will frequently avoid part of the estate passing in intestacy. Of course, if all of the residue fails for any reason, the residuary estate passes by intestacy to the testator's heirs.

D. TESTATOR'S EXPRESSED
CONTRARY INTENTION

As with all of the Code's rules of construction, the provision does not apply if the testator, by the terms of the will, indicates that the provision does not apply. Section 2–603 sets the presumption that mere statements of survivorship such as "if he survives me" are not, "in the absence of additional evidence," sufficient indications of an intent to override the statute's presumption. [2–603(b)(3)]. The justification for this boiled down to two primary arguments. First, the statute is said to be remedial in that it favors family and thus deserves broad interpretation and second, the issue has been litigated enough to have a firm rule. [2–603, Comment]. The Comment notes the conflict among the cases and cites several examples.

It is clear that if the testator adequately expresses an intent to require survivorship, this expression will be given effect. [2–601; 2–603, Comment]. The comment to section 2–603 states that "foolproof" drafting techniques of expressing a contrary intent include adding an additional phrase to a devise that states "and not to [the devisee's] descendants" or a separate clause that states "all lapsed or failed nonresiduary devises are to pass under the residuary clause," or an addition to the residuary clause that states "including all lapsed or failed devises." [2–603, Comment]. Where or how the line is to drawn between "mere words of survivorship" and "express contrary intent" is not explained.

In many lapse situations, no actual intent will be available and the court will be left with only the words of the will to decipher. As mentioned, the Code's substitute devise presumably applies unless a contrary intent is found. When a testator uses survivorship words, however, a presumption stand-off arises: the presumption of statutory application against an expression of contrary intent. In such situations presumptions are frequently and proper-ly used, in a sense, to break the tie. The drafters correctly contend that something has to be said to break the new tie and they opted for testator's "express contrary intent" to rebut the statutory presumption while testator's "mere words of sur-vivorship" will not rebut it.

Without relevant extrinsic evidence to explain the testator's actual intent, however, interpreters of the will are flying blind. In these situations presumptions and rules of construction should con-form to the desires of the average person because there is nothing else on which to rely. Analysis whether the presumption concerning survivorship language conforms to average intent may depend on the class of devisee involved in the devise. For example, it is one thing to say that most persons probably want grandchildren to take by represen-tation in the place of deceased children and quite another to say they probably want their nephews and nieces to take by representation in the place of deceased brothers and sisters. For example one might give an entirely different interpretation to a will that devised "$100,000 to surviving brothers and sisters, and the residue to X charity," than to one that devised "$100,000 to surviving children, and the residue to X charity," One might conclude that testator in the first situation did not want nephews and nieces to take the devise unless all brothers and sisters died * *and* unless the charity was incapable of taking but in the second situation might reach the opposite conclusion and allow descendants of predeceased children to take by representation in the place of deceased children and to the exclusion of the charity. The Code does not make this distinction and applies the same rules to collateral relatives as it does to descendants. From an inheritance standpoint, one's descendants are vastly different from one's collaterals and the statutory presumption should probably recognize this.

* The illustration raises two substitute devise issues under the Code. The first is whether descendants of a predeceased brother or sister take under the section if one or more brothers or sisters survive. The second is whether descendants of predeceased brothers and sisters can take if no brother or sister survives or whether the charity takes instead. If the words "surviving brother and sisters" are mere words of survivorship, the presumption of section 2–603(b)(3) would apply and the descendants of predeceased brothers and sisters might share with surviving brothers and sisters and take in lieu of the charity. [2–603(b)(3)].

E.   FACTUAL ILLUSTRATIONS

CHART 10–1

Applications of Antilapse Provision **

Assumption 1: A. T's properly executed Will provides:
"The grandfather's clock to A,
$10,000 to B, and
the residue to C."

B. A is a neighbor and friend; B is a second cousin; and C is a first cousin.

C. A, B, and C predecease T, each leaving surviving descendants.

Question: Who takes what property?

Analysis: A's devise lapses because A predeceased T. A's descendants do not take a substitute gift because A is not a member of the relational umbrella. A's lapsed devise becomes part of the residue.

B's devise lapses because B predeceased T. Although B is a blood relation, B's descendants will not take a substitute gift because B is not a member of the relational umbrella. B's lapsed devise becomes part of the residue.

C's devise lapses because C predeceased T. C's descendants will take a substitute gift because C is a member of the relational umbrella. C's descendants take the entire residuary estate including the above lapsed devises.

Assumption 2: A. T's properly executed Will provides:
"My 100 shares of XYZ stock to A and B or to the survivor,
$10,000 to C's surviving children, and
the residue to D and E."

B. A and B are T's siblings; C is a first cousin; and D and E are friends of T.

C. A, C, and D predecease T, each leaving surviving descendants: C had three children, F, G, and H. F predeceased T leaving M and N as descendants. M died 100 hours after T leaving no surviving descendants.

Question: Who takes what property?

** When a person is said to survive, it means the person satisfies all requirements of survivorship including the 120 hour rule [2–702] and is not treated as having predeceased. [See 2–702, 2–801(d), 2–803, 2–804].

Analysis: B takes the entire devise of 100 shares. A's devise lapses because A predeceased T. A's descendants are not substituted for A although A is a member of the relational umbrella because the words "or the survivor" create an alternative gift of A's ½ to B. The alternative devise takes precedence over both the substitute gift and the residuary devise.

The devise to C's children is covered by the presumption. The presumption of a substitute devise applies to class devises such as to children and here the children are members of the protected relational umbrella. Consequently, F's descendants, M and N, are eligible to take by representation the substitute devise in place of their ancestor F. The words "surviving children" are considered to be mere words of survivorship and do not on their own rebut the substituted devise. M died without surviving descendants 100 hours after T and under § 2–702 failed to survive T; consequently, M is no longer a substitute devisee leaving N as F's only substitute devisee. The end result is that N, and G and H will share equally the devise. The substitute gift takes precedence over the residuary devise.

D's devise lapses because D predeceased T. D's descendants will not take a substitute devise under 2–603 because D is not a member of the relational umbrella. Even though E is not a member of the relational umbrella, E takes the entire residuary devise including D's lapsed share of the residuary devises because § 2–603 applies and it does not require a particular relationship to the testator. It is a presumption that applies from the circumstance and in order to avoid intestacy.

Assumption 3:   A.   T's properly executed Will provides:
"$10,000 to A, but if A does not survive me, to A's descendants,
$10,000 to B, but if B does not survive me, to C, and
the residue, including all lapsed or failed nonresiduary devises, to D."

       B.   A and B are siblings; C is B's spouse; and D is T's stepchild.

       C.   A, B, C, and D predecease T, each leaving surviving descendants. A's three children, E, F, and G, predecease T but left one, three, and four grandchildren, respectively, who survived T.

Question: Who takes what property?

Analysis:

A's devise lapses because A predeceased T. A's grandchildren will take, by representation or ⅛ each [see 2–705; § 11.05], as alternative devisees. The devise to A's descendants does not become part of the residuary even though the residuary devise specifically includes lapsed devises because devisees take directly as alternative devisees and not as substitute devisees. The substitute devise presumption is not used to protect the grandchildren since the devise is to a multigenerational class gift and such gifts inherently include an antilapse avoidance technique by employing the concept of representation.

B's devise lapses because B predeceased T. C's devise lapses because C predeceased T. The lapsed devise becomes part of the residue. Although B is a member of the protected relational umbrella and a substitute devise is presumed in favor of B's descendants, the devise lapses into the residuary because the specific language included in the residuary clause captures lapsed devises. C's descendants are not entitled to a presumptive substitute devise because C is not a member of the protected relational umbrella; consequently, C's devise would fail even if the residuary devise did not specifically include lapsed devises.

D's devise lapses because D predeceased T. Although D is not a member of the protected relational umbrella, D is separately protected under 2–603 as a stepchild of the testator. Consequently, D's descendants take the entire residuary estate including the above lapsed devises. The specific language concerning lapsed devises applies only to nonresiduary devises and does not apply to residuary devises. The substitute devise presumption will apply to the residuary devise.

Assumption 4:   A.   T's properly executed Will provides:
"$10,000 to A, but if A does not survive me, to A's children,
$10,000 to B's children, and
the residue, including all lapsed or failed nonresiduary devises, to C."

B.   A and B are siblings; C is T's spouse.

C. A, B, and C predecease T, each leaving surviving descendants. A's three children, E, F, and G, predecease T but left one, three, and four grandchildren, respectively. Of B's three children, H, I, and J, H predeceased T but H's child, M, survived T. C's two children survived T but are from a prior marriage and are only T's stepchildren. D, T's adopted child, survived T.

Question: Who takes what property?

Analysis: A's devise lapses because A predeceased T. The alternative devise to A's children also lapses because none survived T. Although A is covered by the relational umbrella and A's grandchildren would be entitled to a substitute devise under the statutory presumption that covers class gifts to children, the presumption is rebutted by specific inclusion of lapsed devises into the residuary devise. The entire lapsed devise becomes part of the residue.

The devise to B's children does not lapse because two of B's children survived T. They take as surviving members of the class thus no part of the devise passes to the residuary devise. A secondary question arises, however, whether M, the child of B's predeceased child, H, may take under the statutory presumption for a substitute devise. Because none of the devise lapses, the specific language in the residuary devise is not applicable to this devise. But does the existence of this language rebut the application of the statutory presumption within the confines of the class gift? All requirements for the substitute devise are satisfied. Considering the remedial nature of the antilapse provision, the provision should be interpreted to protect M, and M should be able to share equally with I and J.

C's devise lapses because C predeceased T. C's children do not take a substitute devise because they are not members of the protected relational umbrella. The protection for a stepchild does not apply because it only applies when a stepchild is the named devisee not a substitute devisee under the statutory presumption. Unfortunately, this means the residue will pass by intestacy and the disinherited adopted child of T will take the entire residuary estate as sole surviving child. [See 2–103; § 5.02]. It is doubtful that the negative will provision of 2–101(b) would apply since the disinheritance was silent. Even if applicable, it would pass the residue to T's collateral relation, by representation and not to T's stepchildren.

Assumption 5: A. D's properly executed and probated Will devised, in relevant part, the residue to T in trust for E's life, remainder to any person or persons T shall appoint by will but in default of such appointment the remainder goes to Charity C.

B. E's properly executed and probated Will, in relevant part, exercises the above power and appoints the trust estate to A.

C. A predeceased E but A's descendants survived E.

D. Charity C is a legally recognized entity capable of holding property.

Question: Who takes what property?

Analysis: As an appointee under a power of appointment, A is a devisee under E's will. If A is a grandparent or descendant of a grandparent, or a stepchild, of either D, the donor of the power, or E, the donee and testator, A's descendants may take by representation a substitute devise under the will because they survived E, the relevant testator.

If A is not a member of the protected relations of either D or E, or is not survived by descendants, the devise lapses and Charity C will take the property as taker in default. Note that in this situation, the property subject to the power of appointment does not pass through the donee's estate if the donee has not effectively exercised the power. It passes directly to the takers in default under the terms of E's instrument, the person who created the power.

§ 10.03 Accessions Regarding Devises of Securities

A substantial amount of the litigation concerning ademption by extinction [see § 10.04] has dealt with devises of securities that, between the time of the will's execution and the testator's death, have undergone changes of form such as stock splits, reformulations or other accessions. The Code provides answers to the common issues raised by such devises. [2–605]. The Code's provision concerns only devises of securities which are broadly defined to include not only all types of notes, stocks, bonds and loans but also mineral interest agreements and leases as well as "any interest or instrument commonly known as a security" and the right to purchase any of the above. [1–201(43)]. The threshold requirements of the provision are:

(1) Testator's will devised securities;

(2) At the time the will was executed, testator owned securities that meet the description of the devised securities;

(3) The additional securities owned by testator at death were acquired after the will was executed; and,

(4) The additional securities owned by testator at death were acquired as a result of testator's ownership of the devised securities.

[2–605(a)]. It makes no difference whether the devise is characterized as specific or general. [2–605, Comment]. If these conditions are satisfied, the devisee, in addition to being entitled to as many of the shares of the devised security as are part of the estate at the testator's death, is entitled to additional or other securities in the following three situations:

(1) when the additional securities of the same entity were issued by reason of action initiated by the entity but not including securities acquired by the exercise of purchase options;

(2) when securities of other entities are the result of a merger, consolidation, reorganization or other similar action; or,

(3) when securities of the same entity are acquired as the result of reinvestment.

[2–605(a)(1)–(3)].

There are exclusions from the protective rule. Cash distributions prior to death are not part of the devise. [2–605(b)]. The latter limitation means that distributions such as cash dividends declared prior to death, although not paid until after death, are not part of the specific devise. [2–605, Comment].

The provision also does not apply to nonsecurity devises that may be subject to accessions. The Comment states that the section is not intended to be exclusive as to accessions affecting securities and assumably it would not preclude similar accession interpretations in regard to other nonsecurity devises that raise similar problems.

Consider the following factual illustrations.

CHART 10–2

Applications of Security Accessions Provision

Assumptions:　A.　T's properly executed Will provides:
"100 shares of W Corporation stock to A,
100 shares of X Corporation stock to B,
100 shares of Y Corporate bonds to C,
100 shares of Z Mutual Fund shares to D
the residue to E."

B. T owned the above securities at the time the will was executed.

C. Between the date of execution and death, W Corporation declared a three for one stock split. Although T sold 200 shares of W Corporation Stock after the stock split, at T's death, T owned 200 shares of W Corporation stock.

D. Between the date of execution and death, X Corporation merged with I Corporation and the combined corporation reissued two shares in the new XI Corporation for each share of the X Corporation stock. At T's death, T owned 200 shares of XI Corporation stock.

E. Between the date of execution and death, Y Corporation converted its outstanding bonds to preferred stock. For every ten bonds, Y Corporation issued one share of preferred stock. At T's death, T owned 10 shares of Y Corporation preferred stock.

F. T held the Z Mutual Fund shares in a reinvestment plan where all earnings, both of income and principal, were reinvested in the fund and the share accumulated. At T's death the 100 shares had grown to a total of 200 shares.

Question: Who takes what property?

Analysis: A will take the 200 shares of W Corporation stock remaining in T's estate. The devise qualifies under section 2–605. It makes no difference whether T sold the original shares devised or some of the dividend shares because A receives what is left of the shares in T's estate. A will not take the 200 shares that T sold before death or their value unless section 2–606 is applicable. [See § 10.04].

B will take the 200 shares of the new XI Corporation because the issuance of the new corporate shares as a result of the merger are protected under section 2–605(a)(2). All actions were initiated by the entity and not by T. It would make no difference to this answer if T had never converted the shares so long as the conversion was by entity action and could be done after T's death.

C will take the 10 shares of Y Corporation preferred stock. Despite the change in security type, the devisee is protected under section 2–605 so long as the conversion was done as a result of entity action.

D will take the full 200 shares of Z Mutual Fund shares owned at T's death because these shares constitute the original 100 shares plus the reinvested shares acquired from the reinvestment plan set up by the entity. It would make no difference if the shares were of an entity other than a mutual fund so long as there is a reinvestment plan.

§ 10.04 Ademption and Nonademption by Extinction

The common law rule of construction regarding ademption by extinction asserts that when a specifically devised item of property is not identified as part of the testator's estate at the time of the testator's death, the devise fails. [Atkinson, Wills § 134]. Although this rule is merely a rule of construction and is subject to control by the testator, many courts severely limit the proof of testator's intent by refusing to admit extrinsic evidence of it. In these decisions, testator's intent to override the rule must be expressed on the face of the will: the will must anticipate the problem and express a solution. For example, T's will might read, "I devise my diamond ring to A, but if I do not own a diamond ring at my death, I devise $10,000 to A." Here, the testator has anticipated ademption by extinction and if the ring is not in the estate, A would take the $10,000 substitute devise. Unfortunately, most testators do not anticipate ademption, and the common law rule precludes A from taking anything from the estate for the devise unless the ring is there regardless of T's intent.

Often courts that follow the strict identity theory employ escape devices to avoid forfeiture for a devisee when the court does not believe testator intended ademption. These devices include tracing efforts to find the asset that testator holds at death which is traceable to the asset described by the specific devise. This worked in situations where the subject of the devise exists in testator's estate but it does not exactly conform to the devise. For example, if T devised "my 1990 Chevrolet to A" but at death owns a 1992 Cadillac, A may be able to take the Cadillac if a court is willing to trace the original devise to the currently owned asset.

Another related and sometimes overlapping escape device concerns changes in form. The common law ademption rule did not cause forfeiture if the specifically devised asset merely changed in form and not in substance between the date of the will and the date of death. The asset as changed passes to the devisee. Depending on the attitude of the court toward the particular devise in question, this approach could often save a devise. For example, if T devised "my 100 shares of XYZ common stock to A," and the corporation converted the shares to preferred stock, A might successfully contend that the 100 shares of common stock had only changed form and, therefore, A should take the 100 preferred shares. Application of this approach might depend of the degree of actual change and whether the change was caused by voluntary or involuntary action by the testator. [See § 10.03].

The Code significantly alters and clarifies the common law rule concerning ademption by extinction of specific devises. [2–606]. In a broad sense, the provision adopts a nonademption rule subject to contravention by extrinsic evidence. In other words, the provision reverses the presumption but makes the presumption rebuttable with extrinsic evidence. In addition, the provision provides specific remedies for several common ademption problems.

First, the specific devisee has a right to specifically devised property or any part of it that exists in testator's estate at death. [2–606(a)]. Concomitantly, the specific devisee has a right to assets that represent, in part or in whole, the remaining interest which the testator retains at death in the specifically devised property. [2–606(a)(1)–(5)]. The provision delineates the following five situations as constituting a testator's remaining interest at death: (1) the unpaid balance of the purchase price, plus any accompanying security agreement, owed to the testator; (2) the unpaid amount of a condemnation award owed to the testator; (3) the unpaid fire or casualty insurance proceeds or recovery for injury to the specifically devise property; (4) the property received by foreclosure or obtained in lieu of foreclosure on a specifically devised obligation; and, (5) the real or personal property acquired by testator as a replacement for the specifically devised property. These rules are not subject to contradiction by extrinsic evidence of testator's unexpressed intent.

Second, in contradiction to the common law rules on ademption by extinction, the Code's "non-ademption" provision reverses the presumption of ademption and adopts a broad extrinsic evidence rule to permit proof of testator's intent concerning ademption. If the specifically devised property is not in the estate at testator's death, the devisee is presumptively entitled to a general pecuniary devise equal to the value of the specifically devised property less the value of any actual portion of the devise remaining in the estate at testator's death and of the five representative remaining interests described above. [2–606(a)(6)]. The presumption may be rebutted either when the facts and circumstances indicate testator intended ademption, or if ademption is consistent with the testator's manifested plan of distribution. The latter proviso permits extrinsic evidence to be admitted to determine T's intent and to permit the court to consider the entire estate plan in order to determine what the testator desired. A related concept that may be relevant to and coordinated with this nonademption rule is the Code's provision concerning abatement. [3–902(a); see § 23.01].

The third ademption by extinction problem for which the Code provides a rule concerns transactions made for an incapacitated testator by or with a lifetime conservator or agent under a durable power of attorney. [2–606(b)–(e)]. The three specific situations covered by the provision include when a conservator or agent: (1) sold the specifically devised property; (2) received a condemnation award for the specifically devised property; and (3) received insurance proceeds for loss of the property due to fire or casualty. In all three situations, the specific devisee is entitled to a general pecuniary devise equal to the net sale price, condemnation award or the value of the insurance proceeds. This right exists even when the conservator has already received the amounts and has integrated these amounts into the testator's other assets. These rules are not subject to contradiction by extrinsic evidence of testator's unexpressed intent. If the testator survives a judicial termination of testator's disability for one year or more, however, the protection provided to the specific devisee by this provision is no longer applicable. Protecting the specific devisee from conservator and agent transactions is consistent with the concept that ademption or nonademption should be related to testator's intent. Acts of a third person, including a testator's conservator or agent under a durable power, do not reveal testator's desires and should not materially and unfairly affect a specific devisee's interest.

Consider the following problems:

CHART 10–3

Ademption by Extinction Under UPC

Assumption 1:   A.   T's properly executed Will provides:
"The grandfather's clock I own at my death to A, but if I do not own one, $1,000 to A;

my automobile to B;

my residence to C;

my 100 shares of XYZ, Inc., common stock to D;

the residue to E."

B.   T sold the grandfather's clock and did not replace it.

T's automobile was destroyed in a major accident; the insurance company has agreed to pay $2,000 but had not paid at T's death.

T sold the residence, moved into an apartment and took $20,000 cash and a note and mortgage for $80,000 from P as payment. P paid the cash but still owes $75,000 on the note and mortgage.

T sold the XYZ, Inc., stock and used the proceeds to buy WVU, Inc., stock.

T's residue is valued at $100,000.

C.   All devisees survived T.

Question: Who takes what property?

Analysis: The specifically devised grandfather's clock is adeemed and T's expressed intent devises A the alternate $1,000.

B is entitled to the unpaid insurance proceeds on the destroyed automobile. Subject to a finding of contrary intent on the part of T, if the unpaid insurance proceeds do not equal the value of the devise, B would be entitled to a pecuniary devise equal to the difference between the value of the devise less the unpaid insurance proceeds from the estate.

C is entitled to the unpaid balance of the sale price, if any, and the security interest held in the estate on the residence. Subject to a finding of contrary intent on the part of T, if the unpaid purchase price and security interest do not equal the value of the devise, C would be entitled to a pecuniary devise equal to the difference between the value of the devise less the unpaid purchase price and security interest.

D is entitled to the WVU stock as T's replacement for the XYZ stock. Subject to a finding of contrary intent on the part of T, if the WVU stock does not equal the value of the devise, D would be entitled to a pecuniary devise equal to the difference between the value of the devise less the value of the WVU stock from the estate.

E is entitled to the residue which is the remaining estate after the deductions for expenses of administration and the payment of all the above devises. If facts and circumstances indicate or it is found that the will manifests an intent to apply ademption, the specific devises will adeem to the extent they are not satisfied by the property remaining in the estate and the adeemed portion would pass to E as part of the residue.

Assumption 2: A. T's properly executed Will provides the same devises as indicated in Assumption 1, above.

               B. Rather than T, all the actions and events in Assumption 1 were performed by T's conservator or attorney in fact under a valid durable power of attorney. T's residue is valued at $100,000.

               C. All devisees survived T.

Question: Who takes what property?

Analysis: The analysis in Assumption 1 is the same with two exceptions. First A would take the greater of the value of the grandfather's clock or the $1,000. The other specific devisees will take whatever remains of their devises plus a general pecuniary devise of the difference of the value of the devise less the value of the remaining portion of the devise. When a conservator or attorney in fact carries out the adeeming action, there is no residual relevance of T's intent. Therefore, the general pecuniary devises would be absolute and not rebuttable with extrinsic evidence.

§ 10.05   Ademption by Satisfaction

The ademption by satisfaction doctrine is the testamentary counterpart of the advancement doctrine under intestate succession. [See § 5.07]. Under the common law, the doctrine provides that a general or residuary devise is adeemed in whole or in part when a testator makes an inter vivos gift to the devisee after the execution of the will. [Atkinson, Wills § 133]. As with advancements, the purpose of the doctrine is to prevent a devisee from receiving a double share. Although its application in any situation depends on proof of the testator's intent, that intent is difficult to judicially establish. When intent is not clearly manifested, courts use presumptions to settle the issue. Under some circumstances a gift might be presumed to be satisfaction; under another situation, it might be presumed to be an unencumbered gift. Unfortunately, the presumptions have not been applied with any significant degree of consistency.

The Code codifies the ademption by satisfaction doctrine and formalizes its proof requirements. [2–609]. Paralleling its provision concerning advancements, the Code provides that a gift is satisfaction of a devise only if one of several formalities is satisfied. A gift is a formal satisfaction if either (1) the will provides for the deduction, or (2) the testator "declared in a contemporaneous writing," or (3) the devisee "acknowledged in writing" that the gift is in satisfaction of the devise. [2–609(a)]. The required writing may, rather than declaring the gift is in satisfaction, merely indicate that the gift must be deducted from the value of the devise. No words of art such as "satisfaction" need be used by the testator. The gist of the declaration must indicate the testator intended that the gift constitutes what lawyers call a gift in satisfaction of a devise. It is also not specifically required that the written expression of intent to make a formal satisfaction be communicated to the devisee at the time of the gift. A qualified formality could be a contemporaneous written note or indication that the gift is a formal satisfaction which is included with the testator's personal records. The writing must be available or provable after the testator's death when distribution decisions are made. It cannot be a blanket written statement that attempts to categorize future gifts as satisfaction. [Estate of McFayden v. Sample (1990)].

Several other features of the Code's provision deserve mention. There is no requirement that the gift must be made to the devisee: if the formality of satisfaction is satisfied and the necessary intent is declared, a gift to someone other than the devisee will be satisfaction of the devise. [2–609, Comment]. Although required by common law, the Code does not require that the relevant actions take place in a certain chronology. Formal satisfaction might be accomplished before the will is executed although most cases will concern the reverse chronology. The Comment states that formal satisfaction need not necessarily be an outright gift. Other will substitutes such as life insurance payable to the devisee may constitute a satisfaction under the Code. [2–609, Comment].

The Code specifically provides that where a devisee of a formal satisfaction fails to survive the donor, the formal satisfaction affects the share that the devisee's descendants take from testator's estate if the descendants take as substitute devisees under the Code's antilapse provisions, unless the testator's contemporaneous writing expressly provides that the gift is not to affect the descendants' devise. [2–609(c); see 2–603, 2–604]. This is the opposite rule from the Code's advancement provision. The distinction is justifiable on the basis that satisfaction concerns the testator's intent whereas advancement concerns intestacy and therefore legislative intent. The gift in satisfaction does not affect the devisee's descendants if they take as alternative devisees unless the testator's contemporaneous writing expressly provides that the gift affects that descendants' devise.

Valuation of formal satisfaction is determined as of the time of the devisee's possession or enjoyment or as of the testator's death, whichever occurs first. [2–609(c)].

CHART 10–4

Satisfaction Calculations

Hypothetical: In all of the following hypotheticals assume decedent, T, made gifts to the named devisee and that these gifts were declared in a proper writing to be a satisfaction to the devisee.

Assumption 1: A. Assume that T's will provided: "I devise $50,000 to each of my children and the residue to my spouse."

B. T made gifts in satisfactions of $20,000 to A, $30,000 to B, and $50,000 to C.

C. T was survived by a spouse, S, two children, A and B, and a grandchild, G. G was C's child: C did not survive T.

D. T's total distributable estate equals $400,000.

Question: Who takes what property?

Analysis: A will take $30,000 or the $50,000 devise less the $20,000 satisfaction. A question may arise whether the $30,000 constituted full satisfaction of the devise. If the satisfaction formality expresses the intent that the gift is full satisfaction, then A would take zero. Because the gift was less than the devise and without outward expression that full satisfaction was intended, a presumption of partial satisfaction would be compatible with the purposes of the Code's provision.

B will take $20,000 or the $50,000 devise less the $30,000 satisfaction. The same analysis is applicable to B's devise as discussed above regarding A's devise.

Because C did not survive T, C does not take from T's estate, but C's satisfaction is not ignored. It affects G's substitute devise because G takes C's devise under the Code's antilapse provision, 2–603. Consequently, because C's devise is apparently fully satisfied by the gift which equals the amount of the devise, G will take zero from the estate.

S takes the residue of $350,000 which now equals the total distributable estate less the devises to A and B. In this situation the reduction of the gifts in satisfaction ran to the benefit of the residuary devisee.

Assumption 2: A. Assume that T's will provided: "I devise $200,000 to my spouse and the residue to my children but if a child does not survive me to that child's descendants."

B. T made gifts in satisfactions of $20,000 to A, $30,000 to B, and $50,000 to C.

C. T was survived by a spouse, S, two children, A and B, and a grandchild, G. G was C's child: C did not survive T.

D. T's total distributable estate equals $300,000.

Question: Who takes what property?

Analysis: S, who takes a general devise, takes $200,000 from the estate leaving a residue equal to $100,000.

Neither C nor C's estate will take from T's estate because C did not survive T.

G is entitled to a full share of the residue as a direct alternative devisee. Because G does not take under the antilapse provision but takes personally, the gift in satisfaction to C, G's ancestor, does not affect G's share.

The calculation of the shares of A, B, and G from the residue requires the construction of a hotchpot.

Satisfaction Hotchpot	Amount	Distribution
Distributable Residuary Estate *	$100,000	
A's Satisfaction	$ 20,000	
B's Satisfaction	$ 30,000	
Total of Hotchpot	$150,000	
Distribution		
A's ⅓ Share	$50,000–$20,000	$ 30,000
B's ⅓ Share	$50,000–$30,000	$ 20,000
G's ⅓ Share	$50,000	$ 50,000
Total Distributed Residuary Estate *		$100,000

* The Distributable Estate and the Total Distributed Residuary Estate amounts must be identical; otherwise, an error in calculation has occurred.

§ 10.06   Miscellaneous Rules of Construction

The Code codifies several other rules of construction that deserve mention. All of the following, of course, are subject to a finding based on the terms of the will or by admissible extrinsic evidence of a contrary intention by the testator. [2–601].

A.   AFTER–ACQUIRED PROPERTY

The Code provides that a will may pass all the testator's property owned at death and acquired by the estate after testator's death. [2–602]. This rule codifies a part of the ambulatory nature of wills. [See § 9.01]. The provision also recognized that decedents' estates may become entitled to property after a testator's death such as inheritance to the estate of a decedent and retirement or other post employment benefits and awards. [See 2–602, Comment].

B.　RIGHT OF NONEXONERATION

The common law rule of right of exoneration of a mortgage on specifically devised real and personal property is abolished regardless of a general directive in the will to pay debts. [2–607]. Consequently, property specifically devised is distributed subject to any mortgage interest attached to it that exists at the testator's death. With the common current practice of mortgaging equity on residences for general borrowing needs because of the current income tax deduction for interest paid on mortgages but not deductible for other paid interest, the nonexoneration rule may be contrary o testator's intent. Extrinsic evidence of such a situation should be admissible to rebut the rule of construction.

CHAPTER 11

RULES OF CONSTRUCTION APPLICABLE TO WILLS AND TO OTHER GOVERNING INSTRUMENTS

§ 11.01 Introduction to Rules of Construction for All Governing Instruments

The Code contains several important provisions dealing with issues raised by questions of survivorship, lapse and related problems. Because of the estate planning importance of will substitutes, the Code extends these constructional rules beyond testamentary instruments and includes constructional rules concerning any "governing instrument." [2–701]. A governing instrument includes deeds, wills, and trusts, life insurance and other related policies, POD accounts, TOD security registrations, pension, retirement and other related plans; any other "dispositive, appointive, or nominative instrument." [1–201(19)]. The Code establishes a set of rules of construction that apply in default but are subject to alteration either by proof of clear and convincing evidence contrary to the default rule or by explicit language superseding the default rule in the governing instrument. [2–701].

For additional discussion of rules of construction, see § 10.01.

§ 11.02 Survivorship Duration Determinations

The Code adopts the rule that a beneficiary under any governing instrument must survive the date and time of the relevant event that determines ownership by 120 hours. [2–702]. This provision applies to a wide range of transfer devices including wills, life insurance policies, multiple-party accounts, transfer on death (TOD) security registrations, and other joint ownership with right of survivorship interests. [See 1–201(19)]. Persons who claim the beneficiary survived by the 120 hours must prove that the beneficiary survived the time period by clear and convincing evidence.

The 120 hours rule for all gratuitous transfers documents including wills, deeds, trusts, appointments and other beneficiary designations tracks the same rule that is applicable in the intestacy situation. [See 2–104; § 5.06]. The difference between these concepts is that in regard to intestacy, the requirement is a rule of law and is not rebuttable whereas the rule applicable to voluntary transfers is alterable by the terms of the document. The Code is very specific, however, in regards to what is necessary to rebut the statutory rule of construction. [2–702(d)]. The Code itemizes four general situations where the statutory rule of construction will not apply. First, it will not apply if the governing instrument contains language that deals explicitly with simultaneous death or with deaths in a common disaster and that language is operable under the facts of the case. Second, the rule of construction is rebutted if the governing instrument expressly indicates that the beneficiary is not required to survive to a particular time or event, by any specific length of time or that expressly requires the individual to survive an event or time by a specific period. The specific period in the above exception includes a reference to the death of another individual. Third, the rule of construction does not apply if application of the rule would cause the transfer to fail to qualify as a valid transfer under the Uniform Statutory Rule Against Perpetuities. [See 2–901]. The fourth rebuttal for the rule of construction applies in the situation where the rule would result in an unintended failure or unintended duplication of a disposition. Notwithstanding the waiver of the 120 hour survivorship requirement, survival of an event or time must be established by clear and convincing evidence.

Third parties dealing with and bona fide purchasers from transferees who subsequently fail to survive the necessary period of time are protected under the Code. [See § 12.05].

The 120 hour survivorship requirement is now part of the new version of the Uniform Simultaneous Death Act of 1991. This Act incorporates the relevant portions of the Code and covers all types of gratuitous transfers. [§ 5.06].

§ 11.03 Antilapse of Beneficiary Designations in Nominative Instruments

The common law rules concerning lapse of testamentary devises and the Code's modifications to them are discussed previously. [2–603, 2–604; § 10.02]. Many of the same issues may arise regarding the interpretation of beneficiary designations in modern will substitutes, e.g., the unanticipated death or failure of a named beneficiary in a governing instrument. The Code incorporates a provision that provides guidance and stability to the interpretation of these beneficiary designations. [1–201(4)]. The Code applies the same substitute gift presumption to these designations as it does to beneficiary designations in wills. [2–706] The range of documents to which the provision applies is set out in the Code's general definitions. [2–706(a)(2), and Comment]. It applies to beneficiary designations included in all insurance and annuity policies, all POD accounts, all TOD security registrations, all pension, profit-sharing, retirement and other benefit plans, and all other nonprobate transfers that occur at death. [1–201(4)]. The last reference is a catch-all reference that makes the provision applicable to all nontestamentary gratuitous transfers that arise at death and that are evidenced by a governing instrument. On the other hand, the 1993 Technical Amendments made it clear that it does not apply to persons who hold interests held in joint tenancy with right of survivorship or to parties of multiple-party joint accounts held with right of survivorship. [2–706(a)(2); see § 34.05].

This provision gives needed substance and predictability to the many types of inter vivos documents that are lacking under current law in most states. For example, if the beneficiary designation on a life insurance policy reads: "to my spouse, but if my spouse does not survive me, to my children," but the insured is survived only by a child and a grandchild of another child that predeceased the insured, this provision creates a substitute gift for the grandchild and allows that person to share equally with the surviving child. This result clearly accords with the intent of most insureds.

The substantive scope and application of the provision are the same as those matters related to lapse of devises in wills. The same protected group, timing and types of designation are employed. A perusal of the text discussing section 2–603 provides the reader with an explanation of how this provision is to be applied and to operate. [See § 10.02].

Because of potential liability for third persons who rely on the named designations, the Code protects third persons who pay proceeds to, receive proceeds in payment for enforceable obligations from, or purchase for value assets from the beneficiary. [See 2–706(d)–(e); § 12.05]. The beneficiary and other gratuitous transferees are not protected and remain liable for the proceeds received.

§ 11.04 Relational Terminology for Dispositive Purposes

A. BENEFICIARY STATUS

In dispositive instruments it is common to use class gifts as a means of describing certain beneficiaries. For example, testators or settlors may use terms of relational classification including "children," "grandchildren," "descendants," "issue," "brothers and sisters," "uncles and aunts," "nephews and nieces" and "cousins." Gifts using this type of terminology are commonly referred to as "class gifts" about which a long list of rules of construction have developed at common law. [See Simes, Future Interests §§ 101–04]. Class gift terminology is used not only for convenience, but also to allow the members in the particular class to fluctuate in number. For example, members in a class may be born and thereby included within, or some may die and predecease the testator and thereby excluded from, the above terminology when distribution is made.

The meaning of this class terminology is as important and determinative when used in dispositive instruments, as it is in defining relational terminology in intestacy situations. Consequently, when a testator in a will uses terms such as "children" or "brothers," it becomes necessary to determine who is to be included within such classes of persons. For full-blooded marital persons the problem of being included within the terminology is merely one of proof of relationship and survivorship. For half-bloods, adopted persons, nonmarital persons, and persons related by affinity, the problem of proof of intended inclusion is problematic. In order for these persons to be included in such class terminology, they must show that the testator intended that they be included. Unfortunately, there is usually no specific indication of intent in the will itself and disputes have developed. The resultant litigation has not only been costly and bitter but has also resulted in uncertainties and inconsistencies.

This determination is a problem of status. Because of the importance of this problem for distribution purposes under the terms of dispositive instruments, the Code includes a specific provision concerning the status of adopted, nonmarital, half blooded individuals and individuals related by affinity. [2–705]. Subject to alteration by the creator of the instrument and to two exceptions, a rule of construction is adopted that class gift language in dispositive instruments is to be construed in a manner similar to the meaning given to similar terms under the status definitions for intestacy. [See § 5.05]. Consequently, relations of the half blood are included in class gifts to collateral reactions but relations by affinity are excluded from class gifts that refer to relationship by blood whether or not the term commonly differentiates between blood and affinity relationship. [2–705(a)]. For example, class gifts to "brothers" or "aunts" will exclude persons who fit the category because of marriage regardless whether the phrase "in law" is commonly added when making reference to the relationship. On the other hand, half blooded brothers or aunts are included in such gifts.

Whereas under intestacy, adopted and nonmarital persons are included with other blood relations, in an effort to address the concern of the over extensions of this provision, the Code incorporates two exceptions from this inclusion. In both situations, the Code includes within appropriate class gift language such persons only if certain conditions are met. [2–705(b), and (c)].

In understanding these exception, it is helpful to distinguish between class gift language used in three situations. The first concerns class gift language used in the instrument of a person who is directly involved in the relationship in question, e.g., a devise to one's "children" in the will of a person who adopted a person. The second concerns a transfer instrument of a person who is not directly involved with the particular relationship situation, but who is an ancestor, collateral, or descendant of a person who is directly involved, e.g., a devise to one's "grandchildren" in the will of the parent of the adopting parent of an adopted child or of the parent of a nonmarital child. The third circumstance concerns the transfer instrument of a person who is neither directly involved nor related to the person directly involved in the relationship situation, e.g., a devise to a nonrelation "A or if A does not survive to A's descendants" in the will of a person where the nonrelation is an adopting parent or parent of a nonmarital child. The issue in all three situations is whether the class gift language includes the adopted or nonmarital persons. As discussed previously, the Code includes such persons when applicable in intestacy. Does the existence of an instrument of transfer change the rule?

If the interpretation of the class gift concerns an instrument executed by the adopting or natural parent, an adopted or nonmarital child of that parent takes unless an intent to exclude is discovered. If the interpretation of the class gift concerns an instrument executed by someone other than the natural parent, however, a nonmarital child of that natural parent will not take under the instrument of a nonparental donor unless such child is expressly included or unless the child lived while a minor with the natural parent or that parent's parent, brother, sister, spouse or surviving spouse. [2–705(b)]. Similarly, if the interpretation of the class gift concerns an instrument executed by someone other than the adopting person, dispositive provisions in instruments made by a stranger to the adoption do not include an adopted person unless the adopted person lived with the adopting parent either before or after the adoption as a regular member of the adopting parent's household. [2–705(c)]. These provisions attempt to accord what some contend conforms to the desires of most people faced with these situations. [2–705, Comment]. Most nonparental transferors do not want to include the adopted or nonmarital persons of others as members of class gifts unless the persons were raised in a manner reasonably similar to that as a child of the parent.

B. MULTIPLE GENERATION CLASS GIFTS

Consistent with the Code's adoption of the per capita at each generation definition of representation for intestacy, it adopts the definition as a rule of construction for class gifts made to "descendants," "issue," and "heirs of the body" for all dispositive instruments that do not otherwise specify the manner of distribution. [2–708; see § 5.04]. In effect, the Code treats the designated ancestor as if the person died intestate as to the property transferred to the class. This definition rejects the per stirpes definition found in the Restatement of

Property. [Restatement (Second) of Property § 28.2 (1988)]. It probably conforms, however, to the desires of the typical testator. [See 2–106, Comment].

C. DETERMINATION OF REPRESENTATION

The terms "representation," "per capita at each generation," and "per stirpes" are used in several provisions in the Code [See 2–603, 2–706, and 2–707] and possibly in other statutes and may also be found in various dispositive instruments. For the purpose of determining their applications, it is necessary to give meaning to them. [2–709]. "Representation" and "per capita at each generation" are given identical definitions and it is the same one provided for these terms in intestacy, i.e., per capita at each generation. [2–709(b), 2–106; see § 5.04]. Per stirpes is given the predominant definition that uses the first generation as the root generation for purposes of the initial and subsequent divisions of the estate distributed even if none survives the ancestor. [2–709(c), and Comment; see § 5.04].

Three other definitions of words used in the provision are also important. The Code defines "deceased" child or descendant to mean a member of the particular class who fails to survive the distribution date by 120 hours. [2–709(a)(1); 2–702]. The Code defines "surviving" ancestor, child or descendant to mean a member of the particular class who neither predeceases the distribution date nor is deemed to predecease within 120 hours of the distribution date. [2–709(a)(3); 2–702]. The "distribution date" means the actual time when the interest in question takes effect in possession or enjoyment, be it the beginning, end, or other time of the day. [2–709(a)(2)].

§ 11.05 Constructional Rules for Future Interests

A. INTRODUCTION TO FUTURE INTERESTS

The trust device is a common estate planning tool. Inherent in the trust is the future interest. The typical trust is established for the term of one or more persons' lives with the undistributed corpus to be transferred free of the trust to the remainder beneficiaries or to the settlor or the settlor's estate as a reversion. Although life interests, remainder interests and reversions are present interests, they are called future interests if they are not also presently possessory or currently enjoyed. Other interests similarly characterized include executory interests, possibilities of reverter and rights of entry. Any of these interests may have problems of construction at the time the interest becomes possessory or ready for present enjoyment, i.e., identifying the particular beneficiaries who will take. As with most matters of construction, the expressed desires of the transferor will be followed if determinable. Unfortunately, the expressed intent is often not expressed, inadequately expressed or inapplicable because of changed circumstances. It then is necessary to fill the intent gap with rules of construction. Generally, these rules should conform to the desires of the average transferor. The common law developed rules of construction for these circumstances but they are often inconsistently applied and result in distributions that many would contend are not consistent with the desires of the average transferor.

The Code, recognizing the importance of future interest in modern estate planning, addresses the major constructional problems that arise when expressed intent is absent and distribution decisions must be made.

B. FUTURE INTERESTS IN TRUST

1. *Survivorship*

The survivorship of the life interests is not a problem. If one is not alive or does not survive the creation of the trust or the interest in trust, the life beneficiary does not take from the trust. Survivorship is most often a problem of the remainder beneficiaries because their interests do not mature in possession or enjoyment until the death of those who hold the life interests. The question of survivorship arises after the death of the transferor or the date of creation of the trust when the life interest or interests end. Must the remainder beneficiaries survive the time of distribution or merely the time of creation? Courts have had numerous problems with this question.

If the transferor clearly indicates that survivorship to the date of distribution is or is not required, the expressed intent will be obeyed. The problem arises when intent is not clearly expressed. What is the default rule? The general common law rule holds that survivorship to date of distribution is not presumed: that is if the remainder beneficiary died between date of creation and date of distribution, the interest passes to the beneficiary's estate for distribution according to the beneficiary's will or by intestacy if no will. This construction requires reopening of estates and the consequent complexities. Because of this courts sometimes strained to avoid application of the general rule but have not developed a consistent response to the problem.

The Code adopts a new rule of construction concerning the survivorship requirement for future interests in trust. [2–707]. It reverses the presumption and provides that there is an implied requirement of survivorship to the date of distribution for future interests held in trust. [2–707(b)]. In addition, the survivorship requirement is extended to 120 hours after the time of distribution. [2–702]. For example, under the Code's provision a simple trust that provides "to T in trust for A for life, remainder to B," B must survive A's death, the date of distribution, by 120 hours in order for B to take the remainder interest.

The new presumption is only applicable to future interests in trust and therefore does not apply to nonequitable interests such as "to A for life, remainder to B." [2–707, Comment]. The common law rule would continue to apply in those cases. Despite the limitation, the new rule will apply to most future interests created today because of the dominance of the trust device as an estate planning tool. One of the arguments for the nonsurvivorship rule is the desire to permit free alienation of property as soon as possible. If persons who hold remainders do not have to survive anyone to take, the interest is more readily transferrable in comparison with a contingent remainder dependent on survivorship to an unknown date. Survivorship contingencies in regard to trust interests are not barriers to property transfer because the trustee may transfer the property of the trust during its administration.

If beneficiaries fail to survive the date of distribution and the antilapse presumption is unavailable, the Code specifies how the lapse will be treated. If the there is a residue devise in transferor's will, the trust corpus passes to those beneficiaries. If no residue exists or the residue is in trust and its remainder beneficiaries fail to survive the date of distribution, the trust corpus passes in intestacy. The 1993 Technical Amendments added that for future interests created by the exercise of a power of appointment, the lapsed property interest passes to the donor's takers in default clause, if any, which is treated as creating a future interest in trust. [2–707(e)(1)]. If still no takers then, the lapsed interest passes as an ordinary future interests except the transferor means the donor of a nongeneral power and the donee of a general power. [2–707(e)(2)].

2. *Antilapse*

The presumption that survivorship is necessary may cause interests to fail and if the nonsurviving beneficiary cannot take, might cut off the beneficiary's stock. The problem of forfeiture served in part as the reasoning behind the common law presumption against a survivorship requirement. Unfortunately, the common law remedy of passing the remainder interest through the nonsurviving beneficiary's estate did not depend upon the existence of descendants surviving the beneficiary. The Code resolves the forfeiture problem by providing an "antilapse" presumption in favor of nonsurviving beneficiary's descendants.

The Code provides that if a remainder beneficiary fails to survive the date of distribution, a substitute gift arises for the beneficiary's descendants, if any survive. [2–707]. This is an "antilapse" rule for future interests in trust. It protects descendants of all remainder beneficiaries regardless of their relationship to the transferor. [See 2–603; § 10.02(B)]. One does not have to be a grandparent or descendant of a grandparent to be entitled to the presumption of the substitute gift. It applies to remainders to specific individuals and to remainders left to classes of persons who are all in a single generation. Examples of single generation class gifts include gifts to "children," "grandchildren," "siblings," and "nephews and nieces." It does not apply to multiple-generation class gifts that inherently possess a nonlapsing affect because representation is allowed for descendants of predeceased ancestors in the class. Examples of such class gifts include gifts to "descendants," "issue," "heirs" and "next of kin." In a sense, the Code converts all single generation class gifts in remainder to multiple generation gifts in remainder. It applies to both irrevocable inter vivos trusts and trusts that are created at death.

The antilapse protection is merely a rule of construction subject to revision by the transferor. Similar to the rule as applied to decedent's estates, a mere survivorship requirement in the instrument will not rebut the presumption.

The common law rule of lapse and the Code's modification to it are discussed previously. [2–604; § 10.02]. A perusal of the text discussing the application of Section 2–603 provides the reader with an explanation of how this provision basically operates. [See § 10.02(C), and (D)]. In addition, the Comment to Section 2–707 contains a comprehensive explanation with illustrations.

C. WORTHIER TITLE

In an effort to clarify an otherwise confused and varied area of the law of future interests, the Code abolishes the Worthier Title doctrine both as a rule of law and of construction. In other words, transfers that pass interests to the transferor's "heirs," "heirs at law," "next of kin," "relatives," "family," and analogous terms do not create, by law or presumption, a reversionary interest in the transferor. The default rule is that a remainder is created. [See 2–710; § 11.06(D)]. Fundamentally, the abolition merely means the transferor's intent must be determined without the assistance of the Worthier Title presumption or rule. Assumably, when specific intent is not indicated, intent may be established by extrinsic evidence. [2–701]].

D. DEFINITION OF "HEIRS"

The Code provides a rule of construction for terms such as "heirs," "heirs at law," "next of kin," "relatives," "family," or analogous terms used in applicable statutes or governing instruments. [2–711]. It applies to both present and future interests. [See Restatement (Second) of Property § 29.4, Comments c and g]. The Code simply and properly provides that these terms when used in relation to a designated individual pass the interests covered by the transfer to those who would take the designated individual's property according to the intestate succession law of the designated individual's domicile. The date to determine this distribution is the time when the disposition takes effect in possession or enjoyment. If applicable under the law of the domicile, the state may take by escheat if other relations can not take. One specific exception in the provision bars a surviving spouse of a designated individual from being an heir if the surviving spouse is remarried at the time of distribution.

§ 11.06 Choice of Law

Choice of law determinations for testamentary and other donative transfers frequently depend upon the type of property involved, the donor's domicile, and the situs of the property. [Atkinson, Wills §§ 94, 145]. Although the Code does not alter the ordinary choice of law rules, it provides the transferor with the discretion to select a local law applicable to the meaning and legal effect of the donative disposition. [2–703]. The Code permits the transferor by the terms of the governing instrument ordinarily to select and specify what local law shall be applied in determining both the meaning and the legal effect of a testamentary disposition of his property. This power in the transferor to select the controlling law is effective regardless: (1) whether the disposition is of personalty or of realty; (2) where the property is located; and (3) whether the testator was domiciled in the state whose law was selected either at the time when the will was executed, at the time of death, or at any time.

The only general limitation is that the law of the selected jurisdiction cannot be contrary to the applicable public policy of the Code state. In addition, the provision specifically prohibits a locally domiciled transferor from making a choice of law that circumvents the Code's elective share [see Art. II, Pt. 2; §§ 6.01–.07] or family protection provisions. [See Art. II, Pt. 4; §§ 8.01–.03]. Other policies that might fit within the general public policy limitation include attempts to avoid taxation, future interest rules with respect to real property, and creditor avoidance devices such as spendthrift clauses.

This provision promotes several policies of the Code. First, by permitting transferors to select the rules and laws to be applicable to their donative instruments, it improves the chances that the transferors' intentions will control the legal effect of their dispositions. Second, it aligns testamentary choice of law rules with what is generally permitted in dealing with inter vivos transactions including trusts. The removal of differences between the way inter vivos transactions and testamentary transactions are treated is one of the goals of the Code and of recent Conflict of Laws theory. [See Restatement (Second), Conflict of Laws §§ 139, 140, 263, 264]. And third, the overall effect of this provision should encourage the use of the will as a dispositive device.

CHAPTER 12

GENERAL MISCELLANEOUS PROVISIONS AND TOPICS

§ 12.01 Introduction to Miscellaneous Matters

Part 8 of Article II of the Code contains four sections that not only are applicable to intestate and testate succession but also have application to other parts of the Code, or to other transfer devices not covered by its content. Briefly, these sections deal with the following matters: (1) the disclaimer of property interests devolving by all means; (2) the effect of various divorces, annulments, and separation decrees upon the issue whether a person is a surviving spouse; (3) the disqualification effect of homicide on intestate succession, wills, trusts, joint survivorship ownership, multiple-party accounts, TOD security registrations, life insurance and other beneficiary designations, and fiduciary nominations; and, (4) the revocation of probate and nonprobate transfers due to divorce of the transferor and the beneficiary.

Another concept that crosses subject matter lines is the protection of bona fide purchasers and third persons who deal with persons whose interests in property or assets in question are extinguished under the Code. The Code contains provisions in several areas dealing with this matter. The meaning and interrelationship of these provisions is discussed in this chapter. [See § 12.05].

Finally, provisions concerning powers of appointment are scattered throughout various parts of the Code. For purposes of clarity and in recognition of the importance of powers of appoint, the discussion of many of these provisions are collected in a single section. [See § 12.06].

§ 12.02   Disclaimer of Property Interests

The doctrine of disclaimer continues to be an important post-mortem planning device. Although the basic doctrine is probably universally recognized, unnecessary limitations and uncertainties have developed. The Code seeks to correct these deficiencies by codifying the scope and effect of the doctrine as it applies to matters related to probate, succession and all other relevant nontestamentary transfers and contracts.

With a few modifications and some restructuring, the Code incorporates the first seven sections of the Uniform Disclaimer of Property Interests Act of 1978. [2–801; Uniform Disclaimer of Property Interests Act]. This 1990 revision replaces the Uniform Disclaimer of Transfers by Will, Intestacy or Appointment Act of 1973 that had been inserted in the 1975 Technical Amendments to the Code and Comments and which had replaced a very similar section which had been made part of the original Official Text. [2–801 (Appendix VII); Uniform Disclaimer of Transfers by Will, Intestacy or Appointment Act]. In recognition of the Code's expanded scope over nonprobate transfers, the new version is broader in coverage than previous Code versions. [2–801, Comment]. The Comment to the new provision, however, only discusses minor changes that were made to the Uniform Act as it was incorporated into the Code. Because this provision mirrors the two companion Uniform Acts dealing with testamentary and nontestamentary disclaimers, official comments are included with those acts only. Comments for the testamentary transfer act can be found in appendix VII of the Code. [See 2–801, Comments, (Appendix VII)].

The Code permits, under defined procedures, all persons to whom property devolves by whatever means to disclaim their interest in the property. [2–801(a)]. The right to disclaim exists regardless whether the transfer instrument permits disclaimers and even if the transfer instrument restricts transfers or prohibits disclaimer or both. The disclaimer may be made either personally by any competent person, or by persons who represent the disclaimant. A representative of a person includes not only a conservator for a disabled person but also a guardian for a minor or incapacitated person, an agent under a durable power of attorney and a deceased person's personal representatives. Any disclaimer by an incapacitated or protected person's representative presumably must be made according to the procedure set out in Article V of the Code. [See 5–407(b)(3), and (c); § 32.01(D)].

A valid disclaimer may be made only by a written instrument that describes the property or interest disclaimed, declares the fact of disclaimer and its extent and is signed by the person renouncing or that person's proper representative. [2–801(c)]. To be effective, particular procedures must be followed depending on the type of interest disclaimed. If the interest concerns devolution at death, the necessary writing must be filed in the court where the deceased owner's or deceased donee of the power's estate is being administered or where it could have been administered if none has been commenced. [2–801(b)(2)]. A copy of the disclaimer must also be delivered or mailed by registered or certified mail to any personal representative or other fiduciary of the decedent or donee. If the interest concerns devolution under a nontestamentary instrument or contract, the necessary writing must be delivered in person or by certified mail to the person holding legal title or possessing the interest disclaimed. Disclaimers of real property interests may also be recorded in the office where deeds are recorded in the county where the real estate is situated. [2–801(b)(4)].

The timing of the disclaimer is also crucial. If the interest concerns devolution at death, the Code requires that the disclaiming instrument must be filed not later than nine months after the death of the decedent or the donee of the power when a present interest is disclaimed or not later than nine months after the event determining the taker of the property or interest is finally ascertained and that interest is indefeasibly vested when a future interest is disclaimed. [2–801(b)(1)–(2)]. These time periods are merely suggested by the draftsmen and may be altered by the enacting state.

Even if the time periods have not run, certain specified actions by the person attempting to disclaim will bar the right to disclaim. [2–801(e)]. Specifically, a person is barred from renouncing if the person: (1) used the property or interest in any commercial manner such as selling or pledging it; (2) waived the right to disclaim in writing; (3) accepted the property or interest or benefits from it; or (4) had the property sold under a judicial sale before the disclaimer becomes effective. Significantly, written waivers of the right to disclaim bind the persons waiving and all persons claiming through or under them. [2–801(d)(3)].

Unless the decedent or the donee has properly indicated otherwise, the disclaimed interest, which devolves by will, by exercise of a power in a will, or by intestacy, passes as if the disclaimant had predeceased the decedent or donee. [2–801(d)(1)]. A similar rule applies to interests devolving by nontestamentary instruments and contracts except the interest devolves as if the disclaimant had predeceased the effective date of the instrument or contract. [2–801(d)(2)]. An exception to this approach applies where the persons who take the disclaimant's interest would share in that interest by representation or other rule if the disclaimant had failed to survive the decedent. In order to prevent manipulation of the size of shares passing to representatives, the disclaimant's actual interest passes by representation to the representative takers. For example, if D died intestate survived by G1 and G2, grandchildren of A and B who are D's two predeceased children, and by C, a surviving child who has two surviving grandchildren, G3 and

G4, C's disclaimer of C's ⅓ intestate share could not be increased effectively to a total of ½ of the estate to G3 and G4 by way of the per capita at each generation rule that would treat all grandchildren equally had no children survived. In this situation, C's ⅓ share would pass equally to G3 and G4. This rule also protects C's ⅓ share for G3 and G4 if A and B had had a total of more than four children.

A similar rule applies to future interests that are to take effect in possession or enjoyment after the termination of the disclaimed interest. For example, if a person disclaims a sole life interest, the remainder is accelerated in possession or enjoyment in the remainder persons. For all purposes including creditors, tax authorities and others who may have interests or claims against the disclaimant, a disclaimer relates back to the date of death of the decedent or the donee of the power.

Although the section constitutes an exclusive remedy for disclaimer of succession, it expressly does not abridge similar rights of persons under other statutes. [2–801(f)]. Any present or future interest, which is in existence, and according to this Section's time limitations, still disclaimable on the effective date of the Code may be disclaimed up to nine months after that date. [2–801(g)].

The Comment warns that if disclaimers are being used for estate and gift savings purposes, disclaimants must scrupulously obey the requirements of I.R.C. 2518 as well as the Code's provision. [2–801, Comment]. Significant differences exist concerning the timing of disclaimers particularly in the disclaiming of future interests. [See Medlin, Examination of Disclaimers, at 1278–90].

§ 12.03 Termination of Marital Status

A. INTRODUCTION

The Code contains two provisions that concern the termination of marital status. The first concerns the determination when a person is a surviving spouse for purposes of receiving the benefits conferred upon a surviving spouse by the Code in Parts 1–4 of Article II and Section 3–203 of Article III. [2–802]. The second concerns the consequences of the termination of a marital relationship on benefits conferred in dispositive instruments. [2–804].

B. DEFINITION OF A SURVIVING SPOUSE

A person's marital status is very important in determining many rights and responsibilities set by the Code. These rights and responsibilities include, for example, distribution in intestacy, elective share rights, revocation of wills, family protection rights, priority for appointment as personal representative, and appointment of a guardian for an incapacitated person. [See 2–802(b)]. Although the Code leaves the requirements for marriage to the law of domestic relations, it includes provisions setting the scope and effect of legal proceedings and other actions which sever the relationship.

Under the Code, a person is not a surviving spouse of the decedent if the person and the decedent have been divorced or their marriage annulled. [2–802(a)]. This rule does not apply, of course, if they remarry and are married on the date of the decedent's death. It also does not apply to a decree of separation that does not terminate the husband-wife status. Notwithstanding the absence of a final divorce or annulment, unless a contrary intent appears on the agreement, a complete property settlement entered into after or in anticipation of separation or divorce operates as a disclaimer of the spouse's elective share, family protections, rights under intestate succession and provisions in wills executed before the property settlement. [2–207].

In addition to a spouse who has obtained a valid divorce or an annulment, the term "surviving spouse" also does not include: (1) a person who obtained or consented to a final decree of divorce or of annulment even though the decree is not valid in the Code state, unless that person has subsequently remarried the decedent, or subsequently lived together as husband and wife [2–802(b)(1)]; (2) a person who participated in a marriage ceremony with a third person following a valid or invalid decree of divorce or annulment [2–802(b)(2)]; or (3) a person who participated as a party to a valid proceeding which terminated all marital property rights. [2–802(b)(3)]. The three above situations recognize a kind of estoppel concept. In each one the surviving person has either consented, participated in, sought or completed some volitional act other than the "divorce" that causes the marital relationship to be terminated as far as the surviving spouse's rights under the Code are concerned. Because the rights of a surviving spouse under the Code are substantial, it is very important that only those who legally and equitably should be considered a surviving spouse are able to take these benefits.

C. REVOCATION OF INTERESTS AND POWERS BY OPERATION OF LAW

At common law, revocation of wills by operation of law was recognized in two situations: a single woman's will was revoked when she subsequently married, and a single man's will was revoked after his marriage and birth of an issue. [Atkinson, Wills § 85]. No other change of circumstances would revoke a will by operation of law.

Taking the modern approach to revocation by operation of law as its guide, the Code rejects these common law situations. In their place it includes a ground for revocation relevant to current societal problems, i.e., termination of the marriage. [2–804]. In addition, recognizing that the problem of a former spouse taking an unintended benefit from a prior spouses arises in more than merely testamentary situations: all gratuitous transfers may include such a result, particularly inter vivos trust. In response the Code expands the revocation concept due to divorce to these instruments. The Code specifically restricts revocation of covered instruments by operation of law to divorce, annulment and homicide. [2–804(f); see 2–803; § 12.04].

By the terms of this provision, a testator's divorce or annulment which occurs after the execution of a will, trust or contract revokes any disposition or appointment of property made by that instrument that will to the former spouse. [2–804(b); see 2–508]. In addition, divorce or annulment revokes any grant of a general or special power of appointment to the former spouse as well as any nomination of the former spouse as executor, trustee, conservator, or guardian. Any grant of a power or nomination for fiduciary office is interpreted and carried out as if the surviving former spouse predeceased the testator. All revoked dispositive provisions are treated as if the former spouse disclaimed them. [2–804(d)]. This permits the property to pass according to the rules relating to the type of transaction or interest involved. Under a will for example, a disclaimer of a general devise is treated as a lapse of the devise and the normal lapse and antilapse provisions of the will or the Code apply to determine the devisee. [See §§ 10.02, 12.02]. Also, for example, disclaimed proceeds under a life insurance policy will be paid to the alternative beneficiaries, if any. [See § 12.02].

The meaning of divorce or annulment under this provision is cross referenced to Section 2–802(b) discussed in the previous part of this section.

Several limitations on the scope and application of this provision are important. First, if by the terms of the instrument the testator anticipates divorce or annulment and still desires to benefit, empower or nominate the former spouse notwithstanding the divorce or annulment, the terms of the provision will be carried out. [2–804(b)]. Second, the testator's remarriage to the former spouse revives all provisions for the former spouse which were revoked solely because of this provision. [2–804(e)]. And third, a mere separation decree does not terminate the marriage and is not a divorce. [2–804(a)(2)]. The latter limitation is not to be confused, however, with the situation where there has been a complete property settlement between the testator and the spouse. Unless the property settlement provides otherwise, such a settlement constitutes a disclaimer by the spouse of all benefits under any prior will. [2–207].

For an explanation of the Code's treatment of the rights between those who claim the property because of the divorce and third persons who dealt with the former spouse, see § 12.05.

§ 12.04   Effect of Homicide

Generally, a person's misconduct does not disqualify the person from inheriting property or from taking property passing from other persons. [Atkinson, Wills § 31]. Consequently, for example, desertion, conviction of a felony, or adultery will not cause a forfeiture of the wrongdoer's property or rights to property passing from those harmed. There are exceptions. A parent who fails to support a nonmarital child while legally obligated to support may be barred in intestacy from inheriting from the nonmarital child or the child's descendants. [See 2–114; § 5.05(E)].

The most pervasive exception to the general rule concerns statutes or court decisions that bar murderers from inheriting or taking property from their victims. The rationale for this rule is to prohibit a wrongdoer from profiting from the wrongful act done to the victim. The substantive and procedural rules for this forfeiture greatly differ among the states which recognize it. In addition, substantial omissions in the rules are commonly present. For example, it is common for a state to bar a murderer from taking in intestacy, testacy and from receiving life insurance proceeds on the victim's life but to ignore other forms of property transfers. Sometimes courts have filled in some of the gaps, but many still exist.

For the sake of clarity and uniformity, the Code includes a substantively and procedurally comprehensive provision concerning the effect of homicide on the rights of murderers to take property from, or assume other privileges granted by, their victims. [2–803]. This provision is applicable, however, only when similar concepts are not in the relevant instruments. [Wilkins v. Fireman's Fund Am. Life Ins. Co. (1985)]. Basically, the Code prohibits a person who feloniously and intentionally kills another from accepting any benefits derived from the victim. The Code deals specifically with statutory benefits conferred as a result of death, benefits conferred in all the decedent's revocable governing instruments, and rights of survivorship in jointly held or community property. [2–803(b), and (c)]. The Code also includes a catch-all clause providing that the same principles are to be applied to the murderer's acquisition of any property or interest from the victim. [2–803(f)]. In addition to forfeiture of property interests, the

Code revokes nominations of the murderer in governing instruments to serve in fiduciary or representative capacities such as personal representative, trustee or agent.

The murderer forfeits all statutory benefits conferred on the murderer by the Code in regard to a decedent's estate. [2–803(b)]. This means the murderer forfeits any intestate share, elective share, pretermitted spouse or heir share, or family protection amounts normally conferred upon a person with the murderer's status due to the death of the decedent.

Concomitantly, due to the wrongful act, the Code's provision revokes all benefits conferred on the murderer by the terms of any and all revocable governing instruments executed by the decedent. [2–803(c)(1)]. This all inclusive application of the forfeiture concept includes benefits bestowed in wills, trusts, contractual agreements, multiple-party accounts, and TOD security registrations. An instrument is revocable if the decedent, alone, held a power at the time or immediately before death to cancel the benefit for the murderer. [2–803(a)(3)]. The decedent, however, need not possess the power to designate the decedent in place of the murderer or the capacity to exercise the power at the time of the murder. This means that the murderer forfeits any testacy share, gift in a revocable trust, POD or TOD survivor benefits, proceeds of life insurance and benefits from other contractual arrangements. [2–803(c)(1)].

Finally, the Code converts an interest held as joint tenancy or community property with right of survivorship into a tenancy in common. [2–803(c)(2)]. Consequently, the victim's share passes as part of the victim's estate and the murderer forfeits the right to survivorship but retains the personal interest in the property. To bind a purchaser of the survivorship property from the murderer, however, persons interested in the decedent's estate who contend a severance of title occurred must file a writing declaring the severance in the appropriate recording office for the type of property in question. [2–803(d)]. For real estate, this means a notice of severance must be filed where deeds to the real estate are filed. If the notice of severance is not filed a third party purchase for value may acquire the property without forfeiture consequences. Because survivorship titles are usually confirmed easily and quickly by filing an affidavit and a death certificate and because there is usually significant delay between the time of the murder and the development of a case accusing a successor of the crime, accused murderers may often have an opportunity to sell the asset to a third person and avoid the claim of severance. Of course, for whatever it may be worth, the murderer would remain liable for the value of the severed interests.

Under the Code the primary method of disposing of the forfeited assets is to treat the murderer as having disclaimed the revoked or forfeited interests. [2–803(e)]. The consequence of disclaimer permits the property to pass according to the rules relating to the type of transaction or interest involved. [See § 12.02]. Under a will, for example, a disclaimer of a general devise is treated as a

lapse of the devise and the normal lapse and antilapse provisions of the will or the Code apply to
determine the devisee. [See §§ 10.02, 12.02].
Also, for example, under a life insurance policy the
disclaimed proceeds would be paid to the alternative beneficiaries, if any. [See § 12.02].

The Code also deals with the problem of proof.
[2–803(g)]. First, for purposes of forfeiture under
this provision, it makes a judgment of conviction,
which establishes criminal accountability, after all
rights of appeal have been exhausted, conclusive
evidence that defendant killed decedent. Second,
notwithstanding an absence of a conviction or even
with the presence of an acquittal, the Code permits, on petition of an interested person, a civil
proceeding against the murderer to take place and
adopts the "preponderance of evidence" test as the
relevant burden of proof that the accused is crimi-
nally accountable for the felonious and intentional
killing of the decedent. If the court determines
the accountability for the murder is proved, the
determination conclusively establishes wrongdoing
for purposes of the application of this provision.
Two particular consequences of these provisions
deserve mention. First, because conviction is not
required for application of the forfeiture provisions, suicide by the murderer does not preclude
their application if the crime can be proved in the
civil proceeding. Second, criminal accountability
includes acting as an accomplice or co-conspirator
as well as the actor or direct perpetrator. [2–803,
Comment].

Under a similar provision in the 1969 Code, a
court held that if the killer was legally insane, he

will not be disinherited. [In re Estate of Vadlamudi (1982)]. On the other hand, acquittal by reason
of insanity in the criminal case is not conclusive on
the probate issue and a civil hearing is necessary
to determine the legal insanity issue. [Id.].

In addition to the notice requirement to bind
purchasers of property sold by a surviving joint
tenant with right of survivorship [2–803(d)], the
Code includes provisions protecting other payors,
bona fide purchasers and other third persons who
deal with the murderer prior to notice of the claim
against the murderer. [2–803(h), and (i); see § 12.-
05]. This protection for bona fide purchasers and
other unknowing third persons recognizes that
there may be a long delay in instituting proceedings accusing a person of murdering another and
even after institution of the case, the result may be
in doubt for a long period of time.

§ 12.05   Protection of Payors and Third Par-
ties

Because the Code creates circumstances that in
effect suspend ownership of assets for a period of
time after a decedent's death, it is concerned with
the validity of transfers between those who hold
these suspended ownership interests and third parties. These third parties are payors who either
hold the interest for or are bona fide purchasers of
the interest from those who hold this suspended
ownership. The Code seeks to protect these third
persons from liability for payment or purchase of
the property. The Code contains five sections specifically dealing with this problem in relationship
to particular property ownership situations. These

include: (1) the problem of the nonprobate transfers to others under the augmented estate concept,
[2–208, 2–204(b); see § 6.03]; (2) the problem of a
beneficiary not surviving the necessary 120 hours,
[2–702(e), and (f); see § 11.02]; (3) the problem of
transactions with a murderer who is a beneficiary
of the victim's estate, [2–803(h), and (i); see § 12.-
04]; (4) the problem of revoked clauses and rights
due to divorce, [2–804(g), and (h); see § 12.03]; and,
(5) the problem of the substitute gift due to lapse in
life insurance, retirement plans and similar transactions, [2–706(d), and (e); § 11.03]. The provisions
are in two parts. The first provision protects persons who are obligated to pay or transfer assets to
a named individual under a governing instrument.
The second provision protects bona fide purchasers
of property from the recipient whose ownership is
in suspension.

The protection for payors and other obligated
third parties is not unlimited but is considerable.
If a payor or a person who is obligated to transfer
or deliver property to another, pays or delivers to
the person designated in the appropriate governing
instrument or agreement, the payor or person
making the transfer is protected from liability unless that person received written notice of the
adverse claim by another. Conversely, the payor
who received written notice of the claim is liable
for making payment or delivery.

Written notice requirements are specified in
each of the sections. Generally, they require that
notice of the claim or triggering event or action
must be a written notice mailed to the payor or
third person by registered or certified mail or

served upon that person as a civil action summons would be served. A mailed notice may be sent to the payor's main office or home. After receipt of written notice, the payor may pay the amount or property over to the proper court for safe keeping purposes. The proper court is defined as the court in which the decedent's estate is being administered or if there is no administration in the court in which the administration could be instituted due to decedent's residency. Payment to the court discharges the payor or person holding the property. Once the court determines the proper ownership or particular time periods expire that settle the ownership, it may transfer the property to the appropriate beneficiaries.

The following Chart graphically outlines the similarities and differences of the five provisions.

CHART 12–1

Comparison of Provisions Protecting Third Parties and Bona Fide Purchasers

Section	Liability Limitation	Protected Act	Basis for Action	Notice Exception
§ 2-202. Augmented Estate.	A payor or other third party is not liable	For having made a payment or transferred to a beneficiary of an item of property, or other benefit, "which is included in the decedent's reclaimable estate,	Designated in a governing instrument	Unless the payor or other third party received prior written notice from the surviving spouse or spouse's representative of an intention to file a petition for the elective share or that a petition for the elective share has been filed.
		For having taken any other action in good faith reliance	On the validity of a governing instrument	
§ 2-702. Requirement of Survival by 120 Hours.	A payor or other third party is not liable	For having made a payment or transfer of an item of property to a beneficiary who is not entitled to the payment or item of property because the beneficiary failed to survive the relevant event by 120 hours	Designated in a governing instrument	Unless the payor or other third party received prior written notice of a claimed lack of entitlement under this section
		For having taken any other action for a beneficiary who is not entitled to the action taken because the beneficiary failed to survive the relevant event by 120 hours "in good faith reliance on the beneficiary's apparent entitlement	Under the terms of the governing instrument	
§ 2-803. Life insurance; Retirement Plan; Account With POD Designation; Transfer-on-Death Registration; Deceased Beneficiary.	A payor is protected from liability	For having made payments to a beneficiary	Under the terms of the beneficiary designation	Unless the payor received prior written notice of a claim to a substitute gift under this section
§ 2-803. Effect of Homicide on Intestate Succession, Wills, Trusts, Joint Assets, Life Insurance, and Beneficiary Designations.	A payor or other third party is not liable	For having made a payment or transferring an item of property or any other benefit to a beneficiary	Designated in a governing instrument affected by an intentional and felonious killing	Unless the payor or other third party received prior written notice of a claimed forfeiture or revocation under this section
§ 2-804. Revocation of Probate and Nonprobate Transfers by Divorce; No Revocation by other Changes of Circumstances.	A payor or other third party is not liable	For having made a payment or transferred an item of property or any other benefit to a beneficiary	Designated in a governing instrument affected by a divorce, annulment, or remarriage	Unless the payor or other third party received prior written notice of the divorce, annulment, or remarriage
		For having taken any other action in good faith reliance	On the validity of the governing instrument	

Purchasers for value and without notice and payees of payments or other property items in partial or full satisfaction of legally enforceable obligations are not obligated to return payment or the property. On the other hand, persons who receive payment or property gratuitously are obligated to return the payment or property and are even personally liable for the payment of property to the person who is determined to be entitled to the property. This rule applies even if federal law preempts the underlying property title or ownership provision. The federal pre-emption relates to the Employee Retirement Income Security Act of 1974 which preempts state law in regard to any employee benefit plan. The drafters of the Code believe that the provision conforms with this pre-emption. [See 2–804, Comment].

§ 12.06 Powers of Appointment

A. INTRODUCTION AND DEFINITIONS

Because the Code's provisions concerning powers of appointment are scattered among several Articles, a single amalgamated discussion of them is helpful for their comprehension. [Kurtz, Powers of Appointment]. Although a complete explanation of the law of powers of appointment is beyond the scope of this Nutshell, a short review of powers and the Code's references to them is appropriate. [See generally, Simes, Future Interests §§ 55–60].

As defined by the Restatement of Property, Second, a power of appointment is the "authority,

other than as an incident of the beneficial ownership of property, to designate recipients of beneficial interest in property." [Restatement (Second)
Property, § 11.1]. There are five principal persons
who are inherently involved in a power: (1) the
donor, who is the creator of the power; (2) the
donee, who is the person who holds the power; (3)
the objects, who are the persons for whom an
appointment can be exercised; (4) the appointees,
who are the persons for whom the powers has been
exercised; and, (5) the takers in default, who are
the persons who will take the property to the
extent that the power is not exercised. [Restate-
ment (Second) Property, § 11.2]. Persons may
function in more than one category. In addition, a
power is personal to the donee and may not be
exercised by other persons. If a donee does not
exercise it, it expires. Two property interests need
identification: (1) the appointive assets which com-
pose the assets that are subject to the exercise of
the power; and, (2) the donee's personal beneficial
interest in the appointive assets other than as an
object of the power. [Restatement (Second) Property, § 11.3].

There are several types of powers that are relevant to the Code's provisions. [Restatement (Second) Property, § 11.4]. First, a general power is
defined as a power that permits the donee to appoint the property to the donee, personally, to the
donee's creditors, to the donee's estate, or to creditors of the donee's estate. If a power contains no
restriction on whom may be an appointee, it is
presumed the power is a general power. Second, a
nongeneral power, or what is sometimes called a

special power, is unhelpfully defined by the Restatement as any power that is not a general power. Usually the donee of a nongeneral power is permitted to appoint only to a particular group of persons, such as one's children or descendants. Because of federal gift and estate tax benefits, nongeneral powers may include as objects everyone except the donee, the donee's creditors, the donee's estate, and the creditors of the donee's estate.

Powers are also categorized as to when they may be exercised. [Restatement (Second) Property, § 11.5]. A power of appointment is presently exercisable if the donee may immediately exercise it at the time in question. It is stated that the donee may exercise it by deed. A "deed" is merely any legally operative act or instrument effective during the donee's lifetime. A power of appointment is not presently exercisable if it may only be exercised by a will (testamentary power) or at the time in question cannot be exercised until some event or passage of time occurs. All powers must be in existence before they are exercisable. [Restatement (Second) Property, § 11.5, Comment a]. A power of appointment created in a living person's will does not come into existence until that person dies and the will becomes effective.

Two other characterizations are also relevant. [Restatement (Second) Property, § 11.4, Comment c]. The donee may hold a purely collateral power if the donee holds no interest in the property except the power. On the other hand, the donee may hold a power in gross if the donee holds both an interest in the property and a power that if exercised would dispose of the interest that the donee does not hold.

B.   EXERCISE OF POWER OF APPOINTMENT

When a testator holds a testamentary power of appointment at death, it becomes essential to determine whether the testator, as donee of the power, has exercised it in testator's will. Most often the instrument that creates the special or general power of appointment specifically names a taker or takers in default of the appointment by the donee. Occasionally, the power does not name takers in default and if a general power is not exercised by the donee, the property reverts to the donor's estate for distribution according to the distribution pattern determined for that estate. The Code includes rules of construction to resolve these issues when a testator's intent is not clearly expressed.

There are several situations that must be distinguished. The following three factors guide the application of the rules of construction adopted in the Code: (1) whether the governing instrument that created the power of appointment expressly requires that a power is exercised by the will only if the donee makes a reference to the power or its source in the will; (2) whether the power of appointment is a general or a nongeneral power; and, (3) whether the testator-donee's will expresses an intention to exercise the power of appointment.

No Specific Reference Requirement: If the document creating a power of appointment is nonexplicit in that it does not include a requirement that the power may only be exercised "by a reference, or by an express or specific reference" to the power in the exercising document, a will that contains a "general residuary clause" or that makes a "general disposition of all the testator's property," exercises the power only if one of two conditions are met. First, a will containing a general residuary clause or a comparable clause exercises a general testamentary nonexplicit power if the document creating the power fails to contain an effective gift in default of exercise. This rule permits the donee's will to control the disposition of the property subject to the power rather than allowing the takers of the donor's estate to take. A contrary rule can create unintended and unanticipated results, including the need to reopen a donor's closed estate and to cause estate tax consequences to an otherwise settled estate. Second, any general and nongeneral nonexplicit testamentary power is exercised if the testator's will manifests an intention to include the property that is subject to the power as part of the residuary or general disposition clause. [2–608].

These rules prevent unintended exercises of powers from occurring merely because a residue clause is included in a donee's will but provide a broad exception if admissible evidence indicates that the testator desired to exercise the power. The distinction between interpretations can be illustrated by comparing its application to two typical drafting examples: (1) if the residuary clause in testators's will merely devises "all the rest, residue and remainder" of testator's estate, presumably the power is not exercised; but (2) if the residuary clause in testators's will devises "all the rest, residue and remainder, including any property over which a power of appointment is held," of testator's estate, presumably the power is exercised. [2–608, Comment]. The latter is called a "blending" or "blanket" clause. The inclusion of such a clause in a will raises a presumption under the Code that testator intended to exercise a power if that power does not require a particular reference to it to be exercised. When the residuary clause omits the reference to powers of appointment, the presumption is that testator does not intend to exercise a power. Either presumption is subject to rebuttal with extrinsic evidence under the principle of Section 2–601. [2–608, Comment; § 10.01].

Specific Reference Requirement: If the document creating a power of appointment is explicit in that it includes a requirement that the power may only be exercised "by a reference, or by an express or specific reference" to the power in the exercising document, the language is presumed to indicate the donor did not desire inadvertent exercise of the power. [2–704] This presumption relates to the exercise of all explicit powers whether they are general or nongeneral and to all exercising documents whether they are wills or other will substitutes. The exact meaning of this provision is not clear on its face. The Comment to the section explains that the section creates a mere presumption against exercise that prevents, for example, a blending clause from automatically exercising the power as such a clause would do when the power is nonexplicit. Beyond the mere presumption, the questions of the donor's intent as to the requirements for exercise, and the donee's intent as to the exercise, of the power, is left to extrinsic evidence. [See 2–701]. Relevant extrinsic evidence may swing the determination either way: in one direction it may show that the donee intended exercise although the donee did not make an otherwise sufficient reference to the power; or, in the other direction, it may show that the donor desired a specific reference to the power and any reference that fails to satisfy this requirement fails to exercise the power. The provision has the apparent purpose of both preventing inadvertent exercise but leaving open the question of proof of intent by inferentially relying on extrinsic evidence to supply that intent.

C. VIRTUAL REPRESENTATION AND GENERAL POWERS OF APPOINTMENT

The Code gives special treatment to the acts of, and to formal court orders binding, the sole holder or all co-holders of a presently exercisable general power of appointment. [1–108, 1–403(2)(i)]. A general power is described as any power of appointment in which the holder of the power is capable of drawing absolute ownership to the holder, personally. [1–108, Comment; see § 12.06(A)]. Although a "holder" of such a power is commonly a donee of a general power of appointment created by the donor, the term is also applicable to the settlor or beneficiary of a trust in which the settlor or beneficiary retains a power to revoke the trust.

A holder or the unanimous co-holders of a presently exercisable general power of appointment can, by granting consent or approval, relieve personal representatives or trustees from a liability or a penalty which these fiduciaries would ordinarily suffer due to a failure to perform a particular duty required by the Code or other law. [1–108]. Similarly, the holder or unanimous co-holders of a general power may consent to modifications or terminations of a trust or to deviations from its terms. The effect of approval or consent of the holder or unanimous co-holders of a general power is to bind the beneficiaries to the extent that the beneficiaries' interests are subject to the power notwithstanding that no court order is obtained. This virtual representation capability can be of crucial significance in nonjudicial settlements of estates and trusts where consent of all those with interests is essential to effectuate the settlement.

The Code also provides that orders resulting from formal court proceedings which bind a holder or all co-holders of such a general power bind other persons to the extent that these persons' interests are subject to the power. [1–403(2)(i)]. This provision has the effect of eliminating the ordinary requirements for notice to and jurisdiction over numerous and unknown, sometime unborn, beneficiaries when litigation occurs. It would not apply, however, if the validity of the general power itself is the issue involved because the power holder or holders cannot represent the others in this type of litigation. [1–403, Comment]. The justification for this ability to bind others is that the holders of presently exercisable general powers of appointment possess the equivalent of full ownership. Furthermore the financial interests between the holder of the power and those persons who have interests subject to the power are sufficiently compatible to satisfy fairness and due process concerns. [Kurtz, Powers of Appointment, at 1154–1151].

The virtual representation power of holders of presently exercisable general powers of appointment does not apply under the Code to holders of nongeneral powers such as special powers and general testamentary powers. There are valid arguments, however, that the donee of a nongeneral power of appointment should have virtual representation capabilities except in limited circumstances. [See Kurtz, Powers of Appointment, at 1155–62].

CHAPTER 13

UNIFORM STATUTORY RULE AGAINST PERPETUITIES

§ 13.01 Introduction

The common law Rule Against Perpetuities has perplexed students, professors, lawyers and judges for centuries. Although the Rule is easy to state, its complexity developed from difficulties in its application. A common formulation of the Rule provides: "No interest is good unless it must vest, if at all, not later than twenty-one years after some life in being at the creation of the interest." [Gray, Rule Against Perpetuities, § 201, at 191]. Its chief purposes are stated to be a desire to curtail the deadhand control of wealth and to facilitate the marketability of property. [Lynn, Modern Rule Against Perpetuities, at 10]. Few would question its goals but many have criticized its methods. Several facets of the Rule's application engender the criticisms.

First, the Rule is really not a rule concerned with the duration of an interest but is concerned with a technical property concept of the vesting of an interest. Comparatively speaking, a relatively short twenty-five year suspended interest could violate the Rule for failure to vest within its confines whereas a suspended interest tested against lives in being could be valid under the Rule even though it actually will last for ninety years or more. This inconsistency in application justifies criticism.

Second, the Rule is enforced with psychic anticipation of contingencies coupled with a draconian "all or nothing" remedy if the contingencies violate the Rule. According to the common law, an interest created in a governing instrument, whether a will or other transfer device, had to be tested against the Rule at its creation. All contingencies in the interest created are tested to see whether they will become vested within the term of the Rule. There must be an initial certainty of vesting of all of the interests. If an interest is not certain of vesting within the Rule, the concept of infective invalidity might cause the entire transfer to fail. Commentators belabor these points in emphasizing the Rule's inconsistency, nonsensical approach, draconian remedy and unjust result. [See, e.g., Leach, Perpetuities in Perspective; Waggoner, Perpetuity Reform].

Despite these compelling criticisms, the Rule proves to endure against reform. A major reason for the lack of reformation derives from disagreements over what form the reform should take. Reformation proposals include: (1) total repeal of the Rule, (2) creation of an immediate judicial reformation power for interests that will not vest within the Rule, (3) creation of wait and see or deferral judicial reformation power for interests that do not vest within the Rule, and (4) substitution of a specific period of time or period in gross within which all conditional interests must vest.

[See generally, Fellows, Testing Perpetuity Reforms, at 602–08].

Checkerboard reform among the states creates more problems than it solves. The multi-state property owner is more numerous than ever before. The possibility that interests will cross state lines has increased significantly during the last fifty years and the need for greater uniformity has concomitantly increased. The force of reform finally gained some momentum in 1979 when the American Law Institute accepted a wait and see doctrine as part of the Restatement (Second) of Property. [See Restatement (Second) of Property, § 1.4]. The Restatement nurtured additional discussion over the Rule and its modifications and this renewed interest reached a crescendo when the National Conference adopted the Uniform Statutory Rule Against Perpetuities Act (hereinafter USRAP) in 1986. Since its promulgation, over twenty states have enacted it as their law. Clearly, it constitutes the best and most politically viable reform proposal made to date. It is important to note that the Act is not without its opponents. [See, Dukeminier, Ninety Years in Limbo; Bloom, Perpetuities Refinement].

In 1990, the USRAP was made a part of the Uniform Probate Code and is found in Part 9 of Article II. Although the comments concerning the provisions are extensive in the Code, the comments and prefatory note materials incorporated into the separate Uniform Act are even more extensive and constitute one of the best sources of information concerning how the act works. For anyone who wishes to peruse the details of USRAP provisions, reference to these materials is essential. The following is but a brief outline of the relevant concepts promoted by the USRAP as well as a brief description of its provisions.

The purposes of the USRAP are broad. Obviously, as part of the Uniform Probate Code and as a separate uniform act, it is designed to bring uniformity of the law to the various states in this country. In addition, promulgation of the provisions reaffirms that there is a need for a Rule Against Perpetuities. Abolition of the Rule was rejected. Another important factor and feature of the provisions is that transfer language in instruments effective prior to enactment of the USRAP continues to be valid after enactment. The USRAP does not enlarge the range of invalidity. It is designed to recognize devices currently valid and to expand the scope of validity to other drafting techniques. Consequently, those who are well versed in the old law will not have to learn new law in order to qualify their transfer techniques.

Finally, a primary purpose of the USRAP is to reduce, and even eliminate in many situations, much of the litigation concerning perpetuity problems. With some limited exceptions, litigation over perpetuity questions cannot arise until the Rule as defined by the statute is violated. Consequently, all transfers which over time become effective despite their technical potential invalidity under the old common law Rule will not produce litigation. Only a transfer device that violates both period testing arms of the USRAP will come before the court except as noted. Even when litigation does occur, the nature and purpose of the litigation will be dramatically different from much litigation under the current common law Rule. Much litigation under the current Rule derives its motivation from a desire to destroy the contingent interest. Actions are brought by those who will gain by the destruction of the transfer device. Under the USRAP, this type of litigation is eliminated. The only litigation that will arise will be litigation to reform an instrument to conform to the Rule. Consequently, only those who wish to settle legitimate concerns and to terminate or to settle ownership of ancient trusts will be able to seek court review. This feature of the USRAP should abolish the common law attribute of granting unjust enrichment to nonintended beneficiaries due to technical failure of transfers due to perpetuity violations. [See Waggoner, Perpetuities Reform].

§ 13.02   Statutory Rule Against Perpetuities

The core of the USRAP is found in its definition of the period of time within which a non-vested interest must vest in order to be valid. Phrased in the disjunctive, a non-vested interest is valid if it is certain to vest or terminate either no later than twenty-one years after the death of a living individual or within ninety years after its creation. [2–901]. The first arm of the rule is merely a codification of the common law Rule. The second arm is a form of a wait and see approach tied to a specific length of time. The combination of these two alternate standards can be summarized as follows:

(1) A transfer which is valid under the common law Rule is valid under the USRAP's provi-

sion and no modification is necessary to forms or instruments that satisfy this standard;

(2) Notwithstanding validity under the common law Rule, no interest is contestable as to validity until ninety years have passed from its creation;

(3) The common "savings" clause which specifically terminates an interest within the common law Rule will also qualify under this provision.

The rules are specifically applicable to non-vested property interests, general powers of appointment that are not presently exercisable because of a condition precedent, and non-general powers of appointment which generally are testamentary powers of appointment. [2–901(a), (b), and (c)].

There is a distinct judicial and practice advantage in validating current methods of estate planning. The positive results will be a decline in litigation concerning previous instruments and techniques used in wills subject to the provision after its enactment. Practitioners will not create invalid transfers under the Rule merely by following old practices. In addition, the second arm of the rule is a remedial safety net for provisions not properly drafted. It basically incorporates a failsafe rule for improper drafting. No interest will fail due to the rule but may require reformation in order to be valid. The draconian remedy of the common law Rule is abolished.

Because of the broad protection provided by the provision, the USRAP specifically restricts the application of lives in being as that definition concerns post-death procreation. In determining whether an interest vests or not, the USRAP disregards the possibility that an individual may have a child born after the individual's death. This exclusion is primarily directed toward the problem raised by post-death procreation due to advances in medical science. [2–901(d), Comment]. It also, however, eliminates the common law lives in being extension granted to children en ventre sa mere. The common law rule was intended to validate interests that might otherwise have been invalid due to the birth of a child after the death of a life in being or transferor. The new rule makes this extension unnecessary for purposes of validating interests under the perpetuity rule and therefore is eliminatable.

Concern has been expressed that the alternative perpetuity periods might be used by drafters using clauses which provide that the maximum time of vesting or termination of an interest or trust must occur no later than the later of the two testing periods. For example, an instrument might use a clause that stated the following or similar to the following: "The non-vested interest is to vest on the later of (a) twenty-one years after the death of the survivor of specified lives in being at the creation of the trust or (b) ninety years after the creation of the trust." To avoid this misuse of the alternate perpetuity periods, the Code converts this type of "later of" clause into a traditional perpetuity saving clause. [2–901(e)]. Basically that limits the length of time to the common law Rule. [Fellows, Testing Perpetuity Reforms, at 657–63]. This section does not apply, however, to a later than clause which does not tack the twenty-one years on to the specific lives and being. [2–901, Comment]. For example, a transfer that creates an interest that is to vest upon "the later of the death of my spouse or thirty years after my death" would not be converted to the common law Rule but would be permitted to vest within the ninety year rule. In addition, it does not prohibit a clause that terminates the trust after 90 years, although this approach is discouraged. [Waggoner, Drafting Under the USRAP, at 248].

§ 13.03 Date of Creation of Interest

Because the perpetuity period refers to the time of creation of the non-vested interest, it is necessary to define when that interest is created. The USRAP codifies the common law on this matter with some clarification. The time of creation for most non-vested property interests or powers of appointment is determined under general principles of property law. [2–902(a)]. This means that non-vested interests created in a will will have the date of the testator's death as its creation date. In regard to inter vivos transfers, an interest or power is created as of the effective date of the transfer. In addition, two special circumstances are resolved. If by the terms of the instrument a person alone and without the consent of any other person may exercise a power to become the unqualified beneficial owner of the property subject to the interest, the non-vested interest or power of appointment is created for purposes of the perpetuity period when that unqualified power terminates. For example, if a person has a power to revoke an inter vivos or testamentary trust, the perpetuity period does not begin to run and is not created until the person no longer is able to exercise the power of revocation. The period then runs from the termination of this power over the interest subject to the USRAP. [2–902(b)].

Occasionally, property arrangements such as trusts, which include interests subject to the US-RAP, may provide that additional property can be added to them during their existence. The question in such situations is at what point do you evaluate the perpetuity period for these new interests transferred to the existing trust. The USRAP, taking the efficient course of action, provides that its perpetuity period begins when the instrument or trust was created not from the date of subsequent transfers to it. [2–902(c)]. Considering the nonforfeiture approach and generous duration of the USRAP's perpetuity periods, this limitation should not deny intent or cause harm to intended beneficiaries.

§ 13.04   Reformation

As mentioned previously, the USRAP includes a judicial reformation procedure exercisable by the courts concerning transfers which are found to violate its perpetuity period. [2–903]. Although this will not occur in most situations because experience informs us that most transfers will qualify under the general rule, the reformation power is reserved to correct those circumstances in which a perpetuity error has indeed been made. The US-RAP adopts a deferred rather than prospective reformation power in the court. This means that there is no power to reform until the transfer is invalid under the perpetuity period. [2–903]. Durationally speaking, this means the non-vested interest has not vested within either of the durational periods of the perpetuity period.

A deferred reformation power was selected for several reasons. First, it will significantly reduce "temperature testing" law suits over a perpetuity question. Second, it permits the transferor's plan to fully work out. As indicated previously, most transfers will vest within one or the other period and thus a law suit is unnecessary. Third, it rejects the prospective analysis of vesting determinations and adopts the retrospective analysis approach. At the time of reformation, the court will know more about how the donor would reform the instrument had the donor known the instrument created an invalid transfer. Should it be when the instrument first is created with a more or less prospective reformation or should it be after the instrument is no longer valid and we know what the actual facts are of the potential distribution? The USRAP elects the latter.

Two exceptions to the post-validity reformation requirement are recognized. The first exception concerns class gifts in which the vesting may still be endowed but the time for actual possession or enjoyment of a share of the estate in a class member has arrived. This exception permits those of the class entitled to immediate possession or enjoyment to seek reformation of the instrument so that their possession or enjoyment may occur immediately. [2–903(2), and Comment].

A second exception concerns the ability to institute a reformation action although the perpetuity periods have not expired if it is clear they will expire before the property vests. [2–903(3)]. This exception would cover the unlikely case where a donor created a transfer that would not vest until a period of time has passed clearly beyond the Rule. For example, consider a transfer of property into a trust from which the income is to be paid by representation among the donor's descendants, from time to time, living for one hundred years: at the end of the one hundred year period the trustee is to distribute the corpus and accumulated income to the donor's living descendants by representation but if none to a charity. It is clear that this transfer violates the USRAP including its ninety year rule. In this situation a prospective reformation action should be permitted to correct the clear undenied violation of the Rule.

When a reformation action is permitted, the court must reform the document. It does not have the discretion to hold that the transfer is invalid.

The USRAP provides information concerning what the court should consider in making the reformation. The statutory requirement is that the court must reform the transfer in a "manner that most closely approximates the transferor's manifested plan of distribution." [2–903]. This provision effectively revokes the common law doctrine of infectious invalidity. [2–903, Comment]. Generally, the recommendation is that courts make as little alteration to the disposition as possible. The goal is to use a scalpel and not a butcher knife. This means that (1) the maximum number of persons who could take at the time of reformation should be permitted to take even though their interests technically were not vested within the period of the rule, and (2) other prohibitory provisions should be altered as little as possible, e.g., an age requirement above twenty-one should be reduced only to the point where it will satisfy the rules. [USRAP, Section 3, Comment].

One of the advantages of the delayed reformation is the opportunity to see how the donor's plan operated and to apply any reformation necessary to the situation as it exists at the current time. There is no need to predict the future. The decision needs to be made at the time it needs to be made and it is final.

§ 13.05 Exclusions From the Rule

The USRAP specifically excludes certain transactions and powers from application of its rule. [2–904]. First, the provision provides that all exceptions recognized at common law or excluded by statute are excluded under the USRAP. The USRAP then defines particular situations that also are excluded. Generally, non-donative transfers are not subject to the Rule. [2–904(1)]. Although not excepted at common law the position of the drafters of the USRAP is that this is the preferred law because a perpetuity rule that concerns gratuitous transfers is not appropriate to apply to transactions with consideration. So that the exclusion is not interpreted beyond its intent, the USRAP excepts from the exclusion certain transactions that are in the nature of donative transfers despite their nongratuitous characterization. This would include prenuptial and postnuptial agreements, separation or divorce settlements, surviving spouses' elections, and other similar types of devices specifically enumerated.

The USRAP codifies the common law determination that nonvested charitable interests held in trusts or by governmental entities are not subject to the perpetuity period so long as they pass from one charitable entity to another charitable entity. [2–904(5)]. Furthermore, with some particular exceptions, nonvested property interests or powers of attorney in regards to trusts or other arrangements dealing with pension, profit sharing, stock bonuses and other types of employee benefit arrangements are excepted from the Rule as well. [2–904(6)].

Purely administrative or management powers that are not related to distribution are excepted from the rule. [2–904(2)]. In addition, a power to appoint a fiduciary [2–904(3)], and a discretionary trustee's power to distribute principal to an indefeasibly vested beneficiary are excepted. [2–904(4)].

The purpose of these exclusions is to draw particular divisions between the types of transfers to which the Rule should apply versus those to which it should not. The USRAP does not indicate that other durational limitations should not be imposed on the excepted transfers. The point being that the Rule Against Perpetuities is the wrong policy to apply against these devices and that particular specialized durational limitations need to be developed for them.

§ 13.06 Date of Application

The USRAP's provisions do not apply retroactively and will not apply prospectively to transfers that occurred before its effective date. [2–905]. Non-vested interests created by the exercise of a power of appointment after the effective date are covered by the USRAP's rule even though the original transfer occurred prior to the effective date. In addition, any power of appointment created subsequent to the effective date is covered by the USRAP rule if exercised after the effective date or if a power to revoke expires after the effective date.

For transfers not covered by the USRAP, the court is encouraged to adopt equitable principles that will incorporate the principles of the Act in order to avoid failure of the transaction. [2–905(b)]. The USRAP also includes a ministerial provision in which a state enacting it would have to repeal or supersede certain other laws in the state.

§ 13.07 Illustrations Using the USRAP

The following Chart 13–1 illustrates how the USRAP deals with several specific situations.

CHART 13-1

USRAP Illustrations

Comment: The following three hypotheticals are merely illustrative of the application of the USRAP. The first hypothetical concerns a conveyance that would be valid under the common law Rule Against Perpetuities. The second and third hypotheticals concern conveyances that would violate the common law Rule but which are validated under the USRAP.

Hypothetical 1: D devises the residue of the estate to T, in trust, with the income to D's children for life, the remainder passes to such of D's grandchildren as attain the age of twenty-one. D's will contains no savings clause. D is survived by three children, ages 12, 7, and 3 years of age, and no grandchildren.

Answer: This trust is valid under the common law Rule. It must vest, if at all, within lives in being (D's children) plus twenty-one years. All interests in the grandchild will vest no later than twenty-one years after the death of the last child to die. The USRAP does not change this analysis. The common law Rule is allowed to play out its requirements. Under this example, if one of the children were to live more than ninety years after D's death, absolute vesting of the transfer will not be known for a longer period than the USRAP's alternative ninety year rule. Because the devise is valid under the common law Rule, the ninety year limitation does not apply.

Hypothetical 2: D devises the residue of the estate to T, in trust, with the income payable to D's children for life. The trust terminates when D's youngest grandchild reaches the age of twenty-five. D's will contains no savings clause. D is survived by three children and seven grandchildren whose ages ranged from eleven to twenty-nine.[1]

Answer: This trust violates the common law Rule Against Perpetuities, because it is possible that D's youngest grandchild may be born after D's death and this grandchild might not reach the age of twenty-five

1. The facts of this hypothetical are basically similar to the facts of Merrill v. Wimmer (1985).

until more than twenty-one years after all the lives in being (D's children and grandchildren living at D's death) are dead. Although the remainder interest probably would vest within the length of the common law rule, it is invalid because of the mere possibility that it will not vest. The USRAP, however, validates the trust. Even if the slim possibility occurred it is likely the remainder interest in the trust will vest within ninety years of D's death and thus the trust will complete its full duration. Even if it has not vested within the ninety year period, the USRAP will cause the interests to be vested at that time by court order. In addition, the USRAP would not permit litigation over the perpetuity period until the later of its two limitation periods passed.

Hypothetical 3: M transferred into an irrevocable inter vivos trust assets the income from which to be paid to M's child, D, for life; D was given a testamentary power of appointment to the remainder. D died thirty years after the date of creation of M's trust. In D's valid will, the power was exercised by transferring the assets into trust. The income and principal from the trust was payable to D's children in the discretion of the trustee. Upon the death of each child, that child's share would be distributed to that child's then living descendants or if none were living, to that child's then living siblings, per stirpes. D was survived by three children ages 24, 22, and 21. All were born after the creation of M's trust.[2]

Answer: This trust violates the common law Rule Against Perpetuities because the trust does not vest until the death of each child of D and D's children are not lives in being. At common law the perpetuity period in this hypothetical would run from the date of the irrevocable inter vivos trust created by M rather than from D's date of death. As the facts state, none of D's children were lives in being at that time. One or more of D's children might not die and thus vesting might not occur until more than twenty-one years after all the lives in being are dead. If held to be invalid, the entire trust might fail. Under the USRAP the trust would be

2. The facts of this hypothetical are basically similar to the facts of Arrowsmith v. Mercantile–Safe Deposit & Trust Co. (1988).

allowed to function for the lives of D's children or sixty years (ninety years less the thirty years that had expired from the running of the perpetuity period) whichever period is shorter. If all of D's children die within the sixty year period, the trust will function and terminate without court involvement according to D's expressed desires. If one or more of D's children lived sixty years beyond D's death, then the Act's alternative ninety year rule applies and the trust will have to be reformed. In this situation, the court would probably vest the income interest in the living children and the remainder of each living child's share on death in that child's descendants, per stirpes, living at that time. [See Waggoner, USRAP in Oregon, at 271–72]. This approach discourages litigation because the trust retains validity, no costs of litigation occur until the relevant periods expire, and thus the donor's intent is carried out in substantial part, if not in whole.

§ 13.08   Honorary Trusts

The Code's 1990 revisions to Article II, as modified by the 1993 Technical Amendments, include an alternative section dealing with what has been vaguely referred to as "honorary trusts." The honorary trust is loosely definable as an "intended trust for a specific noncharitable purpose" where no beneficiary is actually named and the designated purpose cannot be considered charitable. [See Restatement (Second) Trust, § 124, Comment c]. The legality of these devices has been far from secure. [Bogert, Trusts § 35]. The Code in its optional section both legitimatizes and limits the duration of such honorary trusts. [2–907(a)].

Under the Code, any transfer in trust that is for a specific lawful noncharitable purpose, either as specified in the instrument or as selected by the trustee, may be performed by the trustee regardless whether there is a definite or definitely ascertainable beneficiary who can enforce or terminate the trust. [2–907(a)]. The suggested duration is twenty-one years subject to alteration by enacting legislatures. The twenty-one year term is set even if the instruments contemplates a longer period.

The main importance of this section, if enacted by a state, is that it permits a trustee to enforce these types of devices but only for a period of twenty-one years. The Code gives no guidance as to what a noncharitable purpose is. Assumably it would include, for example, trusts for the offering of masses and for the care of personal individual grave sites.

Another provision included in the Code concerns a similar type of transfer, i.e., the trust for pets. [2–907(b)]. Pet owners commonly desire that their pets be well cared for after their deaths. Transfers to and trusts for pets have sometimes been approved as honorary trusts. [See Restatement (Second) Trust, § 124]. The Code gives both recognition and definition to these desires. It specifically permits assets to be transferred in trust for the care of designated domestic or pet animals. [2–907(b)]. Although validity is guaranteed under the provision, it limits the duration of the trust to the lives of the covered animals living when the trust is created. Instruments are to be liberally construed and extrinsic evidence freely admitted to determine transferor's intent.

Several administration provisions are included to regulate the above transfer devices. Income and principal of the trust must be used only for trust purposes or for covered animals unless the instrument expressly provides otherwise. [2–907(c)(1)]. On termination, the trust must be transferred according to its creation instrument or the relevant clauses of the transferor's will or by intestacy. [2–907(c)(2); see 2–711; § 11.05(D)]. The Code makes the intent enforceable by the trustee or other court appointed persons. [2–907(c)(4)]. A court may name a trustee, if none is designated or no one is willing to serve, and order transfer to another trustee in order to see the intended use is carried out. [2–907(c)(7)]. A court may adjust the funds and order the excess distributed as it would be if the trust ended. [2–907(c)(6)].

*

PART THREE

PROBATE OF WILLS AND ADMINISTRATION

CHAPTER 14

INTRODUCTION TO THE FLEXIBLE SYSTEM OF ADMINISTRATION

§ 14.01 Introduction

The process of administration of an estate can be better understood if one knows what matters have to be resolved. A person's financial relationship with his or her property might be characterized as a partnership between the person and the estate. The death of the person causes a dissolution of the partnership and a liquidation of the assets of the estate is necessary. The following outlines the usual necessary steps for this liquidation:

(1) Take care of funeral and burial arrangements;

(2) Gather information concerning the status of the decedent's estate and the extent of the property held;

(3) Make an inventory of the assets in the estate;

(4) Identify creditors and obligations owed to other persons;

(5) Provide basic support for surviving family members during the liquidation process;

(6) Determine taxation obligations and complete and file necessary tax returns;

(7) If necessary, manage the assets of the estate during liquidation;

(8) Liquidate sufficient portions of the estate to pay obligations, debts, and taxes;

(9) Pay obligations, debts and taxes;

(10) Determine shares of eventual successors;

(11) Distribute remaining assets and funds to successors in appropriate shares;

(12) Complete final accounting of transactions during the administration process;

(13) Discharge the personal representative;

(14) Terminate the liquidation process.

The above outlines the basic steps. Most estates will require something more or less.

One of the principal issues in the determining how this process is to operate is who should have control over it. Should the law assume that everyone must follow a specified and standardized process or should the persons in interest control what actions should be taken? The former technique will raise transactional costs for a larger number of estates than will the latter. The latter approach is said to increase the risk of misappropriation and fraud on those who need to be protected. The traditional technique in this country favors the former approach. The Code and similar laws in other jurisdictions take the latter approach.

The current law in most jurisdictions concerning the administration of decedents' estates is typically monolithic, inflexible and formalistic. By contrast the Code provides persons interested in a decedent's estate with substantial flexibility and numerous procedural alternatives and combinations. Reduced to their conceptual characteristics, the three basic types of procedures available are called "informal," "formal" and "supervised." Generally, the informal proceedings for the probate of a will or appointment of a personal representative are administrative in nature and ordinarily require no prior notice to interested persons.   [1–201(23)]. They are initiated by an application to the Registrar who either denies it or issues a written statement of approval. At this moment, the Registrar's decision is considered nonadjudicative and is not appealable. If the application is approved by the Registrar, it permits certain processes to function without continual court involvement and will mature into a final adjudication after the passage of a specific length of time. Formal proceedings are initiated by a petition to the Court and become effective and operational only after notice to interested persons, a hearing and an order of court. [1–201(18)]. They are final adjudications subject only to vacation on limited grounds and reversible only on appeal. In addition, once the order of court is rendered, the Court's involvement ends. Supervised administration functions much as the procedures now existing in non-Code states. [1–201(49)]. Briefly, it is a single continuous proceeding requiring formal procedures and frequent court involvement.

The above three types of proceedings form the framework for the operation of the Code's procedure for the administration of decedents' estates. Significantly, all three proceedings are self-sufficient and interrelated depending upon the desires of the persons interested in the estate. In addition, except for supervised administration, each application to the Registrar or proceeding requiring court action is independent in nature. [3–107]. This attribute of independence permits interested persons to seek judicial review when necessary without affecting the other procedures selected. Naturally, when an informal proceeding and a formal proceeding are in direct conflict, the formal proceeding supersedes its corresponding informal procedure.

In greater detail, the system is composed of the following specific procedural devices: informal appointment, formal appointment, informal probate, formal testacy, formal closing, and supervised administration. Within the above structure, the Code also includes other significant procedural devices and concepts which increase flexibility and predictability. These include, for example, a comprehensive set of statutes of limitations, comprehensive provisions establishing title to property, affidavit and summary procedures for handling very small estates, universal succession, informal procedures, which are in the nature of informal proceedings, for the purposes of accomplishing various tasks such as inventory and appraisement, termination of appointment and closing, and efficient procedures for dealing with the multi-state estates. In addition, after notice and a hearing, the Court may issue formal orders on any range of matters limited only by the court's substantive jurisdiction and the desires of the petitioner. [3–107, Comment]. Except for supervised administration, all proceedings are independent of each other.

The theory behind the Code's proceedings and procedures is to provide interested persons with the option to formalize and seek court action only to the extent they desire. The Court is not involved unless those persons petition for its involvement. If they do so petition, the Court is given the power to deal with the issue or problem presented. Although control is primarily within the domain of those concerned about the decedent's estate, the Code has meaningful provisions for protecting those who may be harmed by wrongful and devious activities of others. The Code was not conceived with any naive thoughts that all persons are honest and fair. An important point to emphasize, however, is that each interested person must exercise affirmative action to be fully protected. One's own self interest is considered a better guardian than is the Court.

Some of the factors that will be considered by interested persons when determining which procedures or devices to use are: (1) the value of the decedent's administrable estate; (2) the statute of limitations applicable; (3) the degree of trust, cooperation and agreement among the interested persons; (4) the testator's express testamentary wishes; (5) the complexities of the administration; (6) the degree of protection from liability needed by the successors or by the personal representative or both; and (7) proof of title to property requirements.

§ 14.02 Illustrative Techniques

An understanding of the Code's procedures and operation for decedents' estates can best be acquired by examining and applying the provisions to hypothetical problems. [See Averill, Administering Decedents' Estates]. The following five hypothetical problems demonstrate how many of the Code's numerous procedures deal with the opening and closing of both a testate and intestate estate, with protective devices available and with the contest of wills. Because two of the Code's outstanding features are its pervasive flexibility and multiplicity of techniques, it is not desirable to structure procedures unnecessarily. To do so would reincarnate much of the evil contained in non-Code probate systems. Consequently, the following suggested techniques should be viewed as mere guideposts and not as dogma.

A. ESTATE VALUED AT LESS THAN $5,000

Hypothetical: Decedent's estate subject to administration is valued at less than $5,000. Decedent is survived by a spouse or a sole heir or a sole devisee.

One obvious course of action for a sole successor is to take no official action under the Code. Presumably, if the successor personally pays off the decedent's creditors, the successor could pocket the remainder of the estate. In fact, if third persons hold possession or title to personal property of the decedent, thirty days after death the title or possession or both can be obtained by the sole successor on the force of a special affidavit so long as no administration has been applied for. [3–1201(a)]. With a similar affidavit, even titles to securities can be changed in this manner. [3–1201(b)]. It also makes no difference whether the decedent died intestate or testate. The effect of the affidavit, however, is merely to protect the third person, not the successor. [3–1202]. Without much additional effort the procedures suggested in the next hypothetical would also be available and may frequently be more desirable.

B.   ESTATE VALUED AT LESS THAN FAMILY PROTECTIONS AND EXPENSES

Hypothetical: Decedent's estate subject to administration after subtracting liens and encumbrances is valued at less than the total of the relevant family protections, reasonable funeral and administration expenses and reasonable medical and hospital expenses of the last illness. Decedent is survived by heirs who are entitled to the relevant family protections.

1. Intestacy

According to the hypothetical, if the appropriate heir or heirs survive the decedent by 120 hours, they are entitled to the whole estate. [See § 5.02]. The Code contains a variety of devices by which the surviving heirs can take the estate. Although, they could do nothing other than to take possession of the estate, it is not practical under this hypothetical if any question of title may be involved. If creditors are the only concern, doing nothing is feasible because after the passage of one year from the date of the decedent's death, unsecured creditors are barred under the limitation on creditor claims provision. [3–803(a)(1)]. There are better alternatives, however.

One alternative for the parties in interest would be to seek universal succession. This procedure permits decedent's heirs or testator's devisee to accept the estate assets without administration by assuming responsibility for discharging those obligations that normally would be discharged by a personal representative. [Art. III, Pt. 3, Succession Without Administration, Prefatory Note to 3–312 to –322]. Although an application to and a written statement of Universal Succession from the Registrar is required, no personal representative is appointed, no administration process is conducted, and no court proceedings are required. [3–313, 3–314]. Universal succession cannot be approved by the Registrar until five days from the decedent's death has passed. [3–315]. Once approved, successors must take upon themselves the responsibility of paying the family protections, reasonable funeral and administration expenses and the reasonable medical and hospital expenses of the last illness. [3–316]. In addition, they may prove title to those assets if requested by purchasers or transfer agents. If our hypothetical small estate is solvent, the universal succession alternative is very appropriate and desirable. If the amount of creditor claims and thus the solvency of the estate is in question, universal succession is not going to satisfy the successors' needs because there will be a definite desire on their part to identify and terminate these creditor claims. Although creditor claims can be paid under universal succession, no procedure is provided for identifying them or for protecting the successors from possible insolvency of the estate. [3–317, Comment]. Consequently, under universal succession there would be no method available for the successors to take advantage of the family protections which protect against such insolvency.

In that case, a sensible alternative is for the heirs to have a person with priority file an application for an informal appointment of a personal representative. [3–301(a)(1), and (4)]. Approval of the application by the Registrar may be obtained five days after decedent's death. [3–307(a)]. Even if nothing else is done, this procedure gives the personal representative full status. [3–307(b)]. The personal representative may make transfers and bona fide purchasers are fully protected even if the transfer is later found to be invalid. [3–714]. In addition, the personal representative is empowered to settle and distribute the estate without court order or supervision. [3–704].

Normally, within thirty days of appointment the personal representative must give notice to all heirs of that appointment. [3–705]. If after inventory and appraisal, however, it appears that the value of the entire estate will not exceed the value of the family protection, costs of administration, reasonable funeral expenses and reasonable and necessary last illness medical and hospital expenses, the personal representative may immediately disburse and distribute the estate to the appropriate persons without giving the normally mandatory notice to creditors. [3–1203]. In this example, therefore, the personal representative could quickly pay the necessary bills, and distribute the remainder to the heirs in satisfaction of their family protection provisions. After the assets are distributed or disbursed, the personal representative can then close the estate by filing a verified statement which recites that to the best of the personal representative's knowledge the value of the entire estate did not exceed the family protection and the other deductible expenses, that disbursement and distribution is complete and that a copy of this statement was sent to all distributees and known unpaid creditors. [3–1204]. The consequences of this filing are that successors and unbarred creditors have only six months from the date of that filing to commence a proceeding against the personal representative and that the personal representative's appointment terminates one year after the filing if no proceedings are pending. [3–1204(b)–(c); see 3–1003(b), 3–1005].

If there is a possibility that additional assets may be discovered that would cause the estate to be valued above the amount permitted under the summary administrative procedure, the personal representative should definitely publish notice to creditors. [3–801]. Publication is advantageous because it reduces the relevant statute of limitations applicable to creditors from one year after death to the later of sixty days after actual notice to known creditors or four months from the date of first publication. [3–803(a)(2)]. Furthermore, publication will not delay administration because the family protection may still be paid before the nonclaim period runs. [2–404, 3–906(a)(2)]. Anytime six months after the date of the original appointment, the personal representative can and should informally close the estate by filing with the Court a certified statement reciting that notice to creditors has been published more than six months before the date of this statement, that the estate has been fully administered and settled (noting claims that remain unpaid), and that a copy of the full accounting of the administration has been sent to all distributees and creditors. [3–1003]. The consequences of this filing are exactly the same as under the summary procedure, that is, successors and unbarred creditors have only six months from the filing to commence a proceeding against the personal representative and the personal representative's appointment terminates one year after the filing if no proceeding is pending. [3–1005, 3–1003(b)].

2. *Testacy*

With the following three exceptions, the fact that decedent died testate rather than intestate would not change the above described procedure. First, if settlement of the estate will be by universal succession, a request for informal probate should be joined with the initiation application. [3–313]. Second, if an executor is nominated in the will, the executor has priority for appointment. [3–203]. Third, if administration is desired, the person who has priority to be personal representative should file an application simultaneously for both informal probate and informal appointment. [3–301(a)(1), (2)]. So long as superseding proceedings are not instituted within the later of three years from death or one year from the date of informal probate, devisees under the will are provided proof of title. [3–108, 3–301(a)(1)(vi), 3–314(a)(5)]. Informally probating the will, therefore, will protect devisees' titles and rights if additional property is discovered.

———

Although the suggested procedures employed for this hypothetical may be all classified as informal or summary procedures, under the circumstances presented, they should be sufficient for efficient administration. The more formal procedures available would seem best used only when necessary. Nonessential use of formal procedures impairs much of the flexibility, efficiency and other benefits of the Code.

C.   ESTATES VALUED IN EXCESS OF FAMILY PROTECTIONS AND EXPENSES

Hypothetical: Decedent's estate is valued above the total of the relevant family protections, if any, reasonable funeral and administration expenses and medical and hospital expenses of the last illness. Presume there is harmony among the appropriate successors, and there is no disagreement about distribution and administration.

One of the outstanding features of the Code is that except for the summary procedures previously discussed for the very small estates, the Code's efficient and flexible procedures are as applicable to the very large, e.g., $1,000,000 plus, estate as it is to the moderate, e.g., $50,000 or less, estate.

1.   Intestacy

Because universal succession is not limited by the value of the estate, it is available to the successors in this hypothetical as well as in the previous hypothetical. Even very large estates may be able to use this technique. As before, the heirs or devisee must be harmonious and serious problems with creditors or claims should not be present. The application to the Registrar would be the same. [3–313]. Once approved, there would be no further proceedings before the court unless desired by the successors or other interested persons.

There may be one or more difficult creditor or tax issues involved, however. The successors may want a conclusive determination of claims and settlement. Therefore, some kind of administration will be required. The Code includes the necessary procedures to satisfy this desire without unduly involving the court.

As with the previous hypothetical, to begin the administration of the estate, the first course of action will be to select the personal representative. Presuming harmony among the heirs, the appropriate or agreed upon person should file an application for informal appointment. [3–301(a)(1), and (4)]. Appointment by the Registrar is probably all that is necessary for administration of the estate. [See 3–307(a)]. Upon approval of appointment by the Registrar, acceptance by the personal representative and issuance of letters, the personal representative possesses full powers to administer the estate without further court approval. [3–307(b)].

Although the personal representative may use only the informal closing procedure, as discussed in the subsection B hypothetical, a more comprehensive alternative, formal closing, would probably be desired. [3–1001(a)]. This procedure is particularly advantageous when there is more than one heir involved. It is desirable both for the protection of the personal representative and for settling various potential issues between the other interested persons. Procedurally, a petition for formal closing may be made at any time after presentation of claims against the estate are barred. After notice to all interested persons is given and a hearing is held, the Court is authorized to issue orders that determine heirship, approve settlement and distribution and discharge the personal representative from further claims by interested persons. Discharge of the personal representative under this procedure would be complete.

Under the procedures described above, the question of whether decedent died leaving a valid will was not considered, therefore such a will could be probated within the three years from death limitation. [3–108]. In order to preclude this, or at least to finally determine the issue, the Code again includes the necessary provisions. Without disturbing the informal characteristics of the administration, the heirs could file a petition for formal testacy seeking a judicial determination of whether the decedent left a will and of decedent's heirs. [3–401, 3–402(b)]. This petition can be made in conjunction with a request for informal appointment, [3–402(a)], or at any other time during administration. Naturally, as is characteristic of formal proceedings, prior notice of the hearing to interested persons is required. [3–403]. The order by the Court that there is no will and the determination of heirship is determinative and binding except as reversed on appeal or as modified or vacated by order of the Court. [3–412, 3–413]. The reasons for vacation are limited and are only available for a maximum of twelve months after the entry of the order.

One of the most imaginative possibilities under the Code for dealing with the additional question of a will is the ability to combine a petition for formal settlement and closing with a petition for formal testacy. [3–1001(a)]. Under this procedure the estate would be informally administered by a full-powered personal representative without the necessity of court proceedings. When the estate is ready for closing, the interested parties, in essentially one proceeding, can have the protection of a court order on the issues of whether there was a valid will, heirship, distribution, settlement, and discharge of the personal representative for the conduct of the administration. Although the requirements for both formal closing and formal testacy proceedings must be followed, the advantages of combining these procedures with informal administration are obvious. Actually from both practical and interpretive standpoints, all formal closing proceedings instituted according to Section 3–1001 should include a determination of testacy so long as that issue has not previously been adjudicated and the limitation period for instituting formal testacy proceedings has not run.

2. *Testacy*

The most obvious additional procedure that must be used if decedent dies testate is that the will must be probated. With only two exceptions, which are not applicable at this point to this situation, the Code provides that title to property passing by will cannot be proved unless the will is declared valid by informal or formal probate. [3–102]. If universal succession is sought, the application must include the information necessary and a request for informal probate of the will. [3–313]. This would be the only additional requirement under this procedure. Similarly, if administration is desired, the named executor or other person with priority should file an application simultaneously for both informal probate and informal appointment. [3–301(a), 3–307]. Three beneficial consequences derive from approval of such an application. Although subject to formal proceedings within the later of three years from death or one year from the date of informal probate, informal probate provides the devisees with proof of title so long as the contingency of a formal probate does not occur. [3–108, 3–302]. In addition, as with intestacy, informal appointment creates a personal representative who upon appointment, acceptance and issuance of letters can administer the estate and can give marketable title to property sold during the administration of the estate. [3–701, 3–711, 3–714]. Furthermore, distributions by the personal representative to persons who the personal representative believes are entitled thereto enable the distributees to give good marketable title to purchasers even though the distributions subsequently prove to be erroneous. [3–910]. Otherwise, the procedures used for opening and closing of the estate would remain the same as those used in intestacy. Combining formal testacy with formal closing is again a very useful procedure to follow. [3–1001(a)].

D.   PROTECTIVE DEVICES

Hypothetical: Decedent died leaving a substantial estate. The successors are not harmonious and show mutual distrust of each other. Suspicions of dishonesty, fraud and other wrongdoings are rampant.

The Code possesses a large number of protective devices. Although interested persons have full discretion to select which protective device to use, they should be advised to use only those that are necessary to ensure the protection desired. The following discussion provides a brief outline of the most significant protective devices.

1. Demand for Notice

Any person who has a financial or property interest in the decedent's estate may file a written demand for notice with the Court anytime after death. [3–204]. This affirmative procedure provides the demandant with the protection of receiving notice of all other filings or orders concerned with the estate, including applications for universal succession, informal probate, or informal appointment, or combination thereof. Under the circumstances presented in this hypothetical, filing a demand for notice should be done as standard operating procedure by those interested in the estate.

2. Formal Proceedings

An interested person can terminate or foreclose universal succession or stay or suspend an informal appointment by petitioning for a formal appointment [3–414], and heirs or devisees under another will can force an informal probate into a formal testacy proceeding. [3–401.] In addition, one year from the date of appointment, and after the time limitation on presenting claims arising before death has expired, interested persons can petition for formal closing, which would include distribution. [3–1001(a), 3–1002]. Significantly, none of the above mentioned formal proceedings will entitle the Court to exercise a continuing supervisory position over the estate and its administration; however, any interested person may petition for supervised administration.

3. Supervised Administration

Supervised administration is a single continuous proceeding before the Court, concerned with the settling of one's estate. [3–501]. Its protective features include formal testacy, formal appointment and formal closing proceedings [3–502, 3–505]; distributions cannot be made without court order [3–504]; and the formal notice requirements must be fulfilled. [See 3–403, 3–414, 3–1001]. It also stays informal applications that are pending and restricts an earlier appointed personal representative from making distributions. [3–503]. Except for the restriction that distributions cannot be made without court order, the supervised personal representative has the same authority or powers as other personal representatives under the Code. [3–504]. Interested persons may request, however, that other restrictions be endorsed on the letters, and when such restrictions are endorsed on these letters, they bind third parties dealing with the personal representative to any violation of the restriction by the latter. The protections afforded by endorsements on the personal representative's letters may represent the principal reason persons would elect to require a supervised administration because all of its other benefits may be employed as needed through individual formal proceedings.

The basic consequence of petitioning for supervised administration is to cause the estate to pass through a procedure similar to that existing in most non-Code states presently. Some attorneys who are accustomed to such a cumbersome procedure may advise its use during the early years after the Code's adoption. As they become more accustomed to the other procedures available under the Code, it is clear that the use of supervised administration will diminish rapidly. In fact, the courts should precipitate such a change in approach by exercising their discretion to refuse such petitions for supervised administration. [3–502].

4. *Other Protective Devices*

Less drastic protective devices provided to interested persons against acts of the personal representative include a petition for an order restraining actions that unreasonably jeopardize the applicant's interests. [3–607]. An illustration of a useful purpose for such an order is one prohibiting the personal representative from selling a particular asset in the estate. Another recourse, if circumstances warrant, is a petition for removal for cause. [3–611]. Causes range from mismanagement and breach of duty to incapacity and the best interest of the estate.

A subtle protective device in the Code is the requirement that, before certain actions may be taken or approved, 120 hours must have elapsed since the decedent's death. This is applicable to acceptance of informal probate, appointment of a personal representative under informal appointment, and the granting of an application for universal succession. [3–302, 3–307(a), 3–315]. This five-day rule permits the notice of death to permeate the relevant communities and thus give most interested persons informal notice that actions related to the death may take place.

5. *Bond*

Under the Code, bond is not required unless a special administrator is appointed, the will requires it, or an interested person petitions for it. [3–603]. Persons who have and retain an interest or a claim valued in excess of 1,000 dollars may file with the Registrar a demand that the personal representative give a bond. [3–605]. The personal representative must then give bond or other suitable security in an amount specified by the Court or, if not specified, in an amount not less than the estimated value of the principal of the estate plus one year's income. [3–604]. This estimate must also be filed with the Registrar and must be under oath. Until the ordered bond is filed, the personal representative must refrain from administering the estate except to preserve it. [3–605].

6. *Improper Distribution*

Interested persons are well protected from improper distribution under an informal closing. Not only must the personal representative file a verified statement indicating that a closing statement and a full account have been sent to all distributees, the personal representative also remains liable for the administration for six months after the filing. [3–1003]. In addition, the distributees remain liable for one year after distribution or three years after death, whichever is later, to return the improperly distributed property and income or its date of distribution value whichever is less. [3–1004; see 3–104].

7. Fraud and Perjury

The Code also includes broad protections against fraud, perjury and other wrongdoing. The limitation periods generally applicable to probate and administration do not apply when fraud has been involved. [1–106]. Instead, the perpetrator is liable for that fraud up to two years after its discovery. Except for bona fide purchasers, even innocent persons who have benefitted by the fraud are liable under the same limitation; however, the period of liability for these persons cannot exceed five years from the time of the commission of the fraud. This provision not only applies to acts by the personal representative but also to anyone else who participates in the administration of an estate.

The penalties of perjury are applicable to any deliberate falsification of any document filed with the Court. [1–310]. The mere filing of an application, petition or demand for notice is deemed to include a verification of its veracity. Consequently, the perjury prosecution threat has broad application.

8. Continuing Jurisdiction over Personal Representatives and Applicants

Once the personal representative accepts appointment, the personal representative submits to the jurisdiction of the Court and remains subject to its jurisdiction until discharged, provided notice of any subsequent proceeding is adequately given. [3–602]. This provision gives interested persons protection from a personal representative who is bent upon being difficult to find or who attempts to leave the state.

In addition, the applicant of any application for informal probate or informal appointment submits personally to the continuing jurisdiction of the Court in any subsequent proceeding brought because of fraud or perjury related to the application. [3–301(b)]. This provision gives interested persons a long arm type basis of jurisdiction over the person who fraudulently or perjuriously files an informal application. Finally, the issuance of the statement of universal succession subjects the universal successors to the personal jurisdiction of the Court in any proceeding instituted relating to the estate or to any liability assumed by the successors. [3–318(a)].

E.   WILL CONTESTS

Hypothetical: Decedent's will disinherits a natural child, X, and devises the entire estate equally to two other natural children, Y and Z. X is very displeased and will try to break the will. P Bank and Trust Co. is nominated as executor under the will.

As indicated, under the Code any interested person may file a formal testacy petition to determine whether a decedent left a valid will. [3–401]. This petition must be filed within three years from death or within twelve months of an earlier informal probate, whichever is later. [3–108].

Many of the Code's provisions concerned with
will contests are similar to the non-Code law in
most states. Jury trials may be demanded by any
party to the formal testacy proceeding. [1–306].
The burdens of proving lack of testamentary capacity, undue influence, fraud and duress are on the
contestants. [3–407]. For ordinary wills, the Code
provides that at least one subscribing witness must
testify, if competent and within the state, and that
due execution may also be proved by other evidence. [3–406(a)]. The Code has special presumptions applicable to self-proved wills. [2–504, 3–
406(b)].

The primary differences between non-Code law
and the Code appear in the mechanics of the procedure itself. First, formal testacy proceedings may
be initiated by heirs as well as by executors and
devisees under a will. [3–401]. In other words,
even though no will has been probated or offered
for probate, this proceeding may determine that
the decedent died intestate. Second, subject to
appeal [1–304, 3–414] and to limited reasons for
vacation and modification [3–412(1)–(2)], the final
order in a formal testacy proceeding is immediately conclusive as to all persons and all issues concerning decedent's testacy and heirs that were or
might have been considered. [3–412]. Third, although a subsequently discovered will may give
cause for vacating a formal testacy order [3–
412(1)], no such will may affect the order after
twelve months from its entry. [3–412(3)(iii)]. It
may be a much shorter time. [3–412(3)(i)–(ii)].
Significantly, this provision is in direct conflict
with the judicial decisions that the probate of a

later discovered will is not a contest of a previously probated will and is not affected by expiration of the contest limitation period.

The strategies to follow when the existence or validity of a will is involved depend upon the desires of the interested persons. It would appear that administration and appointment of a personal representative should be initiated immediately. The devisees, for example, can begin by informally probating the will and informally appointing the named executor who has priority for appointment as personal representative. If a formal probate proceeding is not instituted, the will becomes conclusive three years from death. [3–108].

The devisees, however, may not wish to wait this long before their rights as devisees are secure. Another option would be to combine informal probate and informal appointment, followed immediately by a formal probate proceeding. This approach would start the administration processes and would quickly adjudicate the validity of the will thereby shortening the limitation period within which such issues can be litigated. If the question of validity is a serious problem, the formal probate proceeding litigates this issue at an early time thereby increasing the potential for early distribution.

Combining informal appointment and informal probate at the beginning, and then following it by petitioning for formal settlement at the time of petitioning for formal proceedings terminating administration is also a viable approach. This enables the interested parties to adjudicate all of the issues raised by probate and administration in one proceeding. [3–1001]. The principal questions of testacy, heirship, construction, accounting, settlement, and distribution can all be determined in this proceeding. The final order or orders rendered would fully protect the persons involved.

Significantly, the disinherited heir does not have to wait for the will beneficiaries to act. If formal proceedings are not instituted by the devisees, this interested person can force the issue either by immediately initiating formal appointment and formal probate proceedings or by bringing them anytime within the limitation period.

Another procedure available is to enter into a written compromise agreement if agreement can be reached between the opposing persons. [3–1101]. If approved by the court in formal proceedings, it is binding upon all parties including those (1) who signed it, (2) who are unascertained or unlocated, and (3) who are otherwise represented by parties and fiduciaries involved in the estate. [3–1102].

CHAPTER 15

GENERAL PROVISIONS ON PROBATE OF WILLS AND ADMINISTRATION

§ 15.01 Devolution of Decedents' Estates and the Necessity of Probate and Administration

The Code provides that a decedent's estate, both real and personal property, devolves to decedent's heirs if intestate or to decedent's devisees if testate subject to the family protections, to the rights of creditors, to the elective share of the surviving spouse, and to administration of the estate. [3–101, 3–901]. The identification of the particular person to whom the property devolves is subject to alterations, however, because of lapse, disclaimer, or any other circumstance affecting devolution of the estate involved, depending upon whether it is a testate or an intestate estate. In addition, the scope of testation and the rights of creditors, devisees or heirs to a decedent's estate are subject to the Code's restrictions and limitations that are designed to facilitate prompt settlement of the estate. The Code includes an alternative section for community property estates that substantially applies the same rule to the decedent's half of community property and his separate property. [3–101A].

301

The rule providing that upon death a decedent's title devolves to heirs or devisees, requires further explanation and qualification. First, an heir or devisee will be treated as having predeceased the decedent if that person does not survive the decedent by 120 hours. [2–104, 2–601]. Second, title to property passing by will cannot be proved unless the will is declared valid by informal or formal probate proceedings. [3–102]. Third, except for the administration of ancillary estates, a personal representative must be appointed either formally or informally, accept appointment and be issued letters of that appointment in order to acquire the powers and to undertake the duties and liabilities of the fiduciary office. [3–103]. Fourth, the decedent's unsecured creditors may enforce their claims only after a personal representative is appointed. [3–104]. Even secured creditors are under the same rule as to any deficiency that they may seek above their security interest. After a personal representative has been appointed and has distributed the estate, however, the decedent's creditors may have rights against the distributees and the personal representative individually. [See 3–1004, 3–1005].

The Code contains an exception regarding a devisee's title to property designed to eliminate the requirement that the will be declared valid in small estates and to provide a remedy in certain hardship cases. If proceedings are instituted under the affidavit procedure of Section 3–1201, title to property may be proved by the affidavit and therefore, probate of the will is not required. This exception, of course, applies only to the very small,

$5,000 or less, estates. [See § 16.01]. The clearly preferred and approved procedure to follow under the Code is to informally or formally probate a will notwithstanding that administration of the estate may or may not be sought. [See 3–107].

§ 15.02   Time Limitations on Probate and Administration

One of the key provisions of the Code concerns its time limitations on probate, testacy, and appointment of personal representatives. [3–108]. With five exceptions, this provision provides that no informal or formal proceeding may be commenced beyond three years after the decedent's death. The first exception concerns the request for the probate of a will in the Code state where the will has previously been probated in the decedent's domicile. Under such circumstances the foreign will may be probated.

The next two exceptions concern the missing person. Under the second exception, if failure to prove the fact of decedent's death was the cause of a previous dismissal of a proceeding, appropriate proceedings for probate, appointment, or testacy may be maintained at any time thereafter so long as it is proved that decedent's death occurred before the date of the previous proceeding and that petitioner has not unduly delayed initiation of the new proceeding. The third exception provides that for all other persons whose death cannot be substantiated, a proceeding may be instituted within a three year period after the missing person's conservator is able to establish the death of the missing person. Under the second and third exceptions,

the date of the commencement of the proper proceeding must be considered as the date of the
decedent's death for purposes of other limitations
under the Code that refer to the decedent's date of
death.

The fourth and fifth exceptions were added by
the 1993 Technical Amendments. The fourth exception permits interested persons to commence
informal appointment or formal testacy or appointment proceedings if no proceedings concerning succession or estate administration has occurred within the three year period after decedent's death.
Any appointed personal representative under this
exception is limited to possession of only the property necessary to confirm title in successors and
only expenses of administration may be present
against the estate.

The fifth exception permits formal testacy proceeding to commence after three years from decedent's death to establish an instrument necessary
to control ownership of property. It is not limited
to the situation where the testator's estate was not
administered during the three year period. It does
not provide for appointment of a personal representative, however. An example of its use include
the exercise of a power of appointment in testator's
unprobated will that is not effective until another
person's life ends. It may be helpful anytime title
that is derived from an unprobated will needs to
proved.

It is important to emphasize that these limitations apply only to the Code's prescribed proceedings dealing with probate, testacy, and appoint-

ment. They specifically do not apply to proceedings to construe wills or to determine heirs of an intestate. [3–108]. In addition, inferentially they do not apply to any other proceeding that concerns controversies dealing with an estate currently being administered or with a will that has been properly probated.

The effect of the Code's limitation periods is very important. First, unsecured creditor claims are barred after a maximum of one year after death. [3–803(a)(1)]. Second, when a decedent dies testate and the will is informally probated, if there are no formal testacy proceedings instituted within the later of three years of death or one year after the date of informal probate, devisees under the probated will are provided conclusive proof of their title regardless whether there is administration of the estate. Their titles are not only conclusive as against decedent's heirs, but also as against decedent's devisees under unprobated wills.

§ 15.03 Jurisdiction, Venue and Related Matters for Probate and Administration

A. JURISDICTION OVER THE SUBJECT MATTER

The subject matter jurisdiction of probate courts throughout this country is varied, complicated, and often perplexing. Generally, states confer probate jurisdiction on one of four types of courts: (1) on their chancery court; (2) on a separate probate court that has an equal status with courts of general jurisdiction; (3) on a probate court that definitely is inferior to the court of general jurisdiction; and, (4) on the court of general jurisdiction. [Model Probate Code, 420]. Inevitably, there are variations between those even in the same general category.

In light of this state of confusion, the Code is extremely flexible and is designed to work within the framework of any state in which it is adopted. [See 3–105, 3–106, § 3.01]. Where the state separates probate jurisdiction from the jurisdiction of its other courts, the Code gives the probate court exclusive jurisdiction over formal proceedings to determine how the decedents' estates over which it has territorial jurisdiction are to be administered, expended and distributed and concurrent jurisdiction over any actions or proceedings concerning succession or to which estates are made parties through their personal representatives. [3–105]. If the state does not divide subject matter jurisdiction between its probate courts and other courts, the distinction between exclusive and concurrent jurisdiction is inappropriate. [3–106, Comment]. In such a state, the Court is merely given plenary jurisdiction over all formal proceedings concerned with the administration and distribution of decedents' estates.

B.   JURISDICTION OVER THE PERSON AND NOTICE

When notice is required by the Code or by rule of court, jurisdiction over the person in proceedings within the exclusive jurisdiction of the Court may be obtained by giving notice to interested persons in conformity with Section 1–401. [3–106; see § 4.01]. In addition, those properly notified are bound by the proceedings even though not all interested persons were appropriately notified. Methods of notice and service for obtaining jurisdiction over the person in proceedings within the concurrent jurisdiction of the Court may be governed by the State's general standard of civil practice and not by Section 1–401. [1 UPC Code Practice Manual 31–32]. Whether the general standards of civil practice for notice and jurisdiction or those established in Section 1–401 are applicable to a proceeding under the concurrent jurisdiction of the Court will apparently depend upon whether the proceeding is in personam, quasi in rem, or in rem. The latter two types of jurisdiction would probably be satisfied by Section 1–401. The former type might require the notice and service procedures for ordinary civil cases.

In special circumstances, the Code provides a continuing type of jurisdiction over certain persons. First, once appointment is accepted, the personal representative submits personally to the jurisdiction of the Court and remains subject to its jurisdiction until discharged. [3–602; see 3–1003, Comment]. The only special requirement to sustain this jurisdiction is that adequate notice of any subsequent proceedings must be given to the personal representative. Adequate notice under this provision means that notice of each proceeding must either be delivered to the personal representative or mailed to the personal representative by ordinary first class mail both to the official address listed with the Court and to any other address known to the petitioner.

Second, the applicant of any verified application for informal probate or informal appointment also submits personally to the continuing jurisdiction of the Court in any subsequent proceeding brought because of fraud or perjury related to the application. [3–301(b)]. Presumably, the applicant must also be given adequate notice of any subsequent proceeding. This provision coincides with the Code's provisions concerned with frauds perpetrated in connection with proceedings or filings made under this Code [3–301, Comment; 1–106; see § 2.02(A)], and with its reference to penalties for perjury for deliberate falsification of filings. [1–310; see § 2.02(B)].

Third, the issuance of the statement of universal succession also subjects the universal successors to the personal jurisdiction of the Court in any proceeding instituted relating to the estate or to any liability assumed by the successors. [3–318(a)]. Notice of the proceeding, of course, must be given to the successor.

C.   VENUE

Venue is based upon certain factual contacts existing within the relevant judicial subdivision. The Code lists only two contacts for satisfying venue requirements for informal and formal probate and for administration proceedings. The first and the preferred venue is, of course, the county of the decedent's domicile. [3–201(a)(1)]. Because venue based upon the decedent's domicile has great significance under the Code [see, e.g., 3–203(g), 3–408, 4–201, 4–204], the Code establishes a rule of priority for determining conflicting claims of domicile. This priority is placed in the first court in which the formal proceeding was commenced. [3–202; Truman v. Estate of Collins (1989)]. This court has the exclusive right to determine domicile, and its determination must be accepted in the other courts of the Code state and in the courts of other Code states. Significantly, a Code court without this priority is required to stay or dismiss actions that are duplicative of actions previously filed. These principles should result in beneficially reducing the number of duplicative litigations over domicile. [3–202, Comment].

When the decedent is not domiciled within the state, the second appropriate venue is in any county where the decedent left property. [3–201(a)(2)]. Because the proper location for intangibles is sometimes difficult to determine, the Code explicitly includes rules for this determination. [3–201(d)]. For debts other than those evidenced by investment or commercial paper or other instruments of title, the location of such an asset is where the debtor resides or if not an individual, where the debtor has its principal office. The situs of the instrument sets the location for commercial paper, investment paper and other instruments. Finally, interests in trust property are located wherever the trustee may be sued.

D.   INDEPENDENT PROCEEDINGS
AND JOINDER

As previously discussed, with the exception of supervised administration, proceedings either before the Court or the Registrar are independent of each other in the same estate. [3–107]. On the other hand, if desirable and if undue delay will not occur, informal applications and formal petitions may combine various requests for relief in a single proceeding. Joining claims for relief, however, is optional and unless specifically required by proceedings described in the Code, no petition is defective merely because it does not cover all matters that could have been contained in a final order. At the election of the interested persons, testacy, and appointment proceedings may be combined into one proceeding. For the purpose of emphasizing the nonsupervisory status of the Court, the Code explicitly provides that a formal proceeding for appointment of a personal representative concludes when the Court issues its order either making or declining the appointment.

It might be helpful to emphasize again at this point that, whereas under non-Code law the procedures for probate and for administration are inseparable, the Code explicitly separates them. Probate, be it informal or formal, is solely concerned with the existence or nonexistence of a will. Administration is concerned with the personal representative, that representative's powers, duties and liabilities to creditors and successors and to those things between each other. Consequently, it may be common to find estates where only probate proceedings or where only administration proceedings are instituted. [See Art. III, General Comment].

The above rules need further clarification in one particular regard. Although each proceeding is independent, there necessarily is an interrelationship between informal proceedings and their corresponding formal proceeding. Consequently, informal probate either cannot be instituted or is superseded by formal testacy proceedings in the same state. [3–401]. The same interrelationship exists between informal appointment of a personal representative and its counterpart a formal appointment proceeding [3–414], and between a proceeding in the nature of informal proceedings for closing an estate and its counterpart a formal closing proceeding. [3–1001, 3–1002]. Although universal succession may be combined with informal probate if there is a will, it is foreclosed or terminated if either informal or formal appointment proceedings are filed. [3–314(b)]. Finally, supervised administration precludes any of the above informal proceedings because it generally requires formal appointment, formal probate, formal proceedings for interim distributions, and a formal closing proceeding.

E. DEMAND FOR NOTICE

Any person who has a financial or property interest in the decedent's estate, including creditors and successors, may file a demand for notice with the Court any time after death. [3–204]. Such an affirmative action provides the demandant with the protection of receiving notice of other filings or orders concerning the estate, including applications for universal succession, informal probate, or informal appointment or any combination thereof. Upon the termination of the demandant's interest in the estate, the requirement of notice under this provision ceases. In addition, if circumstances change, the demandant may waive the requirement in writing. Although failure to provide the necessary notice does not affect the validity of an order of Court or accepted filing, the person failing to provide the necessary notice may be liable to the demandant for any damages caused by the failure to notify.

Upon receipt of such a demand, the clerk is to mail a copy of it to any personal representative who has been appointed in the estate. In addition, petitioner must give notice to the demandant or the designated attorney according to the notice procedure prescribed in Section 1–401. [See § 4.01].

F. DECEDENT'S CAUSES OF ACTION

The death of a person is a disrupting event to the successors of the estate. Consequently, delay commonly occurs between the time of death and the time when the interested persons have gathered sufficient facts and have instituted necessary procedures to settle the estate. With these disruption and delay factors in mind, the Code extends any statute of limitations running against a claim belonging to the decedent before death for four months after the date of death. [3–109]. This extension applies, however, only if the statute of limitations ordinarily running against the cause of action was not barred on the date of death. Furthermore, the extension is from the date of death and not from the date of the expiration of the ordinary statute of limitations. [Compare 3–802].

CHAPTER 16

PROCEDURES FOR
SUCCESSION WITHOUT
ADMINISTRATION

§ 16.01 The Passive and Affidavit Procedures for Small Estates

The probate laws of every state include special procedures that simplify the administration processes for small estates. [See Scoles, Succession Without Administration, at 379 & n. 32]. Typically, the use of these procedures is dependent on the net value of the estate, e.g., $5,000, and the nature of the assets, e.g., no real property in estate. Although the Code's ordinary procedures for settling an estate are efficient and uncomplicated without the inclusion of overlapping and potentially conflicting small estate procedures, for purposes of maximum flexibility the Code includes one implied or inherent procedure and two special procedures for dealing with the small estate. [Art. III, Pt. 12, General Comment].

As previously explained, title to property passes to the heirs or devisee, subject only to administration. [§ 15.01]. If an estate consists solely of cash or other tangible personal property, and if the successors pay off all creditors against the estate, it may be inferred that successors may settle the estate without any administration at all. Because title passes automatically and administration is not a necessity, the appropriate successors may simply divide the property according to their desires. [3–102, 3–901]. Small, solvent, and liquid estates, which require no administration, are very common. [See § 16.03].

When decedent's tangible personal property or instruments evidencing a debt, obligation, stock or chose in action are either owed or possessed by a third person, the nonadministration method for settlement is not satisfactory because the third person may refuse to deliver or to pay. When the net value of the decedent's entire probate estate does not exceed $5,000, however, the Code provides that if the sole successor to these assets presents an affidavit to the debtor or possessor, the latter must make payment of the indebtedness or deliver the tangible personal property or other instrument of property to the successor. [3–1201]. The only requirement is that the affidavit must state that: (1) the property does not exceed the prescribed monetary amount; (2) thirty days have elapsed since the death of the decedent; (3) no application or petition for appointment is pending or has been granted in any jurisdiction; and (4) the successor claiming the property is entitled to payment or delivery of it. [3–1201(a)]. With a similar affidavit delivered to security transfer agents, title to securities can also be changed to the successor or successors. [3–1201(b)]. Significantly, the availability and effectiveness of this affidavit procedure does not depend upon the decedent dying domiciled in the Code state where the affidavit is presented. [3–1202, Comment]. Furthermore, a proceeding may be brought by the rightful affiant to force a debtor to pay, possessor to deliver, or the transfer agent to transfer the property. [3–1202].

The effect of the affidavit is to discharge and release the person paying the debt or delivering the property, as if, and to the same extent, the person had dealt with the decedent's personal representative. [3–1202]. This person is further protected by not being required to see to the application of the personal property or to inquire into the truth of the content of the affidavit. The successor who receives payment, delivery or title is, of course, answerable and accountable to any personal representative of the decedent's estate or to any other person having a superior right.

The political popularity of this type of procedure has not waned even in Code states. The trend has been to increase the threshold amount. For example, Arizona's comparable provision sets the amount at $30,000 [Ariz.Rev.Stat. § 14–3971], and New Mexico's provision is at $20,000. [N.M.Stat. Ann.1978, § 45–3–1201].

§ 16.02 The Summary Procedure for Small Estates

Another alternative course of action deals with an estate which, after subtracting liens and encumbrances, is valued at less than the total of the relevant family protections, reasonable funeral and administration expenses and reasonable and necessary medical and hospital expenses of the last illness. If the decedent is survived by persons who are entitled to the relevant family protections, the

Code includes a summary administration procedure that substantially shortens the administration process. [3–1203, 3–1204].

Under this procedure, interested persons would begin the administration process in the ordinary manner. This would include having the person with priority file an application for informal appointment of a personal representative. [See § 20.-02]. Informal appointment gives the personal representative full status. [See 3–307(b)]. If after inventory and appraisal it appears that the value of the entire estate less liens and encumbrances will not exceed the value of the family protections, costs of administration, reasonable funeral expenses, and the last illness' medical and hospital expenses, the personal representative may immediately disburse and distribute the estate to the appropriate persons without giving the normally mandatory notice to creditors. [3–1203]. Consequently, the personal representative may quickly pay the necessary bills and distribute the remainder to the appropriate persons in satisfaction of their family protection provisions. After the assets are distributed or disbursed, the personal representative can then close the estate by filing a sworn statement that to the best of the representative's knowledge the value of the entire estate did not exceed the family protections and the other deductible expenses, that the disbursement and distribution is complete and that a copy of this statement was sent to all distributees and known unpaid creditors. [3–1204(a)]. The consequences of this filing are: (1) successors and unbarred creditors have only six months from the date of that filing to assert a claim [3–1204(c), 3–1005]; and (2) the appointment terminates one year after the filing if no claims are pending.   [3–1204(b)].

With the following two exceptions, the fact that the decedent died testate rather than intestate, would not change the above described procedure. First, the person nominated in the will as executor has priority for appointment. [See § 20.02]. Second, the person who has priority to be personal representative should simultaneously file an application for informal probate and informal appointment. [3–301]. So long as formal proceedings are not instituted within three years of death or one year of informal probate, devises under the will are provided proof of title. [3–108, 3–302]. Informally probating the will, therefore, protects the devisees' titles and rights if additional property is discovered.

§ 16.03   Universal Succession

A.   PURPOSE AND EFFECT OF UNIVERSAL SUCCESSION

Succession without administration, or Universal Succession as it is titled in the Code was added to the Code in 1982 with the addition of eleven sections to Article III, Part 3. [3–312 to –322]. Subsequently, these sections were made part of the freestanding Uniform Succession Without Administration Act promulgated in 1983. Some commentators complained that the Code's original version did not go far enough to provide flexibility to successors. [See, e.g., Martin, Model of Estate Settlement]. They urged the drafters of the Code to incorporate provisions that permit successors of a decedent's estate to succeed to the properties without the formalities of an administrative process. Although the Code was extremely flexible and offered convenient and efficient administration processes, a process without administration was only accorded in the very small estates.

Universal succession provides the successors with the opportunity to settle the estate without proceeding through any administrative process. [See Scoles, Succession Without Administration, at 388–92]. By following the requirements of these provisions, successors can pay creditor claims, distribute assets to the proper successors, and prove title to those assets upon subsequent transfer. Except for the requirement of an application to the Registrar, an informal probate if a will is involved, and a written statement of universal succession from the Registrar, no additional proceeding before the court is required. There is no requirement to notify creditors and, thus, there is no special nonclaim limitation. [See § 22.02]. Significantly, there is no monetary limitation on the availability of this procedure.

Although large and solvent estates may be propelled into some form of administrative processes because of tax complexities, estates in which (1) tax issues are not significant, (2) creditors do not exist or whose claims can be settled without difficulty, (3) assets and obligations owing the estate can be collected without administration processes, and (4) successors are easily identifiable and cooperative, are appropriate candidates for use of this extremely efficient and easy method of settling estates. Good candidates for this technique are also estates that pass all their assets to a surviving spouse and in which the surviving spouse basically assumes all debts and is able to collect all obligations owing the decedent. This situation covers a large number of potential estates. Another common example is the surviving parent who dies leaving little property except personal effects, contractual obligations that pass upon death, and other assets in some form of joint ownership or living trust. These estates could be easily handled through universal succession.

Under universal succession, the heirs of an intestate or the residuary devisee under a will are permitted at their option to become universal successors to the decedent's estate if they agree to assume personal liability for the decedent's taxes, debts and claims against the decedent or the estate and if they agree to make proper distributions due other heirs, devisee and other persons entitled to the property of the decedent. [3–312]. In order to sustain universal succession, all heirs or residuary devisees must join in the application. [3–312, Comment]. Consequently, this process is essentially a consent procedure available when family members are in agreement. Minors and incapacitated, protected, or unascertained persons cannot be universal successors under these provisions. The Code makes the competent heirs and residuary devisees who seek universal succession responsible to the incompetent heirs and legatees. Exclusion of incapacitated and unascertained persons is necessary in order to permit the competent successors to deal with the property of the decedent. [3–312, Comment]. Incompetents and unascertained persons may protect themselves by requesting bond or by forcing the estate into administration.

B. CONTENTS OF APPLICATION FOR UNIVERSAL SUCCESSION

An application for universal succession must conform to the Code's specific requirements. [3–313]. This application must be directed to the Registrar, signed by each applicant and verified to be accurate and complete to the best of the applicant's knowledge and belief. [3–313(a)]. In addition, it must contain the following statements:

(1) (a) If filed by the heirs of an intestate, the same information required for informal appointment under Section 3–301(a)(1) and (4)(i) and that the applicants constitute all the competent heirs;

(b) If filed by residuary devisees under a will, all statements required for informal appointment and informal probate under sections 3–301(a)(1) and (2) and that the applicants include all competent residuary devisees plus all heirs if the estate is partially intestate;

(2) Whether letters of administration are outstanding, whether a petition for appointment of a personal representative is pending in any court in the state, and whether the applicants waive their right to seek appointment as a personal representative of the decedent;

(3) The applicants accept responsibility for the estate and assume personal liability for the dece-

dent's and decedent's estate's taxes, debts, claims, and distributions due to appropriate successors; and,

(4) An optional requirement of describing in general terms the assets of the estate.

[3–313].

C. REGISTRAR'S RESPONSIBILITIES AND FINDINGS IN UNIVERSAL SUCCESSION

The Code grants very little discretion to the Registrar in regards to a universal succession application. The Registrar must grant the application if it finds the following matters satisfied:

(1) A complete application;

(2) All persons necessary have joined and properly verified the statement in the application;

(3) Venue is proper;

(4) Notice necessary under Section 3–204 has been given or waived;

(5) Time limitations for original probate or appointment proceedings have not expired;

(6) If informal probate is requested, the requirements admitting a will to probate have been satisfied; and,

(7) No applicant is a minor, an incapacitated, or a protected person.

[3–314(a)].

A Registrar cannot grant an application unless 120 hours or five days have lapsed since the decedent's death. [3–315]. The Registrar must deny the application under the following two situations:

(1) If letters of administration are outstanding; or

(2) If any creditor, heir or devisee who has an interest in the estate worth in excess of the monetary amount set out by Section 3–605 files an objection to the application.

[3–314(b) & (c)]. The Registrar does not have the same discretionary authority to reject universal succession as it has with regard to informal probate under Section 3–305. [3–314, Comment]. On the other hand, if the universal succession application includes an informal probate application as required in a testate situation, the Registrar's denial of informal probate under Section 3–305 would constitute a reason to deny universal succession.

The Code takes the firm position that if letters of administration are outstanding or pending, universal succession cannot be approved. In addition, if an interested person, who has not waived a personal right to seek appointment as a personal representative, applies or petitions for appointment, universal succession should be foreclosed or terminated unless the application or petition is denied. [3–314, Comment]. Furthermore, devisees under a will that cannot be probated because the time limit for original probate has expired are precluded from requesting universal succession. [3–314(a)(5)].

When the Registrar grants an application, a written statement must be issued describing the estate as set out in the application, and stating that the applicants are the universal successors to the assets of the estate under Section 3–312, that the applicants have assumed liability for the obligations of the decedent, and that the applicants possess the powers and liabilities of universal successors. [3–315]. This statement is considered the evidence of the universal successors' title to the assets in the estate.

D.   POWERS AND LIABILITIES OF UNIVERSAL SUCCESSORS

A statement of universal succession accords the universal successors with full powers of ownership to deal with the assets of the estate in a manner consistent with the responsibilities set out by the Code. [3–316(1)]. The universal successors are required to proceed expeditiously to settle and distribute the estate. No adjudication from a court is necessary unless invoked by the universal successor to resolve questions concerning the estate. In several regards, universal successors are treated the same as are distributees from a personal representative. [3–316(2); see § 23.02]. They have the same powers as distributees. In addition, third persons, who deal with universal successors, are protected to the same extent as are persons who deal with the successors from personal representatives.

In an attempt to extend the universal succession concept beyond state lines, the Code provides that universal successors have the same standing and power to collect assets in another state as personal representatives or distributees have in the Code state. [3–316(3)]. It is not entirely clear whether other states would recognize this standing and power if litigation were to occur in another state not having the Code's universal succession provisions.

E. CREDITORS' RIGHTS UNDER UNIVERSAL SUCCESSION

The universal successors assume all liabilities of the decedent that are not discharged because of the decedent's death and all claims that are incurred after death which would be valid claims against the decedent's estate. [3–317(a)]. This includes, for example, decedent's debts, taxes, and any charges incurred after death for the preservation of the estate. Liability is subject to any defense that would be available to the decedent or the decedent's estate. [3–321]. Generally, the universal successor's personal liability to any creditor, claimant or any other person entitled to the decedent's property may not exceed the proportion of the claim that the universal successor's share bears to the share of all the heirs and residuary devisee. The one notable exception is when the successor's liability arises from fraud, conversion or other wrongful conduct.

Payment to a creditor by a universal successor should be treated the same way as payment by the decedent during his or her lifetime. [3–321, Comment]. In addition, the universal successor is subject to all the rules of fraudulent transfer if insolvency is involved.

Universal succession should not be sought by heirs or devisee unless they are positive that claims and debts against the estate will not exceed the value of the estates assets. Although liability is prorated among heirs and devisee, it is equal in total among all the heirs and devisees to the full amount of the claims. In addition, because notice to creditors is not given, there is no nonclaim limitation cutting off creditor claims. The statute of limitations applicable to creditors under universal succession is limited to the shorter of one year from death provided by Section 2–803(a)(1) or the normal statute of limitations applicable to the claim involved plus the four-month extension provided by Section 3–802(b). [3–317, Comment; see § 22.02]. Because any heir or devisee, who voluntarily joins an application for universal succession, may not subsequently seek appointment of a personal representative and thus administration of the estate, the decision to seek universal succession must be made carefully. Thorough investigation of the value of the estate and its potential liability to creditors, debtors, etc. must be made. Otherwise, liability will not be limited to the value of the decedent's estate. It would seem justified and proper to provide a means by which the heirs and devisees who have sought universal succession may seek the protection of administration if the estate is insolvent due to no fault of their own.

Persons who have claims against the estate may exercise all remedies authorized by law against the universal successors. [3–322]. In addition, where qualified under Section 3–605, claimants may demand bond of the universal successors. Unless the demand for bond is withdrawn, or the claim is satisfied, or the universal successors post bond sufficient to protect the demand, a request for universal succession must be refused or if already granted, the demandant may seek administration of the estate. On the other hand, if the claim is paid, or a sufficient bond is posted, the demandant may not seek administration of the estate. Again, with the authority of the claimant to bring whatever actions permitted by law including suits to enforce a claim and specific performance, the authority to seek bond is more of a threat to force the successors to conform than an actual protective device. Forcing administration would hardly be a punishment to the universal successors if it in fact causes the potential liability to be reduced to the value of the estate less exemptions, homestead and administration costs.

If a personal representative is appointed after universal succession has been granted, the universal successors are personally liable for restitution of any property received from the estate but their liability is limited to that of a distributee. [3–320]. This amount is limited to the value of the property received and its income since receipt or the actual return of the property itself plus income since receipt. [3–320; see 3–909; § 23.02]. Even this liability is limited in time to the later of three years after the decedent's death or one year after receipt of the property. [3–1006]. The latter time limitation does not apply if the property was received as a result of fraud. Notwithstanding, if creditors and claimants become a problem to a universal successor, the best thing that can happen to the successor would be the initiation of administration processes and the appointment of a personal representative.

Issuance of a statement of universal succession confers personal jurisdiction of the court over all persons who join the application for universal succession. [3–318(a)]. This personal jurisdiction, of course, is limited only to proceedings relating to the estate or to any liability assumed by the universal successors.

F. RESPONSIBILITY AMONG UNIVERSAL SUCCESSORS

After the first priority for creditors, the universal successors have the duty to distribute the estate among the appropriate heirs and devisees. [3–316(1)]. Distributions are subject to the normal rules of abatement and to private agreements. [3–902, 3–912]. Any successor who receives a disproportionate portion of the estate is liable to the other heirs or successors. [3–317(b)]. Attorneys' fees and preservation costs have priority only to the extent they are reasonable and properly incurred.

Heirs and devisees who sought universal succession must send information to the heirs and devisees who did not join in the application. [3–319]. The information must be delivered or sent by ordinary mail to the other heirs and devisees and must include the names and addresses of the universal successors, indicate that it is being sent to persons who may have some interest in the estate, and identify the court in which the application and statement of universal succession have been filed. Failure to provide this information is a breach of duty but is not jurisdictional and does not affect the validity of the universal succession processes or the powers or liabilities of the universal successors. [See § 20.04].

The information need only be sent to those for whom an address is reasonably available and may be sent to others if desired. [3–319]. Either delivery or ordinary first class mail may be used as a means of conveying this information. Other heirs, devisees and persons to whom assets are distributed are subjected to the same powers and liabilities as distributees are from a personal representative. [3–317(d); see 3–908, 3–909, and 3–910; § 23.02]. A fiduciary, such as a testamentary trustee, is liable only to the extent of the assets received by the fiduciary unless it has breached its fiduciary obligations or expressly undertaken a greater liability. [3–317(e)].

CHAPTER 17

INFORMAL AND FORMAL APPOINTMENT PROCEEDINGS

§ 17.01 Introduction

Although not required by a substantial number of nations in the world, the administration of a decedent's estate by a so-called personal representative has become an integral part of the law of this country. The primary purpose of administration under the tutelage of a personal representative is to provide protection for the various rights of the decedent's creditors, debtors and successors. [Atkinson, Wills § 103]. This personal representative, consequently, is duty bound to protect the rights among interested persons within these classes and between different members within the same class. At common law, administration was limited to a decedent's personal property, and was not necessary for a decedent's real property because real property was not subject to the decedent's general obligations. Consequently, title descended directly to the decedent's heirs or devisees. In modern times, because real property is subject to the general obligations of the estate, it also is made subject to administration either by the power in the personal representative to sell the real property or by the requirement that the personal representative take possession of it.

With the exceptions previously discussed, the Code adopts the position that the decedent's personal and real property is subject to administration by a personal representative. [3–101]. It is important to emphasize that except for administration of ancillary estates, a personal representative must be appointed in the Code state, either formally or informally, and letters of that appointment must be issued in order for the personal representative to acquire the powers and to undertake the duties and liabilities of the fiduciary office. [3–103]. In fact, administration of an estate commences only upon the issuance of letters to a personal representative. The Code includes two procedures by which a personal representative may obtain the letters. These are informal appointment and formal appointment.

§ 17.02 Informal Appointment

A. INITIATION AND SCOPE

Informal appointment is initiated merely by an applicant filing an application directed to the Registrar. [3–301]. This proceeding is truly non-adversary. The Registrar is only required to see that the application (1) satisfies the statutory requirements, (2) is not statutorily precluded from informal appointment, and (3) is in Registrar's opinion otherwise satisfactory. The informal appointment proceeding does not provide a procedure for persons, who are adversely affected by the appointment, to object. Concomitantly, applicants can not appeal a denial of informal appointment by the Registrar. All disappointed applicants and objectors must rely on the procedures and protections of formal appointment proceedings. [3–309]. If denial of informal appointment was due to an inadvertent failure to satisfy the application requirements, however, an amended application might be filed with the Registrar for review again.

When a person dies intestate, informal appointment will ordinarily be instituted alone. When a person dies testate, informal appointment may, and ordinarily will, be instituted in combination with informal probate proceedings. [See § 18.01].

B. CONTENTS OF APPLICATION

The Code is very precise with respect to the requirements of an application for informal appointment. [3–301]. Substantively identical to an application for informal probate [see § 18.01(B)], the application must contain the following statements and information:

(1) The applicant's interest in the appointment of a personal representative;

(2) Decedent's vital statistics including decedent's name, date of death and age;

(3) The names and addresses of the decedent's spouse, children, heirs and devisees so far as the applicant knows or with reasonable diligence can ascertain and the ages of any who are minors;

(4) The decedent's domicile and if not within the state, the basis of venue;

(5) The identity and address of any unterminated personal representative of the decedent appointed in the state or elsewhere;

(6) Whether the applicant has received a demand for notice or is aware of any demand for notice in any probate or appointment proceeding concerning the decedent which might have been filed in this state or elsewhere; and

(7) That more than three years have not passed since the decedent's death or if such time has elapsed, circumstances exist authorizing tardy informal appointment under Section 3–108.

[3–301(a)(1)(i)–(vi)].

Because appointment of a personal representative may be requested under a number of different situations, the Code accordingly has special additional requirements for the application. When the application for informal appointment concerns an intestate estate, the application must also include the following statements:

(1)(a) The applicant is unaware of any unrevoked testamentary instrument that relates to property within the Code state, or

(b) If such an instrument exists, the reason why it is not being probated;

(2) The priority of the person seeking appointment; and

(3) The name of all other persons who have an equal or prior right to appointment.

[3–301(a)(4)(i)–(ii)].

If the application for informal appointment is for a testate estate, the application must also include the following facts and statements:

(1) A description of the will by date of execution;

(2) The time and place of pending or completed probate proceedings;

(3) Adoption of the statements of the probate application or petition; and

(4) The priority, name and address of the person seeking appointment.

[3–301(a)(3)].

Other similar special requirements are established when the application for appointment concerns the appointment of a successor either due to a change in the estate's testacy status [3–301(a)(5)] or to resignation or termination by death or removal of a prior personal representative. [3–301(a)(6)].

On the application for informal appointment, the applicant must also verify to the best of that person's knowledge and belief that the information provided on the application is accurate and complete. [3–301(a)]. In addition, the applicant must show that notice of the application for informal appointment according to the procedures set out in Section 1–401 was given to: (1) any person who filed a demand for notice under Section 3–204; and (2) any person who has an equal or prior right to appointment and who has not waived that priority in a writing filed with the Court. [3–308(a)(6), 3–310]. This is the only pre-application notice required, and it may be waived by the party to whom it must be given. [See 3–204].

C. REGISTRAR'S RESPONSIBILITIES AND FINDINGS

The Code requires the Registrar to make certain findings upon receipt of an application for informal appointment, and if they are in the affirmative, to appoint the applicant subject to qualification and acceptance. [3–307(a); see 3–601]. Such an appointment, however, may not be made until 120 hours have elapsed since the decedent's death. In addition, an order of appointment must be delayed thirty days when the decedent is a non-resident unless: (1) the decedent's will subjects decedent's estate to the laws of the Code state; or (2) the applicant is the domiciliary personal representative. Issuance of letters under informal appointment gives the personal representative full powers and duties pertaining to the office. [3–307(b)]. Although an appointment and the office of personal representative may be terminated, it is not subject to retroactive vacation. [See § 20.04(D)].

The responsibilities of a Registrar, when considering an application for informal appointment, are not judicial in nature but are purely administrative in nature. Consequently, the Registrar makes no judgment as to the veracity of any statement or facts propounded by the applicant but merely makes a determination whether the proper and necessary statements and facts have been recited by the applicant. If the application meets the statutory requirements, the Registrar should ap-

point and issue letters to the applicant. [3–309].
Notwithstanding these limitations on the Registrar's discretion, an application for informal appointment may be denied by the Registrar for "any
other reason." This unreviewable power is given
to the Registrar to provide flexibility and a sort of
efficient residual protection for unnotified interested persons when the Registrar has knowledge or
justified suspicions that the application is inappropriate. [3–309, Comment]. Because of the extensive power given to an informally appointed personal representative, this discretionary rejection
power over informal appointment applications may
be exercised liberally.

The Code provides a check list for the necessary
findings to be made by the Registrar. If the application fails to contain the proper or necessary
facts, information or statements, the application
must be denied. Accordingly, the Registrar must
determine that:

(1) The application—

(a) Is complete,

(b) Is verified by the applicant,

(c) Is filed by an applicant who appears to be
an interested person as defined in Section 1–
201(24),

(d) Recites facts that indicate venue is proper,

(e) Indicates that the applicant has priority
to the appointment (must be strictly enforced);
[3–308(a)(1)–(4), and (7)], and presumably,

(f) Is filed within the time limits for original appointment;

(2) Except for appointment of a special administrator, the will, under which applicant seeks appointment, must have been probated; and,

(3) Necessary notices under Section 3–204 have been given.

[3–303(a)(5)–(6)].

The Code also designates specific situations justifying denial of the application. These include an application which indicates:

(4) A personal representative, who has not resigned according to the requirements of Section 3–610(c) and whose appointment has not been terminated under Section 3–612, has been appointed in this or another county in the Code state;

(5) An unterminated domiciliary personal representative has been appointed in another state unless the applicant is that domiciliary personal representative;

[3–308(b)], and

(6) An unrevoked testamentary instrument possibly exists that may relate to property subject to the Code state's laws and that has not been filed for probate in this Court.

[3–311].

§ 17.03 Formal Appointment

Formal appointment proceedings are necessary anytime there is a question of the priority or qualification of an applicant for appointment, or of someone who had previously been appointed personal representative in informal proceedings. [3–414]. Formal appointment is also necessary when the Registrar in his or her discretion refuses to approve an informal appointment application. [3–309]. Although such a petition may be made by a person other than the one seeking appointment, the petitioner would have to be an interested person as defined in Section 1–201(24). The format of the petition will be the same as that required for an application for informal probate or for informal appointment. [3–301(a)(1); see §§ 17.02(B), 18.-01(B)]. If formal appointment is combined with formal testacy proceedings, the formal appointment petition must also satisfy the petition for formal testacy. [3–402; see § 18.02(B)].

The filing of a formal appointment petition has certain important consequences. First, after receipt of notice of the petition, any previously appointed personal representative must refrain from exercising any power of administration except such as is necessary to preserve the estate or such as the court otherwise orders. Second, when the filing of the formal appointment petition precedes the informal appointment of a personal representative, the filing has the effect of staying any pending informal appointment proceedings and precluding any such proceedings from commencing thereafter.

Notice must be given to all interested persons including, more specifically, all persons potentially interested in the administration of the estate as successors, any previously appointed personal representative and any person having or claiming priority for appointment. The Court, presumably after a hearing, is required to determine who is entitled to be appointed as personal representative. The priority procedures of Section 3–203 are to be used by the Court. [See § 20.02]. Upon making the selection, the Court must make the proper appointment and terminate any prior appointment if found to be improper. Termination of such an appointment must be made according to the procedures for removal under Section 3–611. [3–414(b); see § 20.09].

It is important to emphasize that although supervised administration may include a formal appointment proceeding, a formal appointment proceeding may be separate and apart from supervised administration. [3–414, Comment].

CHAPTER 18

INFORMAL PROBATE AND FORMAL TESTACY PROCEEDINGS

§ 18.01 Informal Probate

A. INITIATION AND SCOPE

When a decedent dies with a will, the Code ordinarily requires that that will must be probated in order to effectively pass title to the devisees. One method by which this will may become effective is by informal probate. As with informal appointment, informal probate is initiated merely by an applicant filing an application directed to the Registrar. This proceeding is also truly nonadversary. The Registrar is only required to see that the application (1) satisfies the statutory requirements, (2) is not statutorily precluded from informal probate, and (3) is of the opinion it is otherwise satisfactory. The informal probate proceeding does not provide a procedure for persons, who are adversely affected by the probate of the will, to object. Concomitantly, applicants cannot appeal a denial of informal probate by the Registrar. All disappointed applicants and objectors must rely on the procedures and protections of formal testacy. [3–305]. If denial of informal probate was due to an inadvertent failure to satisfy the application requirements, however, an amended application might be filed with the Registrar for review again.

Informal probate may, and usually will be, instituted in combination with informal appointment proceedings. [§ 17.02(A)]. Occasionally, it may even be combined with formal appointment proceedings. [3–107]. Informal probate may also be instituted separately, or even as the sole act taken in a particular estate. This latter type of action would be particularly applicable where devisees are not immediately aware of any property of the decedent but wish to establish their title thereto if any is subsequently discovered. In this situation, informal probate offers such devisees a convenient, efficient and inexpensive method for protecting their interests. Although nonadjudicative, the granting of informal probate becomes conclusive the later of either three years after death or one year after informal probate [3–108], unless it is superseded by formal proceedings. [3–302].

B.   CONTENTS OF APPLICATION

The Code is very precise with respect to the requirements of an application for informal probate. [3–301]. Substantively identical to an application for informal appointment [see § 17.02(B)], the application must contain the following statements and information:

(1) The applicant's interest in probating the will;

(2) Decedent's vital statistics including decedent's name, date of death and age;

(3) The names and addresses of the decedent's spouse, children, heirs and devisees so far as the applicant knows or with reasonable diligence can ascertain and the ages of any who are minors;

(4) The decedent's domicile and if not within the state, the basis of venue;

(5) The identity and address of any unterminated personal representative of the decedent appointed in the state or elsewhere;

(6) Whether the applicant has received a demand for notice or is aware of any demand for notice in any probate or appointment proceeding concerning the decedent filed in this state or elsewhere; and,

(7) That more than three years have not passed since the decedent's death or if such time has elapsed, circumstances exist authorizing tardy informal probate under Section 3–108.

[3–301(a)(1)(i)–(vi)].

In addition, an informal probate application must also include the following statements:

(8) The application includes either the original of the decedent's last will or an authenticated copy of such a will probated in another jurisdiction or that the original is in the possession of the Court;

(9) To the best of the applicant's knowledge, the applicant believes the will to have been validly executed;

(10) The applicant is unaware of any instrument revoking the will after a reasonably diligent search; and

(11) The applicant believes the offered instrument to be the decedent's last will.

[3–301(a)(2)(i)–(iii)].

On the application for informal probate, the applicant also must verify that to the best of the applicant's knowledge and belief the information provided on the application is accurate and complete. [3–301(a)]. In addition, the applicant must show that notice of the application for informal probate according to the procedures set out in Section 1–401 was given: (1) to any person who filed a demand for notice under Section 3–204 and (2) to any unterminated personal representative of the decedent. [3–306[*]]. This is the only preapplication notice required. Presumably, even it may be waived by the party to whom it must be given. [See 3–204].

C. REGISTRAR'S RESPONSIBILITIES AND FINDINGS

The Code requires the Registrar to make certain findings upon receipt of an application for informal probate, and if they are in the affirmative, to issue a written statement of informal probate. [3–302; see § 3.02]. Such a statement, however, may not be made until 120 hours have elapsed since the decedent's death. Issuance of the written statement of informal probate is in essence the approval of informal probate and is conclusive as to all persons until an order in a formal testacy proceeding supersedes it. In addition, an informal probate is not void merely because there is a defect in the application or in the procedure that led to its recognition.

When a Registrar considers an application for informal probate, his or her responsibilities are not judicial in nature but are purely administrative in nature. Consequently, the Registrar is not to make any judgment as to the veracity of any statement or facts propounded by the applicant. The Registrar merely makes a determination whether the proper and necessary statements and facts have been stated by the applicant. If the application meets the statutory requirements, the Registrar should issue a statement of informal probate. [3–305]. Notwithstanding these limitations on the Registrar's discretion, an application for informal probate may be denied by the Registrar for "any other reason." This unreviewable power is given to the Registrar to provide flexibility and a sort of residual protection for unnotified interested persons when the Registrar has knowledge or justified suspicions that the application is inappropriate. This power must be exercised very cautiously by the Registrar; otherwise, the usefulness of informal probate procedures, will be greatly diminished. [3–305, Comment].

The Code provides a check list for the necessary findings to be made by the Registrar. If the application fails to contain the proper or necessary facts, information or statements, the application must be denied. Accordingly, the Registrar must determine that:

(1) The application—

(a) Is complete,

(b) Is verified by the applicant,

(c) Is filed by an applicant who appears to be an interested person as defined in Section 1–201(24),

(d) Recites facts that indicate venue is proper,

(e) Is filed within the time limits for original probate,

[3–303(a)(1)–(4), and (7)],

(f) relates either to (i) a single will, (ii) a will and one or more of its codicils, or (iii) one or more of a known series of independent testamentary instruments the latest of which expressly revoke the earlier;

[3–304],

(2) The original or authenticated copy of a duly executed and apparently unrelated will is in the Registrar's possession; and,

(3) Necessary notices under Section 3–204 have been given.

[3–303(a)(5)–(6)].

The Code also designates specific situations justifying denial of the application. These include an application that indicates:

(4) A personal representative has been appointed in another county in the Code state; and

(5) This or another of decedent's wills has been the subject of a previous probate order in the Code state.

[3–303(b)]. This last restriction does not apply to a will previously probated in another jurisdiction for which probate is being requested in the Code jurisdiction as an ancillary probate. [3–303(d)].

The Code gives the Registrar three separate methods by which to review the execution requirement of the will offered for informal probate. Under these three tests, the will is considered proper and informally probatable if: (1) it contains an attestation clause showing that the execution requirements of Sections 2–502 or 2–506 have been met; or (2) the application includes a sworn statement or affidavit by any person, whether a witness or not, having knowledge of the circumstances surrounding the wills execution; or (3) the Registrar believes the will appears to have been properly executed. [3–303(c)]. Clearly self-proved wills executed according to 2–504 and international wills executed in compliance with Sections 2–1003 through –1005 satisfy one or more of these requirements. Section 3–303(c) includes a reference to wills executed according to section 2–503. Before the 1990 changes to the Code, this section referred to the holographic will execution process. Holographic wills are now included in Section 2–502 and Section 2–503 concerns the Court's dispensing power over execution requirements. Wills offered for probate under Section 2–503 should only be probatable under formal testacy proceedings because they will require a Court determination of validity.

D.　SPECIAL NOTICE REQUIREMENT

Because the pre-application notice for informal probate was considered by many to be inadequate if informal appointment was not also granted, the 1975 Technical Amendments inserted an optional provision. This provision provides that when no personal representative is appointed who would otherwise be required to give written information under Section 3–705, the applicant for informal probate must give written information of the probate to the heirs and the devisees. This writing must include the name and address of the applicant, the name and location of the court granting the informal probate and the date of probate. [3–306[(b)]]. It may either be delivered or sent by ordinary mail to each of the heirs and devisees whose addresses are reasonably available to the applicant. Failure to give this information does not affect the validity of the probate but constitutes merely a breach of duty to the heirs and devisees by the applicant.

§ 18.02　Formal Testacy

A.　PURPOSE AND EFFECT

In contrast to informal probate, formal testacy proceedings are characterizable as litigation. They are initiated only with a petition filed by an interested person, require pre-hearing notice of a hearing and terminate in a final order by the Court. [3–401]. The general purpose for such a proceeding is the determination of a decedent's testacy status. This may mean a finding that the decedent died with a valid will or wills or that the decedent died intestate.

The initiation of formal testacy proceedings may be desirable under several circumstances. The first, and most obvious, is the desire to obtain an order of Court probating a will. Second, such a proceeding may be used to set aside an informal probate. Third, it may be used to prevent a pending application from obtaining informal probate. And fourth, petitioners may seek an order of Court finding the decedent died intestate. Any one of the above specific purposes will also include a determination of heirship. Unless there is a thirty day waiting period because the decedent was a non-resident, it will be rare when formal proceedings are used to prevent informal probate, because the Registrar may ordinarily act immediately upon such an application.

The formal testacy petition may be the initial proceedings instituted concerning the testacy status of the decedent or it may follow informal probate of the same or other conflicting wills. At the petitioner's discretion, the petition may include a request for either informal or formal appointment. Once instituted, however, the pendency of a formal testacy proceeding prohibits the Registrar from acting upon any application for informal probate or for informal appointment.

Depending on the contents of the petition, a formal testacy proceeding has varying effects on a previous informal appointment. If the petition requests confirmation of the previous informal appointment, the appointed personal representative may exercise the powers and responsibilities of the office as if no petition had been filed. If confirmation is not requested and after receipt of notice of the initiation of the proceeding, a petition for formal testacy requires that the previously appointed personal representative refrain from exercising the power to make further distribution of the estate pending the outcome of the proceeding. If the petitioner requests the appointment of a different person to serve as personal representative, the petition may request a restraining order on the acting personal representative that prohibits the latter from exercising any of a normal personal representative's powers and that may request the appointment of a special administrator. When the latter request is absent or denied, the only effect upon a previously appointed personal representative caused by a petition of formal testacy is that the personal representative may not make further distributions until the proceeding is concluded.

B. CONTENTS OF PETITION

The Code is very specific as to the content of a formal testacy petition. Two distinct types of petitions are recognized. One deals with the request for the probate of the will. The other deals with a request for an adjudication of intestacy. Both types must be directed to the Court, request an order of court after notice and hearing and satisfy the other requirements for the particular type of petition.

The petition for formal probate of a will must contain the following requests, information and statements:

(1) A request for an order probating the particular instrument offered in the petition;

(2) A request for determination of heirs;

(3) With the exception that it need not state that the original or authenticated copy of decedent's last will accompanies the application or is in the possession of the Court, it must contain the statement and information required in an application for informal probate; [see § 18.-01(B)].

(4) It must state whether the original of decedent's last will accompanies the petition or is in the possession of the Court; and

(5) If (4) is stated in the negative, it must also state the contents of the will and indicate that it is lost, destroyed, or otherwise unavailable.

[3–402(a)].

A petition for the adjudication of intestacy must include the following requests, statements and information:

(1) A request for a judicial finding and order that decedent died leaving no valid will;

(2) A determination of heirs;

(3) The same information and statements required in every application for informal probate or for informal appointment under Section 3–301(a)(1), and (4) [see § 17.02(B)];

(4)(a) A statement that the applicant is unaware of any unrevoked testamentary instrument that relates to property within the Code state, or

(b) If such an instrument exists, why it is not probated; and

(5) An indication whether supervised administration is requested.

[3–402(b)]. If an appointment of a personal representative is also requested, the petition must also contain the following statements:

(6) The priority of the person seeking appointment; and

(7) The name of all other persons who have an equal or prior right to appointment.

[See 3–301(a)(4)(ii)].

C. PRE–HEARING NOTICE

Being a formal proceeding, notice of a fixed time and place of hearing is essential. The manner of notice is that prescribed by Section 1–401. [See § 4.01]. The Code departs, however, from the normal requirement of giving notice to "interested persons" and specifically enumerates the persons to whom notice must be given. Accordingly, notice must be given to:

(1) Persons who have filed a demand for notice under Section 3–204;

(2) The surviving spouse, children and other heirs;

(3) The devisees and executors of any will that has been probated or offered for informal or formal probate in the Code state or that the petitioner knows has been probated or offered for informal or formal probate elsewhere; and

(4) Any unterminated personal representative appointed for the decedent.

[3–403(a)]. In addition, notice by publication must be given to persons who have an interest in the matters being litigated and who are either unknown or whose addresses are unknown. At the discretion of the petitioner, notice may also be given to other persons such as devisees and executors under known wills that have not been probated or offered for probate. [3–403, Comment].

D.   COURT RESPONSIBILITIES AND CONTENT OF ORDER

The Court's responsibilities are explicitly set out in the Code. Before an order of formal probate can be issued, the Court must be satisfied that all of the following matters have been completed or proved:

(1) The time required for any notice has expired;

(2) Proof of notice was made;

(3) Any necessary hearing was held;

(4) Proof that decedent is dead;

(5) Venue is proper;

(6) The proceeding was commenced within the time limitations prescribed by Section 3–108.

[3–409]. In the order of formal testacy, the Court must determine the decedent's domicile, heirs and state of testacy.

If the petition requests the probate of a will and the will is found to be valid and unrevoked, the Court must order the will formally probated. When a formal testacy proceeding concerns the validity of two or more instruments that do not expressly or impliedly revoke one or the other, the Court may order the probate of more than one of these instruments. Although such an order must indicate what provisions control with respect to the nomination of an executor, it may but need not indicate how each provision of one instrument interrelates or is reconciled with each provision of the other instruments. [3–410]. If the Court does not reconcile the various instruments, subsequent proceedings for interpretation and construction may be necessary. [3–410, Comment]. A formal and final order that a will is formally probated, however, precludes any subsequent petition concerning the probate of any other instrument of the decedent except when a petition to vacate or modify is timely filed under Section 3–412. Even though one or more instruments may be ordered to formal probate, the decedent's estate may still be partially intestate. If this is the case, the Court is required to enter an order to that effect. [3–411].

E. THE UNCONTESTED CASE

When a petition for formal testacy is uncontested, the Court is given discretion as to the proce-

dure to follow to establish the allegations made in
the petition. If the Court is satisfied that the
prerequisites for an order of formal testacy have
been met, it may make the appropriate order of
probate or of intestacy merely on the strength of
the pleadings. [3–405]. On the other hand, the
Court may conduct an open hearing and require
proof by the petitioner of the matters necessary to
support the order requested. If the petition concerns a request to probate a will, an affidavit or
the testimony of one of the attesting witnesses to
the instrument is sufficient to establish due execution. If neither the affidavit nor the testimony of
such person is available, other evidence or affidavit
may be used to prove the due execution of the will.
A special rule is set for a will that has been
previously probated in another state in which at
death decedent was domiciled. Such a will must
be accepted as determinative by the Court if the
following requirements are met: (1) there is a final
order of the court of the state determining testacy,
the validity or construction of a will; (2) notice to
and an opportunity to contest the will was provided to all interested persons; and (3) the order
includes or is based upon a finding that the decedent at death was domiciled in the rendition state.
[3–408]. If the place where the foreign will has
become effective does not provide for probate, the
Court may accept as proof for probate a duly
authenticated certificate from the place's legal custodian reciting that the copy of the will is a true
copy. [3–409].

F. THE CONTESTED CASE

The proof requirements for due execution in the contested case are more stringent. [3–406]. When the will offered for probate is not self-proved, it is necessary in a contested case to introduce the testimony of at least one of the attesting witnesses if that witness is within the state and is competent and able to testify. [3–406(a)]. If such testimony is not available, proof of due execution of an attested or unattested will may be accomplished by other relevant evidence including, for example, affidavits of witnesses and affidavits and testimony of other persons having knowledge of the execution. When a self-proved will is involved, the signature requirement for execution is conclusively presumed. [3–406(b)]. In addition, all other requirements for execution are presumed subject to rebuttal. This means that except where proof of fraud or forgery affecting the acknowledgment or affidavit on the self-proved will is made by the contestants, supportive acknowledgment and affidavits need not be attached to the petition and the testimony of a witness is not necessary.

The Code is very explicit with regard to the burden of proof. Furthermore, when the Code sets the burden of proof on one of the parties, it means that this party has the ultimate burden of persuasion as to the matter involved. The burden of establishing prima facie proof of death and venue falls on the initiating petitioner. Proponents of a will have the same burden of proof for due execution and petitioners seeking to establish intestacy have the burden of proof of heirship. [3–407]. The order in which these issues must be handled is also set out in the Code. If two wills have been petitioned for probate and one revokes the other, the petitioners for the revoking instrument must prove their will is entitled to probate first. When a will is opposed by a petition for a declaration of intestacy, the proponents of the will must establish that it is entitled to probate first. The burdens of proving lack of testamentary capacity, undue influence, fraud and duress are always on the contestants to the will. Evidentiary presumptions used to satisfy the burdens of proof remain unchanged by the Code. [Youngs v. Hitz (1990)].

Any interested person, who desires to contest the probate of a will, must state in pleadings the objections that the person has to the probate of the will. [3–404]. Presumably, if the initial petition for formal testacy is a request for a declaration of intestacy and subsequently the proponents petition for the probate of a will, the initiating petitioner should file a supplemental pleading stating the objections to the proponent's petition for probate. Sometimes the contestant's objection will be obvious such as when the contestant files a petition to probate a will that specifically revokes the initiating petitioner's will. [3–404, Comment]. If the heirs are not the initiating petitioners and wish to contest a will they, of course, will have to file a separate pleading which satisfies this rule.

It is important to note that unless a petition for formal testacy requests the probate or the determination of probate for several instruments, a request for the probate of each instrument must be made in a separate petition which includes the necessary requests, information and statements. The notice requirements for formal testacies must also be satisfied for each petition.

G. EFFECT OF ORDER

The scope of finality of a formal testacy order is very broad under the Code. [3–412]. Such an order is final as to all persons with respect to all issues concerning the decedent's estate that the Court actually considered or might have considered as a part of its decision making process relevant to the question whether the decedent left a valid will or to the determination of heirs or to both. Second, such an order is only subject to appeal and to vacation for a limited period of time and for limited reasons. The time and reasons concerned with an appeal are the same as in any civil case in the Code state and would depend upon the rules of civil procedure in that jurisdiction. [1–304, 1–308].

The reasons and timing for a request for vacating an order in formal testacy are both limited in situation and in time. Proponents of a later discovered will may petition for modification or vacation of such an order and for probate of a will of the decedent when the proponents show they were unaware of the earlier proceeding and were given no notice except by publication. [3–412(1)]. Similarly, heirs may petition for a redetermination of heirship when they show that one or more persons were omitted from the determination and that these persons were: (1) unaware of their relationship to the decedent; (2) unaware of decedent's

death; or (3) given no notice of the formal testacy
proceeding except by publication. [3–412(2)].

Either of the above vacating petitions must be
filed before the earliest of the following time limitations has expired:

(1) The time of entry of any order obtained by
an appointed personal representative for the estate which approves final distribution of the estate;

(2) Six months after an appointed personal
representative for the estate has filed a closing
statement;

(3) No later than the time set for the possible
initiation of an original proceeding to probate a
will of the decedent; or

(4) Twelve months after the entry of the formal testacy order.

[3–412(3)]. If these requirements and limitations
are met, the Court is empowered to order the
appropriate modification or vacation as relevant
under the circumstances. [3–412(4)].

In addition to the above vacation requirements,
the Court, for good cause shown, may modify or
vacate an order in formal testacy within the time
for appeal. [3–413]. It has been held that this
procedure is analogous to a motion to vacate a
default judgment and that cases, which concern
such motions, are relevant authority. [Craig v.
Rider (1982)]. "Good cause shown" is defined to
require proof of at least excusable neglect. [Id.].
It has also been said to require a logical reason or

legal ground, based on fact or law. [DeVries v. Rix (1979)].

H. FORMAL TESTACY AND THE MISSING PERSON

The Code attempts to protect the missing person from improper use of formal testacy proceedings. First, if the petition or other information indicates that the alleged decedent's death is in doubt, petitioners must send a copy of the notice of the hearing on the formal testacy petition by registered mail to the alleged decedent's last known address. [3–403(b)]. Any interested person may also cause such notice to be required upon the filing of a written demand with the Court. When such a notice to the decedent is necessary, the Court is also required to direct the petitioner to make and to report back the results of a reasonably diligent search for the decedent. This search may take the form of any or all of the following approaches:

(1) A general public periodical notice or advertisement requesting information concerning the decedent and decedent's whereabouts;

(2) Notification of the alleged decedent's disappearance to enforcement officials and public welfare agencies in appropriate locales; or

(3) Employment of an investigator to make a search for the alleged decedent.

The cost of any such directed search must be borne by the petitioner when there is to be no administration or by the alleged decedent's estate when there is administration.

The second level of protection occurs at the time when the Court makes its findings. If the Court is not satisfied that petitioners have shown the alleged decedent to be dead, the petition must be dismissed or ordered to be appropriately amended. [3–409]. An appropriate amendment would include a request for a proceeding to protect the estate of a missing person. [3–409, Comment].

Finally, protection is provided with regard to the effect of a final order of testacy. Ordinarily, when notice of the hearing of the petition has been given and the required search has been made as required above, the finding of fact of death is made conclusive on the alleged decedent. This finality is not complete, however, as to the decedent's assets in certain circumstances. [3–412(5)]. If the alleged decedent proves to be alive and not dead as assumed, and notwithstanding any notice sent or search made, the alleged decedent may recover the estate assets possessed by the personal representative. This person may also recover any of the estate or its proceeds that distributees presently possess or their value if equitable in view of all the circumstances. Naturally, the alleged decedent would also have all of the remedies available by reason of fraud or intentional wrongdoing. The finality of a finding of fact of death as far as the alleged decedent is concerned, therefore, is only generally applicable for the protection of creditors of the estate and the good faith actions on the part of the personal representative. [Model Probate Code, at 105].

CHAPTER 19

SUPERVISED ADMINISTRATION

§ 19.01 Supervised Administration

Supervised administration is the most formalistic proceeding included in the Code for the administration of a decedent's estate. It inserts the power and supervision of the Court more directly and more often into the settlement of a decedent's estate. [3–501]. The general philosophy under the Code that self-help is better than continual court involvement is somewhat abandoned under a supervised administration proceeding. The supervised personal representative is not only responsible to the interested parties but also to the Court and is subject to the directions of the Court made either on its own motion or on the motion of any interested persons. Furthermore, the power of the Court to supervise extends from the granting of a petition for supervised administration until the entry of a final distribution and termination order.

Although under the control of the Court and subject to certain other restrictions, a personal representative under supervised administration generally has the same duties and powers as any counterpart who is not supervised. Consequently, supervised administration does not so much subject the personal representative to continuing supervision as much as it subjects the personal representative to potential supervision.

Under the Code, supervised administration is characterized both as an in rem proceeding and as a single proceeding which extends throughout the entire course of administration. [3–501]. The in rem characterization means that it is not necessary to personally serve interested persons in order for the Court to obtain jurisdiction. [Model Probate Code, 91–92]. In addition, the single proceeding concept means that subsequent notices are not necessary throughout the administration. The elimination of personal service and subsequent notices does not apply when the adverse interests of third persons concerning the estate are being litigated. In addition, distribution and closing orders must include the notices required under Section 3–1001. [3–505]. The notice requirements for interim orders including those directing partial distributions or granting other relief are left up to the Court to determine and set. [See, 1 UPC Practice Manual, at 265].

A supervised administration petition may be filed by any interested person or by an appointed personal representative. [3–502]. If the petition constitutes the initial proceeding in the estate, it must be commenced within three years of death. [3–108]. If filed after informal proceedings have been commenced, however, it may be filed anytime before final settlement and distribution. [3–502]. It is permissible to join a petition for supervised administration with a petition for formal testacy and formal appointment proceedings. Actually, if such formal proceedings have not been adjudicated, the supervised administration petition must request that these issues be litigated. When this is the case, the proceeding must satisfy the requirements of formal testacy and formal appointment proceedings including the content of the petition, notice and hearing requirements and other applicable procedures. [See 3–402, 3–403, 3–414; §§ 17.-03, 18.02]. Even if formal proceedings have been adjudicated and are no longer necessary, notice must be given to interested persons presumably in the manner provided in Section 1–401. [3–502]. Presumably, a supervised administration proceeding cannot include a formal testacy or formal appointment proceeding if the time limitation for instituting either or both of the latter proceedings has expired. [3–108; see § 15.02].

The Code gives the Court guidelines in determining whether to grant or to deny a petition for supervised administration. [3–502]. In applying these guidelines, however, the Court is given a great amount of discretion. First, in the ordinary case where the decedent's will states nothing with regard to supervised administration, the Court must order supervised administration only if it finds it "necessary under the circumstances." Second, where the decedent's will expressly directs unsupervised administration, the Court must not order supervised administration unless it finds that persons interested in the estate need its protection. Finally although the Court must ordinarily order supervised administration when the decedent's will directs that the estate proceed in that manner, it is even given discretion to deny such a supervised administration petition if it finds that since the execution of the will circumstances bearing on the need for it have changed and its necessity no longer exists. Significantly, even when a petition for supervised administration is denied, the Court must conduct formal testacy and formal appointment proceedings if such proceedings have not previously been adjudicated or barred.

Because of the direct relationship between the two proceedings, the effect of supervised administration on other proceedings is substantially the same as the effect of a formal testacy proceeding on other proceedings. [3–503; see § 18.02(A)]. First, the pendency of a supervised administration proceeding stays all pending or subsequently filed applications. [3–503(a)]. Second, unless the time limitation has expired, any informally probated will must proceed through a formal testacy proceeding. [3–503(b)]. Finally, an appointed personal representative upon receipt of notice of the filing of a supervised administration petition must refrain from exercising the power of distribution of the estate. [3–503(c)]. There is no other effect on a personal representative's powers and duties, however, unless the Court so restricts by direction following a full hearing on petition. [3–607].

The restriction on the power of a personal representative to distribute continues throughout the supervised administration. [3–504]. Consequently, distributions cannot be made without an interim or final order approving the exercise of the distribution power. If a "distribution" is concomitant with "distributee," it means that no distribution of any of the decedent's property may be made other than to a creditor or purchaser. [See 1–

201(13)]. This would apparently be a prohibition on payment of even the family protections. [1 UPC Practice Manual, at 262–64].

During the pendency of a supervised administration petition an appointed personal representative is not otherwise restricted in the exercise of the office's powers and duties. If any other restriction on the power of a personal representative is desired, it becomes effective against third parties dealing in good faith with the personal representative only upon petition, order of court and endorsement of the restriction on the personal representative's letters of appointment. [3–504]. This third party effect of an endorsement of a restriction on the letters of appointment is probably the most typical reason for supervised administration.

Termination of a supervised administration proceeding will be made according to the rules, notices and procedures established for formal closing proceeding under Section 3–1001. [3–505; see § 24.-03]. On application of the personal representative and at any time during the pendency of a supervised administration proceeding, the Court may issue interim orders which approve or direct partial distribution or which grant other relief. The only explicitly provided pre-notice requirement in the Code for such interim orders would be the notice to those persons who demanded notice under Section 3–204. Any other notice requirements for such orders must be developed and set by the Court. [1 UPC Practice Manual, at 265].

CHAPTER 20

THE PERSONAL REPRESENTATIVE

§ 20.01 Introduction to the Personal Representative

If a decedent's estate is made subject to some form of an official administration, it is essential that a personal representative or multiple personal representatives be appointed. [Atkinson, Wills § 103]. The office of personal representative, therefore, has significant responsibilities and status in the administration of a decedent's estate. Generally and briefly, these responsibilities include collection of assets, settling of claims, and final distribution of the estate. Similarly, the attributes of a personal representative's status include recognition as the estate's legal entity, as officer of the court, as a fiduciary and as title holder of the decedent's personal property. [Atkinson, Wills § 104]. The office, itself, is considered of such extreme importance that the selection of a specific person or entity to serve as personal representative is one of the most important reasons for having a will.

Personal representatives have generally been referred to by specific names depending upon the condition of the estate. [Atkinson, Wills § 104]. A personal representative named in the will is called an "executor." If appointed under an intestate estate, the name is "administrator." Several Latin phrases are added after the term "administrator" to describe the personal representative who is appointed under other circumstances. An administrator cum testamento annexo (c.t.a.) is a personal representative appointed when an executor fails to qualify or is not named in the will. An administrator de bonis non (d.b.n.) is the personal representative who succeeds an administrator. An administrator c.t.a. d.b.n. is the successor to the executor or an administrator c.t.a.

The primary importance of these titles concerns questions of the personal representative's qualification and authority. Many present laws make distinctions between whether the personal representative is an executor or an administrator. For example, persons named in the will as executor may have priority of appointment, less grounds for disqualification, potential bond waiver and potential additional powers during administration. Except for priority of appointment, the Code has abolished these distinctions between a person named in a will as executor and one appointed as an administrator. In fact even the titles have been abolished because all such persons are referred to merely as the "personal representative." [1–201(36)]. This term is used in the Code to refer to all persons who perform substantially the same function including executors, administrators, successor personal representatives and even special administrators.

§ 20.02   Priority and Disqualification for Appointment

Every state has legislation dealing with the qualification and disqualification of executors and administrators. [Atkinson, Wills §§ 108, 109]. Qualification is typically phrased in the form of a priority list and disqualification is phrased with respect to a candidate's particular prohibited status. The Code includes a provision dealing with both issues. [3–203].

CHART 20–1

Priority Order for Appointment of a Domiciliary Personal Representative

Priority Rank	Description of Candidates
1	Persons named in will (including named successors and nominated selectees under a power in the will).
2	Surviving spouse who is a devisee (or the surviving spouse's selectee).
3	Other devisees (or the devisees' selectee).
4	Surviving spouse (or the surviving spouse's selectee).
5	Other heirs (or the heirs' selectee).
6	Any creditor forty-five days after death.

Chart 20–1 describes the priorities set for appointment in both informal and formal proceedings except for the appointment of a special administrator. [3–203(a), and (h)].

Several features of Chart 20–1 deserve additional explanation. The first three priorities concern the estate of a decedent who died testate. The next two priorities concern the decedent who died intestate. Under the last priority, creditors have priority rights only when there are no persons fitting the priority categories or persons with priorities refuse or do not apply for appointment.

Many non-Code states are also very specific as to when a person is disqualified or incompetent to serve either as an administrator or as an executor or both. [Atkinson, Wills §§ 108, 110]. Persons who might be disqualified or barred from appointment, for example, include minors, persons convicted of infamous crimes, or persons adjudged incompetent because of drunkenness, improvidence, mental incapacity or integrity. The additional status of being a non-resident commonly disqualifies a person from becoming an administrator unless a resident agent for service of process is appointed.

The Code eliminates in its disqualification provision any distinction between administrators and executors and most of the specificity. It simply provides that persons under the age of twenty-one and those found unsuitable by a Court in a formal proceeding are disqualified. [3–203(f)]. The Code's suggested age requirement is a legislative option and the term "unsuitable" will have to be defined by the courts. Persons disqualified for either reason do not retain any priority status which they may have otherwise had. One additional temporary disqualification rule worthy of noting is that a non-resident may not be appointed as personal representative in the initial informal appointment proceeding until thirty days have elapsed from the date of the decedent's death. [3–307(a)].

The Code's provision on priority for appointment is applicable to both informal and formal appointment proceedings. In an informal appointment proceeding, the Registrar must strictly comply with the prescribed order of priority. [3–308(a)(7)]. Although the Registrar must rely upon the statements made in the application, the residual rejection authority under Section 3–309 "for any other reason," gives the office an authority to reject an application if the Registrar believes that the person seeking appointment does not possess priority. Persons who object to an appointment, however, can only do so by filing a formal proceeding for appointment. [3–203(b)]. This latter rule permits informal appointment proceedings to always remain nonadjudicative and administrative in nature.

The priority schedule raises no problems when only one person can be classified within the rank having priority. In other words a person named as sole executor in a probated will who is not otherwise disqualified clearly has priority and should be appointed in either informal or formal proceedings. The same can be said for the decedent's surviving spouse who is not otherwise disqualified when decedent has died intestate. When two or more persons share priority, however, an informal appointment can only be made if all with priority who are not otherwise disqualified apply for appointment, or all, except the applicant or applicants, renounce their priority, or all concur in a nominee. [3–203(c)]. Priority can clearly be established by renunciation of all who have priority except those who are applying and by nomination of a selectee by all of those who have priority. [3–203(e)].

When priority of the applicants is not set by the Code's ranking, renunciation or nomination, formal proceedings must be instituted. Significantly, formal proceedings may only be instituted by persons having a substantial interest in the estate, including creditors in insolvent cases. [3–203(b)(1)–(2)]. In any properly instituted formal proceeding, the Court is given guidelines for purposes of making an appointment. First, the Court is to appoint according to the statutory priority order. [3–203(b)]. This means, for example, that when several devisees have equal priority, the Court may merely appoint all such devisees who are not otherwise disqualified as co-personal representatives. Second, the Court must appoint the person specifically given priority by a decedent's will even though heirs and devisees object unless that person is otherwise disqualified. [3–203(b)(2)]. This preference for the person named or nominated in the will is recognition of the maxim "whom the testator will trust, so will the law." Third, when heirs and devisees object to the appointment of a person in any other situation, the Court may appoint the person nominated and acceptable to the heirs and devisees who have in the aggregate interests in the estate apparently equal to more than one half of the probable distributable value of the estate. [3–203(b)(2)]. Fourth, when none of the above rules are applicable, the Court may appoint any suitable person. "Suitable person" is not defined and is left to the discretion of the Court. Fifth, when the value of the estate is worth more than the family protections and the cost of administration, but insufficient to meet all unsecured claims, the Court may appoint any qualified person on petition of the creditors. [3–203(b)(1)]. Finally, before the Court can appoint one without priority, it must determine that those who have priority have been given notice of the proceeding and have failed to request or to nominate another for appointment and that administration is necessary. [3–203(e)].

The Code gives to specific persons the authority to nominate, renounce or agree to appointment even where they would ordinarily be disqualified to serve as a personal representative. First, although persons must normally be twenty-one years of age or older to serve as a personal representative, a person who is otherwise qualified, who is eighteen years of age or over, and who except for the age would have priority, may nominate a qualified person to act as personal representative or may renounce that right to nominate such a person in a writing filed with the Court. [3–203(c)]. Second, conservators of protected persons and guardians other than guardians ad litem for minors and incapacitated persons may exercise their ward's right to nominate, to object to another's appointment or to agree to a selectee when determining the preference of a majority of those who have an interest in the estate. [3–203(d)].

The above discussion of priority is relevant only to the estate of a person who dies domiciled in the Code state or whose estate has not been administered in the state of decedent's domicile. When a personal representative has been appointed in the decedent's domicile, that domiciliary foreign personal representative has priority over all other persons unless the decedent's will nominates different persons for different jurisdictions. [3–203(g)]. In addition, any domiciliary foreign personal representative may nominate another person who immediately assumes first priority for appointment. [See § 26.02].

§ 20.03   Appointment, Bonding and Control

A.   APPOINTMENT

Upon determining the identity of the proper person who is to serve as personal representative, the Court or Registrar must appoint that person by order or statement. Letters of the appointment may be issued to the appointed personal representative, however, only after that person has filed with the appointing Court any bond required and a statement of acceptance of the duties of the office of personal representative. [3–601]. Furthermore, once a person accepts the appointment, the person submits personally to the jurisdiction of the Court for any proceeding instituted by interested persons concerned with the estate. [3–602; see § 15.-03(B)].

Generally, a person must be appropriately appointed, qualified and issued letters in order to possess and to undertake the duties and liabilities of the fiduciary office of personal representative of a decedent. [3–103]. Consequently, administration of an estate does not begin until the letters are issued to the personal representative.

Four exceptions to this rule merit mention. First, it does not apply to a domiciliary foreign personal representative's power given in Article IV. [See § 26.02]. Second, the Code explicitly empowers the named executor in a will to carry out written instructions concerning the decedent's body, funeral and burial even though prior to appointment. [3–701]. Third and probably most importantly, the powers given to a personal representative after appointment can relate back to actions that are beneficial to the estate but that were taken by the person actually appointed prior to the appointment. Fourth, actions by third persons, which a personal representative might have taken, can be ratified by the subsequently appointed personal representative.

The Code also has a special provision dealing with the unusual situation where two or more persons receive general letters of administration. [3–702]. The first person to whom letters are issued is given exclusive authority and is empowered to recover any property of the estate held in the possession of other representatives. Any acts by those subsequently issued letters, however, that are taken in good faith and before notice of the first letters are not void merely because of the lack of validity of the appointment.

B.   BONDING

Under the Code, bond is not required in informal proceedings unless a special administrator is appointed, the will requires it, or an interested person petitions for it. [3–603]. Bond is not required in formal proceedings if the will waives the bonding requirement, unless interested parties have requested a bond and the Court agrees that it is desirable. In all other formal proceedings, bond may be required at the discretion of the Court at the time of appointment. Even if bond is required by the will, the Court may dispense with the bond in formal proceedings if it determines it is not necessary. Finally, professional fiduciaries who have deposited cash or collateral with a state agency according to statutory mandate in order to secure performance of their duties are not required to offer a bond. The Court, upon petition of the personal representative or of any other interested person, is given broad discretion concerning the bonding requirement including the power to excuse such a requirement, increase or reduce the bond's amount, release sureties or permit the substitution by the same or different sureties of another bond. [3–604].

Persons, who have and retain an interest or a claim valued in excess of $1,000, however, may file with the Registrar a demand that the personal representative give bond. [3–605]. If the personal representative has previously been appointed and qualified, a copy of the demand must be mailed to the personal representative. Unless the demandant ceases to have an interest in the estate or the bond is excused under Sections 3–603 or 3–604, the Court must require under such a demand that the personal representative provide bond. Until the ordered bond is filed, the personal representative must also refrain from administering the estate except to preserve it. Failure of the personal representative to give suitable bond within thirty days after receipt of notice of the requirement to do so is cause for removal and for the appointment of a successor.

When bond is required, the amount of the bond may be set in any of the following manners: (1) by the terms of the will; (2) by order of the Court; or (3) in an amount not less than the estimated value of the principal of the estate plus one year's income. [3–604]. The latter estimated value is set by the person seeking to satisfy the bonding requirement by filing a verified statement with the Registrar indicating that person's best estimate of the appropriate values of the estate. The Registrar then has the responsibility of determining whether the bond is properly executed by a corporate security or by one or more individual sureties who have guaranteed their performance by pledging personal property, mortgages on real property or other adequate security with the Court. At the Registrar's discretion, the amount of bond may be reduced or satisfied by the value of estate assets included in accounts that have restrictions placed upon them preventing their unauthorized disposition and that are deposited with domestic financial institutions.

When bond is satisfied by sureties, the Code sets the following terms and conditions:

(1) It must be conditioned upon the faithful discharge of the personal representative's fiduciary duties as set by law;

(2) The state must be named as obligee for the benefit of persons interested in the estate including distributees and creditors;

(3) All sureties must be jointly and severally liable with the personal representative and with each other;

(4) All sureties must state their addresses on the bond;

(5) Each surety by executing an approved bond, consents to the jurisdiction of the Court when named party defendant to proceedings pertaining to the personal representative's fiduciary duties (each surety is entitled to notice of such proceeding by personal delivery or by mail to its filed address and any other known address);

(6) Proceedings for the breach of the bond may be brought against the sureties on petition of a successor personal representative, any other co-personal representative or any interested person; and

(7) Each surety is liable on its bond until the penalty is exhausted regardless of how many proceedings it takes to exhaust it.

[3–606(a)(1)–(5)]. When applicable, sureties are accorded the defenses of res judicata and of any statute of limitations which might be raised by the primary obligor. [3–606(b)].

C. CONTROL PROCEDURES

Although not subject to constant supervision by the Court, a personal representative may be put under the control of the Court upon a filing, at anytime, of a petition by a person who has an interest in the estate. [3–607]. A similar request can also be combined with a timely petition for formal testacy. [3–607, Comment; see 3–401]. Under this procedure, if the Court determines that the personal representative may take some action that would unreasonably jeopardize the applicant's interest or the interest of some other interested person, it may issue a temporary restraining order against the personal representative from performing specific acts. [3–607(a)]. The scope of these restraining orders may relate to all matters of the administration including acts of administration, disbursements, distribution, the exercise of any power, or the discharge of any duties of his office. Under similar circumstances, the petition may request orders that affirmatively require the personal representative to perform a proper function of the personal representative's duties.

Notice as directed by the Court must be given to the personal representative, the attorney of record, if any, and any other party defendants. [3–607(b)]. Unless all parties otherwise consent, the hearing must be set within ten days after the date of the petition. Third persons who may transact business with the personal representative may be made party defendants. It is only by making such third persons party defendants that it can be guaranteed that they will be made bound by the orders on the personal representative.

§ 20.04   Duties, Powers and Liabilities

A. INTRODUCTION TO DUTIES, POWERS AND LIABILITIES

Generally, the law in non-Code states and the provisions in the Code substantially differ with respect to how the personal representative is to carry out the functions of the office. Non–Code law concerned with the administration of decedents' estates frequently include several unmeritorious characteristics. First, nearly every action taken by a personal representative requires an order by the appropriate Court either when initiating the action or when obtaining approval for it or at both times. Second, and even of a greater hindrance to efficient administration, the personal representative lacks any degree of broad powers necessary to administer the estate. Finally, the restrictiveness of the law places a burden of severe potential liability on the personal representative if one attempts to act on one's own without Court order. The consequence of these characteristics is that the prudent, cautious personal representative is forced to obtain Court approval for every action taken thereby substantially increasing the time and cost involved in the administration of an estate. Significantly, provisions limiting Court involvement, broadening the personal representative's powers and exculpating the personal representative from certain liabilities typically constitute a substantial and significant portion of a well drafted will in these states.

The Code incorporates these good estate planning techniques into all administered estates unless specifically restricted by the terms of the will, supervised administration or other formal proceedings brought by interested persons. [3–704; see 3–715]. Except as so restricted, the personal representative is to administer the estate as rapidly as possible without Court supervision or intervention. [3–704]. When the assistance of the Court is desired to resolve a question, however, the personal representative has authority to invoke its jurisdiction.

The Code subjects the personal representative to a pervasive standard of care and performance which is the same as that set for a trustee. It provides that one must act as a prudent person dealing with the property of another. [3–703(a), 7–302]. The general duty in the use of the authority conferred by the Code is properly to distribute and settle the estate in an expeditious and efficient manner which is consistent with the best interests of the estate. [3–703(a)].

B. DUTIES

Upon appointment under the Code, the personal representative, other than a special administrator, has two particular and important notice requirements that must be satisfied. First, and as soon as possible, notice to creditors should be published in order to get the nonclaim period of limitation running. [3–801; see § 22.02]. Second, also within thirty days of appointment, information about the appointment must be delivered or mailed to the heirs and devisees. [3–705]. This information must include the following:

(1) the personal representative's name and address;

(2) whether bond has been filed;

(3) a description of the appointing court

(4) an indication that the recipient has or may have an interest in the estate;

(5) administration in the particular state court is without court supervision;

(6) recipients are entitled to information regarding administration from the personal representative; and,

(7) recipients may petition the court in any matter relating to the estate including distributions and administration expenses.

Only those heirs and devisees whose addresses are reasonably available need receive or be sent this information. At the personal representative's discretion, however, the information may be delivered or sent by first class mail to other persons. It need not be sent to persons who have been held in prior formal testacy proceedings to have no interest in the estate. A failure to publish notice to creditors or to give the appropriate information to the heirs and devisees is a breach of duty on the part of the personal representative but does not affect the validity of the appointment, powers or other duties. [3–801, Comment; 3–705].

Although the Code contains an inventory and appraisal requirement, as compared to typical non-Code states, it materially alters how it is to be accomplished and what is to be done with it when completed. In a traditional manner, the Code provides that the personal representative must prepare an inventory within three months after the appointment. [3–706]. In fact, the personal representative is subject to removal for failure to complete the inventory responsibilities. [3–706, Comment; see 3–611(b)]. This inventory must list the decedent's assets with reasonable detail indicating the fair market value and the amount of any encumbrance existing as to each asset. [3–706]. Once the inventory is prepared, however, the personal representative is only required to mail a copy of it to interested parties who request it. A request may take the form of a demand for notice under Section 3–204 or in any other manner that reasonably informs the personal representative that a proper request has been made. [1 UPC Practice Manual, 315]. In addition to this mailing, the personal representative has discretion whether to file the original of the inventory with the Court. Filing with the Court does not extend its role but merely makes it a public depository.

The Court is also not involved in the appraising process. Actually, there is no procedure established for Court appointed appraisers. The Code provides that the personal representative may personally value the assets at fair market value or may employ other qualified and disinterested appraisers as is required under the circumstances. [3–707]. The Code grants specific authority to hire

different appraisers for different types of assets. If
outside appraisers are employed, their names and
addresses must be included and the item they
appraised must be indicated on the inventory.

If subsequent property is discovered or the value
or description of property on the original inventory
is erroneous or misleading, the personal representative must prepare a supplementary inventory
and appraisement which provides the same information necessary on the original item for the subsequently discovered property or for the property
revalued or redescribed. [3–708]. In addition, this
supplementary inventory must be sent or filed or
both as the original inventory had been.

Several exceptions deserve mention. Special administrators do not have a duty concerning inventory and appraisement. [3–706]. Successor personal representatives also do not have such a duty
unless the duty was not previously discharged, was
improperly discharged or property which was not
listed on the original inventory is discovered. [3–
706; see 3–708].

Ordinarily, the personal representative has a
duty and a right to take control and possession of
the decedent's property. [3–709]. The personal
representative does not, however, hold title to the
property because title immediately vests in the
heirs or devisees or both subject to administration.
[3–101]. If necessary, however, the personal representative may institute proceedings to recover possession of property or to determine its title. Once
in possession, the personal representative must pay

taxes and take all actions reasonably necessary for its management, protection, and preservation.

The Code makes two exceptions to the personal representative's duty to take possession or control of the decedent's property. [3–709]. First, a valid and probated will of the decedent may provide otherwise. It is not unusual in wills to provide that survivors are entitled to remain in possession of decedent's personal effects and residence. Second, the personal representative has discretion to leave or surrender any real property or tangible personal property with or to the person presumptively entitled to the property. Such action by the personal representative is in no way a "distribution" of the property to the recipient. [1 UPC Practice Manual, 317]. It merely constitutes revocable possession in the recipient. In fact, any request by the personal representative for return of the surrendered property is conclusive evidence in a Court proceeding that the personal representative needs possession of the property for purposes of administration. This power in the personal representative to regain possession of the property continues until termination of the appointment. [See 3–608].

The discretion to surrender property to heirs and devisees will be exercised most often when personal effects and residences are left in the control and possession of related and resident survivors and where property otherwise not needed for administration is specifically devised to identifiable beneficiaries. [See 1 UPC Practice Manual, 316–17]. Property, which may have to be sold and property not specifically devised that earns income, should be possessed or controlled by the personal representative.

C. POWERS

In order to permit administration without continual or frequent Court involvement, the Code confers upon a personal representative significant administrative powers. To begin with, the personal representative is given the same power over the title to decedent's property that an absolute owner would have except that it is in a trust-like relationship for the benefit of all interested in the estate including creditors and successors. [3–711]. When exercising this power, the personal representative is not required to give notice, have a hearing, or obtain an order of Court. In addition, for the protection of unsecured creditors, the personal representative has exclusive authority to recover void or voidable transfers made by the decedent during his lifetime. [3–710]. Finally and in a manner similar to proper draftsmanship of testamentary instruments, the Code authorizes the personal representative and any successors to perform twenty-seven specified transactions. [3–715]. The following are examples of powers included within this provision: (1) to make extraordinary repairs or alterations on the estate's structural assets [3–715(7)]; (2) to borrow money [3–715(16)]; (3) to hold securities in the name of a nominee [3–715(14)]; (4) to set reasonable compensation for the personal representative's own services [3–715(18)]; (5) to employ agents who may perform acts of administration whether or not discretionary [3–

715(21)]; and (6) to incorporate any of decedent's businesses or ventures engaged in at the time of his death. [3–715(25)]. All of these powers must be exercised "reasonably for the benefit of interested persons." [3–715]. In other words, the power is given, but it may only be exercised if the latter standard is satisfied.

D. LIABILITIES AND THE EXCULPATORY PROVISION

The Code generally provides that a personal representative is liable to interested persons for any damage or loss that results from a breach of a fiduciary duty in the improper exercise of a power. [3–712]. This liability is characterized as the same as that of a trustee of an express trust. Consequently, prior law concerning the liability of trustees as developed by the statutes and courts are relevant.

In addition to potential liability for loss and damages due to breach of a fiduciary duty, sales or encumbrances of estate property by the personal representative to the personal representative, personally, or to the personal representative's spouse, agent, attorney, or any corporation or trust in which the fiduciary has a substantial beneficial interest are voidable by any person interested in the estate. [3–713]. Similarly, any other transaction that is affected by a substantial conflict of interest on the part of the personal representative is voidable. Only the following three situations are specifically recognized as exceptions to these rules: (1) the person who objects has consented after fair disclosure; (2) the decedent's will or pre-death contract expressly authorizes the transaction; or, (3) the Court approves the transaction after notice to interested persons.

The Code also relieves the personal representative of potential liability under certain special circumstances. If authorized at the time to exercise a power, a personal representative will not be surcharged for the exercise of that power although the power is later determined to have been nonexistent. [3–703(b)]. This has special relevance to distributions made by the personal representative to devisees or heirs in situations when subsequent to the distribution decedent's testacy status changes either because of new informal probate or formal testacy proceedings. Under this situation, the protection only applies if the distribution was made prior to the personal representative's knowledge of a pending proceeding concerned with testacy, vacation, formal appointment or supervised administration. On the other hand, the personal representative is not protected from wrongful distributions because of improper construction of the will or inadequate determination of heirship. [1 UPC Practice Manual, 311–12].

§ 20.05 Liability of Third Persons

As previously discussed, the Code confers upon the personal representative the authority to perform numerous transactions without Court supervision. Under the present law of most non-Code states, any third person who deals with a personal representative faces the possibility of being liable for having participated in the personal representative's breach of the fiduciary responsibilities. [See 4 Scott, Trusts § 279A]. The principal problem for third persons is not the rule but its application. Consequently, third persons have become very cautious and conservative in dealing with fiduciaries such as personal representatives. Without changing or abandoning the basic rule, and for purposes of encouraging third persons to deal with a personal representative, the Code reduces the potential liability of third persons in their dealings with the personal representative. If a person dealt with or assisted a personal representative in good faith and for value, that person is protected as if the personal representative properly exercised a power. [3–714]. In addition, a third person is not required to inquire into the existence of a power or the propriety of its exercise because one knows one is dealing with a personal representative. A third person who pays or delivers assets to the personal representative is also not required to see to its proper application. Finally, unless the person had actual knowledge of a restriction on the personal representative's powers, of restrictive provisions in a will or even of court orders restricting the personal representative's power, restrictions of this nature are ineffective to cause the third person to be liable. The only exception to this rule provides that third persons are bound by restrictions on the powers of a personal representative that have been endorsed on letters of a supervised personal representative under Section 3–504. [See § 19.01].

The reason why the exercised power is improper makes no difference in the application of these protective rules. The impropriety of the action may be because of procedural irregularities, jurisdictional defects occurring in proceedings leading to the issuance of the letters, and even due to the fact decedent is found to be alive. Although this very comprehensive protection for third persons dealing with fiduciaries is much broader than that which generally exists under the law of most non-Code states, it is not intended to replace comparable statutes relating to commercial transactions and security transfers by fiduciaries such as the Uniform Commercial Code and the Uniform Act for the Simplification of Fiduciary Security Transfers.

§ 20.06 Successor and Co-personal Representatives

The Code adopts the rule that successor personal representatives have all of the same powers and duties as their original predecessors. [3–716]. The only exception concerns the decedent's will that specifically makes the power personal to a named executor or person. Successor personal representatives also may be substituted in all actions and proceedings to which the former personal representative was a party. [3–613]. If the former personal representative properly received notice, process or a claim, no further action need be made upon the successor.

When two or more persons serve as co-representatives, generally all must concur on all actions taken during the administration and distribution of the estate. [3–717]. Several exceptions, however, are specifically mentioned. First, the will may

provide that unanimous concurrence is not necessary and may set the basis upon which actions
other than by unanimous consent can be taken.
Second, concurrence is not necessary when it cannot be readily obtained in time to preserve the
estate due to an emergency. Third, any co-representative may receive and give receipts for property due the estate. Fourth, co-representatives may
delegate the responsibilities for certain acts to a
single representative. Finally, third persons dealing with less than all of the co-representatives are
protected as if they had dealt with all of the co-
representatives if these persons are actually unaware that another co-representative has been appointed or if they have been advised by the personal representative with whom they deal that that
person has authority to act alone under any of the
above exceptions.

When there are two or more co-representatives
and when one or more of their appointments terminate for any reason leaving one or more personal
representatives surviving, the survivors may exercise all the powers incident to the office. [3–718].
This applies as well in the situation in which less
than the number nominated as co-executors is appointed. A validly probated will, however, may
restrict or alter the application of these two rules.

§ 20.07 Compensation and Expenses of the Personal Representative and Other Agents

With respect to the determination of compensation to the personal representative and for other
agents employed for the estate, the Code follows a

less structured approach than generally found under non-Code law. The personal representative is simply entitled to reasonable compensation [3–719] and is permitted to personally determine the amount. [3–715(18)]. Unless there is an underlying contract, a personal representative may even renounce a provision in the decedent's will that sets compensation for the personal representative and thereby become entitled to reasonable compensation. [3–719]. Naturally, the personal representative may in a writing filed with the Court renounce all right to all or any part of the compensation.

A personal representative is also given the authority to set the compensation for all agents, including attorneys, employed for purposes of administering the estate. [3–715(18), (21)]. Furthermore, a personal representative is entitled to reimbursement for necessary expenses and disbursements, including reasonable attorney's fees, for any good faith, successful or unsuccessful, defense or prosecution of any proceeding concerning the estate. [3–720].

Protection is provided for interested persons by a provision that permits them to bring a special proceeding solely for the purpose of reviewing the reasonableness of all fees paid the personal representative and other agents, including attorneys. [3–721]. Upon petition and after notice to all interested persons, the Court is empowered to review all disbursements from the estate as payment for services rendered. The Court may order any person who has received excessive compensation from the estate to make appropriate refunds. Because the Court probably has jurisdiction over these matters under Section 3–105, this provision represents more of a psychological restriction on over-charges rather than an additional remedy for interested persons. [3–721, Comment].

The courts are beginning to develop definitions for "reasonable compensation." It is said to require the consideration of several factors including, for example:

(1) Time and labor required, novelty and difficulty of questions involved, and skill needed to resolve issues;

(2) The likelihood that other employment will be precluded by acceptance of this employment;

(3) The fee customarily charged in the locality;

(4) The amount involved and the results obtained;

(5) The time limitations upon such services; and

(6) The experience, reputation and ability of the worker.

[Colorado State Board of Agriculture v. First Nat'l Bank (1977)].

§ 20.08 The Personal Representative's Liability to Third Persons

The Code deals directly with the difficult problem of a personal representative's personal liability to third persons on contracts, from ownership or control of the estate's property and from torts arising out of the administration of the estate. Under the Code the estate is made into a "quasi-corporation" for purposes of such liability. [3–808,

Comment]. Accordingly, the personal representative becomes an agent of this entity and is liable not individually but only as an agent would be liable. [3–808]. More specifically, a personal representative is personally liable under the following circumstances: (1) on contracts properly made in the course of the estate's administration only when expressly provided in the contract or when the representative capacity of the personal representative is not revealed in the contract. [3–808(a)]; and, (2) for torts or for obligations arising from property ownership or control only when the personal representative is personally at fault. [3–808(b)]. Third persons may sue the estate for such claims in the name of the personal representative in a representative capacity regardless of the personal representative's personal liability. [3–808(c)]. The personal representative's personal liability to the estate may be litigated during the third person's initial action against the estate or in any other appropriate proceeding such as a proceeding for an accounting. [3–808(d)].

§ 20.09 Termination and Removal

The Code provides for termination of the appointment of a personal representative for various reasons including death or disability, voluntary action and involuntary removal. Termination of an appointment has a special and important meaning under the Code. With one exception, termination means that the personal representative's rights and powers, which pertain to the office and which are conferred on the office by the Code or in the decedent's will, end. [3–608]. Termination, in other words, refers to the occurrence of events that end a personal representative's authority. [3–1003, Comment]. The exception provides that unless distribution has occurred or a Court has restrained or enjoined the personal representative, a personal representative may exercise all power necessary to protect the estate and to deliver the assets to the successor. [3–608]. Notwithstanding termination, a personal representative may continue to be liable for transactions or omissions occurring prior to termination. A personal representative still must preserve, account for and deliver the assets subject to control, and still is subject to the jurisdiction of the Court.

When a personal representative dies or becomes subject to a conservatorship, the appointment terminates and a qualified successor or special administrator must be appointed. [3–609]. Until such latter appointment, the representative of the deceased or protected person has the duty to protect the estate and is conferred the power to perform all necessary acts to do so. Upon the appointment and qualification of a successor or special administrator, the deceased or protected person's representative must account for and deliver the assets of the estate to the newly appointed representative.

The Code includes three specific methods by which a person may voluntarily terminate an appointment. First, a personal representative's appointment terminates one year after the filing of a closing statement under Section 3–1003. [3–610(a); see § 24.01]. Second, a personal representative's appointment terminates upon a court order closing the estate under the formal closing proceeding of

Sections 3–1001 or 3–1002. [3–610(b); see § 24.03].
The third procedure constitutes a sort of informal
voluntary termination procedure. This procedure
permits a personal representative to file a written
statement of resignation with the Registrar. [3–
610(c)]. Persons known to be interested in the
estate must be given at least fifteen days notice.
Termination occurs if, and only if, a successor
personal representative is appointed and qualifies
and the assets are delivered to the successor. If
within the time indicated in the notice no one
applies or petitions for appointment, the filed resignation statement is ineffective.

The Code also provides a formal proceeding for
the involuntary removal of a personal representative. [3–611]. Any person interested in the estate
may institute such an action at any time by filing
with the Court a petition requesting removal. [3–
611(a)]. Being a formal proceeding, notice of the
time and place for the required hearing must be
given to the personal representative and to other
persons as the Court directs. Upon receipt of
notice of the removal proceeding, the personal representative must not act except to account, to correct maladministration, to preserve the estate or as
ordered by Court under Section 3–607. If the
Court orders the personal representative removed,
it must also direct in its order the disposition of the
assets remaining in the name or control of the
removed personal representative.

A personal representative will only be removed
by the Court for cause. Cause is both generally
and specifically defined in the Code. [3–611(b)].
Generally, the Court should remove a personal

representative for cause when removal would be in the best interest of the estate. The Code then recites the following more specific reasons when a personal representative can be removed for cause:

(1) The appointment was obtained by intentionally misrepresented material facts;

(2) The personal representative—

(a) Disregarded a Court order,

(b) Has become incapable of discharging the responsibilities of the position,

(c) Has mismanaged the estate,

(d) Has failed to perform any duty pertaining to the fiduciary office; or,

(3) A domiciliary personal representative appointed in another state requests removal incident to seeking appointment as ancillary personal representative. [See § 26.02].

[3–611(b)].

Although, during the administration of an estate, a will is discovered that appoints a person as executor who is not serving currently as personal representative, the current personal representative is not immediately removed or replaced but retains the office until another appointment procedure is instituted. [3–612]. If this procedure is not instituted within thirty days after the expiration of time for appeal from the order that changes the nature of the administration, the original personal representative may be appointed again to serve in that capacity. Naturally, termination does occur if the person entitled to appointment under the new testacy proceedings is appointed.

CHAPTER 21

THE SPECIAL ADMINISTRATOR

§ 21.01 The Special Administrator

In the vast number of cases, the Code has eliminated the need for special administrators. The ease and speed by which persons can obtain informal appointment, for example, eliminates the typical reason for having a special administrator appointed. Under the law of many non-Code states, it is often necessary to have a special administrator appointed between the time of filing the petition for probate of a will and the time of decision due to the notice requirements. [Atkinson, Wills § 104]. Another example of a substitute for the special administrator in the Code is the power of a general personal representative to delegate responsibility in order to take care of the situation where the personal representative is temporarily absent or incapacitated. [3–715(21), 3–614, Comment].

Notwithstanding the Code's substitutes for special administrators, there continue to exist situations in which a special administrator is essential or significantly helpful. The following situations are examples:

(1) When informal appointment is not feasible because of a petition for formal appointment or a

formal testacy proceeding requests that a special administrator be appointed;

(2) To perform a function that the general personal representative believes will cause undue friction or hostility between successors and the personal representative;

(3) To perform a function that, if the general personal representative performed or accomplished, would constitute a conflict of interest, e.g., the general personal representative may desire to purchase an asset from the estate; and

(4) To perform the function of a personal representative during an extended time of incapacity or absence where the delegation of authority provision will not satisfy or adequately handle the problem.

[1 UPC Practice Manual, 308–09]. Consequently, the Code contains provisions specifically dealing with the appointment, administration and termination of special administrators. Both informal procedures and formal proceedings are included for their appointment. Significantly, the fiduciary relationship of special administrators is specifically distinguished from the related but broader relationships of general personal representative and successor personal representative. [See 1–201(36), (45) and (47)]. One example of the importance of this difference is that bond is ordinarily required for special administrators in all situations whereas it ordinarily is not required for general and successor personal representatives. [3–603; see § 20.-03(B)].

The informal appointment of a special administrator procedure provides that when it is necessary to protect the estate of a decedent prior to the appointment of a general personal representative, or when a prior appointment has terminated because of death or disability under Section 3–609, the Registrar may appoint a special administrator upon the application of any interested person. [3–614(1)]. When the delay in appointing a general personal representative is due to a pending application or petition for probate, the Registrar may appoint the person named executor in the will if that person is available and qualified. [3–615(a)]. Otherwise, any proper person may be appointed by the Registrar. [3–615(b)]. The duties of an informally appointed special administrator are limited to the collection, management and preservation of the assets of the estate, to account for them and to deliver them to an appointed general personal representative when qualified. [3–616]. Necessarily, the Code gives the special administrator all powers necessary to perform the above duties.

When informal appointment is not available, a special administrator must be appointed by order of the Court. Ordinarily, a formal proceeding to appoint a personal representative begins with the petition of an interested person. [3–614(2)]. After notice and hearing, the petition results in an order appointing a special administrator if the Court finds that the appointment is necessary to preserve the estate or to secure its proper administration. Included within the latter standard are situations in which a general personal representative cannot or should not perform the acts desired. When the appearance of an emergency exists, the Court may order an appointment of a special administrator without notice. Unless the Court orders limits on duties in the appointment, a formally appointed special administrator has all of the powers of a general personal representative. [3–617]. Significantly, the Court may make an appointment limited in time, to the performance of particular acts or on any other terms.

The termination of the appointment of a special administrator occurs (1) on the appointment of a general personal representative, (2) according to the provisions of the order of appointment, or (3) according to the reasons and procedures set for terminating a general personal representative. [3–618].

CHAPTER 22

CREDITORS' CLAIMS

§ 22.01 Introduction to Creditors' Claims

Two of the principal reasons for having administration of a decedent's estate are the protection of creditors and the settlement of their claims. [See 3–101, 3–711]. The Code not only includes provisions concerning the determination and settlement of claims, but it also contains many provisions previously discussed which provide the creditor with protection from misuse of the Code's administration procedures. For example, the creditor may request and use any of the following protective devices:

(1) Demand for notice under Section 3–204;

(2) Demand that a personal representative post bond and be removed for failure to do so under Section 3–605;

(3) Initiate formal appointment proceedings under Sections 3–401 and 3–414;

(4) Initiate supervised administration proceedings under Section 3–502;

(5) Initiate proceedings to obtain further restrictive orders from the Court under Section 3–607; and

401

(6) Initiate proceedings against distributees for improper distribution under Sections 3–909 and 3–1004.

[See 1 UPC Practice Manual, 335–40].

As indicated, the Code includes a set of provisions dealing with the determination and settlement of creditors' claims. The primary issues considered in the following discussion include notice and the time limitations on presenting claims, the procedures for presentation, allowance and rejection of claims, the payment of claims and special issues related to these matters.

§ 22.02 Notice and Nonclaim Limitations

The Code's provision for notice to creditors is one of the special notice procedures in which it departs from using Section 1–401. [3–801, 1–401; see § 4.01]. The Supreme Court decision in Tulsa Professional Collection Services v. Pope (1988) held that a nonclaim statute, which barred creditors' claims not filed within two months after notice by publication only, is unconstitutional as applied to known or reasonably ascertainable creditors. In 1989, the Code was amended to respond to this decision despite a belief that the decision did not affect the Code's notice procedure. [Code, App. IV, Background Comment].

The Code makes a proactive response to the *Tulsa* challenge in adopting three interrelated limitation periods to deal with creditors' claims. First, the Code adopts a one year period in gross after which all claims arising before decedent's death are barred regardless whether any notice was given. [3–803(a)(1)]. This one year period is shorter than the Code's original three year from death period. [3–108; § 15.02]. Mere nonaction by successors for a year after death cuts off creditors if none of the latter seek to force administration.

Second, the Code adopts two special interrelated notice procedures that may be used to reduce the nonclaim period. [3–803(a)(2), 3–801(a), 3–801(b)]. The Code leaves to each enacting state the decision whether to make these procedures mandatory or optional for an appointed personal representative. One procedure sets out a four month nonclaim period following the date of first publication of notice. The other procedure sets out a sixty day nonclaim period following the date of the mailing of a notice to a known creditor. When the two procedures are exercised simultaneously, the mailed notice may refer to the four month nonclaim period used in the notice by publication. If the two notice procedures are not coordinated and exercised concurrently, creditors are barred only after the later of the limitation periods. In other words, if a creditor is given actual notice less than sixty days from the expiration of the four month notice by publication procedure, the creditor that received actual notice has no less than the sixty day period to file the claim. [3–803, Comment]. On the other hand, if the four month period is a date later than the sixty day notice period, a creditor has until the four month period expires to file the claim. Because the one year period requires no action to cut off claims, one would not want to give actual notice or notice by publication any time within sixty days or four months of the expiration of the one year period. Actual mailed and published notice should be used, when appropriate, to shorten the limitation period.

If notice by publication is used, notice must be published once a week for three successive weeks in a newspaper with general circulation and located in the proper governmental subdivision in which appointment has been made. [3–801]. The notice must announce the personal representative's appointment and address and indicate to the estate's creditors that their claims must be presented within four months after the date of first publication or they will be forever barred.

Written notice may be given by the personal representative by mail or other delivery. [3–801(b)]. The notice must provide the same information as the published notice requires. The time limit may state that claims must be presented the later of 60 days after mailing or delivery or the four month after the date of the first publication of notice if relevant.

In summary, creditors with claims that arose before death must properly present their claims within the earlier of:

  1. One year after decedent's death if no notice has been made [3–803(a)(1)]; or,

  2. The later of four months after the date of first notice by publication, or sixty days after mailing or delivery of actual notice [3–803(a)(2)]; or,

3. The nonclaim limitation in the decedent's domiciliary jurisdiction if that time period expires before the procedures for notice to creditors are initiated in the ancillary Code jurisdiction. [3–803(b); see § 26.04].

If a state mandates a personal representative to give proper notice to creditors, failure to give the notice is considered a breach of duty and the personal representative will be liable for any damages due to the breach. [3–801, Comment]. If a state gives the personal representative discretion to give proper notice to creditors, failure to give the notice does not subject the personal representative to liability either to creditors or successors. If effective notice is not given, there is no effective way for the personal representative to close the estate, terminate the appointment or obtain a discharge unless a year has passed from decedent's death. [See 3–1001, 3–1002, 3–1003; §§ 24.01–.03].

Creditors with claims that arose at or after death must present their claims (1) within four months after the personal representative's performance is due on contract claims, or (2) within the later of four months or one year after decedent's death after the claim arises on any other type of claim. [3–803(c)].

All claims that arose before death "whether due or to become due, absolute or contingent, liquidated or unliquidated, founded on contract, tort, or other legal bases" including claims of the Code state and its subdivisions are covered within these nonclaim period limitations. [3–803(a)–(b)]. Claims do not include estate or inheritance taxes or title questions between third persons and the decedent on assets alleged to be included in the estate. [1–201(6)]. Similarly, the nonclaim limitation does not apply to actions for specific performance of pre-death contract claims. [Bradshaw v. McBride (1982)].

The nonclaim limitation period has broad application and overrides other normally relevant limitations. For example, claims are not tolled by reason of a claimant's minority whereas they would be under the usual rule for statutes of limitation. [Estate of Daigle (1981)].

The Code includes the following explicit and limited exceptions from these limitations:

(1) The enforcement of mortgages, pledges, or liens on property [3–803(d)(1); see 3–104, 3–809];

(2) Claims protected by liability insurance up to policy limits [3–803(d)(2)];

(3) The collection of fees and reimbursements for the estate's personal representative, attorney and accountant;

(4) Actions pending at decedent's death [3–804(2)]; and,

(5) Claims against the personal representative concerning any personal liability. [3–803, Comment; but see 3–808].

The strength of the public policy underlying the nonclaim limitation that claims against a decedent's estate should be identified and resolved quickly is evident from the strict enforcement of the time limitation. For example, it has been held that the court has no authority to extend the time for presentment despite possible injustice to the creditor. [Oney v. Odom (1981)].

§ 22.03 Presentation, Allowance and Rejection of Claims

Presentation of a claim by a creditor is made by a written statement of the claim delivered or mailed to the personal representative or filed with the clerk of court. [3–804(1)]. This statement must include the amount claimed and the name and address of the claimant. When presented to the personal representative, an itemized bill containing this information should be sufficient. [Art. III, Pt. 8, General Comment]. The form necessary for a written statement should be liberally construed in favor of the creditor. [See Strong Brothers Enterprises, Inc. v. Estate of Strong (1983)]. A claim not due must also state when it is due and a contingent or unliquidated claim must also state the nature of the uncertainty. [3–804(1)]. Although these two rules are stated as a prerequisite, a failure to contain the required information in the claim does not invalidate an otherwise proper presentation. Claims are deemed effectively presented upon written receipt received from the personal representative or upon filing with the Court, whichever first occurs. When a claim is filed with the Court, the Court performs mere depository and proof of the filing date functions. [3–804, Comment]. Commencement within the nonclaim period of a Court proceeding against the personal representative is also a means of presentation. [3–804(2)].

The personal representative may mail notice to the claimant of either allowance or disallowance. [3–806(a)]. Failure to mail such notice constitutes an allowance sixty days after the expiration of time for original presentation of the claim. Ordinarily, a personal representative can change, in whole or in part, an allowance to a disallowance, or vice verse. [3–806(b); Swett v. Estate of Wakem (1985)]. An allowance cannot be changed to a disallowance, however, after court action directs that it be paid. Also, a disallowance of a claim cannot be changed to an allowance if any limitation period has run against it. A judgment against the personal representative on a claim against the estate, however, constitutes an automatic allowance of it. [3–806(d)].

Proceedings by creditors on rejected claims must be commenced sixty days after notice of disallowance. [3–804(3), 3–806(a)]. The personal representative or the Court on petition may extend this period for an additional sixty days when the claim is not presently due or is contingent or unliquidated although the extension cannot extend beyond the applicable statute of limitations. [3–804(3)].

Claims barred by any statute of limitations must be disallowed by the personal representative when the estate is insolvent or unless waived by all successors whose interests are affected, when the estate is solvent. [3–802]. This rule has broad application to any claim that arose before decedent's death. Such a claim may be barred because of any of the following periods of limitation: (1) the ordinary limitation period for such claims as extended for four months after death [3–802(b)]; (2) the nonclaim periods [3–803(a)]; (3) the sixty day period in which to initiate a proceeding to contest a disallowance [3–804(3), 3–806(a)]; or (4) the one-year-after-death limitation when notice to creditors has not been given. [3–803(a)(1); 3–802, Comment].

§ 22.04 Payment of Claims

The personal representative must pay all claims allowed upon expiration of the earliest relevant non-claim limitation; however, provisions must also be made for the family protections, claims not yet allowed and other unbarred claims. [3–807(a)]. Claimants may obtain court orders directing a personal representative to pay their allowed claims after the above period has run by filing a petition to the court or by motion if the estate is under supervised administration. No execution under a judgment may issue or be levied against property of the estate, however, after death except for the appropriate enforcement of mortgages, pledges or liens. [3–812]. Allowed claims not paid within sixty days after the time for original presentation of claim has expired bear interest at the legal rate or at the rate set in the contract which represents the claim. [3–806(e)].

At any time and for convenience sake, the personal representative may also pay any just claim that has not been barred regardless of presentation. The personal representative, however, is subject to personal liability to other claimants whose claims are allowed and who suffered loss due to the improper payment, if payment is made, without proper security, before the nonclaim period expires or negligently or willfully deprives an injured claimant of a valid priority. [3–807(b)]. So long as the personal representative does not make such a payment in a manner that negligently or willfully deprives other claimants of their priority, the personal representative can confidently make such payments if the nonclaim period has expired and if security for refund from the payee is obtained.

If the estate is not sufficient to pay all claims, the Code sets the following order or priority: (1) costs and expenses of administration; (2) reasonable funeral expenses; (3) federal preferred debts and taxes; (4) reasonable and necessary medical expenses of the last illness including compensation for services rendered; (5) state preferred debts and taxes; (6) all other claims. [3–805(a)]. Claims within the same class share proportionately whether or not due. [3–805(b)].

Allowed or established claims that were not due or were contingent or unliquidated when presented must be paid by the personal representative in the same manner as any other presently due or absolute claim would be paid if they become due or certain before distribution of the estate. [3–810(a)]. When certainty or dueness will not occur before distribution, the personal representative or the claimant may petition the Court to determine the claim in a special proceeding for that purpose. [3–810(b)]. The Court may determine the value of the claim in one of two methods: (1) with the claimant's consent, the claim's present or agreed value may be set taking into account all uncertainties; or (2) an arrangement for future or contingent payment may be made, which for this purpose creates a trust fund, gives the claimant a mortgage, bond or security from the distributee, or sets payment in any other agreed manner.

When it appears to be in the best interests of the estate, the personal representative may compromise any presented claim including claims due or not due, absolute or contingent, liquidated or unliquidated. [3–813]. In addition, the personal representative may deduct from a presented claim any counterclaim that the estate has against the claimant regardless whether the counterclaim is liquidated or unliquidated, arises from a transaction other than one upon which the claim is based or exceeds, or is different from the kind sought in the claim. [3–811]. The Court is given the power to determine the amount of the deduction due to the counterclaim and even to issue a judgment against the claimant in any amount by which the counterclaim exceeds the claim.

§ 22.05 Secured Claims and Encumbered Assets

Secured claims including those entitled mortgages, pledges, or other liens, raise special problems for the personal representative in the administration of the decedent's estate. First, as previously mentioned, the nonclaim period does not apply to proceedings that attempt to enforce a mortgage, pledge or other lien upon the property of the estate. [3–803(d)(1); see 3–104, 3–809]. This means that as to the value of the security interest, the personal representative does not have control over the time or manner of enforcement of the claim against the estate. Consequently, the Code gives the personal representative significant authority in how to deal with such encumbered assets. According to this authority, the personal representative may take any of the following courses of action: (1) pay all or any part of the encumbrance; (2) renew or extend the security obligation; or (3) satisfy the security interest in whole or in part by transferring the asset to the creditor. [3–814]. The personal representative may take any of these actions whether or not the secured creditor presented a claim but in all cases the action taken must be for the best interest of the estate. The share of any distributee of the encumbered property is not increased by payments of the security interest unless the distributee is entitled to exoneration under Section 2–607. [See § 10.06(B)].

If the secured creditor seeks payment of the allowed secured claim, the Code provides three methods by which such claim may be paid. First, if the creditor surrenders the security, the personal representative may base payment upon the amount allowed. Second, when the creditor has exhausted the security before receiving payment, the personal representative may pay the amount allowed less the fair value of the security unless, of course, the creditor is precluded by law from collecting the excess of the claim above the security. [3–809(1)]. Third, when the creditor has not or cannot exhaust the security, the personal representative may also pay the amount of the allowed claim less the value of the security. [3–809(2)]. The value of the security under the latter method must be determined either by converting it into a money value according to the terms of the agreement or by the agreement, arbitration, compromise or litigation between the creditor and personal representative.

CHAPTER 23

SPECIAL DISTRIBUTION PROVISIONS

§ 23.01 General Distribution Rules

The ultimate objective in the administration of a solvent estate is final and complete distribution of the assets to the successors. Because many special problems arise in making distribution determinations, the Code gives the personal representative a set of guidelines to follow.

The personal representative may begin making distributions of property to successors and releases of title to property in the hands of successors as soon as the determination of the probable charges against the estate and its solvency has been made. Distributions are, of course, subject to the fiduciary's responsibility and liability to creditors and taxing authorities. If the personal representative determines that the plan for distribution needs to be reviewed by all of the recipients, the proposal for such distribution may be mailed or delivered to all persons who have a right to object to it. If no written objection is received from any distributee within thirty days of mailing or delivery, the proposal is binding on them as to the kinds or values of the assets in the proposed distribution. [3–906(b)]. This proposal procedure may be very useful where the releases or agreement of all the

413

distributees may be impossible or difficult to obtain.

A problem that arises in some estates is that the estate does not have sufficient funds to satisfy all devises in a will. The cause for this problem of abatement may be due to creditors' claims, an election by the spouse or pretermitted children, expenses of administration, taxes or a general insufficiency of funds. Under the common law, in the absence of a specific order indicated in the testator's will, the order of abatement for personal property was as follows: (1) intestate property; (2) residuary legacies; (3) general legacies; and (4) specific and demonstrative legacies. [Atkinson, Wills § 136]. Within each of the classes of testamentary gifts, the assets would contribute and abate ratably. Although subject to specific statutory or judicial exceptions today, real property was not subject to debts.

Except for the rule that there is no preference between real and personal property, the Code's general rules follow the common law approach. [3–902(a)]. Because the Code does not contain definitions of the various types of testamentary gifts, the common law definitions remain applicable. [See § 10.01]. The Code also continues the rule that a testator may expressly control the order and manner by which devises shall abate. [3–902(b)]. In addition, several exceptions to the general rule must be mentioned. First, if the abatement problem is caused by a surviving spouse taking under the elective share provisions, the Code provides that all beneficiaries under the will are to suffer the reduction pro rata and not according to the Code's general order of abatement. [3–902(a), 2–204]. Second, if the personal representative determines that an express or implied purpose of the testamentary plan would be defeated by following the general order of abatement, the abatement must be made in a manner necessary to carry out the testator's intent. [3–902(b)]. Third, the Code contains a special provision dealing with the apportionment of estate taxes which does not follow the general order of abatement. [3–916; see § 23.03; see also 2–302(a)(2)(iv); § 7.02 (pretermitted children)].

From the personal representative's viewpoint, the second exception is the most important and may cause the most difficulty. A situation in which the exception may be applicable would be in the case when the residuary devisees of a will are the testator's primary beneficiaries. Under these facts, a personal representative could determine that it was the testator's implied purpose to favor the residuary beneficiaries to the detriment of the other general and specific devisees. Although the exception clearly gives an escape device from the rigidity of the general order of abatement, it will just as clearly subject personal representative to the wrath and objection of those who believe the general rule should be applied. When this exception is applied, the personal representative would be wise to seek court approval for such a decision. An efficient way to obtain this approval would be in conjunction with a formal closing proceeding. [See 3–1001, 3–1002; 1 UPC Practice Manual, 380].

If it becomes necessary for the personal representative to sell a devise which is preferred over other interests in the estate, the other interests must be abated in favor of the preferred devisee according to the general rule. [3–902(c)]. The Code also includes a special provision with regard to community property states. This provision provides that in an estate which consists of both separate and community property, debts and expenses of administration must be apportioned or charged against these different kinds of property in proportion to their relative value of the estate. [[3–902A(c)]].

The Code contains several other miscellaneous provisions concerned with distribution. Under its right of retainer provision, a debtor-successor's debt must be offset against her interest in the estate. [3–903]. The successor, however, may take advantage of any defense that could have been raised in a direct proceeding against the successor to collect the debt such as the expiration of any relevant statute of limitations. With regard to interest on the general pecuniary devises, the Code provides that unless the will indicates otherwise such devises bear the legal rate of interest beginning one year after the initial appointment of a personal representative. [3–904]. This differs from the law of most non-Code states which provide that such devises bear interest from the date of death. [3–904, Comment].

The Code also codifies the rule in many states that an anti-contest or anti-claim clause in a will is unenforceable against an interested person if that person had probable cause to institute the proceeding. [3–905; replicated in 2–517]. Under its probable cause test, this clause protects the devisee and other direct or indirect beneficiaries under the will who would receive more if the will were denied probate or, who is also a creditor of the estate and wishes to collect on his claim.

The Code has special provisions dealing with distributions to trustees, distributions to persons under disability and dispositions of unclaimed assets. Under the Code the trustee is treated as a distributee under Section 1–201(13) and therefore has all the privileges and protections accorded distributees in the administration of a decedent's estate. [3–913]. Before distributing assets to the trustee, however, the personal representative may require the trustee to perform certain acts. [See § 39.01]. The Code's provision concerned with unclaimed assets is optional due to the possible existence of and preference for comprehensive legislation on the subject matter. [3–914, Comment]. It requires a personal representative to distribute the share of any missing distributee or claimant to the conservator appointed for that person, if any, or to the appropriate state entity. [3–914(a)]. The state entity must pay the appropriate share to any person who shows proof of entitlement. If it refuses, the Court, on petition of the person entitled to the property and upon notice to the state entity, may make a determination as to the person's right in the property and order payment to that person if such right is established. The petitioner must pay all cost and expenses incident to the proceeding and is not entitled to interest on the assets held by the state entity. No petition and, therefore, no right of recovery is possible after eight years from the date of payment to the state entity. [3–914(b)].

The Code contains a special facility of payment provision for persons under disability. [3–915]. First, if a distributee is a person under disability, the personal representative may discharge the distribution obligations by making distributions to such a person according to the expressed terms of the will. [3–915(b)]. In addition, and unless the will expressly prohibits, distributions to persons under disability according to any statutory facility of payment procedures discharge the personal representative. [See 3–501; § 29.01]. Distribution to an appointed conservator discharges the personal representative, also.

Finally, the Code includes a special facility of payment provision for person under disability other than minors. [3–915(c)]. This provision permits a personal representative to make a distribution for a disabled devisee or heir either to:

(1) an attorney in fact under a valid power of attorney authorizing the receipt of property for the principal; or

(2) a spouse, parent or other close relative with whom the distributee resides if the distribution does not exceed $10,000 per year or $10,000 in a lump sum.

The Court may authorize amounts greater than $10,000 on petition of the personal representative.

If any of the facility of payment conditions are met, the personal representative is discharged from liability for misappropriation by the recipient. Persons to whom the property is delivered or paid must apply the money or property to the disabled person's present needs for support and education. These same recipients are also empowered to reimburse themselves for out of pocket expenses for goods and services necessary for the disable person's support although they may not pay themselves for their own services. The recipient must preserve excess sums for future support. The personal representative is not responsible for supervising the recipient's application of the payments made. If the personal representative knows that an appointed conservator exists or that a proceeding for the appointment of one is pending, payments must be made to the conservator. [3–915(c); see also § 29.01].

§ 23.02   Distribution in Kind

The Code sets a definite preference for distribution in kind notwithstanding the type of gift involved. [3–906]. Obviously, the thing devised to the specific devisee should be distributed to that devisee. [3–906(a)(1)]. Persons entitled to exempt property under Section 2–402 are also entitled to receive the items selected to satisfy this requirement. In addition and with three provisos, the homestead, the family allowance, and all cash devises may be satisfied in kind at their fair market value on the date of distribution. [3–906(a)(2)]. The preference for in kind distribution in these situations can be rebutted if the following two situations exist: (1) the recipient of the distribution demands cash [3–906(a)(2)(i)]; or (2) a residuary devisee requests that the asset to be distributed in kind remain a part of the residue of the estate. [3–906(a)(2)(iii)]. Finally, the residuary estate must be distributed in any manner determined equitable under the particular circumstances. [3–906(a)(4)]. The personal representative possesses wide discretion in this regard. From a practical standpoint, agreement of the residuary devisees is suggested as a recommended, first approach to residuary distribution.

When property is distributed in kind to satisfy the homestead, the family allowance, or cash devises, it is necessary to determine the fair market value of the property distributed as of the date of distribution. [3–906(a)(2)(ii)]. If a security is the type of asset distributed in kind, its value is determined by the price of its last sale on the business day prior to the distribution or the median between the bid and asked prices if no sale was made on that day. [3–906(a)(3)]. A collectible obligation due the estate is valued at its sum due with accrued interest or at its discounted value on the date of distribution. When an asset distributed in kind does not have a readily ascertainable value, a reasonable appraised value set not more than thirty days prior to the date of distribution controls. The personal representative is given the discretionary authority to ascertain valuation in any reasonable way. Appraisers may be hired even if the assets had been previously appraised.

When distribution in kind is made, the personal representative must execute the appropriate instrument which assigns, transfers or releases the assets to the distributee. [3–907]. Proof of receipt of the instrument or of payment in distribution gives the distributee conclusive evidence that the latter has succeeded to that interest in the assets distributed. [3–908]. As these two provisions indicate, the executed instrument or other distribution does not constitute a transfer of title but constitutes evidence of the distributee's title in the property.

Except for the personal representative, no other person interested in the estate may directly attack or set aside the distribution. The personal representative is, therefore, the only person who is entitled to recover the assets or their value for an improper distribution. Even that recovery is barred if the distribution or payment has been adjudicated, the doctrine of estoppel is applicable or any relevant period of the limitations has expired. [3–909; see 3–1006, § 24.02]. When these restrictions do not apply, however, the personal representative may recover from the distributee or from a claimant any improper distribution or payment. [3–909]. The distributee or claimant must either return the property received and its income since distribution, or if not possible, pay the value of the property at the date of distribution and its income and gain received from that date. Under the Code, both trustee and beneficiaries of a testamentary trust are included within the definition of "distributee." [1–201(13)]. Impliedly, the personal representative would be able to obtain the same remedy from donees or other non bona fide purchasers who have received the property from a distributee. [1 UPC Practice Manual, 386–87].

Notwithstanding the potential liability of a distributee, third persons who purchase from or lend to the distributee or the distributee's transferee for value are broadly protected from potential liability. As bona fide purchasers and lenders, they take title free of all rights of any interested person and are not subject to personal liability to the estate or to any interested persons. [3–910]. Even bona fide transactions made with the personal representative who is also a distributee are covered by this restriction. Furthermore, the bona fide party need not inquire into the propriety of the personal representative's distribution in kind even if the personal representative has made the distribution to herself or even when the personal representative's authority has terminated before distribution. If the Code state provides for a state documentary fee on its recorded instruments, the appearance of such documented fee on the recorded instrument constitutes prima facie evidence that the third party dealt with the distributee for value.

If partition of undivided interests in property distributed in kind is necessary, either the personal representative or one or more of the distributees may petition the Court for an order of partition. [3–911]. A petition for partition, however, must be made before formal or informal closing of the estate has been completed. In addition, notice must be made to the distributees and to the personal representative. The Court may order partition or sale if partition cannot be conveniently made.

§ 23.03 Apportionment of Estate Taxes

The Code has a special section dealing with abatement caused by the payment of estate taxes, both federal and state. [3–916]. The Code basically copies the Uniform Estate Tax Apportionment Act except that it tailors the Act to Code terminology and philosophy and packages the Act in one multi-subparagraphed section. [3–916, Comment; see Uniform Estate Tax Apportionment Act]. As with other abatement provisions, the Code's apportionment rule does not apply if decedent's will directs that a different method be applied. [3–916(b)]. Under such a circumstance, the decedent's will controls. Directions in the will, however, must be specific, clear and not susceptible to reasonable contrary interpretation if they are to override this section's tax apportionment scheme. [Estate of Huffaker (1982)]. If the Code's apportionment rule is determined to be inequitable, the Court is given discretion to direct apportionment in any equitable manner it determines appropriate. [3–916(c)(2)]. On petition of the personal representative or other interested persons, the Court in which venue lies for the administration of the decedent's estate may make an apportionment determination. [3–916(c)(1)].

Basically, when the Code's apportionment rule is to be applied, the rule provides that each interest of a person interested in the estate must bear a portion of the tax equal to the proportion of the value of each person's interest as it bears to the total value of all interests in the estate. [3–916(b)]. Values for purposes of the apportionment are the values used for determining the estate tax or taxes. In calculating the apportionment, all allowances, deductions and credits are to be taken into account. [3–916(e)(1)]. Most significantly, interests entitled to deductions such as the marital deduction and the charitable deduction are not subject to apportionment. [3–916(e)(2), (5)]. An exception to the latter rule, is that a life or other temporary interest is not subject to apportionment and the tax on both the temporary and remainder interest is to be paid out of the corpus of the property involved. [3–916(e)(2), 3–916(f)]. This exception is a rule of convenience rather than the rule of equity because it may make a charitable remainder subject to tax even though the property passing to the charity constitutes a legitimate deduction from the tax and is otherwise not taxable. If, because of negligent delay of the fiduciary, penalties or interest or both are assessed by the taxing authorities on the tax, the Court may determine that no apportionment of these additional amounts be charged against the persons with interests in the estate and that the fiduciary be personally responsible for these amounts. [3–916(c)(3)].

The person obligated to pay the tax, including a personal representative, has a variety of remedies available to insure that all obligated persons will pay their fair share of it. First, the person obligated to pay the tax may withhold the amount of tax attributable to an interest from any distribution of property to persons interested in the estate. [3–916(d)(1)]. If the amount possessed by the person obligated to pay the tax is not sufficient to pay the apportioned amount of tax, that person may recover the deficiency from persons interested in the estate. The same recovery possibilities exist even if no property is in the possession of the person obligated to pay the tax. When an action is necessary to recover the apportioned tax from persons interested in the estate, a Court's prior determination of apportionment is considered prima facie correct. [3–916(c)(4)].

The person obligated to pay the taxes is not under a duty to institute an action to recover the apportioned tax from a person interested in an estate during the three month period after the final determination of the tax. [3–916(g)]. After that time, however, that person must bring an action within a reasonable time or be subject to potential liability or surcharge if, because of the unreasonable delay, the apportioned tax was uncollectible. When the uncollectibility is not considered the fault of the person obligated to pay the tax, the additional tax due is equitably apportioned among all remaining who are still subject to apportionment.

Persons obligated to pay the tax who are domiciled or appointed in other jurisdictions are given the authority to institute actions to recover the apportioned tax due from persons who are either domiciled in the Code state or whose property is subject to attachment or execution in the Code state. [3–916(h); see § 26.02]. Again, the prior determinations by the Court having jurisdiction over the administration of the decedent's estate is considered prima facie correct.

CHAPTER 24

CLOSING ESTATES

§ 24.01 Informal Closing Procedure

The Code establishes a procedure by which a personal representative may close an estate without the necessity of obtaining an adjudication from the Court. This informal closing procedure is accomplished only when a general personal representative for the estate files a sworn statement no earlier than six months after the date of the original appointment. [3–1003]. An estate being administered under supervised administration may not be closed in this manner.

The Code is very explicit about the content of the sworn statement. It requires that the verified statement recite that the general personal representative or any predecessors in that position have satisfied the following prerequisites:

(1) The time for presenting claims has expires as proscribed by Section 3–803(a);

(2) Decedent's estate has been fully administered and distributed except as specified;

(3) If some claims remain undischarged, a detailed explanation of how they will be accommodated;

(4) A copy of the statement has been sent to all distributees of the estate;

(5) A copy of the statement has been sent to all creditors whose claims are neither paid nor barred; and

(6) A written full accounting of the administration has been sent to all distributees whose interests are affected.

[3–1003(a)(1)–(3)]. An explicitly approved solution to the problem of undischarged claims is to have the distributees agree to assume liability for their payment. [3–1003(a)(2)].

After the passage of varying periods of time, the filing of the sworn statement has the effect of both terminating the administration and, unless wrongdoing is involved, discharging the personal representative from liability to distributees and creditors. Discharge from liability occurs if successors or unbarred creditors or both have not instituted proceedings against the personal representative for breach of a fiduciary duty within six months after the date the sworn statement was filed. [3–1005]. Necessarily, this limitation period does not apply to actions brought by successors or creditors for the personal representative's fraud, misrepresentation or inadequate disclosure related to the settlement of the decedent's estate.

Termination of the personal representative's authority concerning the estate occurs one year after the date on which the closing statement was filed if no proceedings involving the personal representative are pending in the Court. [3–610(a), 3–1003(b); see § 20.09]. The Code does not terminate the

personal representative's authority upon the filing
of the sworn statement because it was determined
to be necessary to provide the personal representative with continuing authority for a period of time
just in case there was a need to adjust or correct
distributions made to distributees or creditors or
both. [1 UPC Practice Manual, 304]. Obviously, it
would be more convenient and efficient for a personal representative who continued to have authority to make the adjustments or corrections necessary rather than to rely upon individual actions
brought by the aggrieved persons or upon a new
proceeding and appointment of a personal representative under subsequent administration.

§ 24.02 Distributee Liability

When there has not been an appropriate adjudication concerning distribution of a decedent's estate, distributees have potential pass-through liability. They remain potentially liable to a personal representative acting on behalf of the rights of
creditors, heirs or devisees. [3–1006]. The time
limitations set on this liability provides that a
distributee is not liable (1) to a creditor of the
decedent beyond one year from the decedent's
death or (2) to any other claimant beyond three
years after the decedent's death or one year after
the date of distribution, whichever is later in time.
Naturally, in accord with Section 1–106, the limitation period will not bar the liability of a distributee
who received the property as the result of fraud.
[See § 2.02(A)]. In addition, this limitation will
not bar proceedings by an alleged decedent who
proved to be alive. [3–1006, Comment; see § 18.-

02(H)]. Rights of devisees and heirs can also be barred by a previous formal testacy proceeding [3–412; see § 18.02(G)] and all types of claimants including creditors can be cut off by a formal closing proceeding. [See 3–1001, 3–1002; see § 24.-03].

A distributee's liability to undischarged and un-barred creditors is further limited. [3–1004]. First, a distributee is not liable to creditors for amounts received as part of the family protections. Second, total liability cannot exceed the value of the distribution at the time of distribution. Third, distributees are entitled to contribution from other distributees as each would have suffered abate-ment had the claim been paid during administra-tion. A distributee, however, who fails to notify the other distributees of the demand made by a creditor in sufficient time to permit these distribu-tees to join in the proceeding, can lose this right to contribution from other distributees. In addition, the fact that one or more distributees are insolvent or otherwise unable to make contribution does not constitute a justifiable deduction from devisees who are able to pay. [3–1004, Comment].

§ 24.03 Formal Closing Proceedings

The Code provides two related but different pro-cedures for formally closing a decedent's estate. One procedure deals with the estate wholly testate but in which formal testacy proceedings have not been brought and the devisees do not desire to bring such proceedings. [3–1002]. The other pro-cedure deals with all other estates in which a formal closing proceeding is desired by the interested persons. [3–1001].

Formal proceedings terminating testate administration concern the estate wherein a will has been informally probated. [3–1002]. The proceeding must be instituted by petition by the personal representative or any devisee under such will. The petition must not request an adjudication of decedent's testacy status. In addition, no proceeding may be entertained by the Court until the time for presenting creditors' claims which arose before the death of the decedent has expired. Beyond that limitation period, the personal representative may bring the proceeding at any time and devisees may bring it any time after one year from the date of the appointment of the original personal representative.

Although a request for formal testacy may not be made under this proceeding, the petition may request any other determination concerned with the settlement and distribution of the estate including a request for a final accounting, construction of the will and final settlement of the estate. A hearing is to be held only after notice has been given to all devisees and the personal representative. The Court is empowered to issue a broad range of orders including determination of distribution under the will, approval of settlement, approval and direction of distribution and the discharge of the personal representative from creditors, devisees made party to the proceeding and those represented by the personal representative.

If at any time a part of the estate appears to be intestate, the proceeding must be dismissed or amended to conform with the provisions of Section 3-1001. The lack of an adjudication of testacy and the limitation on the scope of the proceeding means that this particular procedure will not be used by interested persons very often. Its principal use arises where it is desired to totally distribute, terminate and discharge the personal representative before the ordinary statute of limitations on initiating proceedings has run, i.e., the later of three years from death or one year after informal probate, and where the petitioners do not want to rouse the interest and curiosity of heirs by providing them notice of a formal closing proceeding. [1 UPC Practice Manual, 392]. Since the passage of time will finalize testacy questions under informal probate, it would appear that letting the time run would be the most practical solution to this problem rather than bringing this type of closing proceeding. [3–108]. After the time has run, there would be no danger in initiating the following comprehensive formal proceeding which includes the determination of testacy.

The Code includes an alternative and unrestricted formal proceeding for terminating and settling administration of decedents' estates. [3–1001]. Many of the requirements are very similar to the above described closing proceedings. The format is for the personal representative or any interested person to petition for an order of complete settlement of the estate. This petition may not be entertained until the time within which creditors may present claims has expired. Upon the expiration of this limitation, the proceeding may be instituted by the personal representative at any time and by any other interested person at any time after the passage of one year from the appointment of the original personal representative. As indicated, the range of requests to the Court is broader than the previously discussed proceedings. Not only may it include a request for final accounting, distribution, construction of the will, and final settlement of the estate, it should also request a determination of formal testacy or of heirs. [1 UPC Practice Manual, 391]. Formal testacy, however, may only be instituted if it has not previously been adjudicated and if the time limit for its institution has not passed. The determination of heirs may be requested at anytime, however, unless previously adjudicated because there is no time limitation, itself, on such a proceeding. [3–108].

Petitioners are required to give notice to all interested persons. If formal testacy proceedings were not previously instituted and adjudicated, notice by publication to unknown and unascertained heirs and devisees will be necessary. In all other cases, notice should be given to all applicable interested persons as defined in Section 1–201(24) and to all unpaid and unbarred creditors. [1 UPC Practice Manual, 391]. After notice and hearing, the Court has the power to issue an order or orders on a broad range of matters concerned with the estate and its settlement depending on what is appropriate under the circumstances and what is requested in the petition. These matters may include an order of formal testacy, a determination of the persons entitled to distribution, approval of settlement, approval and direction of distribution and the discharge of the personal representative.

This formal closing proceeding may also be used as a curative device in situations where notice was not given to one or more heirs or devisees in previous formal proceedings. [3–1001(b)]. Under this device, it is necessary to give notice to the omitted or unnotified persons and to other interested parties. The list of interested parties should be shorter than it was in the prior formal proceeding because it is to be presumed that the prior proceeding was conclusive as to all persons given notice of the earlier proceeding. The Court may determine, confirm or alter its previous order of testacy as it affects all interested persons in light of the new situation. If the omitted or unnotified persons do not object, the evidence received in the original formal testacy proceeding constitutes prima facie proof of its findings as to the due execution of a will admitted to probate or as to the fact that decedent died leaving no valid will. The existence of this curative device will be extremely useful when persons are inadvertently omitted in prior formal proceedings.

The order of the Court under either proceeding is a final adjudication and constitutes both a termination of the administration of the estate and a discharge of the personal representative. Such a judgment is subject only to reversal by appeal and to attack for the perpetration of fraud under Section 1–106. Except for questions of testacy under the former proceeding, distributees under such an order are similarly protected. The final order presumably carries with it all of the protections of res judicata and collateral estoppel.

§ 24.04 Discharge of Security for Fiduciary Performance

When a personal representative's appointment has terminated under the Code [see § 20.09], the personal representative, sureties for the personal representative, or any successor of either, may apply to the Registrar for a certificate that will discharge any lien upon any property given to secure the personal representative's performance. [3–1007]. The filed verified application must show that as far as the applicant knows there are no actions concerning the estate pending in any court. Significantly, the discharging certificate does not affect the liability of the personal representative or the surety, if any, but merely constitutes a release of the security itself. [3–1007, Comment].

§ 24.05 Subsequent Administration

A personal representative, who has been discharged under a formal closing proceeding or whose appointment terminated because a year passed since the filing of a closing statement, has no authority to deal with after-discovered property which requires further administration. [3–1008, 3–608]. Consequently, in order to deal with this property, a successor personal representative must be appointed. This appointment can be accomplished either through informal appointment proceedings [3–401; see § 17.02] or through a special formal appointment proceeding. [3–1008]. Under the latter proceeding upon the petition of an interested person, the Court, after notice that it directs, is empowered to appoint the same or a successor personal representative. Unless the Court orders otherwise, the new formally appointed personal representative is subject to the ordinary and appropriate provisions of the Code in the administration of the subsequently discovered property. A creditor's claim, however, which was previously barred may not be asserted in the subsequent administration.

CHAPTER 25

SETTLEMENT AGREEMENTS

§ 25.01 Settlement Agreements

The Code contains what might be called both formal and informal private settlement procedures. Under the informal procedure, a written private agreement that alters the normal intestate or testate distribution pattern between all of the successors who are affected by the agreement must be followed by the personal representative subject, of course, to any fiduciary obligation. [3–912]. An agreement of this nature is necessarily subject to the rights of creditors and taxing agencies. Because trustees under such an agreement are merely treated as devisees, the personal representative is not responsible for seeing to the performance of any testamentary trust. The trustee, of course, is not relieved of the duties owed to the trust beneficiaries.

The Code also contains a formal procedure for compromising and settling controversies between persons holding the beneficial interests in a decedent's estate. [3–1101, 3–1102]. The types of controversies that may be compromised under this procedure are very broad in scope. They include controversies as to the admissibility of a will to formal probate, to disputes concerning other governing instruments covering gratuitous transfers, to construction, validity or effect of wills or other instruments, to the rights or interests of any successor in the estate and to issues arising during the administration of the estate. A compromise under this procedure is binding on all persons made parties to the procedure so long as it is approved in a formal proceeding before the Court. [3–1101]. Unborn, unascertained, or otherwise unlocatable persons may be bound by the court order if they are virtually represented by other parties with substantially identical interests in the proceeding. [1–403(2)(iii); § 4.02]. This binding effect of an approved compromise is also applicable as against trusts or other inalienable interests. Necessarily, creditors or taxing authorities who are not parties to the compromise cannot have their rights impaired. The comprehensive binding effect of a formal settlement makes it a desirable settlement method where some of the successors are not competent or are unknown.

The Code outlines the procedure to follow in order to get court approval of a compromise. [3–1102]. A petition may be submitted to the Court with the written compromise agreement attached by any interested person including the personal representative or a trustee. [3–1102(2)]. The written agreement must set forth the terms of the compromise and must have been executed by all competent persons and the parents acting for minor children who have a beneficial interest or claim affected by the compromise. [3–1102(1)]. Only those persons affected by the compromise need to execute the compromise. Concomitantly, those persons not executing the compromise or not represented under Section 1–403 by persons executing the compromise are not bound by its terms. [See 3–1102, Comment]. Minor children can be bound by their parents executing the compromise only if other competent persons with similar interests also execute the compromise. [3–1102(3)]. If no other competent person executes the compromise, minor children would have to be represented by guardians ad litem in order to be bound by the approved compromise.

Several prerequisites must be satisfied before the Court can approve a compromise. First, notice must be given to all interested persons or their representatives, including any appointed personal representative of the estate and all trustees of trusts affected by the compromise. Actual notice of the settlement proceedings to all interested parties is essential. [In re Estate of Girod (1982)]. If all are not notified, problems of the finality of the settlement may arise. For example, an heir, who did not receive notice of the settlement, was not barred, in the absence of a showing of prejudice to the other parties by reason of the heir's delay after gaining actual knowledge of the settlement, from challenging the settlement anytime prior to the close of the probate estate. [Id.]. Only those affected by the settlement agreement, however, are interested persons within the notice requirement. [Columbia Union Nat'l Bank & Trust Co. v. Bundschu (1982)].

The second prerequisite is that the Court may approve the compromise only if the underlying controversy is in good faith and the effect of the agreement upon the interests of persons represented by fiduciaries or other representatives is just and reasonable. If satisfied in this regard, the Court then must make an order approving the compromise and directing all fiduciaries subject to its jurisdiction to execute it. [3–1102(3)]. The terms of any approved and executed compromise must be followed by these fiduciaries when making further dispositions of the estate. An advantage of the court approved formal compromise procedure, as compared to the informal compromise procedure, is that it provides the compromising parties a procedure for forcing fiduciaries concerned with the estate to execute the compromise even though the latters' approval might be against their own personal or financial interests, as employees entitled to compensation from the estate or trust. [3–1102, Comment].

*

PART FOUR

FOREIGN PERSONAL REPRESENTATIVE AND ANCILLARY ADMINISTRATION

CHAPTER 26

FOREIGN PERSONAL REPRE-SENTATIVE AND ANCIL-LARY ADMINISTRATION

§ 26.01 The Multi–State Estate

With the mobility of our society today, it is not an uncommon situation for an individual to own property located in two or more states. Although the principal administration will be in the state of the decedent's domicile, ancillary administrations may still be necessary wherever property is situated. Under the law of many non-Code states, this ancillary administration requires a completely separate administration causing undue costs and complexities. The Code includes multiple, less formalistic and more efficient procedures.

Although the Code recognizes the territorial concept of the state's jurisdiction and control over title

441

to its real property [1–301], a primary goal of the Code is a unified administration for a decedent's estate that has multi-state contacts. [1 UPC Practice Manual, 432]. The Code seeks to accomplish this unification by coordinating the laws, actions and decisions of the various states which assume jurisdiction over a decedent's estate. Another technique by which this is accomplished is through the significant powers given to the domiciliary personal representative. Significantly, these rules and techniques which are applicable to ancillary administration control within the Code state regardless of whether the domiciliary state has reciprocal rules and techniques. An inherent limitation in the Code's provisions concerned with multi-state estates is that, with a few exceptions, the Code's provisions only apply to administration, domiciliary or ancillary, in jurisdictions in which it has been enacted. The new and convenient devices included in the Code for ancillary administration, therefore, are available ordinarily only in a Code jurisdiction.

Several exceptions to this limitation deserving mention concern the Code's efforts to give a domiciliary personal representative appointed under its provisions authority and responsibility in other ancillary jurisdictions, whether or not the latter jurisdictions have the Code or similar concepts. First, such a domiciliary personal representative is given the power to prosecute and defend claims of any nature concerning the protection of the estate or of the personal representative's fiduciary responsibilities in any jurisdiction. [3–715(22)]. This provision is contrary to the common holding that a personal representative has no legal status or standing outside the state of appointment. [Atkinson, Wills § 106]. Second, the domiciliary personal representative has the same standing to sue or be sued in any jurisdiction as the decedent would have had immediately before death for claims which survive the decedent's death. [3–703(c)]. This provision not only includes the common case where decedent was in an automobile accident in another state, but also all other types of claims over which the other state can obtain jurisdiction under its long-arm provisions.

§ 26.02 the Domiciliary Foreign Personal Representative

Through the exercise of the powers of the office, the domiciliary personal representative has several options in settling a decedent's estate in a Code ancillary jurisdiction. First, sixty days after the decedent's death and with nothing more than an affidavit, a domiciliary foreign personal representative may solicit or receive payments of debts and deliveries of property held by persons in the Code jurisdiction. [4–201]. This affidavit must recite the date of death, that no local administration is pending and that the domiciliary personal representative is entitled to the payment or delivery. The debtors or possessors, who act in good faith, are released to the same extent as if their payments or deliveries had been made to a local personal representative. [4–202]. Resident creditors may prevent such payments or deliveries, however, by notifying the debtors or possessors that they should not be made. [4–203]. The term "resident creditor" means any claimant against the estate who is domiciled or doing business in the Code ancillary jurisdiction. [4–101(3)].

A concurrent or alternative procedure under the Code provides that by filing in a court in the Code ancillary state authenticated copies of the domiciliary appointment and the official bond, if any, a domiciliary foreign personal representative is entitled to exercise all powers that a local personal representative could exercise. [4–204, 4–205; see § 20.04(C)]. These powers specifically include the power to bring legal proceedings that any non-resident could bring in courts of the Code ancillary jurisdiction. [4–205; see also 3–916(h), § 23.03]. This filing has the above effect only if neither a local administration is pending nor a local personal representative is functioning pursuant to appointment proceedings under Article III. [4–206; see 4–101(1)–(2)]. Actually, the institution by interested persons of informal or formal appointment terminates the domiciliary foreign personal representative's power under this provision except as allowed by the Court. [4–206]. Persons who dealt with the domiciliary foreign personal representative before they received actual notice of a pending local administration proceeding, however, are not to be prejudiced as far as any change of position is concerned. If a local personal representative is appointed, this personal representative assumes all duties and obligations that arose during the exercise of the domiciliary foreign personal representative's powers and may be substituted for the domiciliary foreign personal representative in all actions or proceedings pending in the Code ancillary state.

In an estate where the will has been probated in the testator's domicile, the domiciliary foreign personal representative may also exercise the authority to file for informal probate. [3–303(b)]. Because the Code requires devisees to probate a will in order to prove title, informal probate in the Code ancillary state would at least be necessary if the devolution of real estate is involved. [3–102; see § 15.01]. There is no three year after death limitation on such informal probates. [3–108].

If an interested person petitions for local appointment, the domiciliary foreign personal representative or the representative's nominee is given priority of appointment in the ancillary state. [3–203(g)]. Unless the decedent's will appoints a different person to serve as personal representative in the ancillary jurisdiction, the domiciliary foreign personal representative may obtain removal of anyone else appointed. [3–611(b)]. In addition, the domiciliary foreign personal representative is the only person who may file for an informal appointment in the Code ancillary jurisdiction when an appointment has previously been made in the state of domicile. [3–308(b)].

Locally interested persons are not without protection. Within the Code's rules on statute of limitations and res judicata, interested persons have all of the affirmative action protections accorded interested persons in the domiciliary jurisdiction. [4–207]. These protections would include the possibility of petitioning for formal probate, appointment, or closing, for supervised administration or for any other proceeding or order permissible under Article III. [See § 14.02(D)].

§ 26.03 Jurisdiction Over the Foreign Personal Representative

Significantly, the Code also includes comprehensive provisions dealing with jurisdiction over the foreign personal representative. The foreign personal representative submits himself to personal jurisdiction under the following four situations: (1) when he accepts appointment in a Code jurisdiction [3–602]; (2) when he obtains his powers through the filing of authenticated copies of his domiciliary appointment; (3) although limited to the value of the property collected, when he receives voluntary payments or deliveries; or (4) when he does any other act within the state which would permit that state to assume jurisdiction over him as an individual. [4–301]. A foreign personal representative is also subject to the jurisdiction of any state in which the decedent would have been subject to jurisdiction prior to death. [4–302]. Service of process upon the foreign personal representative may be made in any of three methods: (1) by registered or certified mail addressed to the last reasonably ascertainable address requesting the return receipt be signed only by the addressee; (2) by ordinary mail if method (1) is unavailable; or (3) by a manner permitted by other service of process provisions in the Code state on either the foreign personal representative or the decedent immediately prior to death. [4–303(a)]. Upon proper service, the foreign personal representative must be allowed thirty days to appear or respond. [4–303(b)].

§ 26.04 Coordination of Domiciliary and Ancillary Proceedings

The Code contains numerous provisions that attempt to coordinate laws, actions and decisions between the various states which assume jurisdiction over a decedent's estate. Under the Code, adjudications and actions taken in the domiciliary and other relevant jurisdictions are to be given recognition in local administration and probate proceedings initiated in the ancillary jurisdiction. After proper notice and an opportunity for contest by all interested persons, domiciliary adjudications concerned with testacy, will validity and its construction must also be considered res judicata in a Code, nondomiciliary jurisdiction. [3–408; see § 18.02(E)]. Although a finding of a domicile is required, it may be satisfied through a formal closing proceeding. [3–1001, 3–1002]. Furthermore, adjudications for or against a personal representative either in a domiciliary or ancillary jurisdiction are binding on the local personal representative as if she were a party to the adjudication. [4–401]. Adjudications obtained by fraud or collusion are impliedly excepted. [See 1–106, § 2.02(A)]. Conflicting claims as to the location of the decedent's domicile are also avoided by the Code because the first court in which formal proceedings are commenced has the exclusive right to determine domicile and its determination is binding on all Code courts. [3–202; see § 15.03(C)]. Unsecured creditor's claims that are barred by the domiciliary nonclaim statute are also barred in a Code, nondomiciliary jurisdiction. [3–803(b)]. The nonclaim period may be extended in the ancillary jurisdiction, however, if the first publication for claims in that state occurs before the period has run in the domiciliary state.

The Code also deals with the problems surrounding the settlement and distribution of an estate that is administered in two or more states. First, decedent's assets, wherever their situs and administration, are subject to the properly filed claims of any administration of which the personal representative is aware. [3–815(a)]. Second, in insolvent estates, distributions in Code ancillary administrations are to be coordinated with distributions made in other jurisdictions, including administration in the decedent's domicile. [3–815(b)–(c)]. This coordination includes: (1) satisfying the domicile's family protections if assets in the domicile are insufficient; (2) paying claims and charges in all jurisdictions on a pro rata basis; (3) adjusting claims and charges between creditors who have received a preference payment in other jurisdictions with those creditors who have not received a preference; and (4) transferring any balance remaining after the above payments to the domiciliary personal representative.

With three specific exceptions, the Code provides that in solvent estates the nondomiciliary personal representative must distribute the assets in her possession to the domiciliary personal representative for distribution to the appropriate beneficiaries. [3–816]. The first exception recognizes that either the provisions of a decedent's will or choice of law rules may identify successors according to the local law of the ancillary jurisdiction and to the exclusion of the law of the decedent's domicile. This exception may have significant application where decedent dies with real estate in the ancillary jurisdiction. The second exception anticipates the situation where, after reasonable inquiry, the local personal representative cannot discover the existence or identity of a domiciliary personal representative. This exception may have importance where the decedent died domiciled in a state in which she left no administrable assets. The third exception accords the Court authority in a formal closing proceeding under Section 3–1001 to order distribution other than to the domiciliary personal representative.

*

PART FIVE

THE PROTECTION OF PER-SONS UNDER DISABILI-TY AND THEIR PROP-ERTY

CHAPTER 27

INTRODUCTION TO GUARDIANSHIP AND CONSERVATORSHIP

§ 27.01 Introduction

The concept and necessity of guardianship derive from the circumstance when a person is under some type of disability which causes that person to be unable to manage his or her own personal or business affairs or both. [Woerner, Law of Guardianship § 1]. Through the guardianship device, such a disabled person's rights and interests can be protected. Generally, the person who suffers from such disabilities is either a minor, mental incompetent or other incompetent. The disability of a minor is presumed by legislative determination depending upon the person's age. [Id.]. The other forms of disability require voluntary action by the person or some form of legal proceeding to determine the incompetency status.

An important feature of guardianship is that it serves two distinct functions. The first and most apparent is guardianship of property. Under such a guardianship, the guardian manages (receives and expends) the ward's property or estate for the purposes of the guardianship. The second, which is particularly important in the case of minors, is the guardianship of the person. Here the guardian has custody and, therefore, physical control over the ward. The same person may be permitted to serve in both capacities.

Guardianship laws, with a few exceptions, remained unchanged for many years. [2 UPC Practice Manual, 495]. Consequently, many of the procedures and substantive regulations suffer unreasonably from excessive formality or administrative restrictions or both. In addition, they frequently were antiquated, poorly organized, fragmented and insufficient in coverage. Despite these inadequacies, legislatures have been slow to act and when revisions have occurred the resultant legislation has often been unsatisfactory.

Although in 1946 the draftsmen of the Model Probate Code attempted to improve and modernize guardianship laws, it did not stir reform in the states. [Model Probate Code, at 189–234]. In order to remedy this unfortunate state of affairs, the Code includes a comprehensive and modernized article on the law dealing with the protection of persons under a disability and their property.

§ 27.02 Overview and Policies of the Code

In 1982, the National Conference of Commissioners on Uniform State Laws promulgated the Uniform Guardianship and Protective Proceedings Act as a freestanding act. The provisions in this Act were simultaneously integrated into the Uniform Probate Code as a revision to Article V, Parts 1, 2, 3, and 4. Although many of the Code's provisions in the 1969 version of Article V were merely renumbered or altered in minor ways, a significant number were substantively changed and new concepts were incorporated into the Article. This Nutshell will be concerned with the 1982 Act as it is integrated into the Code.

The Code's approach to these matters is significantly different from prior law. [Effland, Caring for the Elderly, at 376]. For overview purposes, it is helpful to outline the Code's underlying policies. The Code's procedures and rules are designed to:

(1) Allow persons to anticipate incapacity problems and to create their own solutions to them;

(2) Improve and intensify Court involvement when appropriate and necessary;

(3) Limit the invasion into the person's lifetime activities to the least intrusive device or technique;

(4) Protect persons from improper and unnecessary guardianships and conservatorships (require due process and prohibit undue encroachment upon the control of one's lifetime activities);

(5) Provide extensive procedural flexibility and numerous alternatives;

(6) Recognize distinctions between guardianship (custody) and conservatorship (estate management) and minors versus other persons under a disability;

(7) Reduce the stigmatization and embarrassment for those who are subjected to incapacity procedures;

(8) Resolve conflicts between concurrent judicial and quasi judicial proceedings;

(9) Streamline procedures to reduce costs (eliminate redundant and superfluous procedures and remove overpaternalistic court involvement); and

(10) Treat the conservator as a trustee with broad powers to manage the protected person's estate.

It is no small task to offer provisions that will satisfy all of those policies. In fact, some of them are conflicting and require consistent resolution only by individualization of the procedures and remedies.

The comprehensiveness and the number of alternatives and procedural safeguards against misuse or over-use of procedures add a degree of complexity to the Code. Thus, the Code does not provide users with a single and inflexible trail to follow but requires each to cut one's own trail. This attribute does not detract from the Code's merits and benefits; however, it does cause some resistance to its enactment. Chart 27–1 outlines the procedures, techniques, and protections that would be available in a Code state to deal with persons under a disability.

CHART 27–1

Outline of Procedures and Techniques to Deal With Persons Under a Disability

A.	Guardianship	Citation
1	None created except when necessary	5–204(a), 5–306(a)
2	Testamentary/lifetime appointment	5–202, 5–301
3	Limited guardianship	5–204(b), 5–306(a), and (c)
4	Full guardianship	5–207, 5–306(b)
B.	**Conservatorships**	**Citation**
1	Facility of payment or delivery	5–101
2	Multiple-party accounts	Art. 6, Pt. 2
3	Durable powers	Art. 5, Pt. 5
4	Inter vivos trusts	General law of trusts in Code state
5	Single transaction and protective arrangement authorization	5–408
6	Limited conservatorship	5–407(a)
7	Full conservatorship	5–407(b)
C.	**Protection Devices and Concept**	**Citation**
1	Full notice and hearing	5–206(b), 5–304, 5–405, 5–406
2	Representation by counsel	5–406(a)
3	Impartial visitor procedure	5–103(21), 5–406(b), (c)
4	Standard of proof	5–207, 5–103(10), 5–306(b), 5–103(7), 5–401
5	Selection of best person for fiduciary position	5–207, 5–305, 5–409
6	Informal objection procedure by ward	5–203, 5–311(b)

C.	Protection Devices and Concept	Citation
7	Bond	5–410
8	Accounting	5–418

The discussion of Article V of the Code in this Nutshell will not include an analysis of every section or concept. Instead, some of it will be only summarized or generalized.

CHAPTER 28

GENERAL PROVISIONS ON GUARDIANSHIP AND CONSERVATORSHIP

§ 28.01 Organization, Interrelationships, and Definitions

Article V of the Code organizes the many different issues concerning persons under a disability into logical and relevant categories. Part 1 includes general provisions and definitions dealing with the alternative device of facility of payment or delivery, delegation of powers by a parent or guardian, general definitions, and a request for notice by interested persons. All of these provisions are either self-contained or are applicable to all of the other parts of the Article. This makes it convenient to make reference to a single part of the Code.

Parts 2, 3, and 4 are the heart of Article V. They include the provisions concerning guardians of minors, guardians of incapacitated persons other than minors, and conservatorships or the protection of property of persons under disability and minors.

Although Parts 2 and 3 are somewhat duplicative in that each contains provisions for the appointment, removal, termination, venue, court procedures, notice requirements and powers and

457

duties of a guardian and of a guardianship, the drafters of the Code felt that the significant distinctions between the issues relating to minors versus the same issues relating to other incapacitated persons demanded separate treatment. [Compare 5–201 to 5–212 *with* 5–301 to 5–312]. Although separate treatment may increase the size of the Code a small amount, it actually decreases its complexity. By separating the provisions related to minors from the provisions related to other incapacitated persons, the Code clearly indicates what provisions are applicable to each situation. There is no confusion whether a particular provision applies to one case or the other. It has been held that the guardianship of minors and of incapacitated persons are mutually exclusive procedures under the Code. [Guardianship of Evans (1978)]. Part 2 of Article V must be used for the guardianship of minors notwithstanding a minor's other incapacities. Part 3 must be used for the guardianships of all other types of incapacitated persons.

The separation of Part 4, dealing with conservatorships or what are called "protective proceedings," from Parts 2 and 3, dealing with guardianships, is also meritorious. [See 5–401 to 5–431]. This separation clearly defines the range of each of the fiduciary relationships. The guardian is responsible for care and custody of the ward: the guardian is not responsible for money management. [5–103(6), 5–209, 5–309]. The existence of a guardianship indicates the ward is incapacitated from a contractual standpoint. This means that consent of the guardian is necessary for a wide

range of activities in which the ward may participate. On the other hand, the conservator is responsible for the ward's financial management.
[5–103(3), 5–423]. With limited exception, the conservator is not responsible for the care and custody
of the ward. In addition, the existence of a conservatorship does not automatically affect the normal
capacity of the protected person. [See Effland,
Caring for the Elderly, at 398–400]. If that is a
problem, the conservator should seek the appointment of a guardian. Similarly if financial management is necessary, the guardian should seek appointment of a conservator.

It is also important to emphasize that under the
Code, just because a guardian of the person is
necessary, it does not mean that protective proceedings are required, or vice versa. Situations
may arise in which a person may need a guardian
but has no property or assets requiring a conservator. On the other hand, a person may require a
conservator but not require a guardian. For example, a missing person whose assets require management certainly does not need a guardian appointed
to take care and custody of his absent person.

As with other parts of the Code, a large number
of definitions are included that are applicable
throughout Parts 1–4 of Article V. [5–103(1)–(22);
see § 2.02(D)]. For informational and overview
purposes, Chart 28–1 lists them in alphabetical
order.

CHART 28–1

Terms Defined for Provisions
on Disabled Persons

Claims	Organization
Conservator	Parent
Court	Person
Disability	Petition
Estate	Proceeding
Guardian	Property
Incapacitated person	Protected person
Lease	Protective proceeding
Letters	Security
Minor	Visitor
Mortgage	Ward

§ 28.02 Jurisdiction and Venue for Guardianship and Protective Proceedings

A. JURISDICTION OVER THE SUBJECT MATTER

The Code Court is expressly given jurisdiction over the subject matter for guardianship and protective proceedings. [1–302(c); see §§ 3.01, 3.02]. For emphasis and clarity, however, the Code includes several special provisions that are exclusively related to proceedings concerned with persons under disability. First, guardianship and protective proceedings for the same person may be consolidated if they are commenced or pending in the same court. [5–102(b)]. Because the requirements for the above two proceedings are not identical, however, it is necessary that the parties involved take care to satisfy the requirements of both proceedings even though consolidated. [2 UPC Practice Manual, 503–04]. Second, the Code recognizes that in a proceeding subsequent to appointment concerned with a guardian of a minor or a guardian of an incapacitated person, the ward may not reside any more in the judicial subdivision wherein the initial proceeding for appointment was instituted or in which acceptance of a testamentary appointment was filed. Under this circumstance, the Court where the ward presently resides has concurrent jurisdiction over resignation, removal, accounting and other proceedings relating to the guardianship with the court in which the guardian was appointed or the acceptance was filed. [5–211, 5–312]. Generally, the decision whether to retain or to transfer should be based upon concepts similar to those employed under the doctrine of forum non conveniens.

Third, for formal protective proceedings the Code recognizes a distinction between exclusive and concurrent jurisdiction. The Court in which the protective proceeding petition has been filed has until termination exclusive jurisdiction over the following issues:

(1) The determination of the need for a protective order or the appointment of a conservator [5–402(1)];

(2) The determination of the manner in which the protected person's estate that is subject to the laws of the Code state must be managed, expended or distributed to or for the use of the protected person or any of his or her dependents [5–402(2)];

(3) The determination of matters subsequent to appointment such as bonding, accounting, dis-

tribution or any other appropriate relief [5–415(a)];

(4) The determination of instructions requested by the conservator [5–415(b)]; and

(5) The determination of termination of the protective proceeding. [5–429].

The Court also has concurrent jurisdiction with any other court that also may obtain jurisdiction over issues concerned with the determination of the validity of third persons' claims against the protected person individually or against his or her estate and for the determination of his title to any property or claim. [5–402(3); see 5–427].

B. JURISDICTION OVER THE PERSON

Similar to the rule applicable to personal representatives [see § 15.03(B)], the Code provides a continuing type of personal jurisdiction power in the Court of appointment or acceptance over the fiduciaries serving persons under disability. This continuing jurisdiction power is applicable to guardians of minors [5–208], guardians of incapacitated persons [5–307] and conservators of their estates. [5–412]. It subjects these fiduciaries to any proceeding relating to their fiduciary office that may be instituted by any interested person. The only special requirement to sustain this jurisdiction is that a specific notice requirement must be satisfied for each proceeding.

C. VENUE

For proceedings dealing with the guardianship of a minor, venue is in the place where the minor resides or is present. [5–205]. Venue for proceedings dealing with the guardianship of an incapacitated person is also generally in the place where the incapacitated person resides or is present. [5–302]. Venue in such latter proceedings, however, may also be in the Court of competent jurisdiction that had ordered the incapacitated person admitted to an institution. Venue for protective proceedings may be either in the place where the person to be protected resides or if that person does not reside in the Code state, in any place where she has property. [5–403(1)–(2)]. Venue for protective proceedings based upon the person's residence is not affected by a guardian having been appointed in another place. [5–403(1)]. It is important to note that the one appropriate venue recognized for all three types of proceedings concerned with a person under a disability is based upon the disabled person's residence and not her domicile. Reconciliation of identical proceedings in two or more appropriate venues must be made according to Section 1–303. [See § 3.01].

D. REQUEST FOR NOTICE

Using a procedure similar to the demand for notice procedure in Article III, the Code provides that any interested person may file a request for notice with the Registrar. [5–104; see 3–204, § 15.03(E)]. Governmental agencies paying or planning to pay benefits to the protected person are considered interested persons under this procedure. The request must include the following information and statements: (1) the interest of the person making the request; (2) the demandant's address or that of the attorney; and (3) that the request is effective only to matters occurring after the date of its filing. Upon the payment of any required fee, the clerk must mail a copy of the request to any appointed conservator.

CHAPTER 29

AVOIDANCE DEVICES AND DURABLE POWERS OF ATTORNEY

§ 29.01 Miscellaneous Avoidance Devices

One of the goals of the Code's provisions concerned with persons under disabilities is to minimize the necessity for employing the devices and procedures and to simplify these procedures and devices when it is essential to employ them. Several collateral but related devices incorporated within the Code which support this goal deserve discussion at this point.

In the case of a minor, the Code includes a facility of payment provision. Under it, any person who owes the minor $5,000 or less of cash or personal property per year may pay or deliver it either to the minor, if eighteen or married, to the minor's custodian, to the minor's guardian or into a federally insured financial institution savings account in the minor's name and with notice to the minor of the deposit. [5–101]. If these conditions are met, the person making the payment or delivery is discharged from liability for misappropriation by the recipient. Any person to whom the property is delivered or paid, other than the minor and the financial institution, is obligated to apply

the money or property (1) to the minor's present
needs for support and education, (2) to preserve
any excess for future payment for support, and (3)
to preserve any excess above the first two purposes
for delivery to the minor upon attaining majority.
These same recipients are also empowered to reimburse themselves for out of pocket expenses for the
minor's support although they may not pay themselves for their own services. Payments or deliveries may not be made under this section if the
person who owes the minor has actual notice that
an appointed conservator exists or that a proceeding for the appointment of one is pending. This
facility of payment provision will provide a convenient alternative to a conservatorship and other
protective proceedings, for example, where contractual obligors such as insurance companies have
small and annual payments due to a minor. [5–
101, Comment]. The Code also has a special facility of payment provision for distributions from estates by personal representatives. [3–915; § 23.-
01].

The Code includes another provision which, under its limited circumstances, may also avoid the
necessity of the appointment of a guardian for both
a minor and an incapacitated person. Except for
the power to consent to a minor's marriage or
adoption, a parent or guardian may temporarily
delegate to another person any of the care, custody
and property powers exercisable for the benefit of
the ward. [5–102]. The only two requirements for
such a delegation are that the form of the delegation must be made by a properly executed power of
attorney and its term cannot exceed six months in

duration. This provision provides a parent or a guardian with a convenient and simple method to provide continual guardianship protection in case an emergency would arise while the parent or appointed guardian was absent. For example, the delegatee could give consent to an emergency operation. [5–102, Comment]. The delegation of parental powers, however, does not necessarily change the child's legal residence or custody. [Chapp v. High School District No. 1 of Pima County (1978)].

§ 29.02 Durable Powers of Attorney

Durable power statutes exist in all state and equivalent jurisdictions in this country. [See Collin, Moses, & Lombard, Drafting the Durable Power of Attorney]. They have become a significant alternative for conservatorships. They permit persons to anticipate the problem of diminished or full incapacity without the need for court involvement. For many estate planners, the durable power is as an essential document for their clients as is the will.

The Code incorporates the Uniform Durable Power of Attorney Act, as amended, into Part 5 of Article V. [5–501 to 5–505; see Uniform Durable Power of Attorney Act]. Two principles are adopted that make powers of attorney more durable than under the common law. First, the civil law rule with regard to the effect of the principal's death, disability or incompetence applies to all written powers of attorney. [5–504]. It provides that actions by the attorney in fact in good faith and according to the written power of attorney are valid even though such actions take place after the principal's death, disability or incompetence so long as the attorney in fact did not have actual knowledge of the happening of such an event. Any such valid action taken binds the principal and the principal's heirs, devisees and personal representative. For the protection of third parties dealing with the attorney in fact and in the absence of fraud, an affidavit executed by the attorney in fact stating that the attorney in fact did not have knowledge at the time of his action of a revocation or termination caused by death, disability or incompetence is conclusive proof of nonrevocation or nontermination of the power to act at that time. [5–505]. If the action taken requires the execution and delivery of a recordable instrument, the affidavit is also recordable when authenticated. Significantly, this provision does not alter or effect any inconsistent provision in the power of attorney dealing with revocation or termination.

Second, the Code permits the creation of a true durable power of attorney in the instrument creating the power merely by the inclusion of specific provisions. [5–501 to 5–503]. Under the relevant sections, a written power of attorney may specifically provide that the disability of the principal does not affect the power of the appointed attorney in fact to act. [5–502]. The Code offers suggestions for the necessary phrases to create such a power. [5–501]. For a power of attorney that is immediately effective, the phrase suggested is "This power of attorney shall not be affected by disability or incapacity of the principal or lapse of time." For a power which will become effective in the future due to disability, called a "springing power," the suggested phrase is "This power of attorney shall become effective upon the disability or incapacity of the principal." Neither phrase constitutes words of art and the substance of their purpose and effect may be stated with other similar words.

Under a true durable power, all actions taken according to the power by the attorney in fact during a period of disability or incompetence of the principal have the same binding and beneficial effect as if the principal was not disabled. [5–502]. In addition, the same effect applies to actions taken under circumstances where it is uncertain whether the principal is dead or alive. These durable powers remain effective until a time explicitly expressed in the instrument, if any is expressed, or until terminated by the death of the principal, whichever first occurs.

If due to the disability or disappearance a conservator is appointed for the principal, the attorney in fact must account to the conservator as well as the principal. [5–503(a)]. The conservator now has the same power over the attorney in fact as the principal would have had if incapacity or disappearance had not occurred, including the power to revoke, suspend or terminate any part or all of the power. This power over the attorney in fact does not apply to a guardian of the person for the principal.

Significantly, the principal may include in the durable power a nomination of the person whom the principal desires to serve as conservator if

protective proceedings are commenced. [5–503(b)].
Usually, a principal names the attorney in fact as
the nominee in order to prevent any conflict that
might arise between two persons serving in different fiduciary roles. The principal may also nominate in the durable power the person to serve as
guardian of the person. The Court must appoint
the nominee unless good cause or disqualification
is shown.

CHAPTER 30

THE GUARDIAN OF A MINOR

§ 30.01 The Guardian of a Minor

Guardianship of a minor is treated in the Code as a separate relationship. A full set of provisions are provided specifically dealing with the guardian's necessity, selection, appointment, powers, duties, liabilities, duration and termination. [5–201 to 5–212]. Because incapacity due to minority is assumed by law, the procedures provided for the establishment of a guardianship for a minor are not as comprehensive and protective as they are for the creation of guardianships for other persons under a disability.

Under the Code, no guardianship by any method may be created for a person who is incapacitated solely because of minority unless the minor is unmarried and all parental rights of custody have been terminated or suspended. [5–202(b), 5–204(a)]. Consequently, a natural or adoptive parent is automatically the guardian of the person of his or her minor natural and adopted children. There need be no official acceptance or court action taken in these situations. Presumably, any parent would have to be removed according to removal proceedings before any other person could be appointed guardian of that parent's minor children. [5–204(a); see 5–212].

The Code creates a nearly unique procedure for the appointment of a guardian for a minor. This is called parental appointment and is analogous to informal appointment under Article III of the Code. [5-202; see § 17.02]. Under this procedure the parent of an unmarried minor may appoint a guardian for the minor by will or by any other writing which is signed by the parent and attested by at least two witnesses. [5-202(a)]. Under circumstances where a guardian of a minor may be appointed, the mere filing of the parental appointment or the probate of the appointing will in the proper court, constitutes an effective creation of the guardianship. [5-202(b), and (c)]. Upon acceptance, the guardian must give notice to the minor and to any person having the minor's care or the minor's nearest adult relative. [5-202(d)]. A parental appointment may be prevented or terminated by a minor ward who is fourteen or more years of age. [5-203]. The ward must object before the appointment is accepted or within 30 days after receiving notice of its acceptance. If the objection is proper and timely, a guardian may only be appointed by the court.

The court appointment of a guardian of a minor is analogous to formal appointment under Article III of the Code. [5-204; see § 17.03]. It requires the filing of a petition, notice, hearing, and order of appointment. [See 5-204 to 5-206]. The court is duty bound to appoint the person whose appointment would be in the best interest of the minor. [5-207]. The nominee of the minor fourteen or more years of age may but need not necessarily be appointed. Temporary guardians, with full powers of general guardians, may be appointed but their terms may not run more than 6 months. [5–204(b)].

Under the Code, a guardian of a minor has the powers and duties of a parent who properly has custody and whose child is unemancipated. [5–209(a), (b), and (c)]. The guardian is specifically required to become and continue to be personally acquainted with the ward. [5–209(b)(1)]. Although the guardian must protect the ward's assets and use available monies for the benefit of ward's support, care and education, the guardian is not the conservator and is primarily responsible for controlling the minor's personal activities and relationships. This includes, for example, the authority to establish a residence, consent to medical or other professional care, and consent to marriage or adoption of the ward. [5–209(c)]. The guardian has a duty to seek the appointment of a conservator or other protective proceeding, if necessary, and to turn excess monies over to a conservator. Any compensation for services or reimbursement for room, board or clothing, or both, for the guardian must be approved by a court or an independent conservator appointed for the estate of the ward. [5–209(d)].

The Code includes a provision for limited guardianships for minors. [5–209(e)]. This permits the court to restrict the guardian's control over the ward's personal conduct in certain ways. It might, for example, restrict the guardian as to a particular place of abode or residence. [5–209, Comment]. Any limitation placed on the guardian's statutory powers, however, must be endorsed on the letters of guardianship.

The guardian does not have a duty to provide bond or to file periodic or final accountings. Presumably, the Court with its inherent power over these matters could order both to be given. [See 2 UPC Practice Manual, 509–10]. In addition, it is very significant to emphasize that a guardian's duties and powers do not terminate even though she moves herself and ward from the state of appointment. [5–201; 5–209(c)(2)]. The guardian, of course, is liable to ward for injury caused by any breach of duty or improper exercise of a power or both.

A guardianship of a minor continues until the minor dies, is adopted, marries or attains majority and it terminates upon the guardian's death, removal or approved resignation. [5–210]. A testamentary appointment is also terminated if the will which makes the appointment is denied probate in formal testacy proceedings. Although a guardian may resign fiduciary office, the resignation does not terminate the guardianship until it is approved by the Court. Termination means the guardian's authority and responsibility end, but does not affect the guardian's liability for prior acts or her duty to account for the ward's funds and assets.

Removal proceedings may be instituted by any person interested in the ward's welfare or by the ward personally if fourteen years of age or more. [5–212(a)]. The ground for removal is that it would be in the best interest of the ward. Notice of the proceeding must be given to the ward, the

guardian and others as court ordered. [5–212(b)].
After notice and a hearing, the Court may order
termination by removal and may make any other
appropriate orders. [5–212(c)]. If the Court determines that the ward's interests are or may be
inadequately represented, it can appoint a guardian ad litem for the minor at anytime during the
proceeding. [5–212(d)]. When the minor is fourteen or more years of age, the Court is to give
preference to the attorney selected by the minor.

CHAPTER 31

THE GUARDIAN OF AN INCAPACITATED PERSON

§ 31.01 The Guardian of an Incapacitated Person

The Code defines an incapacitated person as one who for any reason except minority is "lacking sufficient understanding or capacity to make or communicate responsible decisions." [5–103(7)]. Although any cause which meets the standard is covered, specifically mentioned examples of the cause of such a condition include mental illness, mental deficiency, physical illness or disability, chronic use of drugs and chronic intoxication. It must be emphasized that this guardian is not the guardian of the incapacitated person's property but is the caretaker of the incapacitated person's person. [See 5–309]. Consequently, the definition of incapacity makes questions concerning the alleged incapacitated person's ability to manage the person's estate irrelevant. [2 UPC Practice Manual, 520].

Similar to the parental appointment procedure for the appointment of a guardian for a minor, the Code includes an appointment procedure for parents or spouses of other incapacitated persons. [5–301; see § 30.01]. Under this procedure the spouse or parent of an incapacitated person may appoint a guardian for the person by will or by any other writing which is signed by the spouse or parent and attested by at least two witnesses. [5–301(a), and (b)]. A spouse's appointment takes priority over a parent's appointment if they conflict. [5–301(b)]. In addition, the appointment in the will of the last parent to die has priority over the first to die unless the surviving parent has been adjudged incapacitated or the will of the last parent to die is denied probate in formal testacy proceedings. [5–301(a)]. Apparently any person can be appointed. [See 5–301(d); 5–301, Comment]. A testamentary guardian who has accepted appointment under a will probated in another state which is the testator's domicile must also be recognized in the Code state. [5–301(c)].

An appointment under this procedure becomes effective upon the nominee's filing of an acceptance of appointment in the Court in which the will has been, either informally or formally probated, or in which the instrument is filed at the place where the incapacitated person resides or is present. [5–301(a), and (b)]. The appointed guardian must give seven days advance notice to the incapacitated person and to the person's caretaker or to the person's nearest adult relative. The notice must state that the appointment may be terminated by the incapacitated person filing a written objection with the Court. Concomitantly, the incapacitated person can prevent the appointment from taking effect or terminate a previous testamentary appointment by filing a written objection with the appropriate Court. [5–301(d)]. This objection would not necessarily foreclose the person from eventually being appointed but would restrict that person's appointment solely to the result of a court appointment procedure.

When testamentary appointment is not available or desired, a guardian for an incapacitated person must be appointed by the Court. The Code's court appointment procedures are meritoriously rigorous and designed to prevent unwanted appointments of such guardians. The procedure is initiated by the incapacitated person, or by any person interested in the person's welfare, filing a petition for a finding of incapacity and for the appointment of a guardian. [5–303(a)]. Although the Code does not state what the contents of the petition must have, it is very explicit with regard to the requirements for notice of the date and time of the hearing on such a petition. [5–304]. The person alleged to be incapacitated must be personally served with notice and waiver of such notice is ineffective unless that person is present at the hearing or a visitor confirms the waiver after an interview with the person. [5–304(c)]. The person's spouse, parents and adult children must also be personally served if they can be found within the state. [5–304(a)(1), (c)]. Finally, any guardian, conservator, caretaker, or custodian, parents and spouse of the person, if not found within the state, must be given notice as provided in Section 1–401. [5–304(a)(2), (c)]. If the alleged incapacitated person's spouse, parents, and adult children are not notified, then one of the person's closest adult relatives must be notified if one can be found. [5–304(a)(3)].

Protection is also provided the alleged incapacitated person throughout the proceeding. First, the person must be represented by personally selected or appointed counsel. [5–303(b)]. Counsel has the duties and powers of a guardian ad litem. Second, the person must be examined by a court appointed physician or other qualified person who must submit a written report on the examination to the Court. Third, the person must be visited before appointment by a "visitor" who has no personal interest in the proceeding and who is either trained in law, nursing or social work. [5–303(b), 5–103(21)]. Finally, the alleged incapacitated person is entitled to be present at the hearing and to have counsel present evidence and cross-examine all relevant witnesses. [5–303(c)].

The scope and necessity of a jury trial in a hearing concerned with the incapacity of a person is left to the option of the enacting jurisdiction. [5–303(c)]. The bracketed phrases grant the alleged incapacitated person an election to have a jury trial or not.

Although any qualified person may be appointed guardian of an incapacitated person, the Code provides a nonmandatory priority list of suggested candidates that will be followed unless a lack of qualification, good cause or the best interest of the incapacitated person dictates otherwise. [5–305(a), and (b)]. The suggested order for consideration is as follows:

(1) Person nominated in the most recent durable power of attorney executed by the incapacitated person;

(2) Incapacitated person's spouse;

(3) Spouse's nominee under 5–301;

(4) An adult child of the incapacitated person;

(5) Incapacitated person's parent;

(6) Parent's nominee under 5–301;

(7) Any relative with whom the incapacitated person resided for more than 6 months;

(8) Person nominated by incapacitated person's caretaker.

[5–305(b), and (c)]. The Court must select the best qualified among candidates of equal priority. [5–306(d)].

Before a guardian for an incapacitated person is appointed, the Court must be satisfied that the person for whom a guardian is sought is actually incapacitated and that the appointment is necessary or at least desirable for the purpose of providing continuing care and supervision of the incapacitated person. [5–306(b)]. If the circumstances do not satisfy these criteria, the Court may dismiss or make any other appropriate order which presumably must be in the incapacitated person's best interest.

The Court is instructed "to encourage the development of maximum self-reliance and independence of the incapacitated person" and thus should tailor the appointments and orders to the specific needs of the incapacitated person. [5–306(a)]. To aid the Court in carrying out these policies, the Code includes a provision for limited guardianships. [5–306(c)]. This permits the court to restrict the guardian's control over the ward's personal conduct in certain ways. It might, for example, limit the guardian to authorization of medical treatment. [See 5–306, Comment]. Any limitation placed on the guardian's statutory powers, however, must be endorsed on the letters of guardianship.

The Code also includes provisions concerning the Court's power to appoint temporary guardians. [5–308]. When an emergency exists for an incapacitated person who has neither a guardian nor any other person with authority to act, the Court may appoint a temporary guardian who may exercise powers granted by the Court. [5–308(a)]. These powers are limited by a specific time period as determined by the enacting state. The Court is empowered to suspend the authority of a court-appointed permanent guardian and to appoint a temporary guardian for a period not to exceed six months, if the Court finds that the appointed guardian is not effectively performing the duties of the office and the welfare of the incapacitated ward requires immediate action. [5–308(b)]. Such an appointment may be made with or without notice.

Except for restrictions imposed on the limited guardian, the guardian of an incapacitated person must take care, custody and control of the ward. [5–309]. The guardian is not liable to third persons, however, merely by reason of those responsibilities. The guardian of an incapacitated person has the same duties, powers and responsibilities as a guardian for a minor. [See § 30.01].

A guardian of an incapacitated person does not have a duty to provide bond or when no conservator is appointed, to file periodic or final accountings. Presumably, the Court with its inherent powers over these matters could order both to be given. As with a guardian of a minor, the duties and powers of a guardian of an incapacitated person do not terminate even though the guardian and ward move from the state of appointment. [5–309, 5–209(c)(2)]. The guardian of an incapacitated person, of course, is liable to the ward for injury caused by a breach of duty or improper exercise of a power or both.

Termination of a guardianship for an incapacitated person occurs when either the guardian or the ward dies, when the guardian is determined to be incapacitated or when the guardian is removed or resigns according to proper procedures and proceedings. [5–310]. A testamentary appointment is also terminated if the will which makes the appointment is denied probate in formal testacy proceedings. Such a termination means the guardian's authority and responsibility end but does not affect the guardian's liability for prior acts or duty to account for the ward's funds and assets.

Removal proceedings may be instituted by the ward or by any other person interested in the ward's welfare. [5–311(a)]. The ward may request a removal order merely by sending an informal letter to the Court or judge and any intentional interference by any person with such a communication may constitute contempt of court. [5–311(b)]. So that a ward who is displeased about being judicially found to be incapacitated does not continually bring new removal proceedings, the order adjudicating incapacity can specify a discretionary restriction on review. This discretionary restriction on review is phrased in terms of time and cannot exceed six months. [See 5–311, Comment]. The procedures for removing a guardian, for accepting the resignation of a guardian and for ordering that the ward is no longer incapacitated contain the same safeguards as the proceedings to appoint a guardian. [5–311(c)].

CHAPTER 32

PROTECTIVE PROCEEDINGS AND THE CONSERVATOR

§ 32.01 Protective Proceedings and the Conservator

A. GENERALLY

As previously emphasized, the Code separates its provisions concerned with the custody and care of the ward's person from its provisions concerned with the management of the protected person's estate. Under the heading "Protective Proceedings," disabled persons who are in need of having their assets and property managed or protected may have a conservator appointed or obtain some other protective court order for such a purpose. [5–401]. The term "disabled person" is not separately defined but means a person who is either a minor or an incapacitated person or who is confined, detained or missing.

Although the provisions dealing with the management of property for minors and for all other disabled persons are combined into a single part of the Code, there are several important differences in treatment. Most important of these is that the standards upon which the Court is to base its decision to act are different. Thus a conservator may be appointed or other protective orders issued by the Court for a minor only when the minor (1) has property needing otherwise unobtainable management or protection, (2) has business affairs which minority may jeopardize or prevent, or (3) has a need for support and education funds better obtainable through a protective proceeding. [5–401(b)]. Whereas for all other disabled persons, similar court action may be taken only when a person for any reason is unable to manage her property and affairs and either (1) the person's property may be wasted or dissipated without proper management, or (2) support, care and welfare funds for that person are necessary and better obtainable through a protective proceeding. [5–401(c)].

The only method by which protective action may be obtained, including the appointment of a conservator, is by formal proceedings before Court. [5–401(a)]. These proceedings are initiated by a petition requesting a protective order or appointment. They may be filed by any of the following persons: (1) the prospective protected person; (2) any person interested in the protected person's estate, affairs or welfare; or (3) any person adversely affected by the lack of effective management. [5–404(a)].

The notice requirements for the date and time of the hearing on such a petition depend on whether a minor or other incapacitated person is involved. [5–405(a)]. The notice is the same as it is for a hearing to appoint a guardian. [5–206 (minors); 5–304 (incapacitated persons)]. If notice by personal service on the proposed protected person is impracticable because of disappearance or other reason, notice must be given by publication as provided in Section 1–401.

The Code attempts to protect a person from misuse of its protective proceedings by requiring representation for the person or review of his condition by independent third persons. In the case of minors, if the Court determines that it would be in the best interest of the minor to have an attorney appointed, it may appoint an attorney who can represent the minor as a guardian ad litem. [5–406(a)]. For other disabled persons, the person to be protected must have his own counsel or the Court must appoint an attorney to represent him as a guardian ad litem. [5–406(b)]. In addition, if the person to be protected is an incapacitated person, the Court may direct that the alleged incapacitated person be examined by a physician or send a visitor to interview him, or both. The physician selected must not be affiliated with any institution in which the person is a patient or is committed. The visitor may either be a guardian ad litem or a court officer or employee. For evaluation purposes, a public or charitable agency may be used as an additional visitor at the Court's discretion. [5–406(c)]. The person to be protected has a right to be at the hearing, be represented by counsel, present evidence, and cross-examine witnesses including those used by the court to evaluate the person. [5–406(d)]. On the Court's determination that it would be in the best interest of the person and according to its conditions, others may be allowed to participate in the proceeding. [5–406(e)]. If requested by the person to be protected or his counsel, the proceeding may be closed or before a jury (if a jury is allowed by the enacting state). [5–406(d)].

The Court may appoint a conservator or make some other protective order only after a hearing and after it is convinced that a need is established. [5–406(f)]. It is important to emphasize that the Court is instructed to order the least intrusive protective device possible under the circumstances. [5–407(a)]. The scope of these orders include what are called both protective arrangements and single transaction authorization. [5–408]. Actually, it is difficult to make a clear distinction between the two devices. Basically, protective arrangements deal with court orders which are designed to set up stable and continuing arrangements for purposes of handling the ward's foreseeable needs with respect to security, service or care. [5–408(a)]. In a non-exclusive list of permissible arrangements, the Code permits the Court under this device to issue orders dealing with payment arrangements concerned with the ward's cash or personal effects, real estate or contractual rights. In addition, the Court is given the authority to establish a suitable trust for the ward. These protective arrangements may be particularly beneficial to third persons including, for example, life insurance or annuity companies that owe the person to be protected sums of money but that do not know to whom or how properly to pay. A protective order is available under these protective arrangements to direct such third persons on these matters and to protect them from potential liability for improper payment.

Basically the single transaction power permits the Court to make any authorization, ratification or other direction which would be in the best interest of the protected person with respect to any transaction relating to the person's financial affairs or estate. [5–408(b)]. Such court orders would include single transactions such as the sale of an asset or may be a series of independent but related transactions. As its name indicates, this power is related to isolated or related transactions and not to a continuing type of an arrangement.

Under the terms of both of these devices, the Court is specifically given the authority to exercise them without appointing a conservator. [5–408(a)–(b)]. Consequently, they have obvious usefulness any time a conservatorship is not necessary. Notwithstanding this usefulness, the Court must give consideration to the interests of the protected person's creditors and dependents as to whether the continuing protection of a conservator is required. [5–408(c)]. In addition, in order to be able to carry out the protective arrangement or authorized single transaction, the Court is given the authority to appoint a special conservator for these purposes. Such a conservator has the authority conferred by the Court, must report to the Court all matters pursuant to the appointment and is discharged only by court order.

B. SELECTION AND BONDING OF THE CONSERVATOR

Because of the authority and power given by the Code to an appointed conservator and the potential for misuse of this device, the Code establishes several guidelines by which one must be appointed. A pervasive requirement is that the conservator must be an individual or a corporation possessing trustee powers. [5–409(a)]. As with other appointment procedures in the Code, it also lists specific priorities for the Court's consideration in making an appointment. [5–409(a)(1)–(7)]. Chart 32–1 describes these priorities for appointment.

CHART 32–1

Priority Order for Appointment of a Conservator

Priority Rank	Description of Candidates
1	Similar kind of fiduciary appointed by an appropriate court in any jurisdiction in which the protected person resides
2	Nominee of the protected person if the latter is at least fourteen years of age and the Court determines the person has sufficient mental capacity to make an intelligent choice
3	The spouse of the protected person
4	Any adult child of the protected person
5	A parent of the protected person including a deceased parent's testamentary nominee
6	Any relative with whom the protected person resided for more than six months prior to the petition
7	Any person nominated by the person caring for or paying benefits to the protected person

Chart 32–1 requires additional explanation. The first priority would apparently include an appropriate fiduciary appointed in a foreign country. Including the nominee of the protected person, persons holding priority through the first six ranks

may nominate in writing another person to serve in the nominator's stead. [5–409(b)]. The seventh priority would include public or governmental agencies such as the Veterans' Administration. [2 UPC Practice Manual, 533]. Between persons of equal priority, the Court has discretion to select the one best qualified if more than one is willing to serve. In addition, for good cause shown, the Court has discretion to ignore these priorities and to appoint anyone, including a person with less or without any priority. [5–409(b)].

If a conservator is appointed, the obligation to furnish a bond is left to the discretion of the Court. [5–410]. If required, the bond must be conditioned upon the faithful discharge of a conservator's fiduciary duties. Unless the Court directs otherwise, the bond must equal in value the aggregate capital value of the property of the estate plus one year's estimated income reduced by the value of court controlled securities deposited under special arrangements and by the value of real estate held by the conservator but which the conservator cannot sell without court authorization. The Court is also given discretion to accept other means of security for the performance of the fiduciary duties. Terms and conditions for bonds required are similar to those required for personal representatives. [5–411; see 3–606; § 20.03(B)]. A conservator is entitled to reasonable compensation. [5–413].

C. POWERS OF THE COURT

In dealing with the estate of a protected person, the Court is given paramount control and authority. [5–407]. During the pendency of a protective proceeding, the Court is given the power to preserve and to apply the property of the person to be protected in any manner necessary for the benefit both of that person or her dependents. [5–407(a)(1)]. Although the Court must have a preliminary hearing, there need not be any notice to other persons of this hearing.

After proper formal proceedings have been completed, the Court has extensive powers over the estates of both minors and other disabled persons. With respect to a minor without other disability, the Court has all powers over the minor's estate and affairs which are or might be necessary to the best interest of the minor, the minor's family and members of the minor's household. [5–407(a)(2)]. Much broader powers are given to the Court with respect to the estate of a person needing protection for a reason other than minority. Here, the Court has all powers over the protected person's estate and affairs which that person could exercise if present and not under the disability. [5–407(b)(3)]. The Court, however, explicitly does not have the power to make a will for the disabled person. Among the specifically mentioned powers which the Court has are the power to make gifts, release property interests, create revocable or irrevocable trusts, exercise the elective share for a surviving spouse and change beneficiaries under insurance or other contractual programs. Any such change of beneficiary, release, disclaimer or gift exceeding twenty per cent of any year's income of the estate may be ordered by the Court only after notice and hearing and after it is determined to be in the best interest of the ward. [5–407(c)]. Significantly, any court order made under this provision must follow and consider any estate plan of the protected person of which the Court has knowledge. [5–426].

Court orders under this provision have no effect upon the capacity of the protected person. [5–407(d)]. Consequently, the protected person is, in spite of any court order, still able to bind herself by contract and transfer her property at least as effectively as any equitable owner of property is able. [2 UPC Practice Manual, 537].

When a conservator is appointed, there is a direct relationship between the powers given to the Court and those given to the conservator. First, the Court is given the authority to exercise its powers either directly or indirectly through a conservator. [5–407]. Second, the Court may in its discretion and subject to the restrictions put upon its own powers, confer upon the conservator any of its own powers or it may give the conservator none of its powers and even limit the powers which a conservator normally possesses. [5–425]. Any such limitation on a conservator's ordinary powers, however, would have to be endorsed upon the conservator's letters of appointment in order to bind third parties.

D. POWERS, DUTIES AND LIABILITIES OF THE CONSERVATOR

The powers, duties and liabilities of a conservator are extensively detailed in the Code. Of the three kinds of fiduciaries provided for persons under disability dealt with in the Code, the conservator is clearly made the most important and is necessarily given the broadest authority as well as being the most supervised by the Court. Generally, the Code treats the conservator's authority over the property of the protected person in a manner very similar to the authority that a trustee has in dealing with the trust estate. [2 UPC Practice Manual, 535]. Because a conservator both is given extensive powers and is dealing with the property of a person by definition unable to effectively manage or apply one's own estate, the Code includes protective devices against overreaching or other abuses by such a fiduciary.

Although the Court has paramount authority over a conservator's powers, in the ordinary case such powers are not exercised by the Court. The conservator is given, therefore, a broad and explicit array of fiduciary powers. [5–423]. Generally, in addition to specifically conferred powers, the conservator is given all powers that a trustee would have under the law of the Code state. [5–423(a)]. Thus, the conservator is specifically accorded the power to invest and reinvest funds of the estate without court authorization or confirmation according to the law applicable to trustees investing trust assets. [5–423(b)]. Finally, when reasonably necessary to carry out the purposes of the conservatorship, a conservator is empowered to take any of a long list of specified actions and transactions without court authorization or confirmation. [5–423(c)]. These enumerated powers accorded a conservator are nearly identical to those given to a personal representative of a decedent's estate under the Code. [Compare 5–423(c)(1)–(26) with 3–715(1)–(27); see § 20.04(C)].

In addition to the above administrative powers, the conservator is accorded substantial and significant distributive powers. Again, without court authorization or confirmation, the conservator is empowered to expend and distribute the estate's income or principal or both for the protected person's support, education, care or benefit. [5–424(a)]. In making such expenditures and distributions, the conservator is given several guidelines. First, the recommendations made by the protected person's parent or guardian must be consider. [5–424(a)(1)]. By acting pursuant to such recommendations, the conservator will be liable only if the conservator knows that a parent or guardian is deriving personal financial benefit from the payment either directly or indirectly as relief from a legal duty of support, or if the recommendations are clearly not in the protected person's best interest. Second, when expending or distributing the protected person's assets, the conservator must consider the size of the estate, the anticipated duration of the conservatorship, the potential for future termination of the conservatorship, the protected person's accustomed standard of living and the latter's other funds or sources of funds. [5–424(a)(2)]. Third, the conservator may also consider the protected person's legal dependents or other members of the relevant household who are in need and are unable to support themselves. [5–424(a)(3)]. Finally, payments may be made to reimburse any person, including the protected person, for proper expenditures or may be made in advance of services when the conservator reasonably expects them to be performed and when advance payment is customary or reasonably necessary. [5–424(a)(4)].

Except for the requirement of court approval for amounts exceeding twenty per cent of the income of the estate for any year, a conservator is permitted to make gifts to charities and to other objects in the same manner as the protected person would be expected to make if the estate is otherwise sufficient for the purposes of the conservatorship. [5–424(b)]. Significantly, this gift-making power does not apply to the conservator of a person who is disabled solely because of minority.

Upon majority for a minor and upon the ceasing of the disability for other protected persons, the conservator is required to pay over all of the unprotected person's funds and properties to him as soon as possible. [5–424(c)–(d)]. Before making payment, however, the conservator must pay all prior claims and expenses of the administration.

A conservator's power may even extend beyond the protected person's death. If the protected person dies and no personal representative is appointed or no application for such appointment is made within forty days from the date of death, the conservator may be authorized by the Court to act as personal representative. [5–424(e)]. Notice must be given to persons demanding notice under Section 3–204 and to any person nominated executor in any known will of the deceased. Under this section there need not be an actual transfer of title from the conservator to the conservator as personal representative.

If a guardian has not been appointed for a minor who is unmarried, under eighteen years of age, and without parents, a conservator has no duty to commence guardianship proceedings and may, if willing, perform the functions of a guardian until the minor becomes eighteen or married. [5–423(a)]. This discretionary power in a conservator may in the appropriate case eliminate the need for the appointment of a guardian of a minor. The same power does not exist in a conservator for a person who is disabled for reasons other than minority.

The conservator's duties are commensurate with the conservator's powers. A conservator's pervasive duty is to exercise the power of the office as a fiduciary according to the standard of care set out in the Code for trustees. [5–416; see 7–302]. In addition, every conservator is required to prepare and to file with the appointing court within ninety days of the appointment a complete inventory of the protected person's estate. [5–417]. Copies of this inventory must be provided to the protected person if the person is fourteen years of age or more and has sufficient mental capacity to understand these matters. A copy of the inventory must also be provided to the parent or guardian with whom the protected person resides.

A conservator also has a record keeping and accounting requirement. Under the Code, the conservator is required to keep suitable records of the administration for the inspection and perusal of any interested person. [5–417]. Not less often than annual and on termination, a conservator is required to account either to the Court or to the protected person or the latter's personal representative. [5–418]. The conservator may voluntarily or involuntarily proceed through formal intermediate and final accountings before the Court. [See § 32.01(I)]. In such an accounting proceeding, the Court may require, in any manner it specifies, the conservator to submit to a physical check of the estate under conservator's control.

In the overall administration of a protected person's estate, including the investment and distribution of assets, the conservator, as is the Court in the exercise of its extensive power, is required to take into account any known estate plan of the protected person. [5–426]. The Code includes the protected person's will, trust and any other will substitutes within the term estate plan. Naturally, the conservator is given the authority to examine the protected person's will. This is a beneficial provision with the goal of reducing unfair and unintentional hardship or loss to the eventual beneficiaries of the protected person's estate.

At any time during the administration of a conservatorship, the Code provides that any person interested in the welfare of the protected person is permitted to file a petition requesting special protection from the conservator's misconduct or for any other appropriate relief. [5–415(a)]. Notice and hearing are necessary for such proceedings. [5–415(c)]. The scope of the petition and of the resultant order is very broad. The conservator may also seek instructions concerning the fiduciary relationship. [5–415(b)].

Although not specifically stated in the Code, a conservator is liable to interested persons for any damage or loss that results from a breach of any fiduciary duty in the improper exercise of a power. This liability should be characterized as the same as a trustee of an express trust. [See 3–712].

In addition to potential liability for loss and damages due to breach of a fiduciary duty, sales or encumbrances of estate property by the conservator to the conservator, personally, or the conservator's spouse, agent, attorney or any corporation or trust in which the conservator has a substantial beneficial interest are voidable unless the Court approves the transaction after notice to interested persons and to others as the Court directs. [5–421]. Similarly, any other transaction involving the estate which is affected by a substantial conflict of interest on the part of the conservator is voidable.

E. THE CONSERVATOR'S TITLE

Contrary to the common law and to the law of most non-Code states today, the Code vests in a conservator a trustee's title to all of the protected person's property. [5–419; see 2 UPC Practice Manual, 537]. This title vests upon appointment and covers not only the property presently held by the protected person but any property thereafter acquired and any property held by custodians or attorneys in fact for the benefit of the protected person. In order that this transfer of title by operation of law does not have unexpected and undesired consequences, the Code specifically provides that the vesting of title in the conservator upon appointment is not a transfer or alienation for purposes of general provisions in statutes, regulations, contracts or other estate planning devices that restrict or penalize the transfer or alienation by the protected person. A specific provision in a contract or other dispositive instrument concerning the effect of the appointment of a conservator will be given effect, however. [See 2 UPC Practice Manual, 537–38]. A spendthrift effect is included with regard to voluntary and involuntary transfers by the protected person. [5–419(b), and (c)].

Proof of the transfer of title between the protected person and the conservator, and vice versa, is handled in an extremely efficient manner in the Code. [5–420(a)]. For the transfer from the protected person to the conservator, the letters of conservatorship represent evidence of the transfer. For the transfer between the conservator and the protected person or the latter's successors, an order of the Court terminating the conservatorship is evidence of the transfer.

For the purpose of being able to give record notice of title as between the conservator and the protected person, the Code permits the letters of conservatorship and the court order terminating a conservatorship to be filed or recorded. [5–420(b)]. The requirements of the filing and recording statutes must be satisfied. This procedure is essential to protect the conservator from third persons claiming title to real estate purchased directly from the protected person. [See 2 UPC Practice

Manual, 538]. This conflict of titles is a possibility because conservatorship, alone does not affect the legal capacity of the protected person. [5–407(d)].

F.   LIABILITY OF THIRD PERSONS

As previously discussed, the Code confers upon the conservator the authority to perform numerous transactions with third persons without court supervision. Under the present law of most non-Code states, any third person who deals with a conservator faces the possibility of being liable for having participated in the conservator's breach of the fiduciary responsibilities. [See § 20.05]. Under the Code, a third person, who has dealt with or assisted a conservator in good faith and for value, is protected as if the conservator properly exercised a power unless the transaction is of the type that requires a court order under Section 5–407. [5–422; see § 32.01(C)]. In addition, the third person is not required to inquire into the existence of a power or into the propriety of its exercise merely because ones knows the other is a conservator. An exception to this rule provides that third persons are bound by restrictions on the powers of a conservator which have been endorsed on the letters of conservatorship under Section 5–425.

G.   CREDITORS' CLAIMS

As with a fiduciary who manages any kind of an estate, one of a conservator's responsibilities is the payment and settlement of claims against the estate. The Code has a provision dealing with this problem which is in some respects similar to its provisions concerned with creditor's claims against a decedent's estate. [5–427; see §§ 22.03, 22.04].

A conservator upon presentation and allowance is required to pay all just claims against the estate and the protected person. [5–427(a)]. This rule applies whether the claim arose before or after the date on which the conservator was appointed. The conservator may either allow or disallow the claim. [5–427(b)]. Failure to mail notice of disallowance constitutes an allowance sixty days after the claim's presentation. Any applicable statute of limitations against a properly presented claim is tolled until thirty days after its disallowance. Consequently, actions on disallowed claims must be instituted by the claimant within the applicable statute of limitations and the tolled period.

If claimants desire, they may forego the presentation procedure and directly petition the Court for determination of the claims. [5–427(c)]. Upon due proof of the claim the creditor may obtain an order for its allowance and payment from the estate. In order for a judgment against a protected person to constitute a claim against protected person's estate, however, the successful litigant must give notice of the proceeding to the conservator. This notice is necessary both for proceedings pending against the protected person at the time of the conservator's appointment and for those initiated against the protected person after the appointment.

If the estate of the protected person is insolvent, the conservator must follow an abatement procedure similar to that required for estates. [5–427(c), and (d); see § 22.04].

H. THE CONSERVATOR'S LIABILITY
TO THIRD PERSONS

The Code deals directly with the difficult problem of a conservator's personal liability to third persons on contracts, from ownership or control of the estate's property and from torts arising out of the administration of the estate. [5–428]. The content of the provision is identical to the provision included for personal representatives in Article III. [3–808; see § 20.08].

I. DURATION, TERMINATION
AND REMOVAL OF THE
CONSERVATOR

When a minor attains majority or when the conservator is satisfied that the protected person's disability no longer exists, the conservator is empowered and required to terminate the conservatorship and to pay over and distribute all funds and assets to the protected person as soon as possible after the payment of claims and expenses of administration. [5–424(c)–(d)]. On such a termination, a conservator is required to account either to the Court or to the protected person or, if deceased, the personal representative. [5–418].

Upon a petition by the protected person, the personal representative if the person is dead, any person interested in the protected person's welfare or the conservator, the Court in its discretion may terminate the conservatorship. [5–429]. Throughout the steps of the termination proceeding, the protected person has the same rights and procedural protections as if it were a proceeding to initiate a protective order. If the Court determines that minority or disability has ceased, it may terminate the conservatorship. Upon termination by Court order, title to the protected person's property passes either to the protected person or to his successors. The order of court may make the title, however, subject to expenses of administration, or for evidence purposes to a conservator's conveyance, or to both conditions.

Removal proceedings may be instituted by any person interested in the welfare of the protected person. [5–415(a)(4)]. The conservator can be removed by the Court for good cause upon notice and a hearing. [5–414]. Although a conservator may resign the fiduciary office, the resignation does not terminate the guardianship until it is approved by the Court. The Court is empowered to appoint another conservator if a vacancy occurs because of resignation, removal or death. If a new conservator is appointed, the successor conservator assumes the title and the powers of the prior conservator. A conservator who has resigned or has been removed must account to the Court. [5–418].

A conservator may end potential liability by petitioning the Court for a reviewed and approved intermediate or final accounting. [5–418]. After notice and hearing, the Court's order concerning such an accounting adjudicates up to the time of the accounting all of the conservator's unsettled liabilities to the protected person and to all the latter's successors subject of course to the ordinary time limitations for appeal or vacation.

§ 32.02　The Foreign Conservator

Similar to the administration of a decedent's estate, the administration of a protected person's estate may require the conservator to administer property in two or more states. [See § 26.01]. Consistent with its general purposes, the Code strives to ease and unify the administration of a protected person's multi-state estate. First, a foreign conservator or similar fiduciary appointed by a court in the state where the protected person resides may collect debts or property from persons within the Code state by presenting to the debtors or possessors proof of the appointment and an affidavit. [5–430; compare 4–201; see § 26.02]. This procedure is available, however, only when there has been no local appointment.

Second, concurrently or alternately, a domiciliary foreign conservator is entitled to exercise all powers which a local conservator could exercise merely by filing in a court in the Code state authenticated copies of the domiciliary appointment and the official bond, if any. [5–431; see § 32.-01(D); compare § 26.02]. These powers specifically include the power to bring legal proceedings which any nonresident could bring in the courts of the Code nondomiciliary jurisdiction. Similarly, this filing has the above effect only if no local protective proceeding is pending and no local conservator has been appointed.

Unlike its comparable provisions in Article IV, there are no supplemental provisions dealing with the protection of locally interested persons [see 4–207, § 26.02] or providing for personal jurisdiction over the foreign conservator. [See 4–301; § 26.03]. Presumably, these deficiencies can be cured by the inherent power of the Court over protective proceeding matters together with the Code state's long-arm statute.

Several other provisions concerned with foreign conservators deserve mention. First, as previously discussed, any foreign conservator or similar fiduciary appointed in the jurisdiction where the protected person resides has priority over all other persons to be appointed conservator in the local Code state. [5–409(a)(1)]. This provision greatly protects the foreign conservator in the administration of the protected person's property in the local jurisdiction. The Code also attempts to give extraterritorial authority to a conservator appointed under its provisions. Such a conservator is given the power to prosecute and defend claims of any nature concerning the protection of the estate or of the conservator's fiduciary responsibilities in any jurisdiction. [5–423(c)(25)]. Although some states may refuse to recognize this power, it should aid conservators greatly in administering the protected person's assets in most jurisdictions.

*

PART SIX
NONPROBATE TRANSFERS

CHAPTER 33

NONTESTAMENTARY CONTRACTUAL ARRANGEMENTS

§ 33.01 Nontestamentary Contractual Arrangements

It is not unusual for persons to insert in various contractual arrangements provisions concerning the consequences of the death of the parties or the primary party to the contract. For example, in a partnership between two persons it may be desirable for each of the partners to provide in the partnership agreement that the partnership will automatically transfer to the surviving partner whomever it may be. Another arrangement that is found particularly in family dealings concerns a parent who has loaned money to a child and received back a promissory note which has a provision that the obligation of the note ceases upon the death of the promisor or promisee or that the obligation on the debt to the promisor is to be paid to another person.

Provisions of this nature have often been held by courts to be invalid because they are characterized as testamentary and unless the instruments were executed with the same formalities as a will including testamentary intent, they are ineffective to pass the interest conveyed upon death. [Atkinson, Wills § 44]. In modern transactions, similar type provisions are often found in life insurance and retirement benefit instruments. They constitute a very convenient way to pass the interest in property outside the probate process and because they are ordinarily represented by a written instrument they carry with them many of the same protections that the statute of wills demands by its execution formalities for wills. It is desirable, therefore, to validate these instruments.

In a broadly phrased provision, the Code accords nontestamentary status to three types of provisions sometimes found in inter vivos transactions. [6–101]. These provisions have often been held by courts to be invalid because they were characterized as testamentary. [Atkinson, Wills § 44]. The three provisions that the Code recognizes as nontestamentary are provisions which in substance provide as follows: (1) to pay money or other benefits due to, controlled, or owned by an obligee to a designated person on the death of the obligee; (2) to waive a debt on the event of the death of the obligee; and (3) to permit the obligee to designate the beneficiary of contractual or property rights which are the subject of an instrument. [6–101(a)(1)–(3)]. The first and third provisions above may be included within either the instrument of creation of the transaction or a separate writing, including a will, executed at the same time or subsequently.

This section will not only establish the validity of many common provisions found in insurance policies, pension plans, annuity contracts, trust agreements and other family arrangements, but it will also validate the use of these provisions in a wide range of commercial transactions including bonds, mortgages, promissory notes, and conveyances. With their guaranteed validity and because the effect of the provision is to avoid the process of the administration of the estate, the use of these provisions in all forms of written instruments may become extremely popular. Although the assets passing by the terms of the provisions are valid and avoid the burden of administration, they do not infringe upon the rights of a creditor established under other laws of the Code state. [6–101(b)].

The Code provision does not intend to bootstrap the validity of the underlying document, financial arrangement, or instrument. [See 6–101, Comment]. For example, it is not intended to validate an ineffective inter vivos gift such as an undelivered deed to real property. The deed transfer is ineffective for lack of delivery and thus the property does not pass or is not transferred to the donee. This provision is not designed to convert the lifetime transfer attempt into a transfer on death. The 1969 version of the Code which made reference to "or any other written instrument effective as a contract, gift, conveyance or trust" was interpreted by the Supreme Court of Washington to eliminate the need for delivery of lifetime gifts of deeds.

[Estate of O'Brien v. Robinson (1988)]. The North Dakota court correctly held that this section did not eliminate the necessity of the delivery of deed to effectuate a lifetime gift of an asset. [First National Bank in Minot v. Bloom (1978)]. In 1989 the offending language was removed and replaced with the phrase "or other written instrument of a similar nature." The comment clearly indicates that this provision is not to validate otherwise invalid transfers or contractual arrangements.

CHAPTER 34

MULTIPLE–PARTY ACCOUNTS

§ 34.01 Introduction to Multiple-Party Accounts

A very common and popular method of holding accounts and deposits with financial institutions is in some form of two or more names. These arrangements are called multiple-party accounts and typically have taken one of the following forms:

(1) Joint accounts, e.g., an account payable to "A or B";

(2) Trust accounts, e.g., an account held as "A in trust for B"; and,

(3) Accounts payable on death or POD accounts, e.g., an account held as "A payable on death to B."

[2 UPC Practice Manual, 564].

Unfortunately, accounts in these forms generate an inordinate amount of litigation concerning various legal problems. [See Scott, Trusts, §§ 58–58.6]. Much of the litigation deals with the determination of the legal foundations for the creation of the multiple accounts. The pervasive issue is whether they are effective to pass property to the non-contributing party at the death of the donor or whether they are testamentary and therefore must satisfy the execution requirements of a Statute of Wills. [1 Page, § 6.18].

All three of the above types of multiple-party accounts generate litigation over other issues as well. These issues relate to problems arising before the donor's death or after donor's death or at both times. Pre-death problems include the rights in the account between the donor and the donee and the rights of the donor's and the donee's creditors in the account. Post-death problems include, in addition to the validity question, the rights of the decedent's creditors and the rights of the donor's surviving spouse or other persons protected from disinheritance. Excluding the many tax issues raised by multiple-party accounts, the other pervasive issues include the manner and time of revocation, the sufficiency of evidence to rebut survivorship and the relationship of the fiduciary institution which holds the account of the persons named on the account and their successors.

The Code addresses the question of the validity of multiple-party, POD, and trust accounts as well as their pre- and post-death problems, including the protection of financial institutions. [Art. VI, Part 2]. The Code's technique (1) eliminates references to the "joint" account and substitutes the more generic term "multiple-party account" and (2) consolidates treatment of the POD account and the trust account so that the same rules apply to both. [Prefatory Note, Art. 6]. Its provisions are divisible into three categories:

(1) General and clarifying definitions of terms;

(2) Ownership issues as between the parties of the multiple-party accounts and other persons including creditors and successors; and

(3) Issues concerning the liability of the financial institutions.

The latter two categories are intentionally separated so that differing intentions of the parties may affect arrangements in the second category without endangering the element of definiteness needed for the third category to induce financial institutions to offer such accounts to their customers. [6–206; see 2 UPC Practice Manual, 565].

§ 34.02 Definitions and General Provisions for Multiple–Party Accounts

Article VI contains twelve special definitions of terms which are applicable to its provisions on multiple-party accounts. [6–201]. A knowledge of these definitions is essential to an understanding of Article VI. For informational and overview purposes Chart 34–1 lists them in alphabetical order.

CHART 34–1

Terms Defined for Multiple Party Accounts

Account	Payment
Agent	POD designation
Beneficiary	Receive
Financial institution	Request
Multiple-party account	Sums on deposit
Party	Terms of the account

With the following noted exceptions, the meaning of each term will be provided only when the definition is necessary and relevant to the discussion in the text. Several terms require separate explanation here because of their pervasive importance to an understanding of the following discussion of Article VI.

First, it is necessary to understand the type of account with which Article VI is concerned. An "account" is defined as any type of contractual arrangement for the deposit of funds between a depositor and a financial institution and includes the ordinary checking account, savings account, certificate of deposit and the share account. The definition of "multiple-party account" is broadly phrased to include any account having more than one owner with a present interest in the account. [6–201, Comment]. Technical distinctions in the wording of the terms of the account are eliminated. Use of terms such as "joint tenancy," "tenancy in common," "or," "and," "right of survivorship," "JTWROS," or "JT TEN," are unnecessary to qualify as a multiple-party account and are covered by the terms of the Code's multiple-party account provisions. Although this broad definition encompasses any account that has two or more names, partnership, joint venture, corporation, charitable organization, or other fiduciary or trust accounts, in which the relationship is established by separate instrument or arrangement, are expressly excluded from coverage of these provisions. [6–202].

An understanding of the terms "party," "POD designation," and "beneficiary" is also essential. A "party" is a person, other than a beneficiary or agent, who has a present right to payment from the multiple-party account, subject to making a proper request for payment. [6–201(6)]. This right to payment must be set forth by the terms of the multiple-party account. A "request" constitutes the prescribed method set by the financial institution for obtaining payment from the account. [6–201(10)].

Although the definition of the word "party" is the same for multiple-party accounts, POD accounts and trust accounts, its application to each of them is different. In a multiple-party account, all of the persons named on the account are parties. [6–201, Comment]. For a POD account and a trust account it means the original payee and the trustee, respectively, who make deposits during their lifetimes. Upon the death of the original payee and trustee, the surviving POD payee and the beneficiary of a trust account, respectively, become parties to the accounts.

A "POD designation" is the designation of a beneficiary in one of two types of accounts. [6–201(8)]. First, it refers to the designation of a beneficiary in an account payable on request (1) to one party during the party's lifetime and upon the party's death to one or more beneficiaries or (2) to multiple parties during their lifetimes and upon the death of all of them to one or more beneficiaries. Second, it refers to the designation of a beneficiary in an account in the name of one or more parties as trustee for the benefit of one or more beneficiaries if the terms of the account state such a relationship and the corpus of the trust is only the sums on deposit in the account. A "beneficiary" is the name of the person to whom sums on deposit in an account are payable on request after the death of all the parties or for whom a party is named as trustee. [2–601(3)].

An agency designation is the designation of an agent who is authorized to make account transactions but who holds no beneficial right to sums in the account. [6–201(2); 6–205(a); 6–211(d)].

Any account may be for a single party or multiple parties. Both types may have a POD designation, an agency designation, or both. [6–203]. Any account with multiple parties may be with or without right of survivorship. On the other hand, a POD designation in a multiple-party account must include a right of survivorship. [6–212(c)].

§ 34.03 Multiple–Party Account Forms for Financial Institutions

In order to provide more uniformity to accounts issued by various financial institutions, the Code includes a suggested form that can be used by financial institutions for their depositors. [6–204(a)]. If an institution uses the suggested form, its actions in accordance to the terms of the form are protected. [6–204, Comment; 6–226]. If an institution uses forms that contain different provisions, the account is governed by the Code's provisions that most closely conforms to the depositor's intent. [6–204(b)].

The form is cast in the nature of a checklist with options provided to the depositor as to how the latter wants the account to be established. By initialing the appropriate options on the checklist, the depositor incorporates the Code's law of multiple-party accounts into the contract of deposit.

Proper use of the form will require a full explanation to the depositor by the financial institution personnel of the meaning and effect of the options.

CHART 34–2

Uniform Single–or Multiple–Party Account Form

Parties [Name one or more parties]:

_____   _____

Ownership [select one and initial]:

____ Single-party account

____ Multiple-party account
Parties own account in proportion to net contributions unless there is clear and convincing evidence of a different intent.

Rights at death [select one and initial]:

____ Single-party account
At death of party, ownership passes as part of party's estate.

____ Single-party account with POD (pay on death) designation
[Name one or more beneficiaries]:

_____   _____

At death of party, ownership passes to POD beneficiaries and is not part of party's estate.

____ Multiple-party account with right of survivorship
At death of party, ownership passes to surviving parties.

____ Multiple-party account with right of survivorship and POD (pay on death) designation
[Name one or more beneficiaries]:

_____   _____

At death of last surviving party, ownership passes to POD beneficiaries and is not part of last surviving party's estate.

____ Multiple-party account without right of survivorship
At death of party, deceased party's ownership passes as part of deceased party's estate.

Agency (power of attorney) designation [optional]

Agents may make account transactions for parties but have no ownership or rights at death unless named as POD beneficiaries.

[To add agency designation to account, name one or more agents]:

_____   _____

[Select one and initial]:

____ Agency designation survives disability or incapacity of parties

____ Agency designation terminates on disability or incapacity of parties

§ 34.04 Ownership During Lifetime of Multiple–Party Accounts

An account is presumed to belong to the parties, during their lifetimes, in proportion to the net contribution of each. [6–211(b)]. This presumption is rebuttable by clear and convincing evidence of a different intent such as an intent to make a gift to the non-contributing party. [6–211, Comment]. A beneficiary in an account with a POD designation has no right to the sums on deposit during the lifetime of any party. [6–211(c)]. Similarly, an agent in an account with an agency designation has no beneficial right to sums on deposit. [6–211(d)].

When, under the above rules, ownership belongs to more than one party, the division of this ownership during the lifetime of the parties is in proportion to the net contribution of each. [6–206(b)]. "Net contribution" of any party at any given time is an amount equal to the sum of all deposits made by or for that party and a pro rata share of any interest or dividends remaining in the account, less any withdrawals from the account made by or for the party that have not been paid to or applied to the use of any other party. [6–211(a)]. Although the drafters deliberately included no provision for the situation where the parties are unable to prove their net contributions, they included a clear rule concerning the amount of "net contribution" as between spouses that cannot estimate the actual amount. [6–211, Comment]. For spouses, the "net contribution" for each is presumed be an equal amount, subject to contrary proof. [6–211(b)].

§ 34.05 Rights at Death for Multiple–Party Accounts

The Code deals with the consequences of the death of one or more of the persons named on the account. Basically, it creates a right of survivorship for interests in the account. On the death of a party to a multiple-party account, ownership to the sums on deposit belong to the surviving party or parties. [6–212(a)]. Ownership of the account's balance in the survivors is presumed unless a non-survivorship arrangement is specified by the terms of the account. [6–212, Comment]. "Sums on deposit" means the remaining balance in the account at the death of a party and includes interest and dividends earned up to that date and deposit life insurance added to the account due to the death. [6–201(11)].

When two or more parties survive and one is the surviving spouse of the decedent, the surviving spouse owns the amount to which the decedent spouse held beneficially immediately before death. [6–212(a); 6–211]. When two or more parties survive and none is the surviving spouse of the decedent, their ownership in the account is the sum of the value of their proportion that they owned in the account before the decedent's death plus an equal share of the interest that the decedent owned immediately before death. In other words, if in a multiple-party account among three persons, A had contributed 50 per cent, B 25 per cent and C 25 per cent and if C died, A's ownership would equal 50 per cent of the account plus one-half of 25 per cent ($12\frac{1}{2}$) and B's ownership would equal 25 per cent plus one-half of 25 per cent ($12\frac{1}{2}$). After C's death, A owns $62\frac{1}{2}$ per cent and B owns $37\frac{1}{2}$ per cent of the account. This presumption of, and calculation for, survivorship continues until only one party survives.

The Code's survivorship rule with regard to accounts with a POD designation is very similar. Upon the death of one of two or more parties, the ownership rights in the sums on deposit are governed by the same provision of the Code described above. [6–212(b)(1)]. When the last survivor of two or more parties dies, ownership belongs to the surviving beneficiary or beneficiaries. [6–212(b)(2)]. If there are two or more beneficiaries, ownership belongs to them in equal and undivided shares, and there is no right of survivorship if a beneficiary later dies. If there is no surviving beneficiary, ownership belongs to the estate of the last surviving party.

Any interest of a decedent, who is a named party in a single-party or multiple-party account that has no effective POD designation or right of survivorship, passes through the decedent's estate. [6–

212(c)]. A tenancy in common designation on an account establishes that the account is without right of survivorship. In addition, a party's proper requests prior to death for payment from the financial institution, e.g., a check written to a named payee, are payable even if not paid at the time of the death. [6–212(d)]. Surviving parties, beneficiaries or the decedent's estate are proportionately liable to the payee to discharge the request if it was not paid by the institution upon proper request for payment by the payee.

Rights of survivorship are determined by the form of the account as it exists at the death of a party. Alteration to this form may be made only by a party who gives written notice of the alteration and this notice must be received by the financial institution during the party's lifetime. [6–213(a)]. Any proper written notice may stop or vary the payment under the terms of the account. Significantly, the right of survivorship cannot be changed by the will of a party or of any other person. [6–213(b)].

Except as the surviving spouse is protected by a spouse's elective share [2–201 to 2–207], and creditors and others are protected in insolvent estates [6–215], transfers resulting from these rules are nontestamentary. [6–214]. This provision means that for purposes of passing an interest to survivors at death, the accounts need not satisfy the execution requirements for wills and are not subject to administration procedures required for assets passing through the decedent's estate. [6–214, Comment].

§ 34.06   Rights of Creditors in Multiple–Party Accounts

When a party to a multiple-party account dies, the account is not subject to the claims of creditors or other claimants unless the estate is insufficient. [6–215(a)]. The account is subject to payment of the estate's debts, taxes, expenses of administration, and the family protections only to the extent of the proportionate share of the amount received necessary to discharge the claims and allowances remaining unpaid after application of the decedent's estate. [6–215(b)]. Consequently, the account is subject to these claims only to the extent of the lesser of (1) the estate's insufficiency of funds or (2) the amount that the decedent owned beneficially immediately before death or (3) the proportionate share necessary to discharge the claims.

Before a proceeding may be instituted to collect from the account, the proper claimants must make a written demand to the personal representative. [6–215(b)]. Thereafter, only the personal representative may bring the proceedings and, in turn, must commence the proceeding within one year from the date of the decedent's death. Significantly, sums recovered by the personal representative become part of the decedent's estate. [6–215(d)]. This provision means that the claim of the initiating claimant gets no priority for the payment. Finally, a financial institution is discharged by payments made according to the terms of the account if made before it is served with process in a proceeding instituted by the personal representative.

Under the multiple-party account provisions, the surviving spouse is not protected from disinheritance above the value of the family protections. A surviving spouse, however, is protected from such disinheritance by the augmented estate concept of the Code's elective share procedure. [2–202; see also § 6.03]. Multiple-party accounts to which the decedent was a party and which pass decedent's interests to third persons are includable within Segment 2 of the augmented estate. [2–202(b)(2)(i)(C); see § 6.03]. Multiple party accounts that pass interests of the decedent to the surviving spouse are includable in Segments 3 or 4 of the augmented estate. [2–202(b)(3), and (4); see § 6.03].

§ 34.07 Protection for Financial Institution Using Multiple–Party Accounts

As previously mentioned, the Code contains separate provisions dealing with the protection of financial institutions. A "financial institution" is very broadly defined to include any organization dealing with financial affairs, including, for example, banks, savings and loan companies, trust companies and credit unions. [6–201(4)]. The basic philosophy of these provisions is that if the financial institution follows the rules set out in making payments, it will not be subsequently liable to other persons even though the payments as between persons named on the account is improper.

First, on proper request, a financial institution may pay funds out of a multiple-party account to any one or more of the parties. [6–221; see also § 34.04]. A proper "request" is simply the manner by which the financial institution permits withdrawals. [6–201(10)]. Second, in spite of the actual net contribution between the parties, the financial institution has no duty to inquire into the source of the deposit or to the application of withdrawals. [6–221].

The Code also segregates its financial institution protection provisions depending on which type of account is involved. As far as the financial institution protection is concerned, payment under a multiple-party account may be made to any one or more of the parties. [6–222(1)]. Payment may not be made, however, to the personal representative or to the heirs of a deceased party unless their proof of death shows the decedent to be the last survivor or that there is no right of survivorship. [6–222(2)].

According to the terms of the account with a POD designation, a financial institution may make payment to (1) one or more of the parties, (2) the beneficiary or beneficiaries if proof of death of all the parties is presented to the financial institution, or (3) the personal representative or heirs upon their proof of death showing that the decedent survived all parties or beneficiaries. [6–223].

Protection is also given to financial institutions for payment to an agent upon request of an agent under an agency designation account [6–224], and to a minor designated as a beneficiary pursuant to the Uniform Transfers to Minors Act. [6–225].

Payments made pursuant to the above rules discharge the financial institution from all claims for amounts paid. [6–226]. This is true although the payment may not be consistent with the beneficial ownership between all persons named on the account or their successors. The above payment rules do not protect a financial institution, however, if it has received written notice from a party altering or limiting the rules for withdrawal set by the terms of the account. The protection of the payment rules can be reacquired if the party making the notice withdraws the notice or concurs in a withdrawal. No other notice or form of information will cause the financial institution to lose the benefit of the protection of the payment rules unless a financial institution has been served with process in an action or proceeding. [6–226(b)].

When a party to a multiple-party account is indebted to the financial institution, the institution may set-off against the account, money owed to it up to the amount of the party's beneficial interest immediately before death. [6–227]. When a party's net contributions are not provable, an equal share with all other parties to the account may be set-off. This set-off provision does not qualify or limit any other statutory right to set-off or lien and is itself subject to any contractual agreement between the party and the institution.

CHAPTER 35

UNIFORM TOD SECURITY REGISTRATION ACT

§ 35.01 Introduction to Securities Registered in Beneficiary Form

The Code incorporates the Uniform TOD Security Registration Act into Part 3 of Article VI. Concurrent ownership principles are different for securities held in joint names than they are for other financial multiple-party accounts. [Art. 6, Pt. 3, Prefatory Note]. While multiple-party accounts permit a cotenant to control the asset, cotenants of securities must act together, thus sharing control of the asset. Many people use the joint titled security, however, as a means to avoid the probate process, despite the troublesome issues attendant with jointly titled securities. The TOD Security Registration Act, now incorporated into the Code, allows owners of securities to make a nontestamentary transfer of securities directly to a designated transferee on the owner's death. [6–309]. Significantly, creditors of security owners do not lose any rights against beneficiaries and other transferees.

§ 35.02 Definitions for Securities Registered in Beneficiary Form

Five special definitions of terms are applicable to the TOD Security Registration Act's provisions.

[6–301]. For informational and overview purposes Chart 35–1 lists them in alphabetical order.

CHART 35–1

TOD Definition of Terms

Beneficiary form	Security
Register	Security account
Registering entity	

First, it is necessary to understand what the Act means when it uses the terms "security" and "security account." The Act adopts the definition of security provided in Section 8–102 of the Uniform Commercial Code. [6–301, Comment]. This definition means any share, participation, or other interest in property, business or in an obligation of an enterprise or other issuer and includes certificated and uncertificated securities and security accounts as well as mutual funds and other investment companies. [6–301(4)]. Because individuals commonly own securities and related interests in security accounts set up by brokers, the Act permits beneficiary form ownership for these accounts. "Security account" is broadly defined to include (1) security operated reinvestment accounts; (2) accounts of securities with a broker; (3) cash balances in brokerage accounts; (4) cash, interest, earnings and dividends earned or declared on a security in security accounts; (5) brokerage reinvestment accounts; (6) all other brokerage accounts; and, (7) all earnings or proceeds from trading transactions due the owner. [6–301(5)]. All payments due an account at the time of the owner's death are also included notwithstanding that the amounts due are unpaid at that time. It does not include securities held in the name of the trust institution for the benefit of a trust. [6–301, Comment].

Under the Act, an individuals is allowed to obtain registration of securities in "beneficiary form." Beneficiary form is defined as a registration that shows the present owner of the security and indicates the owner's intent regarding who becomes the security's owner upon the owner's death. [6–301(1)]. The owner's intent may be shown by the words "transfer on death," the abbreviation "TOD," "pay on death," or the abbreviation "POD," after the name of the registered owner and before the beneficiary's name. [6–305]. A security is deemed registered in beneficiary form when the registration includes a designation of a beneficiary to take ownership at the death of the owner or at the death of all multiple owners. [6–304]. A certificated security is registered when a certificate is issued showing ownership of the security, while an uncertificated security is registered when an account showing ownership is initiated or transferred. [6–301(2)].

§ 35.03 Ownership During Lifetime of the Owner of Securities Registered in Beneficiary Form

Although the purpose of the TOD Act is to permit owners of securities to obtain registration of securities in beneficiary form, there are restrictions as to what type of owner may obtain this registration. The Act specifically limits registration in beneficiary form to individuals. Thus, only natural persons may register as an owner or co-owner of a security. The Act does not restrict the owner's choice of beneficiary, however. Any person, including all legal entities, may be a beneficiary. [6–301; 1–201(35) and (32)].

The individual must have either sole ownership of the security or multiple ownership with right of survivorship. [6–302]. If co-owners fail to specify a survivorship form of ownership, the Act holds them as joint tenants with right of survivorship, tenants by the entireties, or as owners of community property. [6–302, Comment]. Furthermore, registration in beneficiary form negates ownership as tenants in common. The rationale for this is that co-owners who desire to name individual beneficiaries for each individual fractional interest will normally split their holdings into separate registrations. Once divided each co-owner would name a personal choice of beneficiary.

In order to encourage registering entities to permit registration in beneficiary form, the Act adopts an expansive choice of law rule regarding the validity of the beneficiary form transfer technique. [6–303 and Comment]. If any of the listed contacts take place in a state that has enacted the Act or some other similar statute, the forum is to apply that law. The purposes of this provision are twofold. First, it instructs the forum court in a state with the Act to apply forum law when one or more of the listed contacts occurred in the forum. Second, it attempts to attach contractual validity to beneficiary form registration if any of the listed contacts occurred in a state that has the Act or similar law. Accordingly, a forum in a non-Act state is encouraged to apply the law of an Act state so long as any of the listed contacts occurred in the latter state. The specific choice of law contacts are as follows:

(1) the issuer's state of organization;

(2) the registering entity's state of organization;

(3) the registering entity's principal place of business;

(4) the registering entity's office making the registration;

(5) the office of the registering entity's transfer agent; or,

(6) the owner's address listed as of the time of registration.

The range of potentially relevant contacts expands further when considering that a "registering entity" may, as relevant, include the issuer, the issuer's transfer agent or anyone acting for or as the issuer of securities and the broker who maintains security accounts. [6–301(3)]. Even if the proper choice of law for a registration in beneficiary form is to the law of a jurisdiction that has not enacted the TOD Act or similar statute, there is a statutory presumption that the registration is valid and authorized as a matter of contract law. [6–303].

Prior to death of the sole or last surviving owner, the beneficiary holds no ownership interest in a security registered in beneficiary form and the designation of a beneficiary may be canceled or changed at any time by the sole owner or by all surviving owners. [6–306]. Concomitantly, the owner or owners do not need to get the consent of the beneficiary. The Act does not address, however, how a TOD beneficiary designation may be canceled. The terms and conditions of the registering entity for cancellation or alteration are the relevant procedures to observe. If the terms and conditions are silent, cancellation might be effected by reregistration showing a different beneficiary or omitting reference to the beneficiary altogether. [6–306, Comment].

§ 35.04 Ownership on the Death of the Owner of Securities Registered in Beneficiary Form

When the sole owner or the last surviving owner of securities registered in beneficiary form dies, ownership of these securities passes to the beneficiary or beneficiaries who survive all owners. [6–307]. If no beneficiary survives all the owners, the securities held in beneficiary form become the property of the estate of the deceased sole owner or the estate of the last surviving owner. If the beneficiary does survive, however, the security may be reregistered in the beneficiary's name upon proof of the death of all owners and compliance with any transfer requirements of the registering entity. If there are multiple beneficiaries who survive the death of all owners, they hold their interests as tenants in common. Unless the beneficiary designation indicates otherwise, the surviving beneficiaries take an equal share. As amended by the 1993 Technical Amendments, the survival requirement is the Code's pervasive 120 hour survival requirement. [1–201(50); see 2–104, 2–702; §§ 5.06, 11.02].

§ 35.05 Protection for Registering Entities Using Security Registration in Beneficiary Form

The TOD Act makes it clear that the registration of securities in beneficiary form, while valid and authorized, is a privilege and not a right. The owner of securities may only "request" to register securities in beneficiary form. This "request" may be in any form chosen by the registering entity and may include any terms and conditions established by the entity. [6–308, Comment; See also 6–310]. The registering entity is not required to offer or to accept a request, but if the registering entity does offer registration, the owner is deemed to assent to the protections given to the registering entity in the Act. [6–308(a)]. Upon acceptance of a request for registration, the registering entity agrees to implement registration in accordance with the procedures in the TOD Act. So long as the registering entity performs in accordance with certain requirements the registering entity is discharged from all claims to the security by the deceased owners' estate, creditors, heirs, or devisees. [6–308(c)]. On the other hand, the registering entity should not reregister or make payment under the beneficiary form after it has received written notice from a claimant to an interest in the security. In addition, the protection afforded the registering entity has no affect on rights of the beneficiaries in ownership disputes with others. [6–308(d)].

PART SEVEN
TRUST ADMINISTRATION

CHAPTER 36

INTRODUCTION

§ 36.01 Introduction

Although Article VII, Trust Administration, is not a comprehensive codification of the law of trusts, it serves as an integral part of the Code as a whole. [See Article VII, General Comment]. Because the trustee relationship is analogous to the personal representative and conservator relationships under the Code, the Court is given jurisdiction over trustees and their administration of trust estates. Concomitantly, the Code makes the relationship between the Court and trustees consistent with the Code's provisions dealing with the other two fiduciary relationships, i.e., the Court's exercise of jurisdiction over trusts and their administration is not supervisory but must be instituted independently by interested parties only as needed. The other general purposes for this jurisdiction are: (1) to make procedural requirements similarly applicable to both testamentary and inter vivos trusts; (2) to provide an identifiable forum where jurisdiction may be obtained over the trustee and the beneficiaries by notice and where all issues by and between them can be litigated; (3) to remove or reduce legal barriers facing foreign trustees of foreign trusts; (4) to remove restrictions on the place of administration; (5) to substitute in lieu of the present often unnecessary routine judicial proceedings, clear judicial remedies and statutory duties; and (6) to provide the beneficiaries with some evidence of the trust's existence. [Article VII, General Comment].

§ 36.02 Definitions

Because the word "trust" does not have a singular meaning, the Code is very specific with respect to the type of trust to which it applies. Both inclusions and exclusions are illustrated. [1–201(45)]. First, it includes all private and charitable express trusts, including all trusts created or determined by judicial action, which are in the nature of an express trust. Second, the word excludes a large number of specific devices or transactions that have occasionally been characterized as similar to an express trust. Several important exclusions mentioned are "other constructive trusts," resulting trusts, conservatorships, the administration of a decedent's estate, trust accounts, custodial devices, business trusts, common trust funds, voting trusts, security arrangements, employee benefit trusts and nominee arrangements. Basically, everything is excluded that is not an express trust or truly in the nature of an express trust. [1–201, Comment].

The Code also includes a comprehensive definition of the word "trustee." [1–201(54)]. It not only specifically includes the original trustee but also additional and successor trustees. Significantly, it makes no difference whether any of these trustees were appointed or confirmed by a court. Corporations, as well as natural persons, may serve as trustee. [See 7–101, 7–105; see also 1–201(35)].

CHAPTER 37

TRUST REGISTRATION

§ 37.01   Trust Registration

Trust registration is a relatively unique concept and procedure established in the Code. [Article VII, Pt. 1, General Comment]. Registration is accomplished merely by filing with the proper Court a statement which includes the following information:

(1) The name and address of the trustee;

(2) An acknowledgment of trusteeship by the trustee;

(3) A statement whether the trust has been registered elsewhere; and

(4) A brief identification of the trust.

[7–102]. Identification specifications differ depending upon whether the trust is inter vivos or testamentary. If the trust is inter vivos, the statement must give the name of each settlor, the name of the original trustee and the date of the instrument. If the trust is testamentary, the statement must give the name of the settlor-testator and the date and location of the domiciliary probate. With the exception of oral inter vivos trusts, the registration statement does not require revelation of the beneficiaries or of the terms of the trusts.

The registration statement for oral inter vivos trusts, however, not only must include information identifying the settlor, or any other source of the trust's corpus, but also must include information describing the time and manner of the trust's creation and its terms including a description of its subject matter, beneficiaries and time of performance. This additional information greatly assists all of the parties, i.e., settlor, trustee and beneficiaries, in identifying and establishing their rights and duties as far as these trusts are concerned.

Generally, a registration statement must be filed for any trust that has its principal place of administration in the Code state. [7-101]. Registration may be waived only when a person or several persons hold a presently exercisable general power of appointment over the trust, and when the holder or all co-holders direct or agree with the trustee to refrain from registration. [1-108]. A common example when the above waiver will be available to the trustee will be when the settlor of the trust retains the power of amendment or revocation. [7-104, Comment]. Any attempt by the settlor to merely waive the registration requirement, even by the express terms of the trust instrument, is void. [7-104]. Furthermore, a trustee is subject to removal, denial of compensation or surcharge for failure to register a trust within thirty days after receipt of a written demand to register made by the trust's settlor or beneficiary. Notwithstanding a failure to register, the trustee is still subject to the personal jurisdiction of any court in which the trust could have been registered.

When required, the registration statement must be filed in the Court where the principal place of administration is located. [7–101]. The principal place of administration is specifically set out as the place which is designated in the trust instrument or which, if not designated, is the trustee's usual place of business where the trust records are kept. When co-trustees from more than one place are involved and when the trust instrument fails to designate, the Code provides an order of priority for determining the principal place of administration: (1) the usual place of business of a sole corporate trustee, if any; (2) if no corporate trustee is involved, the usual place of business or residence of a sole professional individual fiduciary, if any; and (3) under all other circumstances, the usual place of business or residence of any of the co-trustees as they agree among themselves. Significantly, the principal place of administration may or may not be the place where the trust was created.

The primary effect of registration is to establish a Court where after appropriate notice, the trustee and the beneficiaries are subject to the jurisdiction of the Court with respect to their affairs and interests in the trust. [7–103]. Basically then, registration establishes a single jurisdictional forum for determining litigable issues dealing with the internal affairs of the trust. [See 7–201]. As mentioned above, the registration Court is not authorized to maintain continuing supervision over the trust or to require periodic accounting from the trustee. [7–201(b); see also Art. VII, Pt. 1, General Comment]. All assumptions of jurisdiction by the

Court occur only when a proceeding is brought at the sole option of interested persons.

CHAPTER 38

JURISDICTION, VENUE AND OTHER COURT PROCE-DURES FOR TRUSTS

§ 38.01 General Purpose for Trust Provisions

The general purpose of the Code's provisions dealing with the jurisdiction of the Court over trusts is to enhance unity of administration and litigation. This purpose is achieved in several ways. First, the Court's "exclusive" jurisdiction concerned with the internal affairs of the trust is distinguished from its "concurrent" jurisdiction concerned primarily with matters between the trustee and third persons such as creditors, adverse possessors, etc. Second, the trustee and beneficiaries are subject to continual personal jurisdiction in subject matter litigation under the exclusive jurisdiction of the Court. Third, a sound venue rule is established for exclusive jurisdiction proceedings. And fourth, a mandatory forum non conveniens rule is established for Code Courts dealing with the internal affairs of foreign trusts.

§ 38.02 Jurisdiction and Venue Over Trusts

A. JURISDICTION OVER THE SUBJECT MATTER

The Court with the proper venue has exclusive jurisdiction over the "internal" affairs of the trust. [7–201(a)]. Generally, the internal affairs of a trust include issues dealing with the administration and distribution of the trust and with determination of rights, responsibilities, and other matters between the trustee and the trust beneficiaries. Proceedings brought under the exclusive jurisdiction of the Court are instituted by petition after notice to interested parties. [7–206]. Additional persons may be notified at the discretion of the Court, but any decree is valid against those who were given notice even though fewer than all the interested persons had been notified. Because of its importance, the Code provides separately that interested persons may also petition this Court for review of the propriety of any employment of any person by the trustee and the reasonableness of compensation for any person so employed, including the reasonableness of the trustee's own compensation. [7–205]. The court, under this proceeding, may order refunds for any excessive compensation paid from the trust. Significantly, exclusive jurisdiction proceedings do not result in court proceedings of a continuing supervisory nature. [7–201(b)].

B. JURISDICTION OVER THE PERSON

Similar to the rule applicable to personal representatives, the Code provides a continuing type of personal jurisdiction power over the trustee in the Court in which a trustee registered a trust or accepted a trusteeship of a previously registered trust. [7–103(a)]. The beneficiaries are similarly under the continuing jurisdiction of this Court, too. [7–103(b)]. These rules of personal jurisdiction subject the trustee and the beneficiaries to any proceeding brought under the Court's exclusive subject matter jurisdiction. [See 7–201, § 38.-02(A)]. The only special requirements to sustain this personal jurisdiction is that specific notice requirements must be satisfied for each proceeding. For a trustee, notice of each proceeding must either be delivered to the trustee or mailed to the trustee by ordinary mail both to the official address listed with the Court and to any other address known to the petitioner. [7–103(a)]. The beneficiaries must be notified of any proceeding brought against them by notice given pursuant to Section 1–401. [7–103(b); see § 4.01].

C. VENUE

Venue for exclusive jurisdiction proceedings is set in the Court wherein the trust is registered. [7–202]. If a trust is not registered, venue is in the Court where the trust could have been registered properly or otherwise by the rules of civil procedure.

This Court is also given concurrent jurisdiction with other courts in the Code state to deal with litigation between third parties and the trust. [7–204]. Such litigation would include actions to determine the existence of inter vivos trusts, by or against debtors and creditors of the trust and any other actions between the trustee and nonbeneficiary third parties.

§ 38.03   Forum Non Conveniens in Trust Litigation

The Code includes a special statutory forum non conveniens rule applicable to foreign trusts. This rule applies to exclusive jurisdiction proceedings concerned with trusts that are registered or have their principal place of administration in another state. [7–203]. If the rule applies, the Court must refuse to entertain the proceeding when a party objects to the jurisdiction. The only two mentioned situations that would cause the Court not to employ this rule are: (1) when the state of registration or principal place of administration is unable to bind by litigation in its court all appropriate parties; or (2) when the interests of justice are potentially seriously impaired. Frequent use of the rule is encouraged by the power of the Court to suspend proceedings or to make conditional dismissals subject to jurisdiction being obtained in the court in the other state.

§ 38.04   Virtual Representation in Trust Litigation

A related problem to the jurisdiction of the Court over trust matters is that of virtual representation. The specific typical issue is whether an order that is binding against the trustee is also binding against all of the beneficiaries although some or all of the beneficiaries were not made parties to the suit. The Code provides that an order which binds the trustee also binds the beneficiary in three specific situations: (1) when the proceeding is to probate a will establishing or adding to a trust; (2) when the proceeding is to review the acts or accounts of a prior fiduciary; and (3) when the proceeding involves creditors or other third parties. [1–403(2)(ii); see § 4.02].

CHAPTER 39

TRUSTEE'S DUTIES, LIABIL-
ITIES, PROTECTIONS
AND POWERS

§ 39.01 Duties of a Trustee

The Code covers several areas of a trustee's duties and liabilities. It codifies the trustee's standard of care and performance, the duty to keep the beneficiaries informed and to account, to provide bond, and to continually administer the trust efficiently and soundly in the most appropriate location. [7–302 to 7–307]. These duties are not exclusive in that the trustee continues to have the general duty to administer the trust expeditiously for the beneficiaries' benefit. [7–301].

With respect to the standard of care and performance, the Code adopts a standard that relates to "a prudent man dealing with the property of another," [7–302] rather than the Second Restatement of Trusts' standard that relates to a "man of ordinary prudence * * * dealing with his own property." [See Restatement, (Second), Trusts § 174 (1959)]. Because the word "prudence" in the Restatement test has frequently been interpreted to be the prudence one would use in dealing with the property of another, the Code actually does not attempt to change the law but merely to

545

clarify it. [7–302, Comment]. Trustees, who have special skills or who are named trustees because of representations of special skills, are specifically under a duty to exercise such skills. [7–302].

Generally, the Code requires the trustee to keep the beneficiaries reasonably informed. [7–303]. More specifically, the trustee must provide the following information:

(1) Notify in writing the current and prospective beneficiaries of the Court in which the trust is registered and of the trustee's name and address within thirty days after acceptance of the trust;

(2) Upon a beneficiary's reasonable request, provide a copy of the trust, information about trust assets, and any other trust matters concerned with its administration;

(3) Upon a beneficiary's reasonable request, account annually; and

(4) Account at termination or upon a change of trustee.

[7–303(a)–(c)]. Because the above information need not be filed with the Court, these requirements create merely an informal type of information and accounting procedure. [7–303, Comment].

Under the Code, a trustee is not required to provide a performance security bond unless the trust instrument requires it, a beneficiary reasonably requests it, or the Court finds that a bond is necessary to protect the interests of incapacitated or unrepresented beneficiaries. [7–304; see also 3–913]. If the bond is required, it must be filed in the registration Court, if any, or in any other appropriate court. The amount and other requirements for the bond are the same as those for personal representatives. [See 3–604 to 3–606; see § 20.03(B)]. Upon the petition of an appropriate or interested person, the Court may alter the bonding requirements.

The Code makes it a trustee's affirmative duty to administer the trust in the most appropriate location considering the purposes of the trust and its sound, efficient management. [7–305]. If according to this standard a trust should be administered in another more appropriate location, the trustee must request a change in the place of administration. Upon such a request the Court is given the authority to release registration, remove a trustee and appoint a trustee in another place in the Code state or even in another state. If contrary to efficient administration or the purposes of the trust, the Court may order a deviation from clauses in the trust instrument which expressly set the place of administration or explain changes in such places. The Court is to give "weight" to the opinions of adult beneficiaries in making any decision as far as the suitability of the trustee or the place of administration or both are concerned.

§ 39.02 The Trustee's Liability to Third Persons

The Code deals directly with the difficult problem of the trustee's personal liability to third persons on contracts from ownership or control of the trust's property and for torts arising out of the administration of the trust. [7–306]. The content of the provision is identical to the provision included for a personal representative in Article III. [3–808; see § 20.08]. Under the Code the trust estate is made into a "quasi-corporation" for purposes of such liability. [See 3–808, Comment]. Accordingly, the trustee becomes an agent of this entity and is liable not individually but only as an agent would be liable. More specifically, a trustee is personally liable under the following circumstances: (1) on contracts properly made in the course of a trust's administration only when expressly provided in the contract or when the representative capacity of the trustee is not revealed in the contract [7–306(a)]; and, (2) for torts or for obligations arising from property ownership or control only when the trustee is personally at fault. [7–306(b)]. Third persons may sue the trust estate for such claims in the name of the trustee in its representative capacity regardless of the trustee's own personal liability. [7–306(c)]. The trustee's personal liability to the trust may be litigated during the third person's initial action against the trust estate or in any other appropriate proceeding such as a proceeding for an accounting. [7–306(d)].

§ 39.03 The Trustee's Accounts

As a part of the Court's exclusive jurisdiction, under the Code the Court has authority to review and settle a trustee's interim and final accounts. [7–201(a)(2)]. Such proceedings can be characterized as a formal proceeding and would carry with them the normal limitations concerning appeal and res judicata. [See 1–304].

The Code also accords nonadjudicated informal type final accounts or statements a limited degree of recognition and finality. [7–307]. If a beneficiary has received an informal final account from the trustee, the beneficiary is barred from instituting a suit for breach of trust against the trustee more than six months after receipt of the account. This six month limitation only applies, however, if the account makes a full disclosure of the administration and recites that the trust relationship has ceased between the trustee and the beneficiary. So long as the beneficiary has received from the trustee a final account and was informed of the location and availability of the trustee's record, an alternate three year limitation period bars beneficiaries' claims even without full disclosure. Significantly, these periods of limitation do not bar actions based upon the trustee's fraud or evasion because an overriding provision covers such events. [1–106; see § 2.02(A)]. Both the six month and the three year limitations run from the date of receipt of the final account by the beneficiary. Receipt is defined as actual personal receipt by adult beneficiaries and as receipt by the appropriate representatives for minors and other disabled persons. There is no similar statute of limitations for informal type interim accounts, however, and claims concerning such accounts can only be barred by adjudication or consent. [2 UPC Practice Manual, 598].

§ 39.04 Powers of a Trustee

Part 4 of Article VII of the Code deals with powers of trustees and is left blank so that each state may insert either the Uniform Trustees' Powers Act, some modification of this act or its own version of trustees' powers legislation. [See Uniform Trustees' Powers Act]. Discussion of powers legislation for trustees is beyond the scope of this Nutshell.

CHAPTER 40

THE FOREIGN TRUSTEE

§ 40.01 The Foreign Trustee

Other important and related problems of trust administration concern the registration, qualification and powers of a nonresident or foreign trustee. Several different fact situations are involved and for clarity need to be distinguished from each other. The first situation involves the nonresident who serves as trustee of a trust that has its principal place of administration within the Code state. The second involves the foreign trustee of a foreign trust who has to administer assets or to bring legal proceedings within the Code state. The third situation involves the locally domiciled testator whose will creates a foreign trust and appoints a foreign trustee. When analyzing the above situations, it is also often important under non-Code law to determine whether the foreign trustee is an individual or a corporation. The Code addresses itself in some manner to all three situations and to the importance of the type of trustee involved. Generally, the Code eliminates restrictions frequently imposed on foreign trustees and removes discriminations frequently applied against foreign corporate trustees. [7–105, Comment].

Because any trust that has its principal place of administration within the Code state must be regis-

tered in the proper Court, any individual or corporate foreign trustee who maintains the principal
place of administration of the trust within the
state must register that trust. [7–101]. Under
such a situation, a foreign corporate trustee must
also qualify as a foreign corporation doing business
within the state. [7–105]. This foreign corporate
qualification requirement, however, does not apply
to a foreign corporate co-trustee solely because a
co-trustee of the trust maintains the principal
place of administration of the trust in the Code
state. When a trust is registered in the Code state,
however, it has the effect of submitting all of its
foreign trustees to the personal jurisdiction of the
registration Court. [7–103(a)].

With respect to the first situation, some states
have statutes that bar a foreign corporate trustee
from acting as a local trustee unless the law of the
jurisdiction in which the foreign corporation is
organized or has its principal office permits local
corporate fiduciaries to perform in a similar manner. These are called reciprocity statutes and
have been enacted in several states. [See 5 Scott,
Trusts § 588]. These statutes do not apply to a
foreign trustee who is an individual. The Code
does not have such a reciprocity requirement with
respect to either a nonresident individual or a
foreign corporate trustee.

With reference to the second situation, the Code
gives both the nonresident individual and the foreign corporate trustee of a foreign trust broad
authority to deal with trust matters within the
Code state. These powers include the authority to
hold, invest in, manage or acquire property locat-

ed, and to maintain litigation, in the Code state. [7–105]. Significantly, unless otherwise required by law, a foreign corporate trustee is not required to qualify as a foreign corporation doing business in the state merely to perform one or more of the above acts.

Finally, the Code also permits a nonresident individual or foreign corporate trustee to receive distributions of assets under a will from a domiciliary estate and to remove these assets to the foreign jurisdiction. [7–105]. Fear that such a trustee-devisee [1–201(11)] may take its distributive share and never be heard from again, motivated the inclusion of some protection for the trust's beneficiary. Before making distribution to a nonresident or foreign trustee named devisee under a will, the personal representative of an estate, in the personal representative's exonerated discretion, may either (1) require the trustee to register if registration is possible in the state of administration; (2) require the trustee to give notice and information to the beneficiary concerning the trust; or, (3) require the trustee to post bond if it would appear necessary for the protection of persons and beneficiaries unable to protect themselves. [3–913]. If appropriate, all three actions by the trustee may be required before any distribution.

*

INDEX

References are to Pages

ABATEMENT, ORDER OF, 414–15
Caused by,
    Elective share, 101–02, 414–15
    Pretermitted child, 118, 414
    Pretermitted spouse, 115–16

ACCESSIONS
Devises of securities, 191–95

ACCOUNTING
Attorney in fact, 469
Conservator, 496–97
Guardian of minor, 474
Personal Representative, formal closing, 430
Trustee, 546

ADEMPTION
By extinction, 195–201
By satisfaction, 201–06
Nonademption, 197–201

ADMINISTRATION, DECEDENTS' ESTATES
    See also Ancillary Administration; Courts; Jurisdiction over
        Subject Matter; Personal Representative; Universal
        Succession; Venue
Claims, necessity of administration, 302
Commencement, by issuance of letters, 331

ADMINISTRATION, DECEDENTS' ESTATES—Cont'd
Flexible system,
    Illustrative techniques, 280–300
    Overview, 275–80
Probate necessary, exceptions, 302–03
Subsequent administration, 434–35
Succession without administration, 281–86, 301–03, 383–84
Summary administrative procedures, small estates, 316–18
Transfer of small estates by affidavit, 281, 302, 315–16

ADMINISTRATION, PROTECTED PERSONS' ESTATES
See Conservator and Conservatorship; Disability, Persons Under; Protective Proceedings

ADMINISTRATION, TRUSTS
See Trusts and Trustees

ADMINISTRATOR
See Personal Representative

ADOPTED PERSONS
See Child; Class Gifts; Guardians of Minors; Intestate Succession

ADVANCEMENT, 64–71

AFFIDAVITS
Collection of property,
    By foreign conservator, 504
    By foreign personal representative, 443–44
    Small estates, by successor, 281, 302, 315–16
Durable powers of attorney, 467–68
Wills, proof of due execution,
    Formal probate, 354, 355
    Informal probate, 346
    Self-proved will, 144–45

AFTER ACQUIRED PROPERTY, 207

AFTERBORN HEIRS
See Intestate Succession

ALIENS
See Intestate Succession

ALLOWANCES
See Family Protections

ANCILLARY ADMINISTRATION, 441–49
    See also Foreign Personal Representative; Jurisdiction Over
        Persons
Creditors, resident,
    Claims, 406, 447–48
    Notice, 444
Distribution to domiciliary personal representative, 448–49
Domicile, conflicting claims of, 447–48
Judgments, binding effect, 447
Local administration, 445
    Effect on powers of foreign personal representative, 444
No local administration, 443–44

ANTENUPTIAL CONTRACTS
    See also Succession Contracts
Waiver of rights, 95, 122, 234

ANTILAPSE STATUTE
See Beneficiary Designation; Class Gifts; Governing Instru-
    ment; Wills, Devises

APPOINTMENT PROCEEDINGS
See Informal Appointment Proceedings; Formal Appointment
    Proceedings

APPRAISALS
    See also Inventory and Appraisement
Personal representative, duty of, 382

AUGMENTED ESTATE
See Elective Share

BANK ACCOUNTS
See Multiple–Person Accounts

BENEFICIARY DESIGNATION
Antilapse, 210–12
Defined, 211

BONDS
Conservator, 490
Foreign conservator, 504
Personal representative, 295, 374–77
    Certificate discharge liens securing performance, 434
Trustee, 546–47

CHILD
    See also Guardians of Minors; Intestate Succession

CHILD—Cont'd
Assumed dead, omitted from will, 120
Rights to family protections, 123–24

CHILDREN BORN OUT OF WEDLOCK
See Class Gifts; Intestate Succession

CHOICE OF LAW
As to family protections, 121
As to meaning, effect of will, 224–25
As to the elective share, 79
As to TOD security registrations, 529–30
As to validity of will, 139–41
    Comparison with the International Will Act, 141–42

CLAIMS AGAINST DECEDENTS' ESTATES
Administration,
    Costs and expenses, priority as claim, 410
    Necessity of, 302
Allowance, 407–08
Compromise, 411
Counterclaims, 411
Definition, 405–06
Disallowance, 407–08
Distributee's liability to creditors, 429
Execution prohibited, 409
Family protections, priority as claim, 122
Funeral expenses, priority as claim, 410
Interest, allowed claims, 409
Nonclaim limitations,
    Constitutionality, 402
    Limitations after notice, 402–04
    Period in gross, 402–03
    Strictly imposed, 406
Notice,
    Actual notice, 403
    Notice by publication, 403
    Of disallowance, 407–08
    Small estates excepted, 284, 317
    To creditors, 402–06
Payment, 409–10
    Insufficient assets,
        Priority, 410
        Proportional in multiple administration, 448
    Secured claims, 411–12

CLAIMS AGAINST DECEDENTS' ESTATES—Cont'd
Presentation, 407–09
  Time, 405
Proceedings,
  Between personal representative and estate, 392–93
  By claimant injured by payment, 409
  By creditor on rejected claims, 408
    Time extensions, 408
  Counterclaim deducted, 411
Secured claims,
  Execution permitted, 409
  Nonclaim ineffective against, 406, 411
  Payments, 411–12
Statute of limitations, 408–09
Unpaid claims, liabilities,
  Of distributee, 295
  Of personal representative, 392–93, 409
    Limitations, proceeding against, 284, 317–18, 427

CLAIMS AGAINST PROTECTED PERSONS AND THEIR ESTATES
  See also Conservator and Conservatorship; Protective Proceedings
Allowance, 501
Payment,
  Conservator's duty, 501
  Priority, 502
Presentation, limitation tolled by, 501

CLAIMS AGAINST TRUSTEES AND TRUST ESTATES
Liability, trustee to third person, 547–48
Limitations, 548–49

CLASS GIFTS
Adopted, halfblooded and nonmarital persons, inclusion of, 212–16
Antilapse, 179–80, 212–13

CLOSING DECEDENTS' ESTATES
  See also Distribution, Decedents' Estates; Personal Representative
Formal closing proceedings, 429–34
Informal closing procedure, 426–28
  Closing statements, 426–27
Proceedings after closing,
  Against distributees, liability and limitations, 428–29

CLOSING DECEDENTS' ESTATES—Cont'd
Proceedings after closing—Cont'd
    Against personal representatives, limitations, 429
    Subsequent administration, 434–35
Small estates, 317–18
Termination of appointment, 393–94
    Effect on authority, liability, 393–94, 433–34
    Time effective,
        After closing statement, 427
        Upon order closing estate, 433–34

COMMUNITY PROPERTY STATES, PROVISION FOR
Devolution, 301
Distribution, abatement, 415–16
Elective share of spouse, 77
Intestate share of spouse, 36

COMPROMISE OF ESTATE CONTROVERSIES
See Settlement Agreements

CONSERVATOR AND CONSERVATORSHIP
    See also Claims Against Protected Persons and Their Estates; Protective Proceedings
Alternatives to full conservatorship, 487
Appointment, 489–90
    Cause for, 471
    Proceeding for, 485
Bond, 490
Conflict of interest, 498
Court, relation to conservator, 492–93
    Initiation of proceedings, 462
Definitions,
    Conservator, 459
    Protected persons, 486–87
    Protective proceeding, 471
Foreign conservator, 504–05
Letters of conservatorship,
    Recording of, 499
    Restrictions endorsed on, 492, 500
Liability,
    Accounts, 496–97
    Claims, fiduciary and individual, 502
Limited conservatorship, 487
Persons dealing with conservator, protection, 500

CONSERVATOR AND CONSERVATORSHIP—Cont'd
Powers and duties,
    Accounts, 496–97
    Administrative powers, 493–94
        Parental powers and duties as guardian, 496
    Court enlargement or limitation, 492
    Distributive powers and duties, 494–96
    Estate plan, duty to preserve, 491, 497
    Fiduciary duty, generally, 496
    Inventory and records, 496
    Personal representative, powers as, 493–94
    Will of protected person, authority to examine, 171
Removal, 503
Resignation, 502–03
Termination, 502–03
Title, as between conservator and protected person, 498–99

CONTEST OF WILLS
    See also Formal Testacy Proceedings; Wills
Burden of proof, 355–56
No contest clause, 173, 416–17
Notice, 351–52

COURTS
    See also Jurisdiction Over Subject Matter; Registrar; Venue
Appeals, 24
Jury trial,
    Guardianship proceedings, incapacitated person, 479
    Will contests, 298
Rules of practice, 24

CREDITORS
See Claims Against Decedents' Estates; Claims Against Protected Persons and Their Estates; Claims Against Trustees and Trust Estates; Multiple–Person Accounts

CUSTODY
See Guardians of Incapacitated Persons; Guardians of Minors

DEATH
Evidence of death, rules, 19–20
Missing persons, testacy proceedings, 359–60
Simultaneous death, 62–64

DEBTS
    See also Abatement, Order of; Claims Against Decedents' Estates; Claims Against Protected Persons and Their Estates; Claims Against Trustees and Trust Estates; Multiple–Person Accounts

DEBTS—Cont'd
Place of indebtedness, venue, 309
Priority among claims, 410

DEMAND FOR NOTICE
See Notice

DESCENT AND DISTRIBUTION
See Intestate Succession

DISABILITY, PERSONS UNDER
    See also Incapacitated Persons; Minors; Protective Proceed-
        ings
Defined, 471, 476, 484
Personal representative's disability, effect, 393–94
Powers of attorney affected by disability, 467–68
Procedures available, outline, 453–55
Underlying policies, 453–55
Virtual representation, 26–28, 252–54, 437–38, 543–44

DISCLAIMER, 228–32
Court power to disclaim protected person's interest, 491

DISTRIBUTEE
    See also Distribution, Decedents' Estates
Agreement among successors, 436–39
Liability for improper distribution, 428–29
Universal succession, 324–25

DISTRIBUTION, DECEDENTS' ESTATES
    See also Abatement, Order of; Closing Decedents' Estates;
        Title
Court, orders directing distribution,
    Formal settlements, 431–32
    Supervised administration, 364
Deed as proof of distributee's title, 420–21
Distributee, 364, 416, 421
Improper distributions,
    Distributee's liability, 428–29
    Personal representative's liability, 387
    Purchasers protected, 421–22
In kind, 419–22
Partition, proceeding, 422
Personal representative,
    Authority, 387
    Restrained from distribution, 377–78

DISTRIBUTION, DECEDENTS' ESTATES—Cont'd
Personal representative—Cont'd
  Restricted, in supervised administration, 364
  Successors' agreement binding, 436
Persons under disability, authorized distribution, 418–19
Right of retainer, 416
Small estates, summary distribution, 317
Types of testamentary gifts, 175–76
Unclaimed property, 417

DIVORCE AND ANNULMENT
See Marital Status

DOMICILE
Choice of law, standard rule, 224
  Elective share, 79
  Family protections, 121
Decedents' estates,
  Priority of domiciliary administration, 447–48
  Venue, 308–09
Domiciliary foreign conservator, authority, 504
Domiciliary foreign personal representative, authority, 443–44

DOWER
See Elective Share

ELECTIVE SHARE
  Generally, 73–78
Accrual method, 79–81
Augmented estate defined, 84–95
Curtesy abolished, 79
Custodial trust, 104–05
Domicile of decedent governs right, 79
Dower abolished, 79
Elective share percentage, 78–82
Exclusions, 95–98
Funding the elective share, 98–102
  Charges to spouse, 99–100
  Contribution, 100–01
Nonprobate assets,
  Surviving Spouse's personal estate, 93–94
  Transfers to others, 85–92
  Transfers to the surviving spouse, 92–93
Procedure for election, 102–05
Protected person's right of election, 104
Supplemental amount, 83

ELECTIVE SHARE—Cont'd
Third party, protection from liability, 242–46
Time limit, 102
Waiver of right, 95–96
Will disposition, choice of law, limitation, 225

ESCHEAT, 34, 417

ESTATE TAX APPORTIONMENT, 415, 422–25

EXECUTOR
See Personal Representative; Wills

EXEMPT PROPERTY AND ALLOWANCES
See Family Protections

EXONERATION
Construction against, nonexoneration, 207, 412

FAMILY PROTECTIONS, 121–25
Claims, priority over, 122–23, 429
Distribution in kind, 419
Elective share, effect, 79, 85, 121–22
Exempt property, 124
Family allowance, 123–24
Homestead allowance, 123
Waiver of rights, 95, 122

FEES
Agents, 385–86, 391
Attorney for estate, 391–92
Conservator, 490
Guardian, 473
Personal representative, 385, 390–91

FORCED SHARE
See Elective Share

FOREIGN PERSONAL REPRESENTATIVE, 443–46
See also Ancillary Administration; Jurisdiction Over Persons

FORMAL APPOINTMENT PROCEEDINGS, 337–39, 371–72
See also Personal Representative; Special Administrator
Order of appointment, 371–72
Termination of previous appointment, 395
Subsequent administration, 434

FORMAL TESTACY PROCEEDINGS, 347–60
See also Probate of Wills

FORMAL TESTACY PROCEEDINGS—Cont'd
Contested cases, 355–57
Notice requirements, 351–52
Order,
    Content, 352–53
    Effect, 357
    Vacation, 357–59
Petition, contents required, 349–51
Purposes and effects, 347–49
Uncontested cases, 353–54

FRAUD, 16–17, 296, 308, 327, 428, 433, 447, 549

FUNERAL EXPENSES, 316, 410

FUTURE INTERESTS
See Trusts and Trustees

GIFTS
    See also Class Gifts
Ademption by satisfaction, 201–04
Advancement, 64–71
Augmented estate, part of, 85–94
Nontestamentary provisions in, 507–10

GOVERNING INSTRUMENT, 208

GUARDIAN AD LITEM, 28, 438, 475, 479, 486

GUARDIANS OF INCAPACITATED PERSONS, 476–83
    See also Incapacitated Persons; Jurisdiction Over Persons;
        Jurisdiction Over Subject Matter; Venue
Appointment, 476–80
Physician, duties, 479
Powers and duties, 481
    Restrictions on powers, 480–81
Temporary guardian, 481–82
Termination, 482
Visitor, 479

GUARDIANS OF MINORS, 471–75
    See also Jurisdiction Over Persons; Jurisdiction Over Sub-
        ject Matter; Minors; Venue
Delegation of authority, 466–67

HALF BLOODS
See Class Gifts; Intestate Succession

HEIRS, 224
Determination of,
    Judicial proceedings, 353
    Unadministered estates, 314–15, 432

HOLOGRAPHIC WILLS
See Wills

HOMESTEAD ALLOWANCE
See Family Protections

HOMICIDE
Effect on succession, 237–42

HONORARY TRUSTS, 271–73

ILLEGITIMATES
See Class Gifts; Intestate Succession

INCAPACITATED PERSONS
    See also Disability, Persons Under; Guardians of Incapaci-
        tated Persons; Protective Proceedings
Defined, 476
Incapacity, determined, 478, 482
Rights, 477–81, 482–83

INCORPORATION BY REFERENCE
See Wills

INDEPENDENT ACTS, EVENTS AFFECTING DISPOSITION
See Wills

INFORMAL APPOINTMENT PROCEEDINGS, 330–33
    See also Jurisdiction Over Persons; Notice; Personal Repre-
        sentative
Contents of application, 332–35
Findings required, 335–37
Formal appointment proceedings, effect on, 338
Special administrator, 399
Supervised administration, effect on, 364
Waiting period required, 335

INFORMAL PROBATE PROCEEDINGS, 340–47
    See also Jurisdiction Over Persons; Notice; Probate of Wills
Contents of application, 341–43
Findings required, 343–46
Proceedings blocking informal probate,
    Formal testacy proceedings, 348

INFORMAL PROBATE PROCEEDINGS—Cont'd
Proceedings blocking informal probate—Cont'd
    Supervised administration, 364
Special notice requirement, 347
Waiting period required, 343

INTERESTED PERSON
Defined, 25
Notice to, 25–26

INTERNATIONAL WILLS
See Wills

INTESTATE SUCCESSION, 29–72
    See also Administration, Decedents' Estate; Child; Heirs;
        Representation, Taking By
Adopted persons, 54–58
Advancement, 64–71
Affinity, relationship by, 60
Afterborn persons, 59
Aliens not disqualified, 61–62
Ancestors, share, 39–41
Collateral relations, share, 39–41
Contracts to die intestate, 168–71
Curtesy abolished, 79
Debts to decedent, charged against share, 71
Descendants, 37–39
Disclaiming succession, 228–33
Divorce, effect, 233–37
Dower abolished, 79
Escheat, 40
Foster children, 61
Halfbloods, 59
Heirs, 224
Homicide, effect on succession, 237–42
Issue, 32
Negative will, disinheritance, 71–72
Nonmarital issue, 59–60
Posthumous heirs, 59
Pretermitted children, share, 116–20
Pretermitted spouse, share, 113–16
Representation, taking by, 44–53
Surviving spouse, share, 37–38
Survivorship requirement, 62–64

INVENTORY AND APPRAISEMENT
Decedent's estate, 382
Employment of appraisers, 382–83
Protected person's estate, 496

ISSUE
See Intestate Succession

JOINT ACCOUNTS
See Multiple–Person Accounts; Security Registration

JURISDICTION OVER PERSONS
Applicants for informal proceedings, 308
Conservator, 462
Foreign personal representative, 446–47
Guardians, 462
Personal representative, 307–08
Trustee and trust beneficiaries, 541

JURISDICTION OVER SUBJECT MATTER
Generally, 22–23
Decedents' estates, 305–06
Protective proceedings and guardianship, 460–62
Trusts and trustees, 541

LAPSE
Generally, 176–77
Antilapse provision, 178–95
Beneficiary designations, nominative instruments, 210–12
Failure in residuary devise, 183
Pour-over will, 165
Survivorship requirements, 209–10

MARITAL STATUS, 233–37
See also Spouse
Waiver of marital rights, 95–96

MINORS
See also Disability, Persons Under; Guardians of Minors; Protective Proceedings

MISSING PERSONS
See Death; Distribution, Decedents' Estates

MISTAKE, IN INDUCEMENT
See Wills

MULTIPLE–PERSON ACCOUNTS, 511–25
Account defined, 514
Claims against, 522–23
Creditors' rights, 522–23
Death, rights at, 519–21
Financial institutions, protection, 523–25
Lifetime, rights, 518–19

MULTI–STATE ESTATES
See Ancillary Administration; Foreign Personal Representative

NEGATIVE WILLS
See Wills

NONMARITAL CHILDREN
See Class Gifts; Intestate Succession

NONPROBATE TRANSFERS
    See also Multiple–Person Accounts; TOD Security Registration
Contractual arrangements, 507–10

NONTESTAMENTARY CONTRACTUAL ARRANGEMENTS,
    507–10

NOTICE
Alleged decedent, 359–60
Creditors, 402–06
Demand for notice,
    Estate proceedings, 311–12
    Persons under a disability, proceedings, 463–64
Elective share proceeding, 103
Formal appointment, 338
Formal testacy proceeding, 351–52
Guardianship, incapacitated persons, 477–78
Informal appointment, 334
Informal probate, 343
Method of giving, 25–26
Proof of notice, 26
Protective proceedings, 485–86
Settlement agreements, 438
Supervised administration, 363
Third party protection, loss of, 243–44
Waiver of notice, 26

OMITTED CHILDREN
See Wills

PARENTS
See Intestate Succession

PERJURY, 17–18

PERPETUITIES, STATUTORY RULE OF, 259–71
    Generally, 255–59
Alternative periods, 259
Creation, date of interest, 262–63
Exclusions from, 266–67
Interests covered, 260
Prospective application, 268
Reformation, 263–66

PERSONAL REPRESENTATIVE, 366–96
    See also Distribution, Decedents' Estates; Foreign Personal
           Representative; Formal Appointment Proceedings;
           Informal Appointment Proceedings; Jurisdiction Over
           Persons; Special Administrator
Appointment, 373–74
Bond, 374–77
Compensation and expenses, 390–92
Conservator,
    Acquiring powers as personal representative, 495–96
Co-representatives, 389–90
Court control, 377–78
Duties in administration, 380–85
Letters, 373–74
Liability,
    Breach of duty, 386
    Conflict of interest, 386–87
    Personal, 392–93
Notice,
    By personal representative,
        To creditors, 380, 403–04
        To heirs and devisees, 380–81
    To personal representative, of proceedings, 307–08
Powers in administration, 385–86
Priority and disqualification for appointment, 368–73
Protection of persons dealing with representative, 387–89
Successor personal representative, 389
Termination of appointment, 393–96

POSTHUMOUS HEIRS
See Intestate Succession

POUR–OVER WILLS
See Wills

POWER OF APPOINTMENT
Defined, 246–49
Exercise, 249–52
Virtual representation, general powers of appointment, 252–54

POWER OF ATTORNEY
Delegated by parent or guardian, 466–67
Durable powers of attorney, 467–70

PRETERMITTED CHILDREN
See Wills

PROBATE OF WILLS
See also Formal Testacy Proceedings; Informal Probate Pro-
ceedings; Wills
Late-discovered wills,
Barred after final orders, 357
Cause for vacation, 357–58
Probate after limitation on administration, 304
Lost or destroyed wills, formal probate only, 152–53, 350
Previously probated wills, 346, 354
Self proved wills, contested cases, 355

PROTECTIVE PROCEEDINGS, 484–505
See also Claims Against Protected Persons and Their
Estates; Conservator and Conservatorship; Dis-
ability, Persons Under; Jurisdiction Over Subject
Matter; Notice
Generally, 484–88
Appointment of conservator, 485–90
Avoidance devices, 465–70
Creditors' claims, 500–02
Powers of Court, 490–92
Termination, 502–04
Third person liability, 500

REGISTRAR
Designation by Court order, 24
Responsibility, 335–37, 343–46, 399

RENUNCIATION OF SUCCESSION
See Disclaimer

REPRESENTATION, TAKING BY, 44–52
Per capita at each generation, 48–49
Per capita with per capita representation, 48
Per stirpes, 48
Principles of, 46–47
Root generation, 47
Stocks and generations, defined, 44–45

REVIVAL OF REVOKED WILLS
See Wills

REVOCATION OF WILLS
See Wills

RULE AGAINST PERPETUITIES
See Perpetuities, Statutory Rule of

SECURITIES
  See also Security Registration
Accessions, 191–95
Specifically devised, ademption, 195–201
Transfer, no administration, 315
Valuation, for distribution in kind, 420

SECURITY REGISTRATION, 526–32
Beneficiary form, 526–28
Choice of law, 529–30
Creditors, rights,
    Lifetime ownership, 528–31
Ownership on death, 531
Registering entity protection, 532
Security and security account, defined, 527
Uniform TOD Security Registration Act, 526

SELF–PROVED WILLS
See Probate of Wills; Wills

SETTLEMENT AGREEMENTS, 436–39
Court approval, proceeding, 437–39
Private agreements among successors, 436–37

SIMULTANEOUS DEATH
See Death

SMALL ESTATES, 314–18

SPECIAL ADMINISTRATOR, 397–400

SPOUSE
See Elective Share; Intestate Succession; Marital Status; Wills

SUCCESSION
See Intestate Succession

SUCCESSION CONTRACTS, 168–71

SUCCESSION WITHOUT ADMINISTRATION
See Universal Succession

SUPERVISED ADMINISTRATION, 361–65
See also Notice

SURETY
See Bonds

SURVIVORSHIP, 62–64, 209–10
See also Death; Multiple–Person Accounts
Antilapse, 178–91
Family Protections, 121
Heirs, 121
Lapse, 176–77

TITLE
Conservator, title by appointment, 498–500
Deed of distribution, 420–21
Devolution of, on death, 301
Personal representative, 383
Third person protection, 242–46, 387–89, 500

TOD SECURITY REGISTRATION
See Security Registration

TRUST ACCOUNTS
See Multiple–Person Accounts

TRUST REGISTRATION, 536–39
See also Jurisdiction Over Persons; Trusts and Trustees

TRUSTS AND TRUSTEES, 536–50
See also Jurisdiction Over Persons; Jurisdiction Over Subject Matter; Trust Registration; Venue
Accounts, 548–49
Compromise agreement, binding effect, 436
Duties of Trustee, 545–47
Foreign trusts and trustees, 551–53
Forum non conveniens, 543

TRUSTS AND TRUSTEES—Cont'd
Future interests, rules of construction, 218–24
    Antilapse, 221–23
    Heirs, definition, 224
    Survivorship, 219–21
    Worthier Title, 223
Honorary trusts, 271–73
Intervivos trusts, pour-overs, 163–65
Subject matter jurisdiction, 541
Trustees,
    Duties, 545–47
    Liability, 547–48
    Powers, 549–50
Virtual representation, 543–44

UNIFORM LAWS
See Table of Collateral Authorities–Uniform Laws

UNIVERSAL SUCCESSION, 318–29
    Generally, 318–21
Application requirements, 321–22
Creditors' rights, 325–28
Duty of universal successors, 328–29
Liability of successors, 324–25
Powers of universal successors, 324–25
Registrar's responsibility, 322–23

VENUE
Decedents' estates, 308–09
Guardianship of incapacitated persons, 463
Guardianship of minors, 463
Multiple venues, 23
Protective proceedings, 463
Trusts and trustees, 542–43

VERIFICATIONS, 18, 334, 343

WILLS
    See also Probate of Wills; Succession Contracts
    Generally, 126–32
Anti-contest and anti-claim clauses, 173
Capacity,
    Testators, 132
    Witnesses, 136
Conservator, authority to examine, 171
Contract to make or not to revoke, 168–71
Custodian of will, 172–73

WILLS—Cont'd
Dependent relative revocation, 157–58
Devises,
  Abatement order, 414
  Disclaimer of, 229
  Types, 175–76
Dispensing power, 130–32
Divorce or annulment, spousal provisions revoked by, 236
Foreign wills, 139–41
Formalities, theory of, 128–32
Holographic wills, 137–39
Homicide, forfeiture effect, 238
Incorporation by reference, 160–63
Independent significance, 165–66
International will, 141–44
Mistake, in inducement, omitted child assumed dead, 120
Negative will, 71–72
Ordinary witnessed wills, 133–37
Pour-over wills, 163–65
Pretermitted child, effect, 116–20
Pretermitted spouse, effect, 113–16
Public depository, 171–72
  International will, 172
Revival of revoked wills, 153–58
  By remarriage to former spouse, 237
Revocation,
  By operation of law, 151
  By physical act, 147–48
  By subsequent will, 149–51
  Lost or destroyed, 151–53
  Of spousal provisions by annulment or divorce, 236
  Partial revocation, 147–49
Rules of construction,
  Generally, 147–76
  Ademption by extinction, 195–201
  Ademption by satisfaction, 201–04
  After-acquired property, 207
  Antilapse, 176–93
  Class gifts,
    Antilapse applicable, 179
    Multigeneration gifts, 216–17
    Relational terminology, 212–16
  Exercise of power of appointment, 249–52
  Exoneration, construction against, 207
  Failure of devise, effect, 183

WILLS—Cont'd
Rules of construction—Cont'd
  Intention of testator controls, 174
  Nonademption, specific devises, 195–201
  Representation, meaning, 217–18
  Survivorship requirement, 209–10
Self-proved wills, 144–46
Separate list of bequests affecting disposition, 166–68
Supersession, 158–60
Testamentary additions to trusts, 163–65

†